BLACKWELL'S POLITICAL TEXTS
General Editors: C. H. WILSON and R. B. McCALLUM

PATRIARCHA

PATRIARCHA

and

Other Political Works

of

SIR ROBERT FILMER

Edited from the original sources
and with an Introduction by

PETER LASLETT

*Research Fellow of St. John's College,
late student of Peterhouse, Cambridge*

BASIL BLACKWELL
OXFORD
1949

JC 153, F513

PRINTED IN GREAT BRITAIN IN THE CITY OF OXFORD
AT THE ALDEN PRESS

CONTENTS

8905

INTRODUCTION

FOR over two hundred years the name of Sir Robert Filmer has been a byword — a byword for obscurity. None, or almost none, of the thinkers or historians who have examined Filmerism, refuted it, anatomized it or simply dismissed it as stupidity have known exactly who Sir Robert Filmer was, when he lived, what he did and what he wrote. It so happens that all the important evidence about his life and his writings was preserved by the line of English baronets which descended from him and which persisted until 1916. It is set out here with two objectives. First, to fix him in his historical context and to make it easier to understand why he wrote as he did. Second, to correct the inaccuracies and misconceptions caused by this lengthy story of contemptuous neglect.

He was born in or about the year 1588 — the year of the Great Armada and the year of the birth of Thomas Hobbes. His father was Edward Filmer, gent., lord of the manor of Little Charlton in the parish of East Sutton near Maidstone in Kent, and later Sir Edward Filmer, Kt., owner of the whole of East Sutton, Sheriff of Kent and county notable. He was Sir Edward's eldest son and the heir to three other Kentish manors and much landed property. Most of it had been accumulated by his grandfather, Robert Filmer, who had been a registrar or prothonotary of Queen Elizabeth's Court of the Common Pleas and a typical sixteenth-century lawyer on the make.

His mother was Elizabeth Argall, a member of another recently established county family with its origins in the City of London. But the Filmers were an older family than the Argalls and Sir Robert Filmer inherited a name which can be traced back to the early fourteenth century and a coat of arms of genuine antiquity. Both families were connected with the gentry of Essex and with the society of merchant venturers which founded the first community of Englishmen overseas — the Virginia Company of London. Sir Robert Filmer's uncle was Captain Sir Samuel Argall, first discoverer of the direct sea route to Virginia, first surveyor of the coast of New England, reputed conqueror of the site of the modern city of New York.

He spent the first forty-one of his sixty-five years as the eldest son of a family of eighteen children. He was educated first (probably) at the village school, then at Trinity College, Cambridge, where his associates were high church clergymen, and finally at Lincoln's Inn. His intellectual life began in the community of Kentish county families, whose learning and cultivation at this period were truly astonishing. He reached maturity in Westminster in the early years of James I, where he was a friend of Camden, Spelman and the rest of the group of early Stuart historians.

In 1610 he married Anne Heton, a child heiress. She and her sister shared the estate of their father, Martin Heton, Elizabeth's last nominee to the despoiled bishopric of Ely. He probably did not live with his wife for the first few years. He had a brother at Court, another in the City 'trading beyond the seas', a third who was trained for the Church but who emigrated to Virginia and set up a manorial establishment and a line of American cousins. His sisters married into Kentish county families and became the ultimate great aunts and great grandmothers of many of the dynasties of the Old South. He was knighted in January 1618/19. Up to this point the major activity of Sir Robert Filmer was as heir and elder brother: he was his own example of the rights and duties of primogeniture.

In 1629 he succeeded to his father's encumbered estate and from then on the eldest son became the patriarch of the household at East Sutton. It was two households in fact because he kept up his own establishment of 'The Porter's Lodge, in the Close of the Collegiate Church at Westminster' as well as the rambling manor house with its magnificent view over the luxuriant Weald of Kent. In this way he continued his connection with the lawyers, historians and High Churchmen of Westminster. But he took over his father's place in the community of Kentish gentry, as a magistrate and an officer of the county defence forces, though he was neither rich enough nor healthy enough to serve as Sheriff or to become an active leader in county affairs.

At their meetings and over their morning draughts the members of the bench of justices at Maidstone discussed more than local administration and the affairs of the most important local military organization in the kingdom. The gentlemen who met there came from families of writers, poets, historians, lawyers, courtiers, clerics, theologians and men of business. They bore names which appeared in far more interesting and important places than the Quarter Sessions Book. Nearly half of them left their mark on the intellectual life of their generation and even more on the life of the colony of Virginia. These county gentry turned Westminster lawyers and London merchants were caught up in most of the commercial ventures, political controversies and intellectual activities of their day. They corresponded with each other and with their sons and cousins in the capital on all these subjects. They even maintained a form of limited publication and circulation of their views on the problems of the time by means of manuscript treatises, passed from hand to hand and manor house to manor house. Sir Robert Filmer's career as a writer began as the author of one of these hand-written and hand-copied essays.

The subject he chose, or which was forced upon him by the troubled conscience of his acquaintance and his relations, was the vexed problem of the ethics of lending money at interest. In about 1630, or perhaps earlier, he wrote 'Quaestio Quodlibetica, or a discourse whether it may be lawful to take interest for money'. Its style and the treatment it received bear all the marks of the purposes for which it was written. In 1611 Roger Fenton had published *A Treatise of Usurie*, an important stumbling block to those of Sir Robert's friends who wanted to set their minds at rest about the uses they were making of their money. 'Quaestio Quodlibetica' was a commentary on this book and upon all the recognized authorities on the subject. It was courteous, moderate and extensively learned. Reasonable interest was justifiable: Sir Robert himself would pay it but he would not take it. Manuscript copies of this work passed from hand to hand for twenty years, until in 1653 Sir Roger Twysden 'adventured the putting of it to the press'.

Some time during the next twelve years he wrote an exactly similar manuscript for an exactly similar purpose and for the same reading public. This was an essay on another crucial question exercising the minds of all his intellectually responsible contemporaries — the problem of political obligation. The question of the historical origin and ethical basis of political power had become in the 1630s a pressing personal issue for all his friends. Sir Robert Filmer's declaration to his contemporaries on this subject was entitled, *Patriarcha: a Defence of the Natural Power of Kings against the Unnatural Liberty of the People*.

This treatise may have been inspired by the Ship Money controversy of 1634-38, and therefore composed before 1640. It certainly existed in one or more manuscript versions before the breach between King and Parliament led to Civil War in 1642. This can be proved from the statement (page 95) that the Barons' War and the Wars of the Roses were the only occasions when 'This Kingdom hath been wasted with civil war'. It must certainly be dated after 1635, since it quotes Selden's *Mare Clausum*, which was published in that year.

The writing of *Patriarcha* made no recorded difference in his life. It must have marked him once for all as an extreme supporter of the Royal Prerogative and as an enemy to constitutional change of any kind. But he was never at any time willing to allow the work to be printed, so that his reputation for absolutism cannot have spread much further than his circle of friends. The closest of these was Peter Heylyn, the Royalist canon of Westminster, who tells us a little of his character and of his determination never to publish the work which has always been regarded as his *magnum opus*: 'So affable was his conversation, his discourse so rational, his judgment so exact in most parts of learning and his affections to the Church so exemplary in him, that I never enjoyed a greater felicity in the company of any man living than I did in his. Had he been pleased to have suffered his excellent discourse called Patriarcha to appear in public, it would have given such satisfaction to all our great masters in the schools of polity that all other tractates in that kind had been found unnecessary. But he did not think fit while he was alive to gratify the nation in publishing that excellent piece.'

In his portrait Sir Robert Filmer's features are small and delicate, his nose aquiline and prominent: his complexion is pale, but his straggling hair and wispy, tapered moustache are ruddy and almost ginger. His other intimate friends re-echo Heylyn's tribute to his learning. There was Sir Roger Twysden, his lifelong associate amongst the Kentish gentry and one of the titans of early seventeenth-century historical scholarship. He calls him 'a very learned gentleman'. There is evidence that he 'was very intimately acquainted with Mr. Camden', that he knew Cotton, Selden, Spelman and Sir Edward Dering, the discoverer of a new manuscript of Magna Carta, Fludd the Rosicrucian and Culpeper the herbalist. But society at East Sutton Park had grace and polish as well as erudition. Filmer himself refers to his intimacy with George Herbert, while his brother at Court was an associate of Ben Jonson. The circle included Henry King, George Sandys, Isaac Walton, Richard Lovelace, even John Donne himself. One of them was that little known phenomenon, Ambrose Fisher, clergyman, dramatist and classical scholar, yet totally blind from birth. Music must have been an abiding passion. There was an exquisite collection of Italian, French and English music and Sir Robert's private estimate of a wife's wisdom was 'first for pleasure, then for musique'.

The Civil War shattered this community as it shattered Lord Falkland's at Great Tew. Filmer's family, brothers, sons and cousins, were Royalist to a man. But the Kentish county community was divided into an active Parliamentarian minority, which took charge of the county from the first, and a passive Royalist majority, which only exerted its strength twice and failed both times. In the spring of 1642 and the summer of 1648, the two crises of the Great Rebellion, the intervention of the body of the Kentish gentry on the side of the King was nearly fatal to the Parliament. Sir Robert Filmer himself, as far as can be discovered, took no active part in either effort for the King. He appears to have maintained a deliberate attitude of non-intervention throughout the whole struggle: all he did was to write a little and to publish less.

This creates a suspicion of faithlessness to his own declared principles, but there is not enough evidence to prove a charge of personal inconsistency. He was certainly getting old — he was fifty-four in 1642. He was certainly ill — he had suffered from the stone all his life and he died of it in 1653. Kent, moreover, was for the most part so firmly in the hands of Parliament and its county committees at Knowle and Rochester that there was very little chance for him to do more than he did. It is also true that he suffered considerable material losses and that he was imprisoned by Parliament from winter 1643 until summer 1645 or later. Nevertheless it is a little difficult to explain either his declarations of neutrality or his apparent failure to assist in the desperate efforts of his neighbours, his friends and his family in 1642 and 1648.

This is what happened in 1642. Sir Robert Filmer had played his part with the rest of the county administration in co-operating with the measures taken by the Long Parliament in 1640 and 1641. Kent and its M.P.s had so far supported Pym. But at the Assizes in March 1642 the Royalist majority decided to make the real feelings of the county known at Westminster and to do so very forcibly. They agreed on a strongly worded petition and determined to assemble in a body at Blackheath and to go *en masse* to the House of Commons and present it. This was obviously a threat of revolt and vigorous action was taken against them. Notwithstanding, the march to Whitehall did take place and at the next Assizes in July an even more extreme petition was adopted in defiance of the alarmed Commons and Kent Committee. The result was the imprisonment of the ringleaders, the hurried flight of the younger men to the King's headquarters and the outbreak of petty violence against the Royalist gentry all over the county. Richard Lovelace was one of those who went to prison, hence the loveliest of all Royalist lyrics 'To Althea from Prison'. Sir Robert Filmer's eldest son was one of those who fled to the King. His only action was to go bail for Sir Roger Twysden: it was notorious that this sort of bail was purely nominal.

He did not escape harrowing by the Parliamentary troops and East

Sutton Church and manor house were ransacked on September 1st, 1642. Arms and horses were requisitioned and he was heavily taxed on his property both in Westminster and Kent. Yet almost a year of the Civil War went by, with Sir Robert carrying on his routine duties 'in these times of trouble'. But the Kentish Committee was evidently suspicious of him. He was seized and examined while riding to London in July 1643, but allowed to go on without his horse. In his absence the soldiery reappeared at East Sutton and spent four days sacking it, opposed only by the spirited protests of Dame Anne Filmer and her servants. Then followed a direct threat of sequestration. Finally in the winter of 1643 he got word of an order to imprison him.

It is not known whether the Parliamentary authorities had any reason for these attacks other than the information laid by one of Filmer's tenants that he was hoarding arms. It is just possible, but not at all likely, that they objected to his notoriety as a Royalist writer. The following letter from his wife to the head of the Committee illustrates his attitude at this time and the condition of his affairs: 'I am at this present in such a condition that I cannot waight on you and the rest of the comitee as I desire, my coach I have not once sett foot in these 14 monethes, my coach horses and five other horses having been taken from us all for the parliament. I understand there is an order of par: for securing the persons of divers gentlemen of this county: if I were not confident that my husbands dangerous and painfull infirmity of the stone of wch his father died were not as greate security of his person as may be, myselfe should be the first sutor to you and these other gentlemen yr assotiatts for his restrainte: I that can best wittnes how far he hath binn from medling on either side in deed or so much as words: take myself bound in duty to offer my testimony for his innocency so far as it may be accepted from a woman in the cause of her husband: but if there be so strange a resolution for confinement of these that have not offended, I hope I shall not fail in making request that it may be to a place of wholesome and pure aire (for to an infirme body in the winter season, an ill aire may turne a restrainte into an execution) and that it may be at such a distance that I may be able these shortt daies to goe and return without indangering my owne health to give my nessisary attendance on him who hath binn a trew prisonner ever since he came from you, so much did that small iorny shake him that he hath taken phisik ever since. If these trew reasons may be considered you shall doe a charity wch I am confident will hereafter be pleasing to yr. selves and oblige me to acknowledge myselfe, Sr. yr humble servant. A. Filmer.'

To prison he went, though the committee took to heart Anne Filmer's appeal and sent him to Leeds Castle, only three miles from East Sutton. It was, and is, a huge medieval castle in the middle of a lake. Here he busied himself writing theology and trying to keep control of his decaying estate. He was probably released after the Parliament had finally won the First Civil War—in the middle of 1645. He is not definitely known to have been at liberty until April 1647 and by that date he had made the decision which gives him his historical importance — he had decided to publish. His first printed work was a theological tract, 'Of the Blasphemie against the Holy Ghost' and it was on sale by February 1646/47. A year later he publicly entered the field of constitutional controversy and began his career in the history of English political thought. In February 1647/48 Richard Royston, 'the constant factor for all scandalous books and papers against the proceedings of Parliament', began to sell 'The Freeholder's Grand Inquest touching our Soveraigne Lord the King and his Parliament'. This was a revision and extension of the final passages of Sir Robert Filmer's Patriarcha MS. He had brought it up to date with reference to the works on constitutional history and theory which had appeared since the original was written and he published it as a complete Royalist's answer to the claims of Army and Parliament alike.

When Sir Robert Filmer came out of prison he had only six or seven years to live, but these years were the only really active period of his life as a writer. Now that he had decided to address an audience wider than the readers of manuscript treatises circulated between the manor houses of Kent, it was as an old man with set convictions and with his reading and thinking complete. The 'Freeholder' had made only passing reference to political obligation. He followed it up almost at once, in April 1648, with the first of his critical essays on the books which were forming the opinions of his contemporaries upon the ethical basis and the historical origins of political power. The book he chose was Philip Hunton's *Treatise of Monarchie* which had been published in 1643 and which was already the centre of an extensive controversy. In 'The Anarchy of a Limited or Mixed Monarchy' he swept away all Hunton's arguments by reference to a thesis which he nowhere stated but occasionally summarized — the general theory of the Patriarcha MS. These first three tracts, like all his published work, were anonymously printed.

Immediately after this came his second chance to play a personal part in the military struggle for his principles and for the constitution he was defending. In June 1648 the Scottish army was on the way to restore the King, Cromwell was occupied in rebellious Wales, most of the Navy had joined the future Charles II. It was she crisis of the Second Civil War. In Kent a sudden mass uprising of the gentry and their following had been engineered by Sir Robert Filmer's neighbour, Sir Edward Hales. If they could succeed in a quick descent on a wavering London, the imprisoned Charles I would be restored. The Kentish leaders invited, even implored, Sir Robert Filmer's help: 'Not that they expect any actuall service from you, having taken your age into serious consideration. Sr., they conceive your presence will much conduce to the public good, and we hope that you who have ever been a wellwisher to such an act, will not now draw back.' But it does not appear that either he or any of his family did take any part in the desperate fight which was lost to Fairfax at Maidstone on June 2nd, 1648. On August 21st appeared the most outspoken work he wrote, 'The Necessity of the Absolute Power of all Kings, and in particular of the King of England'. The inference seems inescapable: he was content to wage his war for the King by the publication of essays.

For the next four years he was silent, apart from the writing of some considerations on the proper attitude to the rebel government which were never published. Some of the defeated Royalist soldiers were emigrating to Virginia where 'Sir William Barkley, the Governor there, industriously invited many gentlemen and others thither as to a place of security'. Sir Robert Filmer is known to have helped one settler in the colony and in 1652 his brother Henry returned from his plantation of Laus Deo for a visit to his birthplace. Though his tracts had no perceptible effect on opinion, he could not remain indifferent to all the works which were coming from the presses in such numbers. In 1650 appeared Milton's first defence of the Puritan Revolution against Salmasius, who voiced the shocked conscience of Europe at the execution of Charles I. And in 1651 Thomas Hobbes published the greatest of all vindications of sovereignty, indeed 'the sole masterpiece of political philosophy in the English language'. Leviathan expressed an absolutist doctrine which Filmer completely agreed with, but based it upon a theory of politics which was quite unacceptable. He seems to have felt that neither of these works should go unchallenged and in February 1651/52 he published three critical reviews under the title 'Observations concerning the Originall of Government, upon Mr. Hobs Leviathan, Mr. Milton against Salmasius, H. Grotius "De Jure Belli"'. It was followed in May 1652 by the last of his political works,

'Observations upon Aristotle's Politiques touching Forms of Government'.

In these two pamphlets he set up his destructive criticism of contemporary theories of obligation and his naturalistic, patriarchal presuppositions against the great books of the greatest writers known to him. Both works quoted extensively from the Patriarcha MS., and ten whole pages of the review of Grotius were copied verbatim from that source. There is something impressive in his determination in this last year of his life to analyse and annihilate the major works of his ablest contemporaries. But the final essay of all is, perhaps, even more surprising and attractive. Its subject was Witchcraft.

It is notorious that the belief in witchcraft and the practice of it grew perceptibly in the sixteenth and seventeenth centuries and that the periods of crisis were under Elizabeth and under Cromwell. It was another case of conscience for the local magistrate, called upon to pass judgment on wretched old women, hysterical girls and neurotic youths hounded by the superstitions of their neighbours. Such experiences on the bench had led an ancestor of Filmer's, Reginald Scott, to write the first rationalist treatment of this subject in 1584. In July 1652 Sir Robert himself was present at the Maidstone Assizes and saw six witches examined, with the usual discovery of revolting witch marks on their bodies. He heard the evidence, which was the usual mixture of hearsay and hysterical confession, and he saw the execution of all six by hanging, though there was a demand that the witches should be burnt — a thing which never actually happened in England.

There is ample evidence that up to this time Sir Robert Filmer had believed, and the belief was conventional in his day, that the executing of witches was theologically justified. But what he saw and heard at Maidstone so worked on him that he abandoned the conviction that the witches of England in 1652 were the same as the witches of the Old Testament. He published his doubts to the jurymen of the whole country in 'An Advertisement to the Jurymen of England, touching Witches. Together with a Difference between an English and a Hebrew Witch'. This was published in March 1653. Three months later he died and was buried in the fourteenth-century church behind his own manor house at East Sutton on May 30th, 1653.

He had never been very important outside his own circle in Kent, Westminster and Virginia, and there is no doubt that he would have been completely forgotten had it not been for the storm raised when his *Patriarcha* was finally published in 1680. But his family did not forget him and in this case the House of Stuart did not forget his family. His eldest son, Sir Edward Filmer, had been Gentleman of the Privy Chamber to Charles I, and he was given the same office by Charles II. He died unmarried in 1669, and East Sutton passed to his brother, Robert. In 1674 this second son was created the first baronet of the Filmer line in consideration, it was said, of his father's sufferings for the crown. From him sprang a house of nine further baronets, who were seated at East Sutton in increasing wealth and splendour until 1916. In Virginia the Filmers and the Filmer connections were associated with all the great families which finally gave to the thirteen colonies their Revolutionary leadership in the 1770s — the Washingtons, the Byrds, the Berkelys and the Randolphs and so the Jeffersons. Whatever the subsequent literary and philosophical reputation of Sir Robert Filmer, he had been a great genealogical success.

Such are the known facts about the life of Sir Robert Filmer. They do not show him up as a forgotten genius, nor as a man of more than considerable ability in any field. But they do clear him of the insinuations and outright accusations made by his Whig critics. Sidney calls him 'a vicious wretch', a 'court flatterer' with all the faults of 'Bawds, Whores, Buffoons, Players, Slaves and other base people'. Tyrell and Locke are less outrageous, but it is curious that no one thought of fastening on him the only reproach that might have stuck — that of disloyalty to his own cause. The notoriety they gave him has created a persisting caricature of a reactionary country gentleman, the autocratic father of a large family, with no knowledge of the world other than that he would get from his duties as a magistrate, and with his intellectual interests confined to what he had picked up at the University and mulled over in his library of scholastic authors. He was none of these things, except, possibly, a domineering father. He was a man of genuine culture, a seventeenth-century literary and intellectual critic. He was personally acquainted with poets, lawyers, theologians, politicians, playwrights and historians and he bought the books of his contemporaries and wrote judicious, critical and often humorous notices of them for his own amusement and for the satisfaction of a small circle of friends. The political events of his last years forced him into more serious controversy and into publication, but he was probably a little ashamed of the dogmatic generalizations of *Patriarcha*, which was the only work he wrote positively and not as an appreciation of someone else's ideas. The worst of the injustices which have been done to him is that he should have been judged almost exclusively on *Patriarcha* alone.

FILMER'S ARGUMENT

Patriarcha is not the anatomy of a political system, but an essay on political obligation and the historical origin of political power. The published tracts are extensions, applications and modifications of the arguments of *Patriarcha*. Even when fitted together, the corpus of Filmer's political writings does not present anything like a coherent theory of politics. It is impossible therefore to write a systematic survey of Filmer's doctrines and call it his argument. All that can be attempted is a summary of the propositions attacked by Locke and his companions when they worked out the theory of Liberalism.

Sir Robert Filmer's prime assumption was that the Bible was the true, the unique and complete revelation of God's will on all things. It contained the whole truth about the nature of the world and the nature of society. The details of recorded history from the beginning to the death of the Apostles were to be found in it, and also the laws which would govern history from that time to the end of the world. This first assumption was shared by Puritan and High Churchman alike, in fact by nearly every member of Christendom: it needed no defence. Although Filmer recognized that there were those who did not conform, and that it was possible to talk about the world and its history without reference to the Scriptures, he refused to examine such an alternative: it was blasphemy. All the evidence about man and society came from the Bible: even such work of the Greek philosophers as might be admitted as evidence — in particular the thought of Aristotle — must be assumed to have been based on some mysterious communication to them of the content of the Scriptures.

Given such a datum about Holy Writ, what did the Bible say about human society? To Filmer it was perfectly definite on two points — the origin of human society and the nature of the relationship between the people who composed human society. Human society originated in one man — Adam. There had been a time before the creation of Eve when Adam was the only human being in existence. He had owned the whole world, all the land and all the creatures in it. It was the expressed will of God that human society should begin in this way, with one man and not with two humans, or with a multitude of humans. And having willed that the human race should begin in this way, God must be supposed to have meant something by it. Filmer inferred that God's meaning was to show that all other human beings were to be subordinated to this first human, Adam. Furthermore, since all these subsequent humans sprang from the same source, they were all naturally, physiologically, related to each other. By this

God meant to show that the relationship between all human beings was to be naturalistic; it was a physical bond. Society was a family, and a family descended from one, single, male individual.

These two inferences from Scripture had several very important implications. First, the inferiority of women. Eve had been created after Adam, she had been fashioned out of Adam and God had specifically subjected her to Adam. Therefore in any situation the female was always inferior to the male: sisters were inferior to brothers, wives to husbands, princesses to princes. In all systems of authority, then, the females could be disregarded, except when, in the failure of a male, a female transmitted a relationship and the authority which went with it. Second, the inequality of all humans, the absolute primacy of authority. God, by creating Adam first, gave him authority over everyone who came after him. All men were born of fathers and were subjected to their fathers for two reasons. One was because they were created, under God, by the volition of their fathers, and the other was because they were created after their fathers in time. It was this second point which established the law of primogeniture. Younger brothers were inferior to elder brothers because they came after them in time, but elder sisters were inferior to younger brothers because women were in all situations inferior to men. All this meant that the concept of a free human being subject to no authority but his own will was absolutely impossible. All men were born, and always remained, unfree and unequal; they were subject to their fathers and inferior to their elders. No theory of political association which started with free and equal individuals made any sense at all.

Another implication of Filmer's reading of Scripture concerned the origin of the right to possessions — of property. He recognized that to establish the true nature of society it was as important to discover the laws governing the relation of individuals to their possessions as it was to discover the relation of individual to individual. To him the teaching of the Bible was equally clear on this point — property had always been private property, no other sort of property existed. Adam had been given possession of the whole world and everything in it, indeed it had been created for him to possess and to do with as he wished. So Adam's eldest son had enjoyed during Adam's lifetime just as much property as Adam had voluntarily given him. After Adam's death he inherited all his property as he inherited all his power. So it was with all Adam's other sons, only they had no right to inherit any of Adam's property and had to be content with what their father or elder brother had voluntarily given them. So it was with all men who had existed since Adam: they had absolute right to just that property which they had lawfully inherited or which had been alienated to them by those who had likewise lawfully inherited it. There had been no stage of primitive communism and there could be no such thing as communally owned, public property. Such things as belonged to no man in particular still belonged to the king, who had inherited them as property in the same way as he had inherited political power.

Perhaps the most important implication of biblical revelation about human society was about the nature of consent. Society was not based on agreement between individuals, or indeed on consciously thought out relationships at all. The consent of an individual to live in any society was simply irrelevant: he had been placed in that society as arbitrarily as he had been placed in his father's family. Indeed the two relationships were the same thing, that between each member of a family and that between any two members of a political society. Society was not an intellectual construct at all, its members had not created it by taking thought, it was a given, natural phenomenon. All thought of contract between individuals as the origin of society was, therefore, simply nonsense. So also was any concept of a state of nature before society, or political society, had existed. Political society had always existed, or it had existed since the creation of Eve, because the family had always existed and the family *was* political society. Political society was also universal. There were no living humans who were not descended from Adam and who did not live in families, so there were no human beings who lived outside political society. A state of nature simply did not exist, and it never had existed.

So much for Filmer's deductions from the Bible about the origin of human society and the nature of social relationships. How did all this apply to the political society he lived in himself? How did it apply to the monarchies of England and France, to the Republic of Venice and to the Confederation of the Netherlands? All this was a matter of history: mainly of biblical history, which, it must be remembered, contained for him and his generation the greatest part of the history of the whole human race. Such history as was subsequent to the Bible was very much shorter than that which had gone before and must be supposed to illustrate the same principles as were so plainly evident in biblical history. Early history in the Old Testament can be briefly summarized. Adam's position as father and as supreme political potentate — as patriarch — was inherited by his eldest son and so by succeeding patriarchs down to Noah. With Noah the whole process started over again, because his family was all that was left of the human race after the Flood. But Noah made a very important decision. Instead of keeping to himself the governance of the whole world which his family was to populate, he decided to divide it up between his sons and to retain for himself and his direct line only that territory which was to belong to the Chosen People. It was at this point that all the separate states of the world were founded and that the political units outside Mesopotamia, outside the Mediterranean area and outside Europe were set up. Now Noah was within his rights in doing this, because his power was absolutely supreme: he could, and did, relegate it completely to any one of his descendants for a particular area.

It must be insisted that these new states were families, and that their heads, their patriarchs, were fathers. These patriarchates finally became the separate states of the world of the seventeenth century. Filmer emphasized that the heads of these states, whether kings, or protectors, or doges with their councils, derived their power from their succession to one or other of the sons or nephews of Noah, and so finally from the supreme fatherly power of Adam. He admitted that there had been revolutions and usurpations and that it was no longer possible in his day to find the line of succession of a ruling monarch from Noah. But he never admitted that there had been any subsequent origin of political power, or that any usurping mayor of the palace or conquering general or representative assembly had ever been able to set up an authority on a different basis or a power of a different kind from that originally enjoyed by the primeval patriarch of that particular family of the world's peoples. In particular he denied that popular elections had ever been able to constitute political power, or limit it, or do anything to change it from the paternal authority on which political subjection rested. The enormous variety of political constitutions in the world as he knew it, and the obvious fact that political authority was being exercised in a way which contradicted his theory about its origin, he explained by the fact that truth about politics had been preserved in only one of the world's peoples — that is amongst God's Chosen People — amongst the Israelites. Everywhere else heathenism had obliterated all knowledge of the origins of political power and nearly all the world's peoples had forgotten both why they were in subjection to their government and who had the right to exercise political power.

But even amongst the Jews the story was extremely complicated and the true succession very difficult to trace. Filmer's only hope of making history consistent was to assume the constant interference of

God Himself in the governance of His people. It was difficult to maintain his case in face of the history of the Royal House of Israel, but he upheld two important positions. One was that the nature of political power in the Jewish state, whether exercised by God Himself, by the Judges or by the House of David, was patriarchal. He made a great deal out of the texts on the Princes of Israel as fathers of families and tribes. The second point was that the Old Testament gave no grounds whatsoever for supposing that governors were ever elected or that the people could do anything to limit the power of their rulers, who were sovereign and absolute.

This was as much as he could extract from biblical history to demonstrate patriarchalism. He went on to use the recorded history of the European nations to establish the absolute nature of kingship wherever it is found. He dealt at length with the history of Rome to prove that it was for most of its history a monarchy and that there never was a true Roman democracy. He laid it down that there could be found no recorded instance of a state where the people had been able to set up a stable political system, that no form of government except monarchy had governed, or could ever govern, any area larger than a city and that all authorities really agreed that monarchy was the best and democracy the worst form of government. He made a minute analysis of Aristotle to prove these points, and all his historical arguments were intended to demonstrate the absolute necessity of supreme sovereignty in all states. He examined the whole of British constitutional history with this aim in view and concluded that the King of England was an absolute, sovereign monarch of this ideal pattern. He nowhere tried to show how Charles I was a direct heir of one of the sons of Noah, but he obviously assumed it, and he went into detail to prove that the English Parliament had no moral or legal rights which infringed the sovereignty of monarchs, any more than the French States General or the Polish Earthly Messengers.[1]

Such was the positive evidence that Filmer found to support his argument from Revelation and human history to establish the truth of the patriarchal principle of political obligation. He did not actually present his case in this positive way, however. His method was to demonstrate the impossibility of all other accounts of political obligation and to show how only patriarchalism as summarized above would meet all the difficulties.

His main concern was to show that if you did not assume a natural bond between individuals as the basis for society you could never

---

[1] See 'Anarchy'—infra pp. 310-11.

hope to reach any stage higher than primitive anarchy and communism.
Supposing that the human race had been created differently from the
way supposed by Filmer and that each individual was so independent
that no political authority had any right over him unless it could be
shown that he had given his free consent to its establishment, then the
first insuperable difficulty would be to show how the human race had
ever been divided up into separate societies at all. In such a situation
only unanimous consent of all individuals could result in any action
being taken at all and therefore the division of the human race into
separate societies must be supposed to have required the consent of
every human being. It could not be assumed that any given group of
independent individuals could themselves agree to set up their own
political society without reference to the rest of mankind, because that
would give every conceivable collection of humans, or even a single
human, the right to set up a separate political society. Since the unanimous consent of all humanity was an impossibility, the implication
of absolute equality and independence for the individual was universal,
world-wide anarchy.

But given that societies smaller than the whole human race did exist
by moral right, how could it be shown that political authority with a
moral right to obedience could be established within them? The only
possible procedure which would preserve the absolute independence
of every individual within the society was by means of an assembly
of the whole population. But who had the right to call such an assembly and to preside over it? Furthermore, how could it be supposed
that all the people could ever meet together: what about the invalids,
the women and the children? Then, even if such an assembly did meet
it could only make decisions if the people were unanimous. No
majority rule or representation by proxy could possibly overcome
these difficulties. This was so because the decisions to be made affected
the fundamental rights to independence of every member of the society
and could only be morally binding if every member gave his consent to
them. It was impossible to show that such assemblies had ever met in
historical fact and Filmer maintained that even if they had, they could
never have solved this moral problem of establishing political authority
without overriding the independence of individuals. Once more we
are left with anarchy.

By anarchy, therefore, he meant in the first place the absence of
any morally valid political authority. This anarchy extended down-
wards from the generation which supposedly instituted the authority.
Our 'contracting' forefathers could only have bound themselves to

obedience, and, unless it be granted that obligation can be transferred by fatherhood, every individual in every succeeding generation must have been born with his natural freedom and equality, absolved from all obligation to political authority. For if you once allow that a child is born with his freedom limited by his father's natural right of proxy, you have abandoned the principle of absolute freedom and equality and you have granted Filmer his first principle of a natural bond between individuals. Patriarchalism was as necessary to establish the continuity of political society as it had been to give validity to the division of humanity into political societies.

He showed that no possible constitutional solution can be found to this problem of anarchy. This was made apparent in his analysis of mixed constitutions, where the power of the monarch is tempered in some way by the rights of the people or of the aristocracy. He followed Hunton step by step in his justification of such a constitution to the point where it was admitted that the only final judge of such an arrangement in case of dispute must be the conscience of all mankind. This, said Filmer, in triumph, was nothing but anarchy. The consciences of a world of discrete individuals cannot be expected to be anything else. His refutation of mixed monarchy, however, involved more than the demonstration of the inevitable necessity of patriarchalism in politics. It rested in the main on the principle of sovereignty which he adopted unaltered from the French thinker Jean Bodin. By anarchy he meant, in the second place, the absence of a sovereign authority.

With anarchy went communism. In the same way as it was impossible for a people to escape from political anarchy once it was assumed that all individuals were independent and equal, so it was impossible for them to escape from communism if once it were granted that everyone had a moral right to an equal share of the gifts of nature. All the same arguments applied. Division of communal into private property could only be done by unanimous consent of all humankind; majority decisions and votes by proxy were inadmissible because the right to a share in all property must be assumed to be natural in the same way as the right to be treated as independent and equal. In short, Filmer found it impossible for his opponents to extricate themselves from the dilemma created for them by their own first principles.

His own solution was, of course, the assumption of natural inequality, the rule of a patriarchal monarch and the patriarchal rules of succession to property. The supremacy in all things of the Heir of Adam followed logically from his interpretation of the Bible, both of its teachings on the nature of human relationships, and of the account it gave of

biblical and other history. The patriarchal king ruled by divine right
for two reasons. God had specifically granted all social power to His
direct ancestor, Adam, and He had created the social order in such a
way that the continuance of the hierarchy founded by Adam was
indispensable. But Filmer presented a quite separate argument to
justify monarchy, an argument from the relation of authority to will.
He stated that the exercise of will was the only form of authority, that
only one mind could will effectively and continuously, that there
could be no such thing as an agreed or common will, therefore
authority must belong as a possession to one individual who only can
do the willing. All law, Divine, Natural, Political, Constitutional,
Social or Domestic, was the exercise of such will by some one person.
This argument can be regarded as an extension of his dogma that
agreement means nothing politically and that the social bond is not
intellectual. It is not presented in this way, however, but is argued as
a part of the doctrine of the indispensability to society of a supreme
sovereign, which Filmer took over verbatim from Bodin.

This combination of patriarchalism with Bodinian sovereignty
raised one important difficulty. Granted that the basis of all power
was in the fatherhood, how could the absolute, arbitrary power of the
king be reconciled with the absolute, arbitrary power of each individual
father? Each was equally natural, each was equally established by
God. Filmer's answer was to refer the king and the father each to his
position in the hierarchy which started in Adam: he invoked the same
principle which explained primogeniture. Each political state was a
rightfully constituted human family, and authority in that family
belonged to its eldest member, to the direct descendant of Adam — in
fact to the king. But each individual family within that political
society was headed by a man who exercised authority not only as
paterfamilias, but also (especially over those not naturally related to him)
in virtue of a similar, but more distant, relation to Adam. Such individual fathers were therefore subordinate to the king. It must be noted
that the power of such subordinate fathers was not constituted by the
king, it was still natural. This was of major importance in reconciling
his theory with the actual facts of political society, for it covered the
difficult case of the failure of the royal line, of what happened when
there was no recognized heir of Adam.

Such a position was strictly speaking simply the result of ignorance:
there always was at any one time an eldest heir of Adam in any one
society. But if he could not be found, then, Filmer said, power
devolved to the chief heads of families, who by virtue of their natural

power, should appoint the new royal house. This was the nearest approach he ever made to permitting election. The same reference to the universal hierarchy also showed why the subjection of sons to their fathers was almost abrogated when they themselves grew up and became fathers. This was because the Supreme Father, the king, was content to allow subordinate fathers to retain their natural power over children who were minors, but when they grew up it was his will that their subjection should be transferred to the king himself, to the state in fact. The king was within his right in doing this because he could abrogate natural power, though he could not create it. He could, of course, delegate it and the king's ministers enjoyed such delegated natural power.

Since this was the nature of the position occupied by the king in patriarchal society, it was inevitable that his power should be absolute and arbitrary. All law was the expression of one indivisible will, and the king's will was the only legally constituted supreme will in society: therefore law was simply the expression of the king's will. It was he who had enacted it, it was he who kept it in being and he was at liberty to amend or abrogate it at his discretion. Similarly all custom, even the Common Law, had its force from the allowance by the king that it was natural: it also could be modified or set aside by the exercise of his fatherly will. But it must be remembered that the king as a father would only interfere with such customs for the good of his subjects and that the king himself was under Divine Law. The fatherly nature of his power and the content of the Divine Law made it imperative that the king should do his utmost to preserve his subjects and to consult their benefit. That was why he had allowed in England the growth of good laws and good customs, that was why he had assembled Parliaments. The whole mechanism of the constitution existed to enable the king to exercise his absolute and arbitrary power in a fatherly way and in obedience to God's law.

Nevertheless the subjects of the patriarchal monarch had no remedy whatsoever against him. Resistance to his commands could not be contemplated: it was inconceivable that there should be valid grounds to justify any opposition to natural subjection. Similarly the question of punishing the king for breaking the law, even the Divine Law, simply did not arise: the only remedy for outraged subjects was the confidence that an erring king would be Divinely punished for unfatherly conduct. It followed also that neither Aristocracy nor Democracy could exist as forms of government with a moral right to obedience. Nobody in society had a right to rule as an aristocrat or to elect anyone else to rule as a democrat. Filmer had hinted at an aristocracy in the remedy he proposed for the failure of the royal line, but the chief fathers who were to meet on that occasion exercised their power only once and as the result of an anachronism: they had no right to limit or even define the natural power of the new dynasty. Aristocracy and Democracy were not only entirely illegal, they were impossible. They were impossible because no plurality of voices could ever join in the exercise of the supreme will which was essential to sovereignty, and sovereignty was essential to political power. On the other hand there could be no such thing as tyranny, because it implied that the fatherly king could behave in an unfatherly manner in defiance of the law of God.

Filmer has himself summed up his conclusions about the nature of government from his interpretation of the evidence of the Bible and human history in the six following negative propositions. They were probably the last words he wrote on politics.[1]

1. That there is no Form of Government, but Monarchy only.
2. That there is no Monarchy, but Paternal.
3. That there is no Paternal Monarchy, but Absolute, or Arbitrary.
4. That there is no such thing as an Aristocraty or Democraty.
5. That there is no such Form of Government as a Tyranny.
6. That the People are not born Free by Nature.

PATRIARCHALISM IN SEVENTEENTH-CENTURY THINKING: FILMER AND HIS CONTEMPORARIES

Such was the substance of the most refuted theory of politics in the language. It presents an obvious problem to the modern reader, a problem which demands attention before any attempt is made to relate it to the thought of its era. Why, it might well be asked, were the works of Sir Robert Filmer of any importance at all? Why, above all, should a thinker of the stature of John Locke have found it necessary to analyse Filmer almost word for word before he could present his own argument? *Patriarcha* cannot bear comparison as philosophy or as history with the *Leviathan*, with Harington's *Oceana*, or even with many of the ephemeral tracts of the times. What, then, is it doing alongside all these illustrious names in English thinking and English politics?

[1] See the end of the Forms, infra, p. 229.

It must be pointed out at once that such a reflection does far less than justice to the thesis, or rather the implied thesis, of Filmer's thinking. No less an authority than J. W. Allen has stated that 'as a political thinker he was far more profound and far more original than was Locke'.[1] His critique of the assumptions his contemporaries were making about political obligation went to the bottom of the most difficult problem in the whole field of inquiry. It will be seen that neither Locke nor Sidney nor any of a host of others who attacked *Patriarcha* ever attempted to meet the force of these criticisms and that none of them even realized what he meant by his naturalism.

Furthermore it must be emphasized that a great deal of the fantastic in his writings simply comes from the remote and unfamiliar vocabulary of the age. We do not quarrel with Isaac Walton for believing that fish could be engendered out of mud, or even with Gilbert White for seriously considering the view that swallows hibernated at the bottom of ponds. Why then should we be outraged at Filmer's seriously believing that Charles I was a direct heir of Adam or that 'most of the civilest nations of the world labour to fetch their original from one of the sons or nephews of Noah'? It so happened that his view of monarchy involved a large amount of history and biblical criticism both of which must seem to us as unscientific and improbable as does the natural history of the same generation. This is no reason for dismissing Filmer as fantastic whilst we take more seriously the works of men who did not happen to appeal to so much historical or biblical evidence.

Finally, in explaining why Filmer was both important and influential, it must be admitted that his reputation owed a great deal to the fortuitous circumstances of the time at which his works were resuscitated. They passed almost unnoticed when they were first issued and it will be shown that it was only the position of the Tory party between 1680 and 1690 which identified them with an important segment of English opinion.

Nevertheless the writings of Filmer have a significance in the history of European social thinking which is quite independent of the relation they bear to Locke's theory of obligation and of the position of the English Tories in later Stuart times. The value of *Patriarcha* as a historical document consists primarily in its revelation of the strength and persistence in European culture of the patriarchal family form and the patriarchal attitude to political problems. It was because of

[1] In *The Social and Political Ideas of some English Thinkers of the Augustan Age*, ed. Hearnshaw, London, 1928.

patriarchalism that Sir Robert Filmer was read, not because of his literary or philosophical ability. It was because of patriarchalism that Locke and Sidney had to answer him, for in appealing to the power of the father and the relevance of the family to the state he touched the assumptions of all his own readers and of most of Locke's. Some attention must be given to patriarchalism as a feature of European culture in general, and of Sir Robert's generation and class in particular, if his importance and effectiveness are to be properly understood.

The words Patriarch and Patriarchal, with the modern generalized term Patriarchalism, have more than one definition and are used to cover both a particular institution and a general attitude. They are technical terms in theology, where they refer to the Old Testament tribal leaders and also to the ecclesiastical office of the patriarchate. In anthropology they are used to describe a specific form of the family and the social attitudes which go with it. The patriarchal *family* is marked by the supremacy of the father, the inferiority of women, rules of primogeniture and so on. In fully developed patriarchalism the family extends itself into the patriarchal *household* where the eldest father rules not simply over his wife and children but also over his younger brothers, his sisters, grandchildren, nephews, nieces and over a large household of retainers and servants. The anthropologist recognizes patriarchal *societies*, which may consist of associations of such households, and the distinction between patriarchal and other institutional forms, e.g. matriarchal forms, is of fundamental importance to the whole study of Social Anthropology. It helps to determine the political structure of societies, and in this way patriarchal is also a term in political science. It has an important influence over property institutions and has therefore a place in economics and economic history. It even affects the typical development of the personality of the individuals comprising a society, so that the psychologist is also interested in whether a man's emotional upbringing has been patriarchal or otherwise. Filmer himself, of course, only used the terms in one of their theological senses and occasionally in their extended political sense. But in analysing the patriarchal background to seventeenth-century European thinking and in assessing Filmer's role as a theorist of patriarchalism we shall have to take into account all the relevant evidence, anthropological, sociological and even psychological, as well as political and economic.

Now the social anthropologist classifies European culture of all periods, even in the present era of self-conscious rationalism, as markedly patriarchal. It is patriarchal in its family forms, it is patriarchal in its emotional attitudes: it is even patriarchal in its politics and economics. In none of these respects, of course, is it as extreme in its patriarchalism as are many other cultures, ancient or modern, primitive or advanced. The European cannot sympathize, for example, with contemporary Japanese society which builds its whole political philosophy on the Emperor as the literal ancestor of all the Japanese. Nevertheless we need go no further than our vocabulary of political and religious authority to see how closely we still associate all forms of power with the power of the father. God is still the Father, the Pope is still Papa, we still talk of paternal despots, even of paternal bureaucracies. In fact, in the view of the most influential school of social psychologists, the emotional attitude of the contemporary American to political authority is identical in character with his emotional attitude to the father of his family.

But it is in the economic field that the evidence for the survival of patriarchal institutions into present day European society is most marked. It is astonishing to realize that in this respect the Europe of today is almost exactly the same as the Europe of Sir Robert Filmer's generation. In all parts of the world where European law and culture prevail, with the exception of the areas which have adopted communism, there is a general presumption which favours of the inheritance of a father's property by his eldest son. There is also a tendency to subordinate the interests of women to men in the possession of property and above all there is an assumption that a man has a right before all other men to the possessions of his dead father. All these assumptions about the transference of property are the assumptions of patriarchalism. To patriarchalism is due the very possibility of a man's identifying himself with his posterity and so striving to build up his wealth for the benefit of his son and his son's son. In this form patriarchalism is readily recognized as an essential feature of the European tradition, and it is easy to see how differently modern society would have developed if the patriarchal rules of property had become as archaic as the patriarchal rules of politics. It is clear, for example, that patriarchalism has always been an essential, perhaps the essential, presupposition of capitalism.

Three hundred years ago, before the coming of the liberal view of society and the acceptance of the absolutely autonomous and independent individual, European patriarchalism was naturally far stronger. It was not expressed then, as it never has been since, in a series of formulated propositions about society to which nearly everyone would have agreed. Such traditions as these are generally present in a culture in the form of assumptions which need no formulation since it is almost inconceivable that they could ever be challenged. Indeed it is just at the point when they get written down that a search must be made for the decay of the institution which the intellectual traditions represent. Filmer's *Patriarcha* may not, in fact, indicate a climax in the growth of patriarchal institutions and ideas: it may quite as easily mark their incipient decline. It is certain however that the institutions of patriarchalism — the patriarchal family and the patriarchal household — were widespread in the society he lived in and that the intellectual tradition of patriarchalism, which placed the family at the centre of all social institutions, can be traced in all the thinkers of his period.

The patriarchal family came down to Filmer as one of the stablest features of European culture. There is not enough evidence to show whether the great culture change which took place over the much debated period between medieval and modern times was accompanied, or perhaps partially caused, by a change in the ethical pattern of family life. A revolution which manifested itself in such conspicuous religious changes and which was accompanied by such important economic developments could hardly fail to be reflected in some modification of domestic relationships. The little that is known points to an increase in the power of the parents, and especially of the father, rather than a decrease. In England at any rate the theological changes did nothing to soften the rigidity of the marriage and divorce laws and probably ended by strengthening them still further. It is true that extreme Puritanism, especially in the Low Countries and the New World, was ameliorating the position of women and breaking down the bonds which bound the adult son or daughter to the father. Nevertheless the Puritan theology deepened the emotional authoritarianism within the family group. Puritan family worship, Puritan fundamentalism — literally receiving every precept of Moses' declaration of the Law to the patriarchal society of the Hebrews — powerfully reinforced the patriarchal tradition of Christianity. In assuming that the family always had been and always would be patriarchal, Filmer could be justifiably confident that he would never be challenged.

The seventeenth-century patriarchal family, moreover, had many of the features of the patriarchal household. It included not only wife and children, but often younger brothers, sisters, nephews and nieces: male superiority and primogeniture were unquestioned. More striking was the presence of a very large number of servants, whose subjection to the head of the household was as absolute and unquestioned as that of the infant heir. The size of the household varied with the wealth, importance and profession of its master. A gentleman like Sir Robert would have in his domestic society not only manservants and maid-servants for the house, but also many of the workers on the home farm, the carters, the huntsman, the coachmen, perhaps a brewer, a carpenter or even a blacksmith. If the head of the family were a nobleman, the number of such dependants would be proportionately larger, but the landed gentry were not the only heads of patriarchal households: The merchant in the city had a similar entourage of apprentices and journeymen: even a professional man like Pepys refers to his 'family', which on New Year's Day 1661 was 'myself, my wife, Jane, Will. Hewer, and Wayneman, my girl's brother'. The tenant farmer had an establishment smaller in size but similar in arrangement. In fact there can have been few individuals in seventeenth-century England who did not belong to one or other of these patriarchal households. All but a very small number were in 'natural subjection' to men to whom they were not necessarily connected by blood. The smaller tradesfolk cannot be reckoned as members: otherwise the only exceptions were the patriarchs themselves, who were, of course, the directive minority. Nevertheless, in most of the places where the word 'people' is mentioned in the political writings of the time, even in such authors as Milton himself, it is possible to substitute the word 'patriarchs' or 'heads of households'.

It has been seen how important a part such a patriarchal household, played in Sir Robert's own experience. It is obvious from the contents of *Patriarcha* that he assumed in his readers the presuppositions of the head of East Sutton Park. It must also be remembered that in the traditions and even in some of the practice of the Royal Household, where his brother and son held posts of ceremonial importance, he and his readers had before them an example which certainly lent itself to the view that political society at large was nothing more than an extension of the patriarchal household. The officers of the King's Household had become the heads of the national civil service, and the subjection of the whole of the nobility with their own households derived in part from the personal service which they did in the house-hold of the king. The medieval, even the primitive and barbaric, origins of these customs were important illustrations of the European tradition which placed the patriarchal household at the very centre of society. To this day the Royal Household is a survival of the greatest significance in the history of social institutions: it is preserved not only in the constitutions of Great Britain and other European monarchies, but also over the whole range of European dramatic literature. The

c

modern reader is only familiar with the patriarchal household in such
contexts as the Court of Hamlet, King of Denmark, and it is this
archaism which makes Filmer's work so anachronistic. It is worth
pointing out, however, that the descendants of the Virginian planters,
who became the slaveowners of the Southern States, were the heads
of a classic type of patriarchal household, so that it survived until the
middle of the nineteenth century even in such a rationalistic and
egalitarian society as the U.S.A.

Such was the institutional background against which *Patriarcha* was
intended to be read. It will be remembered that it was actually composed in the first place for a community of such heads of patriarchal
households. It would be surprising to find that this essay of Filmer's
was the first to appeal to patriarchal assumptions and in fact it is
representative of a whole tradition of speculation about politics. But
a phrase like 'the intellectual tradition of patriarchalism', though it is
useful in indicating that there was a specific patriarchal strand in the
thinking of the time, in no sense accurately expresses the reality of the
case. As has already been emphasized, it was not a series of propositions, it was more a condition of all political thinking; a limitation on
the ideas which might come into any thinker's head, as much as a
source of specific social conceptions. There were writers, of whom
Filmer was one, who made deliberate use of patriarchal conceptions
to sanction a particular view about political obligation. But all writers,
whatever their attitude to this problem, shared this preoccupation with
the family as the fundamental unit of social relationships.

There is a vivid illustration of this in the traditional and universally
accepted approach to Biblical evidence on political obedience. It was
assumed, of course, that the Scripture must contain a definite direction
to Christians on their duty to obey the state, since there must be in
Revelation a complete statement of the whole duty of man. The text
which was accepted as the Divine pronouncement was the fifth commandment 'Honour thy father and thy mother'. It was in terms of
the patriarchal family, therefore, that all forms of social obedience were
construed, from submission in the nursery and in the school, to the
deference required by the magistrate and the king himself. This
traditional interpretation of the Scripture was adopted as a dogma of
the Church of England at the very outset of the Reformation, for it
appears in the 'Institution of a Christian man' in 1537. During Filmer's
lifetime it would seem to have been a universally accepted maxim of
casuistry. It appears in the sermons, in the systems of theology, in the
commentaries on Scripture. The convention was so commonplace

that it is introduced into *Patriarcha* almost incidentally, as if it were taken for granted: 'We find in the decalogue that the law which enjoins obedience to Kings is delivered in the terms of "Honour thy Father".' It should be noted, however, that such an assumption did not necessarily imply that domestic and political society were the same; rather it insisted on the *analogy* between the two.

This analogy between the family and the state is, of course, so obvious that it would be dangerous to read too much into its use by political thinkers. But it appears so frequently in the writings of the sixteenth and seventeenth centuries, and it occupies such an important place in so many of them, that it can be justifiably supposed that its use during this period was one of the reflections of patriarchal institutions. It derived in the first place from the Greek philosophers, and is frequently presented in the form of a commentary on Aristotle: in fact the whole concept of naturalistic politics is part of the Aristotelian tradition, as Filmer himself fully realized. Whatever their views on Aristotle, however, the politicians and lawyers of the period were all greatly exercised by the problem of the proper constitution of the family and its relation to the state.

The outstanding example of the insistence on the family as the point of departure of political society is Jean Bodin. In fact he defined the state as a government of households and his work is full of cross analogies between the two sorts of society. But Hooker is no less insistent, and he is also a good example of the way in which the argument was introduced as a reference to Aristotle: 'It is no improbable opinion therefore which the arch-philosopher [Aristotle] was of, that as the chiefest person in every household was always as it were a king, so when numbers of households joined themselves in civil society together, kings were the first kind of governors among them.' The most strictly contractarian and individualistic of the seventeenth-century writers also argued in this way. Grotius is quoted by Filmer as maintaining that political subjection is analogous both to the subjection of a woman to her husband and to the obedience due from pupils to tutors, also conceived as a domestic relationship. In fact the *De Jure Belli et Pacis* is much concerned with the laws of the family and leaves its readers in no doubt of the importance of arguments by analogy between those laws and the laws of political society. These are not isolated examples: Bellarmine, Suarez, Arnisaeus and many others before Filmer, Hobbes, Locke, Pufendorf and many others after him, could be used to illustrate the same point.

The laws of the family and the rights of the father enjoyed a gratuitous prestige at this epoch because of the great influence of Roman law. Filmer himself depended extensively on the 'Civil Law' for his arguments about Patria Potestas, though in this also it is possible that his thinking was simply derivative from his master Bodin. Bodin in fact went so far as to recommend that the father have restored to him the power of condemning his children to death which he possessed in Roman Law. The lawyers of the time, and particularly the French school of legal thinkers, were beginning to interpret the Roman legal system in terms of Roman society, and were also tending to interpret their own society into the highly patriarchal institutions of the Roman people. This is the element in political speculation which may have been responsible for much of its unreality. Filmer did not adopt the capital punishment of children by their fathers, but he quoted examples of it from Bodin with approval, and much of his discussion of fatherly rights is expressed in Roman legal terms. If in such things as this *Patriarcha* as a whole implies a great deal more power in the hands of Elizabethan fathers than we know from other sources that they actually possessed, it is because he saw in himself and his fellows the Roman *paterfamilias*.

It is possible, therefore, to trace the patriarchal family in all these respects in the conventional theology, the political thinking and the legal opinion of the age. It is obvious, if only from the quotation from Hooker, that the use of the family analogy created a presumption in favour of monarchy. It is also to be expected that sooner or later the two societies would be merged into one, and that thinkers would be found who could claim that the king *was* the father and the family *was* the state. Filmer's originality, in so far as he was an original writer at all, consisted in the boldness and clarity with which he formulated these two propositions. The necessary logical step had been taken, however, long before he wrote *Patriarcha*. It was implicit in the proposition that Adam, the first man, was the first king.

The conception of the kingship of Adam had entered the political thought of Europe in the late sixteenth century as a weapon in the great controversy which was then in progress on the subject of political obedience. It is not as yet clear who first adopted it, but it was familiar to the early Spanish Jesuits and Suarez considered the proposition, together with its attendant argument from the history of the Old Testament Patriarchs. It was certainly no novelty, since it was referred to by Josephus in one of those apologetic asides which he found necessary in vindicating Judaism to the Greeks. It was probably from Josephus that the concept was taken over, since he had been extensively read throughout the century after his first being printed in 1470. It was so familiar in England by 1606 that Bishop Overall was able to get the whole body of the English clergy to agree on an unequivocal statement of the proposition as one of the canons of the English Church. Overall's *Convocation Book* (dated 1606 but not printed until 1690) contains an almost complete anticipation of the account given in *Patriarcha* of the descent of patriarchal power from Adam to the crowned heads of Europe. There are even repetitions of Overall's phraseology in Filmer's books.

It is a little surprising that this argument should have made so little appeal to those who were interested in vindicating the absolute rights of legitimate monarchs. It might have been expected that the royal defender of royal rights, King James I, would have used it. But his *Trew Law of a Free Monarchy* contains no more than a strong statement of the argument by analogy between the power of the individual king and the individual father. The German thinker, Arnisaeus, comes nearest to the conception of the identity of the two, but even in his thought it does not appear that domestic and political society have definitely coalesced. It was left to Filmer to work out the theory of patriarchalism as a series of propositions in political thinking. He did so, of course, with reference to one particular society with its monarchy, that of England, and in respect of a particular constitutional situation, the situation which led to the English Civil War.

He presented his case as an ordinary argument in political obligation and in addition to his statements about fatherhood and kingship he wrote out all the conventional claims which were being made to substantiate the absolute power of monarchs. It has been shown that his statements about the patriarchal basis of political power were to a large extent derivative, original only in presentation and in coherence. But in the well-argued field of the relative merits of monarchy, aristocracy and democracy, or of the justifiability of resistance, he had nothing further to say than to repeat the well-worn clichés of the last two or three generations of Englishmen and Frenchmen. Nevertheless there were instances in which the combination of patriarchal and naturalistic assumptions with the traditional arguments led to a novel approach to the old positions, and even to some change of attitude. This was particularly true of the ancient tradition of the Divine Right of Kings.

Patriarcha is usually classified as a development of the theory that kings rule by the appointment of God and that resistance to them is forbidden by Divine Law. As is well known, the theory had been worked out as a justification for the resistance of the Emperor to the claims of the Pope during the Middle Ages, and had developed during the sixteenth century as a defence of the Catholic king against Protestant insurgents, or of the Protestant king against Catholic insurgents. Filmer's patriarchalism added a great deal of. precision to this claim. Once accepted, it made it impossible to doubt that kings and kings only could enjoy Divine Right, because only kings could be patriarchs. It also complicated the theory, for it raised the question of queens as metaphorical or literal 'fathers' and many intricate problems of succession. More valuable was the fact that it made the theory to some extent independent of Scriptural texts. It showed that monarchy was natural to man and, assuming that what was natural expressed the Divine Will, so provided an autonomous verification of the divinity of monarchy.

It is true that this was no great advance on the position already occupied by the Divine Righters, but there is a different meaning of the Divine Right for which Filmerism was far more significant. There is a sense in which in the seventeenth century all political power was divine. The ability to command all the people, the right to legislate for a whole society, the exercise of a morally valid will above all other wills — all these things must derive from God's power. The divinity of kingship was, in fact, still to some extent the magic of kingship; it will be remembered that the English kings retained their power to heal scrofula by touching. Filmer's theories certainly added a great deal to this *mystique* of kingship — indeed of government in general. His historical arguments are exactly parallel to the arguments used by the Japanese to vindicate the Emperor's claim to divinity. They assigned an origin of remote antiquity to the Royal line and they connected the ruler of today with ancestors possessed of heroic, if not divine, attributes. They referred the necessity of obedience to the early emotional submission of the child to its parents and they provided an easy Divine vindication of all these things by reference to Scripture. Filmer's patriarchal mystique of kingship could almost be said to have provided for the Stuart monarchs the sort of political mythology which the doctrine of the 'Volk' provided for the Nazi dictatorship of Germany. *Patriarcha* certainly exercised that sort of influence under James II and for the Jacobites.

For the most part, nevertheless, his references to Divine Right consisted of the same old well-worn phrases. There is not a trace of originality in the use he made of the familiar Biblical texts — the statement about the inscription on Caesar's penny, the directions about submission to the 'Higher Powers' in the battle-scarred thirteenth chapter of the Romans and the Epistles of St. Peter. All these arguments could be paralleled in scores of writers in sixteenth-century France or in seventeenth-century England, in Heywood, Barclay, Overall, James I, Manwaring and so on. This is particularly true of Filmer's statements justifying passive obedience and forbidding all resistance to the divinely appointed monarch. It will be obvious from the footnotes to *Patriarcha* that the text itself is very largely a tissue of quotations from other authors, some of them acknowledged, some unacknowledged, some accurately quoted, others so jumbled that they misrepresent the originals. Most surprising is the fact that Filmer seems to have lifted his history complete from a small group of the obvious English authors, and though his whole position rested on an interpretation of historical evidence, he was apparently satisfied with second-hand historical evidence wherever he could find it. He even plagiarizes the authors whom he wishes to refute, as when he borrows from Suarez a quotation out of St. Chrysostom and uses it in a different context, where it misrepresents the original author. He goes to the length of using the words of the men he was attacking to state his own point of view. In all these respects he was a profoundly unoriginal writer, although originality may consist in the juxtaposition of other men's notions as well as in notions of one's own.

His great advantage as a thinker was the ability to combine the subtleties of the doctrine of sovereignty with the crude assumptions of conventional patriarchalism, and he might have been less effective had he been less naive. It was this combination which led to his devastating attack on the assumptions of the contractual school about the nature of society and the justification of political obligation. We have seen that he questioned the principle which was essential to all accounts of obligation other than his own, the principle of consent. This to Filmer was an obvious contradiction of the social reality around him. It was simply not true that authority was being exercised by consent. How could it be pretended that the son consented to being commanded by his father? What conceivable sophistry could justify the obedience of the apprentice in going to church at his master's bidding, or the submission of the schoolboy to a beating, on the ground that they had given their assent? If authority could be exercised without consent, if in fact it was perpetually being so exercised, then there must be some other source of obligation. This other sort of obligation could only be by nature, not by choice, and observation showed that it was patriarchal.

But once granted that authority of any sort could be exercised by patriarchal right, it was difficult to see why political authority should be exercised by consent. There was no better case for the members of political society having historically consented to the establishment of an authority over them than there was in the case of the family. On the contrary, all the evidence pointed to a patriarchal origin of political power. It is in the patriarch, therefore, that we must seek the Bodinian sovereign. It is in the patriarch's will that we can find the supreme power which will maintain society. The patriarch inherited his power by the ordinary laws of property: it was his while he lived, to do what he liked with, to lend, to alienate, to retain undiminished against everyone else. No subject then can have any share of political power except what the patriarch confers on him: no law can have any validity except what the patriarch's will has created and which can continue only so long as the patriarch goes on willing it. There are no such things as political rights. There can be no such thing as the people's will. Neither limited monarchy, constitutional safeguards, nor the principles of democracy have any meaning whatsoever.

The general implication of Filmer's writings was a series of statements of this kind and this was the position which Locke attacked. But it would be difficult to believe that Filmer realized that he implied all these things or that he even consciously meant all that he said in so many words. His was the genuinely conservative mind: the sort of mind that so much wanted to prove that the traditional reality was the only conceivable political order, that he looked no further than to its vindication in just the form in which it existed. The *Patriarcha* is a rambling and incoherent work, without any progressive structure and no proper conclusion. But in one way it is extraordinarily complete; it left out none of the cherished political institutions of Englishmen. It justified the Houses of Parliament as well as the Kingship, the Common Law as well as the Prerogative. All he wanted was to state a principle that would make it impossible for people to defend change of any sort and he evidently believed that he had hit upon such a principle in patriarchalism. He uses it to attack the position set up by his antagonists, and not to establish his own. He uses it in defence of the *status quo* and never to suggest a reform. He never seemed to realize that his principle could be used to set up a despotism utterly different from the absolute monarchy he was defending. At times he even seems to be embarrassed at the possibility that he might be proving too much, and he often introduces his more extreme remarks with an apology.

It is perhaps typical of English society, in Filmer's generation as in any other, that he should have been so unconscious of being a disturbing radical. It might seem at first that it would need a social upheaval of the most violent kind to reveal the patriarchal roots of English and -European political institutions in the form of a treatise on politics. It is true of course that important alterations were going forward in English society when Filmer wrote and that he might have been dimly conscious that the social order to which the patriarchal household belonged was very soon to disappear. But it is obvious that he wrote with no sense of urgency and that issues did not press him to recognize the logical implications of what he was writing. Had he been alive to face the sort of question which Locke forced upon him, he might perhaps have given the sort of answer that Locke attributed to him. He might, in 1680, have favoured a Bourbon despotism for England. But he certainly had neither the imagination nor the motive to realize that such an issue could ever arise.

THE REPUBLICATION OF FILMER'S WORKS
FILMER, LOCKE AND LIBERALISM

What Filmer wrote down for his Kentish friends and for Charles I in the 1630s was first read by Sancroft, Shaftesbury and Locke in 1680. Half a century went by between the time of the formulation of his position and the time of its entrance into the tradition of political thinking. Yet when *Patriarcha* appeared in print in 1680 its thesis had a cogency which it might have lacked in any other year in English history. Charles II, his Court and ministers and the whole body of opinion which favoured the continuance of the Restoration stood in desperate need of an argument which would vindicate legitimacy. Without it it looked as if the monarchy would be swept away.

The opposition to Charles II's government, led by Shaftesbury and the Country Party, had engineered the political crisis in 1678 with the fabrication of the Popish Plot. Their first object was the removal of the Catholic Duke of York, the future James II, from succession to the throne. They had made such skilful use of these 'revelations' of Catholic designs on the British monarchy and on British independence that their Exclusion Bill would have passed both Houses by the middle of 1679 if the king had not prorogued and then dissolved Parliament. In the autumn of that year the country came nearer than ever again to its condition in 1641: it seemed to be on the verge of the same sort of long term, irreconcilable civil conflict, a conflict which could only be settled by force of arms.

It was at this very moment that the first collected edition of Filmer's works was bundled through the press, so hastily that its pages were wrongly numbered and its title page did not tally with its contents. This volume contained all the political tracts which had been printed in his lifetime, except the 'Power of Kings'. The political storm continued throughout 1680, and, when the new Parliament met, a second Exclusion Bill was introduced, and defeated in the Lords. It was in this year that *Patriarcha* was first printed, from an imperfect copy. Meanwhile there had been a new issue of the collected tracts, and the 'Power of Kings' had been separately published, with a foreword introducing Filmer to his rapidly growing reading public. So the whole body of his political writings was in print, and in the hands of the pamphleteers and propagandists on both sides, when the third and final Exclusion Bill was passed at the tumultuous Oxford Parliament in 1681, and nullified by its dissolution.

There succeeded four years of monarchical autocracy under Charles II, vindictive, repressive and reactionary, and then the reign of James. In this period of seven years the thought of Sir Robert Filmer formed the *ipsissima verba* of the established order. His collected tracts were again reprinted in 1684, now complete in one volume, and in 1685 the *Patriarcha* appeared for the first time in a tolerably complete form in the edition of Edmund Bohun. By 1688, therefore, the cult of Filmer had become an organic part of the cult of monarchical legitimism, and his political principles a major obstacle to the Whig theory of the Glorious Revolution. When the rightful heir went into exile, and the cult he upheld retired into the country houses of the Tory squires and into the studies of the non-juring parsons, the works of Filmer went with it. They were still in such demand that in 1696 (and possibly in 1695) they were all printed yet again, this time with *Patriarcha* bound up in the same volume. These two final decades of the seventeenth century were the formative years of the principles of British and American liberalism. Although he had been dead for thirty years, Sir Robert Filmer was the most important single influence to oppose them.

The reasons for this paradox, that a man who had had a negligible effect on his own generation should have become of such importance to the generation of his grandson, must be sought in the position occupied throughout these twenty years by the supporters of tradition and the crown — or the Tories as they came to be called. The Exclusion controversy is recognized as the birthplace of the much prized Anglo-

Saxon party systems: it was the first issue to be debated on recognizably party lines, and the names Whig and Tory first appeared in the course of it. Exclusion was a typically party issue because it raised questions of fundamental principle as well as of immediate policy. The Whigs claimed that James II must not be allowed to succeed because it was obvious that the majority of the people did not want him as king: it was Parliament's duty to alter the succession, because Parliament represented the people and so had the right to determine who should be king. This implied that government rested on consent: in fact the Whig case followed logically from original premise to practical policy. To oppose it effectively the Tories wanted a statement which denied its first principle, that consent was the basis of government. In the writings of Filmer they found it.

But the reply to the Whigs had to be more than a statement of first principles — it must also be good propaganda. The threat to the restored monarchy and the sudden spectre of the Long Parliament were the result of an extremely skilful propaganda campaign. It was for propaganda purposes that the Country Party had been run by Lord Shaftesbury: newspapers, pamphlets, scare rumours and stunts, the whole apparatus for influencing opinion had been brought into action to promote Exclusion. What was wanted was a propagandist case with a ready and striking appeal, an appeal if possible to the irrational, one that would provide slogans to answer the cries of 'No Popish Successor' which were being raised all over the country. Patriarchalism provided just such a propagandist answer. Its invocation of the mystique of monarchy had considerable emotive power and 'Pater Patriae' was an effective slogan, not only against Shaftesbury but right down to 1688 and beyond. In playing upon the tradition of patriarchalism it struck just the right note with the directive minority whose support was important: they were patriarchs themselves, to almost the extent to which Sir Robert had been.

The Tories, therefore, needed Filmer in 1680 because the crown was in peril, because their opponents had raised the question of political obligation and because they were faced with a propaganda scoop. It is not in itself surprising that someone should have hit upon this series of forgotten Royalist tracts as the answer to their difficulties, for republication was a common thing in seventeenth-century literary history. The political controversies of the 1680s and 1690s called forth the reprinting, and in some cases the first impression, of large numbers of works written for quite other purposes. The work of Parsons the Jesuit was reprinted in 1681, Hunton's *Treatise of Monarchy* was issued

twice in 1689, and it was in 1690 that *Convocation Book* was first
published. It is not yet certain who it was who remembered Filmer
well enough to realize how valuable his writings might be. There are
several candidates. It might have been Archbishop Sancroft: he is
known to have handled some of Filmer's MSS., and he helped Bohun
in his edition of *Patriarcha*. It might have been one of Filmer's grand-
sons or grandnephews: it is likely that a descendant wrote the bio-
graphical notice in the 1680 'Power of Kings'. It might even have been
his own publisher, Richard Royston, still bookseller to the King and
certainly responsible for the 1684 Collection. But whoever was
responsible for initiating the republication, its immediate and enduring
success was a pathetic reflection of the absence of any truly critical
element in the conservative thinking of the time. Filmer had no serious
rivals on his own side: most of them were content with the vaguest
assertion of indefeasible right, the thinnest of theories of conquest as
the basis of power, or the silliest statement of 'lachrymism'. The only
exception was Thomas Hobbes, and he had almost every possible dis-
qualification for being the champion of the Exclusion Tories.

From the moment that the works of Sir Robert Filmer had become
the expression of the declared attitude of the House of Stuart and its
adherents, it became inevitable that they would be the centre of a
major controversy in political thinking, and even that the Revolution
of 1688 would have to be justified by a denial of the thesis which they
put forward. Within a few months of the publication of *Patriarcha*
three of the ablest minds on the Whig side had set to work to refute
patriarchalism, James Tyrell the historian, Algernon Sidney the doyen
of the statesmen of the 'Old Cause', and John Locke. The controversy,
of course, spread far wider than these three men, and Filmer's name is
constantly recurring in the pamphlets and journals of the period. The
argumentation bore all the characteristics of such disputes: there was
a great deal of question begging, misrepresentation and downright
abuse: no logical conclusion was reached and the whole body of the
literature is now unreadable in its tedious repetitiveness. The importance of this debate, however, must be measured in terms of the constitutional principles of 1688 and the influence of Locke's *Two Treatises*,
both of which derive from it. Furthermore it was marked by an event
which has been happily unusual in English disagreements of opinion:
it was a contributory cause of the condemnation to death of Algernon
Sidney, one of the chief antagonists.

He was tried in November 1683, at the height of Charles II's
vengeance on the promoters of Exclusion. The charge was treason and

it was proved upon him before Judge Jeffreys from evidence of two separate acts of treason. The first of them was consulting with the Rye House plotters, especially with Argyll in Scotland. The second charge was that he wrote a 'libel' stating 'that we may change and take away Kings'. In his defence Sidney openly maintained that this book, which was in fact the manuscript of his *Discourses*, was simply a refutation of Sir Robert Filmer, but Jeffreys summed up by saying to the jury: 'If you believe that this is Colonel Sidney's book, no one can doubt but that he is guilty of compassing the King's death.' He was found guilty and executed on December 7th, 1683. He handed a paper to the executioner on the scaffold which reaffirmed his defiance of Filmer and of the authorities who had made of *Patriarcha* the canonical scripture of political obedience.

It is not granted to every writer that a republication of his works shall be a cause of the death of a conventional hero. The fate of Sidney adds an almost dramatic notoriety to Filmer's name. Meanwhile the Tory publicists were creating an orthodoxy out of his writings which was far more extreme and ridiculous than anything he ever published himself. It has been shown that Sir Robert was a little shy of giving his *Patriarcha* to the world in the form in which it had circulated among his friends, probably because it contains the direct assimilation of the English constitution into the patriarchal scheme. This argument appears only by implication in the works he himself had consented to publish, and it must be insisted that neither in them nor in the *Patriarcha* does he actually say that Charles Stuart was the literal father of all the English in virtue of his unique relationship with Adam or Noah. But his champions in the 1680s showed no such diffidence. They were using Filmerism in a political war to the knife, and they took the whole of *Patriarcha* for their text and its most improbable implications for their dogmatic assertions.

The circumstances of this political warfare by propaganda, and such events as the fate of Sidney, determined the nature of Whig criticism of Filmer's case. The Whigs were forced to concentrate their first attack on his character as a gentleman, his capacity as writer, the honesty of his motives and the sincerity of his protestantism. All of this could be done of course without any reference to the facts of his biography or to his actual reputation with his contemporaries. Then they found it essential that his every single inconsistency or improbability should be held up to ridicule. For this, likewise, it was not necessary to keep to what Filmer had actually said, but to seize on anything he might have implied or could be made to imply. Above all, it was not his statements which were under attack, but the statements made in defence or in explanation of him by his Tory defenders. It was only after all this had been done that any attention needed to be given to the logical consideration and refutation of his actual propositions about political obligation.

In all these respects the controversy over Filmerism was typical of all other political controversies. But the subsequent importance of Locke's *Two Treatises*, and to a lesser extent of Sidney's *Discourses*, has tended to obscure the primary purposes for which they were both written. It has made it easy to overlook the fact that they were judged by their contemporaries first of all for their effectiveness as controversial propaganda, and only secondarily as statements of belief about political obligation. An examination of either of the two books will quickly show how much of them was given to the tasks of discrediting Filmer as a man and as a writer and in countering the case made by Filmer's supporters rather than by Filmer himself. When they did get to grips with the central propositions of patriarchalism, however, it is interesting to see that their arguments contained little more than had been said a quarter of a century previously by an author who had no such pressures upon him to write political propaganda.

Edward Gee is the only writer of standing known to have dealt with Filmer's tracts on their first appearance, though Gee's arguments against patriarchalism can be paralleled in many other contexts. Writing in 1658 he characterized the patriarchal school as follows: 'The drift of their opinion is to make the rise and right of government *natural* and *native*, not *voluntary* and *conventional*.' Such a succinct statement of the real issue between those who could believe in a contractual society and those who could not, shows that Gee fully realized what was at stake and took Filmer perfectly seriously, which none of the Whigs could bring himself to do. Gee justified his disagreement with Filmer by challenging his belief in the kingship of Adam. This damaged the patriarchal case in two important ways. It removed the possibility of contemporary kings being related to the father of all mankind and it reduced patriarchal society to an anarchy of independent families. But Gee went on to use the patriarchal principle to establish a society which was an odd mixture of the 'natural and native' with the 'voluntary and conventional'.

Now all that we get against Filmer in the works of Sidney and Tyrell and the other Whigs is a restatement of this case at greater length, but without Gee's deep appreciation of what was at stake and with the addition of a great deal of propagandist denigration of Filmer.

Sidney's vast work is unreadable precisely because this is so. All of its 420 folio pages are taken up with the minutiae of Filmer's exegetical and historical errors. The whole of his thinking is bounded by the scope of Filmer's works and without a detailed acquaintance with them it is impossible to understand the *Discourses* at all. It is true that in going to such lengths to prove negatives against Filmer, Sidney did go out of his way to assert their positives. His theory of popular sovereignty is established by Filmer's statements in reverse. But he gave no sign that he realized how difficult it might be to establish his own political principles, given the individualistic view of human nature which they implied. Nor did he seem to know that this was the issue with which Filmer was concerned. In fact all he accomplished was the statement of a theory of history on principles which he did not attempt to demonstrate. The fact that Sidney had nothing to say on the subject of political obligation as conceived by Filmer does not, of course, dispose of the importance of the *Discourses* as a protest, and a very necessary protest, against Stuart patriarchal despotism.

The relation of Locke to Filmer is more complicated, complicated in fact by the perpetual presence between and above the two men of the Great Leviathan of Thomas Hobbes. But the *Two Treatises* can accurately be given a first classification with the works of Sidney, Tyrell and the lesser Whigs. There is the same initial determination to discredit Filmer by all available means. The difference is, of course, that Locke's quiet irony and smoothly flowing argument did the job a great deal better than Sidney's outraged blusterings or Tyrell's laborious pedantry. Filmer's reputation has never recovered from what he said: Locke nonchalantly flicked him off the ridge of a temporary notoriety into permanent obscurity. It cannot be claimed that Locke was much more economical either in language or in space in achieving this result, for the *First Treatise* in its original form was far longer than we have it now and must have been very like Sidney's *Discourses*, though it could hardly have been so bulky. There is also, in this primary effort to discredit his opponent, the same refusal to meet him on his own ground. Locke certainly made no attempt to overcome the dilemma posed by Filmer, when he challenged those who disagreed with him to get their free and equal individuals out of the state of nature into any sort of society by means of contract. Most of the arguments first systematized by Gee also reappear. And this section of the two essays was certainly not directed against Hobbes, except in so far as the following statement by Filmer involved him. 'With no small content I read Mr. Hobs Book "De Cive", and his "Leviathan"; about the Rights of Sovereignty, which no man, that I know, hath so amply and judiciously handled: I consent with him about the Rights of *exercising* Government but I cannot agree to his means of *acquiring* it.'

It is quite unrealistic to overlook the avowed objective of a practical man like Locke and to assume that he was not writing against Filmer, who was being used by the authorities to persuade men to believe that government had no relation to consent, but against Hobbes, whose reputation was philosophical and whose political influence was negligible. It was Filmer and Patriarchalism which were the enemy, not Hobbes and the despotism of egoistic timorousness. This applies not only to the *First Treatise*, which was written with the specific object of refuting Filmer, but to the *Second Treatise* also. But there is a difference here between Locke and his companions in arms. He was not circumscribed as they were in the range of his arguments by what Filmer had written. The frequent veiled references and coincidences in vocabulary show that he had the arguments of *Leviathan* in mind as well as of *Patriarcha*. Nevertheless this must not be allowed to obscure the fact that Locke was arguing with his terms of reference chosen by Filmer, and not by Hobbes or even by himself: the incidental influences of the form of Filmer's thinking are remarkable, even throughout the *Second Treatise*. Much of the misunderstanding and consequent depreciation of Locke have resulted from a failure to recognize that he did not, in writing the *Two Treatises*, choose a format to present a view of politics *sub specie aeternitatis*, as did Hobbes in writing *Leviathan*. The form his works should take was forced on him by inescapable political and intellectual circumstance.

Locke did not succeed in establishing against Filmer that consent pervaded all social relationships. He did not appear to realize that this would have to be done if naturalism were to be refuted. He explained family relationships by saying that they were based on contract and not on status, though he allowed that natural sociability was one of the stages leading up to social contract. He was evidently embarrassed by the force of some of Filmer's arguments, in particular his claim that only patriarchalism can give continuity to society. In disallowing that the successive generations which make up a community were connected by nature, Locke was forced to suppose that the true bond between father and son, between the English in 1688 and the English in 1588, was a bond of inherited property together with the consent to fulfil obligations that go with the inheritance of property. But in most cases he seemed to have been unconscious that he was making assumptions which he would have to prove if he was to be consistent in disagreeing with Filmer. This can be illustrated by the discrepancies which are obvious in his treatment of the problem of establishing the rule of majorities, which as we have seen was one of Filmer's major criticisms of the contractarians.

In the end, of course, the logical relationship between the two cases did not matter. Filmer was overwhelmed by the concentrated campaign to discredit him on all grounds and, which was the only really important thing, political events justified Locke. It was the success of the Revolution Settlement which exploded patriarchalism, far more than political argumentation. But it did not mean that Filmer's works were immediately consigned to the limbo from which they had been rescued in 1679. They played their part in the politics of the Jacobites and non-jurors and in the great Sacheverell affair under Queen Anne; indeed faint echoes of the Exclusion controversy can be heard throughout the eighteenth century. More surprising is it to find that the theories of *Patriarcha* found a place in the tradition of political thinking as a whole. It is probable that Bossuet was directly influenced by Filmer and Rousseau makes a reference to patriarchalism which seems to be aimed particularly at him. Most striking is the use made of his works during the American Revolution, for it indicates that even at that time and in that society the conservative cast of mind found patriarchalism satisfactory. His champion was the Virginian Tory parson, Jonathan Boucher, who expounded his philosophy in sermons preached against the American rebels and dedicated to George Washington.

Boucher's was in fact the best common-sense defence of Filmer that ever was made. But by 1750 almost all other common-sense influences were against him and his name had already become a rather dreary appendage to the name of John Locke. The reason of course was the triumph of Whig principles and of Whig institutions, the growth of rationalism and the steady expansion of urban, commercial and bourgeois culture. Retreating perpetually before them were the political institutions and political prejudices of European patriarchalism. This process had been going on in the period between the composition of *Patriarcha* and its publication, which is itself a justification of the somewhat contemptuous attitude of Locke.

The triple relationship of the three men, Filmer, Locke and Hobbes, is interesting in itself. Filmer, for all his brash naivety and his obviously amateur outlook, was that extremely rare phenomenon — the codifier of conscious and unconscious prejudice. Hobbes was even rarer, though he belonged to a far commoner type of thinker: he was the

D

really able rationalizer, the creator of a genuine philosophy out of an active realization that the social condition was a condition of danger. But Locke in his way was the rarest of them all, for he had, in a less degree, the qualities of both and in addition a strong vein of sterling common sense. He sensed at once, and all his readers sense it, that a political theory must correspond to something self-evident about ordinary men, something which does not need complicated demonstration but which cannot be used to lead them into improbable situations. He saw that neither Hobbes' *Artificial Man* nor Filmer's patriarchal family state would ever be accepted on the common-sense grounds which justify really important beliefs. It was for these reasons, as well as because of the victory of the forces in society which Locke represented, that he has a far more important place in the texture of political society than either of the other two.

The comparative study of the three thinkers can also be used to demonstrate how Filmer's psychological assumptions were never examined either by Locke or by Hobbes and have not subsequently been disposed of. He insisted that society was not created by conscious thinking and that it is not kept in being, kept working, by conscious thought. Hobbes' *Leviathan* was created by agreement amongst a society of entirely selfish and independent individuals. They obeyed it because it represented them and had been carefully constructed so as to embody their conscious purposes and to fulfil their conscious needs. Locke's contractual government was erected on an even more limited agreement between individuals, but nonetheless it was an embodiment of thinking, it assumed that the stuff of society was conscious ratiocination. Both Hobbes and Locke presupposed that individuals were psychologically constructed so as to be able to do this. Filmer dogmatically supposed that this was untrue and nothing they said was of a nature to convict him of being wrong. Society for him was physically natural to man. It had not grown up out of men's conscious thinking, it could not be altered by further thinking, it was simply a part of human nature.

The rational, liberal theory of politics is an attempt to demonstrate that political society is a human artifact, and that in obeying political authority men are obeying themselves. This thesis was established and elaborated in the early modern period by a series of thinkers, and John Locke was one of the really important names amongst them. But it was a difficult thesis to maintain, and some of the difficulties must have been due to a failure to take into account Filmer's type of scepticism. There were radical questionings and there were reformulations, particularly by Rousseau and by Hegel. Nevertheless the assumption that human society itself partook of the nature of intellectual activity, that it actually worked by way of syllogisms as well as being open to examination by the use of logical propositions, was basic to the political thinking of our immediate historical hinterland in the nineteenth century, to the thinking of Bentham and Mill, even of T. H. Green and Bosanquet. It is still fundamental to the tradition behind the democratic institutions of the modern world. It is even more important to Marxian sociological theory, and especially to those of its implications which issue in the pure political theory of a classless, stateless society.

But the political experience and the scientific observation of the twentieth century have shown up this assumption for what it is — a working hypothesis. The change has come about because of the evidence of anthropology and of sociology and above all because of our tragic experience of government by deliberate invocation of the irrational. We have been forced to recognize that this statement — the statement that social arrangements rest on mental agreement — is an hypothesis, an hypothesis which may prove to be accurate, but which cannot be dogmatically assumed. Our definition of nature may be different from Filmer's and Locke's, and in particular we no longer assume that we possess in Revelation a detailed account of what nature is, in their sense or in our own. But we should now be disposed to grant to Filmer that it is more accurate, or in our language it is more scientific, it leads to greater economy of hypothesis, to think of society as natural rather than as created by thinking and willing. We must agree with Locke that the only way to examine social phenomena is by the method of logical argument. But we may also agree with Filmer that it is wrong to assume that the association of men in civil society is itself the consequence of such ratiocination.

BIBLIOGRAPHICAL NOTE

THE text of *Patriarcha* printed here is a word for word copy of the Patriarcha Manuscript in the Cambridge University Library (Additional MS. 7078). Slight verbal emendations have been made from the printed versions of 1680 and 1685, both based on a different original. Spelling and punctuation have been modernized, since it was found that they are completely arbitrary. The chapter headings which have appeared in the previous printings of this work have been omitted since it was found that they had no authorization in the MS.: the 'Heads of the Discourse' which are prefixed to the manuscript text have been substituted. The only modern version is that edited by Henry Morley for his Universal Library in 1884: for the reasons given below that text has no claims to represent the authentic version of *Patriarcha*.

The manuscript reproduced here is the only handwritten version known to have survived. It was discovered by the author at East Sutton Park in 1939.[1] Its existence had been effectively concealed by its being described by the Historical Manuscript Commission as 'Palicanta' in their report on their visit to East Sutton Park in 1872 (3 Rep. App., p. 246). It is known that *Patriarcha* circulated in various manuscript copies after its composition and before its first printing. The Cambridge Manuscript is not one of those copies. It is an exquisitely written and magnificently bound quarto volume in Sir Robert Filmer's own show hand — a fine example of seventeenth-century English penmanship. The tooled calf binding is elaborately decorated with gold leaf, and on both faces there is an achievement of the Stuart Arms surrounded by the Garter. The volume has every mark of a show copy for presentation to Royalty. Thomas Hobbes made such a manuscript copy of *Leviathan* for presentation to Charles II 'engrossed in vellum in a marvellous fair hand'. It is a fair assumption that Sir Robert Filmer wrote out this version of his major work and had it suitably bound as a present for Charles I.

There is a complicated relationship between this manuscript and the versions of *Patriarcha* previously printed. When the work first appeared

---

[1] It was then in the possession of the last descendant of Sir Robert to live at East Sutton, the late Mrs. Stanley Wilson. Grateful acknowledgments are due to Arthur Wilson Filmer, Esq., for free access to the Filmer Collections when they were at East Sutton Park before the war.

in 1680 the version used was one of the manuscripts which had been passing from hand to hand for forty years. The copy selected was particularly corrupt and incomplete: paragraphs, sentences and words were missing or mistranscribed, Filmer's numerous quotations were seldom marked as such, the text had been interfered with so as to conceal its date. Archbishop Sancroft thereupon 'Obtained the Original Manuscript from Sir Robert's son' and lent it to Edmund Bohun, who issued a corrected version in 1685. This 1685 edition was the most accurate text available before the discovery of the MS. now at Cambridge, but when Henry Morley edited *Patriarcha* in 1884 he completely ignored it and reproduced the 1680 printing, with some further inaccuracies. The 'Original Manuscript of the Author'[1] used by Bohun was of later origin than the Cambridge Manuscript and the evidence goes to show that both were based on a yet earlier text.

Collation of the Cambridge Manuscript with the other versions has shown it to be far more accurate than Bohun's text and to represent a much earlier state of the work as a whole. Most of the verbal anomalies present in all the printings can be solved, many more marginal references and indications of quotations are shown up, and the internal evidence which dates the work before the Civil War appears for the first time. The ten pages which were printed as part of the 'Observations on Grotius' are included where they logically belong. All this goes to show that the Cambridge MS. version was a copy of the treatise which existed before Filmer decided to print anything on the subject of political obligation. It also illustrates very clearly the use he made of this essay when he did begin to write tracts for the press. Perhaps the major difference between the Cambridge MS. and the MS. used by Bohun lies in the different placing of several passages and the presence of several new paragraphs. But there are instances where the sense of a passage requires the use of Bohun's version in preference to the Cambridge version, and the general conclusion must be that there was a succession of manuscripts. The one result which seems to be established by the comparative study of the versions which have survived is that the Cambridge MS. is certainly the earliest source now extant, as it is far and away the most reliable. It seems very unlikely that the discovery of a still earlier version could do much to disturb the claim that the text presented here is substantially the authentic original of *Patriarcha*, as it was written down by Sir Robert Filmer.

Footnotes, mainly references to Filmer's sources, will be found in this edition in the case of *Patriarcha* but not for the other tracts. All

[1] See the Preface to Bohun's edition of *Patriarcha*, 1685.

the works written by Sir Robert which could be called political in content are included. The tracts on usury and on witchcraft have no proper place in an edition of Sir Robert's political writings. The political tracts have been reprinted from the 1684 republication, corrected from the first editions of 1648 and 1652. They are arranged in the same order in which they appeared in all the collected editions. Archaistic spelling and punctuation have been brought up to date, but the texts have not been modernized in the same way as *Patriarcha*. Each is prefaced with a short bibliographical note.

It has not been possible in an Introduction of this nature and of this brevity to provide documentation. This is particularly unfortunate because many of the statements made are based on original research, much of it amongst unpublished materials. A brief bibliography of Filmer's published works is provided, however, and the footnotes to *Patriarcha* cover most of Sir Robert's own sources. Further reference can be made to two articles by the present writer: 'The Gentry of Kent in 1640' in the *Cambridge Historical Journal* for 1948 and 'Sir Robert Filmer' in the October 1948 issue of *The William and Mary Quarterly* (Third Series, Vol. V, No. 4), published by the Institute of Early American History and Culture, Williamsburg, Virginia, U.S.A.

ACKNOWLEDGEMENTS

For the introduction to these texts, slight as it is, I should like to acknowledge the help of the following:

The governing bodies of St. John's College and Peterhouse, Cambridge, and St. Deiniol's Library, Hawarden, Cheshire, have supported my researches. In addition to the late Mrs. Wilson and to Mr. Wilson Filmer, Mr. Holworthy (Archivist of the Kent County Council), Mr. Pink (of the Cambridge University Library), Mr. Keen of Cliffords Inn and the staff of the Library of Congress have all given freely of their time and resources to make accessible the scattered evidence on the Filmers. I should also like to acknowledge my debt to Professor Herbert Butterfield, to the late Professor Karl Mannheim, to Canon Charles Smyth, to Sir Ernest Barker and to the Rev. Hardenfeldt, Chaplain of Sutton Valence School, Kent.

CONCISE BIBLIOGRAPHY
OF THE WORKS OF SIR ROBERT FILMER

A. COLLECTED EDITIONS

1. 1679. THE FREEHOLDERS GRAND INQUEST . . ., London. No printer or publisher, MDCLXXIX (Omits 'Patriarcha', 'Necessity', 'Quaestio Quodlibetica').
2. 1679/80. POLITICAL DISCOURSES OF SIR ROBERT FILMER. No printer or publisher, MDCLXXX (Omits 'Necessity' and 'Qu. Quod.').
3. 1680. THE FREEHOLDERS GRAND INQUEST . . ., London. No printer or publisher, MDCLXXX (Omits 'Patriarcha', 'Necessity' and 'Qu. Quod.').
4. 1684. THE FREEHOLDERS GRAND INQUEST . . ., London. Printed for Rich. Royston, at the Angel in Amen Corner, 1684 (Omits 'Patriarcha' and 'Qu. Quod'.).
5. 1695. OBSERVATIONS UPON ARISTOTLES POLITICKS . . . (1695) (Not seen).
6. 1696. OBSERVATIONS CONCERNING THE ORIGINAL AND VARIOUS FORMS OF GOVERNMENT . . ., London. Printed for RRC., sold by Sam. Keble, 1696 (Omits 'Qu. Quod.').

B. INDIVIDUAL WORKS (in alphabetical order)

ADVERTISEMENT — 'An Advertisement to the Jurymen of England, Touching Witches. Together with a Difference between an English and Hebrew Witch', London. Printed by I.G. for Richard Royston, at the Angel in Ivie Lane, 1653.

ANARCHY — 'The Anarchy of a Limited or Mixed Monarchy . . .', 1648. No printer or publisher [Royston].

BLASPHEMY (Never included in the Collected Editions)
1. 'Of the Blasphemie Against the Holy Ghost.' Printed in the Yeare 1646, no printer or publisher.
2. 'A tract concerning the Sin Against the Holy Ghost. By . . . John Hales . . .', London, 1677.

DIRECTIONS — 'Directions for Obedience to Governors in Dangerous and Doubtful Times' (Always printed with 'Forms', q.v.).

FORMS — 'Observations upon Aristotles Politiques touching Forms of Government. Together with Directions . . .', London, Royston . . ., 1652.

FREEHOLDER — 'The Freeholders Grand Inquest touching our Soveraigne Lord the King and His Parliament.' Printed in the 23rd year of Charles I, no printer or publisher [Royston].

NECESSITY (or 'Power')

1. 'The Necessity of the Absolute Power of all Kings: and in particular of the Kings of England', London, 1648. No printer or publisher [Royston].

2. 'The Power of Kings, and in Particular of the King of England, Learnedly asserted by . . . With a preface giving an account of the Author and his Works', London. Printed by WH & TF, sold by Walter Davis, 1680.

ORIGINAL — 'Observations concerning the Original of Government, upon Mr. Hobs Leviathan, Mr. Milton against Salmasius, H. Grotius De Jure Belli', London. Printed for R. Royston at the Angel in Ivie Lane, 1652. (Milton Section photostatically reproduced by W. R. Parker, Ihio University Press, 1940.)

ORIGINAL AND ANARCHY (Joint publication) — 'Observations upon the Originall . . . Hobs . . . Milton . . . Grotius . . . Mr. Hunton's Treatise of Monarchy', London, Royston, 1652.

PATRIARCHA

1. 1680 — Davis Patriarcha.
'Patriarcha, or the Natural Power of Kings', London. Printed for Walter Davis, 1680.

2. ?1680 — Chiswell Patriarcha.
'Patriarcha, or the Natural Power of Kings', London. Printed for Ric. Chiswell, Matthew Gillyflower & Wm. Henchman, 1680 (not seen).

3. 1685 — Bohun Patriarcha.
'Patriarcha, or the Natural Power of Kings . . . The 2nd Edition, Corrected according to the Original Manuscript of the Author . . .' By Edmund Bohun, London. Printed for Chiswell, Gillyflower, G. Wells, 1685.

4. 1884 — Morley Patriarcha.
'Two Treatises of Civil Government by John Locke. Preceded by Sir Robert Filmer's "Patriarcha"', with an Introduction by Henry Morley, London, Morley's Universal Library, 1884.

QUAESTIO QUODLIBETICA

1. 'Quaestio Quodlibetica, or a Discourse Whether it may be lawful to take Use for Money', London. Printed for Humphrey Moseley, 1653.

2. 'A Discourse whether it may be lawful to take Use for Money', London. Printed for Will. Crook, 1678.

3. 'Harleian Miscellany', Vol. X, pp. 105-38. Introduction Thos. Park, 1813.

PATRIARCHA

and other

POLITICAL WORKS

of

SIR ROBERT FILMER

PATRIARCHA

THE HEADS OF THE DISCOURSE

PATRIARCHA

A DEFENCE OF THE NATURAL POWER OF KINGS AGAINST THE UNNATURAL LIBERTY OF THE PEOPLE

I The Natural Freedom of Mankind, a New, Plausible and Dangerous Opinion

WITHIN the last hundred years many of the Schoolmen and other Divines have published and maintained an opinion that:[1]

'Mankind is naturally endowed and born with freedom from all subjection, and at liberty to choose what form of government it please, and that the power which any one man hath over others was at the first by human right bestowed according to the discretion of the multitude.'

This tenet was first hatched in the Schools for good Divinity, and hath been fostered by succeeding Papists. The Divines of the Reformed Churches have entertained it, and the common people everywhere tenderly embrace it as being most plausible to flesh and blood, for that it prodigally distributes a portion of liberty to the meanest of the multitude, who magnify liberty as if the height of human felicity were only to be found in it, never remembering that the desire of liberty was the cause of the fall of Adam.

But howsoever this opinion hath of late obtained great reputation, yet it is not to be found in the ancient fathers and doctors of the primitive Church. It contradicts the doctrine and history of the Holy Scriptures, the constant practice of all ancient monarchies, and the very principles of the law of nature. It is hard to say whether it be more erroneous in Divinity or dangerous in policy.

Upon the grounds of this doctrine, both Jesuits and some zealous favourers of the Geneva discipline have built a perilous conclusion, which is, 'that the people or multitude have power to punish or deprive the Prince if he transgress the laws of the kingdom'. Witness Parsons and Buchanan. The first, under the name of Dolman, in the third chapter of his first book,[2] labours to prove that Kings have been lawfully chastised by their commonwealths. The latter, in his book *De Jure Regni apud Scotos*,[3] maintained a liberty of the people to depose

---

[1] 'Within the last hundred years' — in the printed versions—'since the time school divinity began to flourish'.

[2] See PARSONS, ROBERT, under the name R. DOLEMAN: *A conference about the next succession to the crowne of Ingland . . .*, 1594, pp. 37 ff.

[3] See BUCHANAN, GEORGE: *De jure regni apud Scotos . . .*, Edinburgh, 1580.

their Prince. Cardinal Bellarmine and Mr. Calvin both look asquint this way.*

This desperate assertion whereby Kings are made subject to the censures and deprivations of their subjects follows (as the authors of it conceive) as a necessary consequence of that former position of the supposed natural equality and freedom of mankind, and liberty to choose what form of government it please.†

And though Sir John Heywood,[1] Adam Blackwood,[2] John Barclay[3] and some others have learnedly confuted both Buchanan and Parsons, and vindicated the right of Kings in most points, yet all of them, when they come to the argument drawn from the natural liberty and equality of mankind, they do with one consent admit it for a principle unquestionable, not so much as once denying or opposing it. Whereas if they did but confute this first erroneous principle, the main foundation of popular sedition would be taken away.

The rebellious consequence which follows this prime article of the natural freedom of mankind may be my sufficient warrant for a modest examination of the original truth of it; much hath been said, and by many, for the affirmative; equity requires that an ear be reserved a little for the negative.

In this discourse I shall give myself these cautions:

First, I have nothing to do to meddle with mysteries of the present state. Such arcana imperii, or cabinet councils, the vulgar may not pry into. An implicit faith is given to the meanest artificer in his own craft; how much more is it, then, due to a Prince in the profound secrets of government: the causes and ends of the greatest politic actions and motions of state dazzle the eyes and exceed the capacities of all men, save only those that are hourly versed in managing public affairs: yet since the rule for each man to know in what to obey his Prince cannot be learnt without a relative knowledge of those points wherein a sovereign may command, it is necessary when the commands and pleasures of superiors come abroad and call for an obedience that every man inform himself how to regulate his actions or his

---

* *Lib.* 3, *De-Laicis, c.* 6.[4]   † Calvin, *Institutes, Lib.* 4, *c.* 10.[5]

---

[1] See HAYWARD, SIR JOHN: *An answer to the first part of a certain conference concerning succession* . . ., 1603.

[2] See BLACKWOOD, ADAM: *Adversus G. Buchanani dialogum 'De Jure Regni'.* . ., Paris, 1588.

[3] See BARCLAY, WILLIAM, author of *De Regno et Regnali Potestate,* 1600, etc.

[4] See BELLARMINUS, ROBERTUS: *Opera Omnia,* Naples, 1856-62, vol. II, p. 317.

[5] See CALVIN's *Institutes.*

sufferings, for according to the quality of the thing commanded an active or passive obedience is to be yielded, and this is not to limit the Prince's power, but the extent of the subject's obedience, by giving to Caesar the things that are Caesar's, etc.

Secondly, I am not to question or quarrel at the rights or liberties of this or any other nation; my task is chiefly to inquire from whom these came, not to dispute what or how many they are, but whether they are derived from the laws of natural liberty or from the grace and bounty of Princes. My desire and hope is that the people of England may and do enjoy as ample privileges as any nation under heaven; the greatest liberty in the world (if it be duly considered) is for a people to live under a monarch. It is the Magna Charta of this kingdom; all other shows or pretexts of liberty are but several degrees of slavery, and a liberty only to destroy liberty.

If such as maintain the natural liberty of mankind take offence at the liberty I take to examine it, they must take heed that they do not deny by retail that liberty which they affirm by wholesale; for if their thesis be true, the hypothesis will follow, that all men may examine their own charters, deeds, or evidences by which they claim and hold the inheritance or freehold of their liberties.

Thirdly, I detract not from the worth of all those learned men who are of a contrary opinion in the point of natural liberty. The profoundest scholar that ever was known hath not been able to search out every truth that is discoverable; neither Aristotle in natural philosophy, nor Mr. Hooker in Divinity. They were but men, yet I reverence their judgments in most points, and confess myself beholding even to their errors in this; something that I found amiss in their opinions guided me in the discovery of that truth which (I persuade myself) they missed. A dwarf sometimes may see that which a giant looks over: for whilst one truth is curiously searched after, another must necessarily be neglected. Late writers have taken up too much upon trust from the subtle Schoolmen, who to be sure to thrust down the King below the Pope, thought it the safest course to advance the people above the King; that so the papal power may more easily take place of the regal. Many an ignorant subject hath been fooled into this faith, that a man may become a martyr for his country by being a traitor to his Prince; whereas the new coined distinction into Royalists and Patriots is most unnatural, since the relation between King and people is so great that their well-being is reciprocal.

II   The Question Stated out of Bellarmine: and some Contradictions of his Noted

To make evident the grounds of this question about the natural
liberty of mankind, I will lay down some passages of Cardinal Bellarmine, that may best unfold the state of this controversy. 'Secular or
civil power' (saith he) 'is instituted by men; it is in the people unless
they bestow it on a Prince. This power is immediately in the whole
multitude, as in the subject of it; for this power is by the Divine law,
but the Divine law hath given this power to no particular man. If the
positive law be taken away, there is left no reason why amongst a
multitude (who are equal) one rather than another should bear rule
over the rest. Power is given by the multitude to one man, or to more
by the same law of nature; for the commonwealth of itself cannot
exercise this power, therefore it is bound to bestow it upon some one
man, or some few. It depends upon the consent of the multitude to
ordain over themselves a King, or consul, or other magistrate; and if
there be a lawful cause, the multitude may change the kingdom into
an aristocracy or democracy.'* Thus far Bellarmine, in which passages
are comprised the strength of all that ever I have read or heard produced
for the natural liberty of the subject.

Before I examine or refute these doctrines, I must make an observation upon his words.

First, he saith, that by the law of God, power is immediately in the
people; hereby he makes God the author of a democratical estate; for
a democracy is nothing else but the power of the multitude. If this be
true, not only aristocracies but all monarchies are altogether unlawful,
as being ordained (as he thinks) by men, when as God himself hath
chosen a democracy.

Secondly, he holds, that although a democracy be the ordinance of
God, yet the people have no power to use the power which God hath
given them, but only power to make away their power; whereby it
follows, that there can be no democratical government, because the
people (he saith) 'must give their power to one man, or to some few';
which maketh either a regal or aristocratical estate, which the multitude is tied to do, even by the same law of nature which originally
gave them the power. And why then doth he say, the multitude may
change the kingdom into a democracy?

Thirdly, he concludes, that 'if there be a lawful cause the multitude

* Lib. 3, De Laicis, c. 4.[1]

---

[1] op. cit., II, 317.

may change the kingdom into an aristocracy or democracy'. Here I would fain know who shall judge of this cause? If the multitude (for I see nobody else can) then this is a pestilent and dangerous conclusion.

III The Argument of Bellarmine Answered out of Bellarmine himself: and of the Regal Authority of the Patriarchs before the Flood

I come now to examine that argument which is used by Bellarmine, and is the one and only argument I can find produced by any author for the proof of the natural liberty of the people. It is thus framed: That God hath given or ordained power, is evident by Scripture; but God hath given it to no particular man, because by nature all men are equal; therefore he hath given power to the people or multitude.

To answer this reason, drawn from the equality of mankind by nature, I will first use the help of Bellarmine himself, whose words are these: 'If many men had been created out of the earth, all they ought to have been Princes over their posterity.'* In these words we have an evident confession, that creation made man Prince of his posterity.[1] And indeed not only Adam, but the succeeding Patriarchs had, by right of fatherhood, royal authority over their children. Nor dares Bellarmine deny this also. 'That the patriarchs' (saith he) 'were endowed with Kingly power, their deeds do testify.'[2] For as Adam was lord of his children, so his children under him had a command over their own children, but still with subordination to the first parent, who is lord paramount over his children's children to all generations, as being the grandfather of his people.[3]

I see not then how the children of Adam, or of any man else, can be free from subjection to their parents. And this subordination of children is the fountain of all regal authority, by the ordination of God himself. From whence it follows, that civil power, not only in general is by Divine institution, but even the assigning of it specifically to the eldest parent. Which quite takes away that new and common distinction which refers only power universal or absolute to God, but power respective in regard of the special form of government to the choice of the people. Nor leaves it any place for such imaginary pactions between Kings and their people as many dream of.

* Lib. 1, De Pontif. Rom. c. 2.[4]

---

[1] This sentence omitted in MS.   [2] loc. cit.   [3] This last phrase omitted in MS.
[4] op. cit., I, 313.

E

This lordship which Adam by creation had over the whole world, and by right descending from him the Patriarchs did enjoy, was as large and ample as the absolutest dominion of any monarch which hath been since the creation. For power of life and death we find that Judah, the Father, pronounced sentence of death against Thamar, his daughter-in-law, for playing the harlot, 'Bring her forth' (saith he) 'that she may be burnt'.[1] Touching war, we see that Abraham commanded an army of 318 soldiers of his own family.[2] And Esau met his brother Jacob with 400 men at arms.[3] For matter of peace, Abraham made a league with Abimelech, and ratified the articles with an oath.[4] These acts of judging in capital crimes, of making war, and concluding peace, are the chiefest works of sovereignty that are found in any monarch. Not only until the Flood, but after it, this patriarchal power did continue, as the very name of Patriarch doth in part prove.[5]

IV   The Dispersion of Nations after the Flood was by Entire Families over which the Fathers were Kings, and from those Kings, all Kings are Descended

The three sons of Noah had the whole world divided amongst them by their Father; for of them was the whole world overspread, according to the benediction given to him and his sons: 'Be fruitful and multiply and replenish the earth.'* Most of the civilest nations of the world labour to fetch their original from some one of the sons or nephews of Noah, which were scattered abroad after the confusion of Babel. In this dispersion we must certainly find the establishment of regal power throughout the kingdoms of the world.

It is a common opinion that at the confusion of tongues there were seventy-two distinct nations erected. All which were not confused multitudes, without heads or governors, and at liberty to choose what governors or government they pleased, but they were distinct families, which had Fathers for rulers over them, whereby it appears that even in the confusion God was careful to preserve the fatherly authority by distributing the diversity of languages according to the diversity of families. For so it plainly appears by the text. First, after the enumeration of the sons of Japhet, the conclusion is: 'By these were the isles of

* Gen. ix.

---

[1] Gen. xxxviii, 24.   [2] ditto, xiv, 14.   [3] ditto, xxxiii, 1.   [4] ditto, xxi, 23-4.
[5] This chapter is quoted very frequently by Locke and all Filmer's opponents. It is very closely paralleled by OVERALL, JOHN, Convocation Book, 1606, pub. 1690, Canons, I, II.

the Gentiles divided in their lands; every one after his tongue, after their families, in their nations.'* So it is said: 'These are the sons of Ham after their families, after their tongues, in their countries, and in their nations.' The like we read: 'These are the sons of Shem after their families, after their tongues, in their lands, after their nations. These are the families of the sons of Noah after their generations in their nations, and by these were the nations divided in the earth after the Flood.'

In this division of the world, some are of the opinion that Noah used lots for the distribution of it. Others affirm he sailed about the Mediterranean Sea in ten years, and as he went about, pointed to each son his part, and so made the division of the then known world into Asia, Africa, and Europe, according to the number of his sons, the limits of which three parts are all found in that Midland Sea. But howsoever the manner of this division be uncertain, yet it is most certain the division itself was by families from Noah and his children, over which the parents were heads and Princes.

Amongst these was Nimrod, who no doubt (as Sir Walter Raleigh affirms[1]) was by right lord or King over his family. Yet against right did he enlarge his empire by seizing violently on the rights of other lords of families, and in this sense he may be said to be the author and first founder of monarchy. And all those that do attribute unto him the original of regal power do hold he got it by tyranny or usurpation, and not by any due election of the people or multitude, nor by any paction with them. As this patriarchal power continued in Abraham, Isaac and Jacob, even until the Egyptian bondage, so we find it amongst the sons of Ishmael and Esau. It is said: 'These are the sons of Ishmael, and these are their names of their castles and towns, twelve Princes of their tribes or families.† And these are the names of the dukes that came of Esau, according to their families and their places by their nations.'‡

Some, perhaps, may think that these Princes and dukes of families were but some petty lords under some greater Kings, because the number of them are so many that their particular territories could be but small, and not worthy the title of kingdoms. But we must consider that at first Kings had no such large dominions as they have nowadays. We find in the time of Abraham, which was about 300 years after the Flood, that in a little corner of Asia nine Kings at once

* Gen. x, 5.   † Gen. xxv, 16.   ‡ Gen. xxxvi, 40.

---

[1] RALEIGH, SIR W., *Works*, 8 vols. 1829, vol. II, p. 353.

met in battle, most of which were but Kings of cities apiece, with the adjacent territories, as Sodom, Gomorrha, Shinar, etc. In the same chapter is mention made of Melchisedek, King of Salem, which was but the city of Jerusalem.* And in the catalogue of the Kings of Edom, the name of each King's city is recorded, as the only mark to distinguish their dominions.† In the land of Canaan, which was but a small circuit, Joshua destroyed thirty-one Kings, and about the same time Adonibesek had seventy Kings whose fingers and toes he had cut off, and made them feed under his table.[1] A few years after this, thirty-two Kings came to aid Benhadad, King of Syria,[2] and about seventy Kings of Greece went to the Wars of Troy. Caesar found more Kings in France than there be now provinces there, and at his sailing over into this island he found four Kings in our county of Kent.[3] These heaps of Kings in each nation are an argument their territories were but small, and strongly confirm our assertion that erection of kingdoms came at first only by distinction of families.

By manifest footsteps we may trace this paternal government unto the Israelites coming into Egypt, where the exercise of [supreme][4] patriarchal jurisdiction was intermitted, because they were in subjection to a stronger Prince. After the return of these Israelites out of bondage, God, out of a special care of them, chose Moses and Joshua successively to govern as Princes in the place and stead of the supreme Fathers, and after them likewise for a time He raised up Judges to defend His people in times of peril. But when God gave the Israelites Kings, He re-established the ancient and prime right of lineal succession to paternal government. And whensoever He made choice of any special person to be King, He intended that the issue should have benefit thereof, as being comprehended sufficiently in the person of the Father, although the Father only were named in the grant.

V   Kings are either Fathers of their People, or Heirs of such
      Fathers, or the Usurpers of the Rights of such Fathers

It may seem absurd to maintain that Kings now are the fathers of their people, since experience shows the contrary. It is true, all Kings be not the natural parents of their subjects, yet they all either are, or

* Gen. xiv.   † Gen. xxxvi.

---

[1] Judges i, 7.   [2] 1 Kings xx, 16.
[3] This phrase marks *Patriarcha* as addressed to the gentry of Kent, cf. Introduction.
[4] Omitted in MS.

are to be reputed, as the next heirs of those progenitors who were at first the natural parents of the whole people, and in their right succeed to the exercise of supreme jurisdiction. And such heirs are not only lords of their own children, but also of their brethren, and all others that were subject to their Fathers.

And therefore we find that God told Cain of his brother Abel: 'His desires shall be subject unto thee, and thou shalt rule over him.'[1] Accordingly, when Jacob had bought his brother's birthright, Isaac blessed him thus: 'Be lord over thy brethren, and let the sons of thy mother bow before thee.'[2] So we find that at the offering of Princes at the dedication of the tabernacle the Princes of Israel are said to be heads of the houses of their Fathers, as Eliab the son of Helon was Prince of the children of his Father Zebulun. Numbers vii, 2 and 24.

As long as the first Fathers of families lived, the name of Patriarchs did aptly belong unto them. But after a few descents, when the true fatherhood itself was extinct, and only the right of the Father descended to the true heir, then the title of Prince or King was more significant to express the power of him who succeeds only to the right of that fatherhood which his ancestors did *naturally* enjoy. By this means it comes to pass, that many a child, by succeeding a King, hath the right of a Father over many a grey-headed multitude, [and hath the title of Pater Patriae.][3]

VI Of the Escheating of Kingdoms

It may be demanded what becomes of the right of fatherhood in case the Crown does escheat for want of an heir, whether it doth not then devolve to the people. The answer is:

First, it is but the negligence or ignorance of the people to lose the knowledge of the true heir, for an heir there always is. If Adam himself were still living, and now ready to die, it is certain that there is one man, and but one in the world, who is next heir, although the knowledge who should be that one man be quite lost.

Secondly, this ignorance of the people being admitted, it doth not by any means follow that, for want of heirs, the supreme power devolves to the multitude, and that they have power to rule or choose what rulers they please. No: the Kingly power escheats in such cases to the prime and independent heads of families, for every kingdom is resolved into those principles whereof at first it was made. By the uniting of great families or petty Princedoms, we find the greater

----

[1] Gen. iv, 7.　　　[2] Gen. xxvii, 29.　　　[3] Omitted in MS.

monarchies were at the first erected, and into such again, as into their
first matter, many times they return. And because the dependency of
ancient families is oft obscure or worn out of knowledge, therefore the
wisdom of all or most Princes have thought fit to adopt many times
those for heads of families and Princes of provinces whose merits,
abilities, or fortunes have enabled them, or made them fit and capable
of such royal favours. All such prime heads and Fathers have power
to consent in the uniting or conferring of their fatherly right of
sovereign authority on whom they please. And he that is so elected
claims not his power as a donative from the people, but as being substituted properly by God, from whom he receives his royal charter of
an universal Father, though testified by the ministry of the heads of the
people.

If it please God, for the correction of the Prince or punishment of
the people, to suffer Princes to be removed and others to be placed in
their rooms, either by the factions of the nobility or rebellion of the
people, in all such cases the judgment of God, who hath power to give
and take away kingdoms, is most just. Yet the ministry of men who
execute God's judgments without commission is sinful and damnable.
God doth but use and turn men's unrighteous acts to the performance
of His righteous decrees.

In all kingdoms or commonwealths in the world, whether the Prince
be the supreme Father of the people or but the true heir of such a
Father, or whether he come to the Crown by usurpation, or by election of the nobles or of the people, or by any other way whatsoever,
or whether some few or a multitude govern the commonwealth, yet
still the authority that is in any one, or in many, or in all of these, is
the only right and natural authority of a supreme Father. There is,
and always shall be continued to the end of the world, a natural right
of a supreme Father over every multitude, although, by the secret will
of God, many at first do most unjustly obtain the exercise of it.

To confirm this natural right of regal power, we find in the Decalogue that the law which enjoins obedience to Kings is delivered in the
terms of 'Honour thy Father', as if all power were originally in the
Father. If obedience to parents be immediately due by a natural law,
and subjection to Princes but by the mediation of a human ordinance,
what reason is there that the law of nature should give place to the
laws of men, as we see the power of the Father over his child gives
place and is subordinate to the power of the magistrate?[1]

[1] This chapter is much used by Locke against Filmer. Its arguments are repeated and
expanded in the Original and the Anarchy.

VII Of the Agreement of Paternal and Regal Power

If we compare the natural duties[1] of a Father with those of a King, we find them to be all one, without any difference at all but only in the latitude or extent of them. As the Father over one family, so the King, as Father over many families, extends his care to preserve, feed, clothe, instruct and defend the whole commonwealth. His wars, his peace, his courts of justice, and all his acts of sovereignty, tend only to preserve and distribute to every subordinate and inferior Father, and to their children, their rights and privileges, so that all the duties of a King are summed up in an universal fatherly care of his people. By conferring these proofs and reasons drawn from the authority of Scripture, it appears little less than a paradox which Bellarmine and others affirm of the freedom of the multitude to choose what rulers they please.

Had the Patriarchs their power given them by their own children? Bellarmine dares not say it, but the contrary. If then, the fatherhood enjoyed this authority for so many ages by the law of nature, when was it lost, or when forfeited, or how is it devolved to the liberty of the multitude?[2]

VIII The Opinions of Hugo Grotius, and Mr. Selden, about Natural Community and Voluntary Propriety Examined

The doctrine of Grotius is that 'God immediately after the Creation, did bestow upon mankind in general a right over things of inferior nature . . . From whence it came to pass that presently every man might snatch what he would for his own use, and spend what he could: and such an universal right was then instead of property, for what every one so catched another could not take from him but by injury'.*

How repugnant this assertion of Grotius is to the truth of Holy Scripture, Mr. Selden teacheth us in his *Mare Clausum*,† saying that Adam 'by donation from God', Genesis i, 28, 'was made the general lord of all things, not without such a private dominion to himself, as (without his grant) did exclude his children. And by donation and

---

* *De Jure Belli, lib. 2, c. 2.*[3] † *Lib. 1, c. 4.*[4]

[1] 'Duties' — printed versions have 'rights'.
[2] At this point the MS. version has the passage omitted in all the printed versions but later published by Filmer as pp. 31-43 of the Original — Observations on Grotius; see below, page 268
[3] See GROTIUS, HUGO, *De Jure Belli et Pacis . . .*, Paris, 1625, p. 138.
[4] See SELDEN, JOHN, *Mare Clausum . . .*, 1635, translated Nedham, M., 1652, p. 20.

assignation, or some kind of cession (before he was dead or left any heir to succeed him) his children had their distinct territories by right of private dominion. Abel had his flocks, and pastures for them. Cain had his fields for corn, and the land of Nod where he built himself a city'. .

This determination of Mr. Selden's being consonant to the history of the Bible, and to natural reason, doth contradict the doctrine of Grotius. I cannot conceive why Mr. Selden should afterwards affirm that, 'neither the law of Nature, nor the Divine law, do command or forbid either communion of all things or private dominion, but permitteth both'.[1]

As for the general community between Noah and his sons which Mr. Selden will have to be granted to them,[2] Genesis ix, 2, the text doth not warrant it. For although the sons are there mentioned with Noah in the blessing, yet it may best be understood with a subordination or a benediction in succession. The blessing might truly be fulfilled, if the sons either under, or after, their Father, enjoyed a private dominion. It is not probable that the private dominion which God gave to Adam, and, by his donation, assignation or cession, to his children, was abrogated, and a community of all things instituted between Noah and his sons. At the time of the Flood Noah was left the sole heir of the world. Why should it be thought that God would disinherit him of his birthright, and make him of all the men in the world the only tenant in common with his children? If the blessing given to Adam, Genesis i, 28, be compared to that given to Noah and his sons, Genesis ix, 2, there will be found a considerable difference between those two texts. In the benediction of Adam, we find expressed a 'subduing of the earth, and a dominion over the creatures', neither of which are expressed in the blessing of Noah, nor the earth there once named. It is only said, 'The fear of you shall be upon the creatures, and into your hands are they delivered.' Then immediately it follows, 'Every moving thing shall be meat for you, as the green herb.' The first blessing gave Adam dominion over the earth and all creatures, the later allows Noah liberty to use the living creatures for food. Here is no alteration or diminishing of his title to a propriety of all things, but an enlargement only of his commons.

But whether with Grotius, community came in at the Creation, or with Mr. Selden at the Flood, they both agree it did not long continue. 'Sed veri non est simile hujusmodi communionem diu obtinuisse',[3] is

[1] See SELDEN, JOHN. *Mare Clausum* . . ., 1635, translated Nedham, M., 1652, p. 20.
[2] ibid., p. 18. [3] loc. cit., p. 18.

the confession of Mr. Selden.[1] It seems strange that Grotius should maintain that community of all things should be by the law of nature, of which God is the author, and yet such community should not be able to continue. Doth it not derogate from the providence of God Almighty, to ordain a community which could not continue? Or doth it not make the act of our forefathers, in abrogating the natural law of community by introducing that of propriety, to be a sin of a high presumption?

The prime duties of the second table[1] are conversant about the right of propriety. But if propriety be brought in by a human law (as Grotius teacheth), then the moral law depends upon the will of man. There could be no law against adultery or theft, if women and all things were common.

Mr. Selden saith that the law of nature or of God 'nec vetuit nec jubebat, sed permisit utrumque, tam nempe rerum communionem quam privatum dominium'.[2] And yet for propriety (which he terms 'primaeva rerum dominia') he teacheth that 'Adam received it from God, a numine acceperat'.[3] And for community he saith: 'We meet with evident footsteps of the community of things in that donation of God, by which Noah and his three sons are made domini pro indiviso rerum omnium.' Thus he makes the private dominion of Adam as well as the common dominion of Noah and his sons to be both by the will of God. Nor doth he show how Noah or his sons, or their posterity, had any authority to alter the law of community which was given them by God.

'In distributing territories' (Mr. Selden saith) 'the consent as it were of mankind, (passing their promise which should also bind their posterity), did intervene. So that men departed from their common right of communion of those things, which were so distributed to particular lords or masters.'[4] This distribution by consent of mankind we must take upon credit, for there is not the least proof offered for it out of antiquity.

How the consent of mankind could bind posterity when all things were common, is a point not so evident. Where children take nothing by gift or by descent from their parents, but have an equal and common interest with them, there is no reason in such cases, that the acts of the fathers should bind the sons.

---

[1] 'Second table'. Moral as distinct from religious commandments.
[2] loc. cit., p. 20, 'neither forbade nor ordained but permitted both community of things and private dominion equally'.
[3] ibid., p. 19.
[4] loc. cit., p. 21.

I find no cause why Mr. Selden should call community a pristine right, since he makes it but to begin in Noah and to end in Noah's children or grandchildren at the most. For he confesseth the earth: 'a Noachidis seculis aliquot post diluvium esse divisam'.[1]

That ancient tradition which by Mr. Selden's acknowledgment hath received reputation everywhere, seems most reasonable, in that it tells us that 'Noah himself, as lord of all, was author of the distribution of the world, and of private dominion, and that by the appointment of an oracle from God he did confirm this distribution by his last will and testament, which at his death he left in the hands of his eldest son Shem. And also warned all his sons, that none of them should invade any of their brothers' dominions, or injure one another, because from thence discord and civil war would necessarily follow'.[2]

IX Dangerous Conclusions of Grotius against Monarchy Censured

Many conclusions in Grotius his book *De Jure Belli et Pacis* are built upon the foundation of these two principles.

1. The first is that 'Communis rerum usus naturalis fuit'.

2. The second is that 'Dominium quale nunc in usu est, voluntas humana introduxit'.

Upon these two propositions of natural community and voluntary propriety, depend divers dangerous and seditious conclusions, which are dispersed in several places. In the fourth chapter of the first book, the title of which chapter is of the war of subjects against their superiors, Grotius handleth the question: 'Whether the law of not resisting superiors do bind us in most grievous and most certain danger', and his determination is that: 'This law of not resisting superiors seems to depend upon the will of those men who at first joined themselves in a civil society, from whom the right of government doth come to them that govern. If those had been at first asked if their will were to impose this burden upon all, that they should choose rather to die, than in any case by arms to repell the force of superiors, I know not whether they would answer that it was their will, unless perhaps with this addition: if resistance cannot be made but with great disturbance of the commonwealth, and destruction of many innocents.'[3] Here we

---

[1] loc. cit., p. 18.
[2] ditto, p. 19. Locke makes great play with this chapter, quoting it from the Original.
[3] GROTIUS, op. cit., pp. 104, 105.

have his resolution, that in great and certain danger, men may resist their governors, if it be without disturbance of the commonwealth. If you would know who should be judge of the greatness and certainty of the danger, or how we may know it, Grotius hath not one word of it. So that for ought appears to the contrary, his mind may be that every private man may be judge of the danger, for other judge he appoints none. It had been a foul fault in so desperate a piece of service as the resisting of superiors, to have concealed the lawful means by which we may judge of the greatness or certainty of public danger, before we lift up our hands against authority, considering how prone most of us are to censure and mistake those things for great and certain dangers which in truth many times are no dangers at all, or at the most very small ones. And to flatter ourselves, that by resisting our superiors we may do our country laudable service, without disturbance of the commonwealth, since the effects of sedition cannot be certainly judged of but by the events only.

Grotius proceeds to answer an objection against this doctrine of resisting superiors. 'If' (saith he) 'any man shall say that this rigid doctrine of dying rather than resisting any injuries of superiors is no human but a Divine law, it is to be noted that men at first, not by any precept of God, but of their own accord, led by experience of the infirmities of separated families against violence, did meet together in civil society, from whence civil power took beginning. Which therefore St. Peter calls an human ordinance, although elsewhere it be called a Divine ordinance, because God approveth the wholesome institutions of men. God in approving a human law is to be thought to approve it as human, and in a human manner.'[1]

And again in another place he goeth further, and teacheth us that: 'If the question happen to be concerning the primitive will of the people, it will not be amiss for the people that now are, and which are accounted the same with them that were long ago, to express their meaning in this matter which is to be followed, unless it certainly appear that the people long ago willed otherwise.'*

For fuller explication of his judgment about resisting superiors, he concludes thus: 'The greater the thing is which is to be preserved, the greater is the equity which reacheth forth an exception against the words of the law. Yet I dare not' (saith Grotius) 'without difference condemn either single men or a lesser part of the people, who in the

---

* Lib. 2, c. 2.

[1] ibid., p. 105.

last refuge of necessity, do so use this equity, as in the meantime, they do not forsake the respect of the common good.'[1]

Another doctrine of Grotius is that: 'The empire which is exercised by Kings doth not cease to be the empire of the people. That Kings who in a lawful manner succeed those men who were elected, have the supreme power by an usufructuary right only and no propriety.'

Furthermore, he teacheth that: 'The people may choose what form of government they please, and their will is the rule of right.* Populus eligere potest qualem vult gubernationis formam, neque ex praestantia formae, sed ex voluntate jus metiendum est.'

Also that: 'The people, choosing a King may reserve some acts to themselves, and may bestow others upon the King, with full authority, if either an express partition be appointed, or if the people being yet free do command their future King, by way of a standing command, or if anything be added by which it may be understood, that the King may be compelled or else punished.'

In these passages of Grotius which I have cited, we find evidently these doctrines.

1 That civil power depends on the will of the people.

2 That private men or petty multitudes may take up arms against their Princes.

3 That the lawful Kings have no propriety in their kingdoms, but an usufructuary right only, as if the people were the lords, and the Kings but their tenants.

4 That the law of not resisting superiors is a human law, depending on the will of the people at first.

5 That the will of the first people, if it be not known, may be expounded by the people that now are.

No doubt but Grotius foresaw what uses the people might make of these doctrines by concluding, if the chief power be in the people, that then it is lawful for them to compel and punish Kings as oft as they misuse their power. Therefore he tells us he: 'Rejects the opinion of them, who everywhere and without exception will have the chief power to be so the peoples, that it is lawful for them to compel and punish Kings as oft as they misuse their power.' And 'this opinion', he confesseth, 'if it be altogether received, hath been and may be the cause of many evils'.† This cautelous rejection qualified with these

---

* Lib. 1, c. 3.[2]   † Lib. 1, c. 3.[3]

[1] GROTIUS, op. cit., p. 106.   [2] ibid., p. 68.   [3] ibid., pp. 67, 68.

terms of *everywhere*, *without exception* and *altogether*, makes but a mixed negation, partly negative and partly affirmative (which our lawyers call a negative pregnant). Which brings forth this modal proposition, *that in some places with some exception, and in some sort, the people may compel and punish their Kings.*

But let us see how Grotius doth refute the general opinion that people may correct Kings. He frames his argument in these words: 'It is lawful for every man to yield himself to be a private servant to whom he please. What should hinder but that also it may be lawful for a free people so to yield themselves to one or more, that the right of governing them be fully set over without retaining any part of the right? And you must not say, "That this may not be presumed", for we do not now seek what in a doubtful case may be presumed, but what by right may be done.'[1] Thus far is the argument, in which the most that is proved (if we gratify him and yield his whole argument for good) is this, *that the people may grant away their power without retaining any part.* But what is this to what the people have done? For though the people may give away their power without reservation of any part to themselves, yet if they have not so done, but have reserved a part, Grotius must confess that the people may compel and punish their Kings if they transgress. So that, by his favour, the point will be, not what by right may be done, but what in this doubtful case hath been done, since by his own rule it is the will and meaning of the first people that joined in society that must regulate the power of their successors.

But on Grotius' side it may be urged, that in all presumption the people have given away their whole power to Kings, unless they can prove they have reserved a part. For if they will have any benefit of a reservation or exception, it lies on their part to prove their exception, and not on the Kings' parts who are in possession.

This answer, though in itself it be most just and good, yet of all men, Grotius may not use it. For he saves the people the labour of proving the primitive reservation of their forefathers, by making the people that now are competent expositors of the meaning of those first ancestors, who may justly be presumed not to have been either so improvident for themselves or so negligent of all their posterity, when, by the law of nature, they were free and had all things common, at an instant without any condition or limitation, to give away that liberty and right of community, and to make themselves and their children

[1] ibid., p. 68.

eternally subject to the will of such governors as might misuse them without control.

On the behalf of the people it may be further answered to Grotius, that although our ancestors had made an absolute grant of their liberty, without any condition expressed, yet it must necessarily be implied that it was upon condition to be well governed, and that the non-performance of that implied condition makes the grant void. Or, if we will not allow an implicit condition, then it may be said that the grant in itself was a void grant, for being unreasonable and a violation of the law of Nature, without any valuable consideration. What sound reply Grotius can return to such answers, I cannot conceive, if he keep himself to his first principle of natural community.

As Grotius' argument against the people is not sound, so his answer to the argument that is made for the people is not satisfactory. It is objected that: 'He that ordains is above him that is ordained.' Grotius answers: 'Verum duntaxat est in ea constitutione cujus effectus perpetuo pendet a voluntate constituentis, non etiam in ea qua ab initio est voluntatis, postea vero effectum habet necessitatis: quomodo mulier virum sibi constituit, cui parere semper habet necesse.'[1] The reply may be, that by Grotius' former doctrine the very effect of the constitution of Kings by the people depends perpetually upon the will of them that constitute, and upon no other necessity. He will not say that it is by any necessity of the law of nature, or by any positive law of God. He teacheth that: *Non Dei precepto sed sponte*, men entered into civil society, that it is an human ordinance that God doth only approve it *ut humanum*, and *humano modo*. He tells us further that: 'Populus potest eligere qualem vult gubernationis formam, et ex voluntate jus metiendum est.'[2] That the people may give the King 'as little power as they will and for as little time as they please, that they may make temporary Kings as dictators and protectors: jus quovis tempore revocabile, id est precarium';[3] as the Vandals in Africa and the Goths in Spain would depose their Kings as oft as they displeased them, 'horum enim actus irriti possunt reddi ab his, qui potestatem revocabiliter dederunt, ac proinde non idem est effectus, nec jus idem'.[4] Here he doth teach in

---

[1] GROTIUS, op. cit., pp. 71-2. 'This may indeed be true in a constitution whose effect depends in perpetuity on the will of those who compose it, but it is not so in a constitution whose effect, though at the beginning it depends upon will, afterwards is of necessity. It is like a woman who appoints herself a husband whom she must necessarily always obey.'

[2] ibid.; p. 68.

[3] 'Whose power is revocable at any time, that is, it is temporary.'

[4] ibid., p. 77, adds 'singuli' after 'enim' – 'For their acts can be rendered null by those who gave them power revocably, and therefore the effect is not the same nor the legal right.'

plain words, the effect doth depend upon the will of the people. By this we may judge how improperly he useth the instance of a woman that appoints herself a husband, who she must always necessarily obey, since the necessity of the continuance of the wife's obedience depends upon the law of God, which hath made the bond of matrimony indissolvable. Grotius will not say the like for the continuance of the subject's obedience to the Prince, neither will he say that women may choose husbands, as he tells us the people may choose Kings, by giving their husbands as little power, and for as little time, as they please.

Next it is objected that: 'Tutors who are set over pupils may be removed if they abuse their power.' Grotius answers: 'In tutore hoc procedit qui superiorem habet, at in imperiis quia progressus non datur in infinitum, omnino in aliqua persona, aut caetu consistendum est. We must stay in some one person, or in a multitude, whose faults (because they have no superior judge above them) God hath witnessed that He will have a particular care of, either to revenge them if He judge it needful, or to tolerate them either for the punishment, or trial of the people.'[1] It is true in kingdoms we cannot proceed *in infinitum*, yet we may and must go to the highest, which by Grotius' rule is the people, because they first made Kings. So that there is no need to stay *in aliqua persona*, but *in caetu*, in the people, so that by his doctrine Kings may be punished by the people, but the faults of the people must be left to the judgment of God.

I have briefly presented here the desperate inconveniences which attend upon the doctrine *of the natural freedom and community of all things*. These and many more absurdities are easily removed if on the contrary we maintain *the natural and private dominion of Adam* to be the fountain of all government and propriety. And if we mark it well, we shall find that Grotius doth in part grant as much. The ground why those that now live do obey their governors is the will of their fore-fathers, who at the first ordained Princes, and in obedience to that will the children continue in subjection. This is according to the mind of Grotius, so that the question is not *whether Kings have a fatherly power over their subjects*, but *how Kings first came by it*. Grotius will have it that our forefathers, being all free, made an assignment of their power to Kings. The other opinion denies any such general freedom to our forefathers, but derives the power of Kings from the original dominion of Adam.

This natural dominion of Adam may be proved out of Grotius himself, who teacheth that: 'generatione jus acquiritur parentibus in liberis',

[1] ibid., p. 73.

and that 'naturally no other can be found but the parents to whom the government should belong, and the right of ruling and compelling them doth belong to parents'. And in another place he hath these words, speaking of the fifth commandment: 'Parentum nomine qui naturales sunt magistratus, etiam alios rectores par est intelligi quorum authoritas societatem humanam continet.'[1] And if parents be natural magistrates, children must needs be born natural subjects.

But though Grotius acknowledges parents to be natural magistrates, yet he will have it that children, when they come to full age and are separated from their parents, are free from natural subjection. For this he offers proof out of Aristotle and out of Scripture.

1. First, for Aristotle. We must note he doth not teach that every separation of children of full age is an obtaining of liberty, as if that men when they come to years might voluntarily separate themselves and cast off their natural obedience. But Aristotle speaks only of a passive separation. For he doth not say that children are subject to parents *until they do separate*, but he saith *until they be separated* in the verb of the passive voice. That is, until by law they be separated, for the law (which is nothing else but the will of him that hath the power of the supreme Father) doth in many cases, for the public benefit of society, free children from subjection to the subordinate parent. So that the natural subjection, by such emancipation of children, is not extinguished, but only assumed and regulated by the parent paramount.

2. Secondly, Grotius cites Numbers xxx to prove that the 'power of the Fathers over the sons and daughters, to dissolve their vows, was not perpetual, but during the time only whilst the children were part of the Father's family'.[2] But if we turn to the chapter we may find that Grotius either deceives himself or us. For there is not one word in that chapter concerning vows of sons, but of daughters only, being in their Father's family. And the being of the daughter in the Father's house meaneth only the daughter's being a virgin and not married, which may be gathered by the argument of the whole chapter, which taketh particular order for the vows of women of all estates. First, for virgins, in the third verse. Secondly, for wives in general, in the sixth verse. Thirdly, for widows and women divorced, in the ninth verse. There is no law for virgins out of their Fathers' houses: we may not think they would have been omitted if they had been free from

<hr />

[1] GROTIUS, op. cit., pp. 176; 177. 'By the word parents, who are the natural magistrates, we ought to understand the other rulers also by whose authority human society is held together.'
[2] ibid., p. 178.

their Fathers. We find no freedom in the text for women till after marriage, and if they were married, though they were in their Fathers' houses, yet the Fathers had no power of their vows, but their husbands.

If, by the law of nature, departure from the Father's house had emancipated children, why doth the Civil Law, contrary to the law of nature, give power and remedy to Fathers to recover by action of law their children that depart, or are taken from them without their consent? Without the consent of parents the Civil Law allows no emancipation.[1]

X   Two Passages in the Civil Law Cleared[2]

There are two places cited out of the Civil Law which do seem much to strengthen the opinion of Grotius about natural community, though they be not alleged by him, yet they are fit to be considered because they are authorities of the greatest antiquity in this point and the foundation upon which the late Schoolmen have built. In the Digests there is first this principle: 'Jure naturali omnes homines liberi nascuntur.'[3] Secondly, the Law there, speaking of the Prince, saith: 'Populus ei et in eum omne suum imperium et potestatem confert.'[4] For a general answer to these two texts of the Civil Law, it must be remembered that the grounds of this Law are but the opinions and sayings of heathens that knew not, or at least believed not, the history of the Scriptures or of the Creation, and that this Law was fitted properly for the commonwealth and empire of the Romans. For these causes it is no great wonder if the principles of the Roman Laws vary from the rules of Scripture, and customs of other nations.

To answer in particular to the first text. It may be said the sense of these words, 'by the law of nature all are born free', must needs mean a freedom only that is opposite to such subjection as was between *master* and *servant*, and not a freedom from such subjection as is between *Father* and *son*. This is made manifest by the text of the Law, for Ulpian in that place speaketh only of manumission, which is a setting at liberty of servants from servitude, and not of emancipation, which is the freeing of children from their Fathers' tuition. 'Servitude', as the Law teacheth, 'is a constitution of the law of nations, by which a man

---

[1] This is the end of the passage printed by Filmer in the Original (See below p. 268), but omitted in all printed versions of *Patriarcha*.

[2] The whole of this chapter is missing from the edition of Filmer used by Locke and for Morley's reprint. It is present in the 1685 edition.

[3] See MOMMSEN, *Digesta Justiniani*, 2 vols., Berlin, 1866–70, vol. I, p. 2.

[4] ibid., p. 14.

F

is subjected to the dominion of any other man against nature'.[1] So not every subjection is servitude, but subjection contrary to the law of nature. No man is born a servant or subject to the power of a master by the law of nature, yet every man is born subject to the power of a Father. This the Law itself saith: 'In potestate nostra liberi nostri sunt.' And Ulpian teacheth that the education of children is by the law of nature, so that 'quicquid ex me et uxore mea nascitur in potestate mea est'.[2]

For answer to the second text, 'that the people bestow all the power upon the Prince'. Certainly the Law there intends no more than to note *the particular fact* of the people of Rome, and not *a general right* of all other people. When Julius and Augustus had successively taken power into their hands, the people of Rome very bountifully, by a Royal Law, bestowed that power upon Augustus which he before had taken upon him. This act of the people the Law mentioned, not to prove the right of all people to give power to Princes, but produceth it against the people to show them that, by their own act, the Prince was free from all laws. And therefore in the very same place the Civil Law doth conclude that 'what pleaseth the Prince hath the vigour of the Law, or whatsoever the emperor ordained by his Epistles, or Rescripts, or commanded upon mature deliberation, or by edict, was a law'. The title of the Law 'De Constitutione Principum' is not concerning the ordaining of Princes by the people, but the ordaining of laws by the Princes.[3]

XI Suarez' Dispute against the Regality of Adam. Families diversely Defined, Suarez Contradicting Bellarmine

Suarez[4] the Jesuit riseth up against the royal authority of Adam in defence of the freedom and liberty of the people, and thus argues. 'By right of creation' (saith he) 'Adam had only economical power, but not political. He had power over his wife, and a fatherly power over his sons, whilst they were not made free. He might also, in process of time, have servants and a complete family, and in that family he might have complete economical power. But after that families began to be multiplied, and men to be separated and become heads of several families, they had the same power over their families. But political power did not begin until families began to be gathered to-

[1] See MOMMSEN, *Digesta Justiniani*, 2 vols., Berlin, 1866-70, vol. I, p. 15.
[2] ibid., p. 18.　　　[3] ibid., p. 14.
[4] The printed text resumes here, but with some re-arrangement of paragraphs.

gether into one perfect community. Wherefore, as the community did not begin by the creation of Adam, nor by his will alone, but of all them which did agree in this community, so we cannot say that Adam naturally had political primacy in that community. For that cannot be gathered by any natural principles, because by the force of the law of nature alone it is not due to any progenitor to be also King of his posterity. And if this be not gathered out of the principles of nature, we cannot say, "God by a special gift or providence gave him this power", for there is no revelation of this, nor testimony of Scripture.* Hitherto Suarez.

Whereas he makes Adam to have a fatherly power over his sons, and yet shuts up this power within one family, he seems either to imagine that all Adam's children lived within one house and under a roof with their Father, or else, that as soon as any of his children lived out of his house, they ceased to be subject, and did thereby become free. For my part I cannot believe that Adam, although he were sole monarch of the world, had any such spacious palace as might contain any considerable part of his children. It is likelier that some mean cottage or tent did serve him to keep his court in. It were a hard case he should lose part of his authority because his children lay not within the walls of his house. But if Suarez will allow all Adam's children to be of his family, howsoever they were separate in dwellings, if their habitations were contiguous or at such a distance as might easily receive his fatherly commands, and that all that were under his commands were of his family, although they had many children or servants married, having themselves also children, then I see no reason but that we may call Adam's family a commonwealth, except we will wrangle about words. For Adam, living 930 years and seeing seven or eight descents from himself, he might live to command of his children and his posterity a multitude far bigger than many commonwealths or kingdoms.

I know politicians and civil lawyers do not agree well about the definition of a family, and Bodin doth seem in one place to confine it to a house. Yet in his definition he doth enlarge his meaning to 'all persons under the obedience of one and the same head of the family',† and he approves better of the propriety of the Hebrew word for a family, which is derived from a word that signifies a head, a Prince or

* De Legibus, lib. 3, c. 2.[1]   † Lib. 1, c. 2.[2]

---

[1] See SUAREZ, FRANCISCO, Tractatus de Legibus . . ., Coimbra, 1612, p. 202.
[2] See BODIN, JEAN, Les Six Livres de la Republique, Paris, 1583, etc., translated Knolles, R., The six bookes of a commonweale, 1606, p. 8.

lord, than the Greek word for a family, which is derived from 'oikos', which signifies a house. Nor doth Aristotle confine a family to one house, but esteems it to be made of those *that daily converse together.* Whereas, before him, Charondas called a family *homosypioi*, those that feed together *out of one common pannier*, and Epimenides, the Cretan, terms a family *homocapnoi*, '*those that sit by one common fire or smoke*'.[1] But let Suarez understand what he please by Adam's family, if he will but confess, as he needs must, that Adam and the Patriarchs had absolute power of life and death, of peace and war and the like, within their houses or families, he must give us leave, at least, to call them Kings of their houses or families. And if they be so by the law of nature, what liberty will be left to their children to dispose of?

Aristotle gives the lie to Plato, and those that say that political and economical societies are all one, and do not differ *specie*, but only *multitudine et paucitate*, as if there were 'no difference betwixt a great house and a little city'.* All the argument I find he brings against them is this: 'The community of man and wife differs from the community of master and servant, because they have several ends. The intention of nature, by conjunction of male and female, is generation. But the scope of master and servant is only preservation, so that a wife and a servant are by nature distinguished. Because nature does not work like the cutlers at Delphos, for she makes but one thing for one use.' If we allow this argument to be sound, nothing doth follow but only this, that conjugal and despotical communities do differ. But it is no consequence that therefore economical and political societies do the like. For, though it prove a family to consist of two distinct communities, yet it follows not that a family and a commonwealth are distinct, because, as well in the commonweal as in the family, both these communities are found.

And as this argument comes not home to our point, so it is not able to prove that little which it shows for. For if it should be granted (which yet is false) that generation and preservation differ about the *individuum*, yet they agree in the *general*, and serve both for the conservation of mankind. Even as several servants differ in their particular ends or offices, as one to brew and another to bake, yet they agree in the general preservation of the family. Besides Aristotle himself confesseth that among the barbarians (as he calls them that are not Grecians) 'a wife and a servant are the same, because by nature no barbarian

* *Politics, lib. 1, c. 2.*[2]

---

[1] cf. ARISTOTLE, *Politics*, translated Sir Ernest Barker, 1946, p. 4.   [2] ibid., p. 3.

is fit to govern. It is fit the Grecians should rule over the barbarians, for by nature a servant and a barbarian is all one. Their family
consists only of an ox for a manservant and a wife for a maid, so they
are fit only to rule their wives and their beasts'.[1] Lastly Aristotle, if
it had pleased him, might have remembered that nature doth not
always make *one thing but for one use*. He knows the tongue serves both
to speak and to taste.

But to leave Aristotle and to return to Suarez. He saith that 'Adam
had fatherly power over his sons whilst they were not made free'.
Here I could wish that the Jesuit had taught us how and when sons
become free. I know no means by the law of nature. It is the favour, I
think, of the parents only, who, when their children are of age and
discretion to ease their parents of part of their fatherly care, are then
content to remit some part of their fatherly authority. Therefore the
customs of some countries do in some cases enfranchise the children
of inferior parents, but many nations have no such custom, but on the
contrary have strict laws for the obedience of children.* The Judaical
law of Moses giveth full power to the Father to stone his disobedient
son, so it be done in the presence of a magistrate. And yet it did not
belong to the magistrate to inquire or examine the justness of the
cause, but it was so decreed lest the Father should in his anger suddenly
or secretly kill his son. Also by the laws of the Persians and of the people
of Upper Asia, and of the Gauls, and by the laws of all the West Indies,
the parents have power of life and death over their children. The
Romans, even in their most popular estate, had this law in force, and
this power of parents was ratified and amplified by the laws of the
Twelve Tables, to the enabling of parents to sell their children two or
three times over. By the help of this fatherly power Rome long
flourished, and often times was freed from great dangers. The Fathers
have drawn out of the very assemblies their own sons, when, being
Tribunes, they have published laws tending to sedition.

Memorable is the example of Cassius, who threw his son headlong
out of the Consistory, publishing the law 'Agraria' for the division of
lands in behoof of the people. And afterwards, by his own private
judgment, put him to death by throwing him down headlong from
the Tarpeian Rock, the magistrates and people standing thereat amazed
and not daring to resist his fatherly authority, although they would
with all their hearts have had that law for the division of land. By

* BODIN, *lib.* 1, *c.* 4.[2]

---

[1] ibid.   [2] cf. KNOLLES, p. 20 ff.

which it appears it was lawful for the Father to dispose of the life of his child contrary to the will of the magistrates or people.[1] The Romans also had a law that what the children got was not their own, but their Father's, although Solon made a law which acquitted the son from nourishing of his Father if his Father had taught him no trade whereby to get his living.

Suarez proceeds, and tells us that 'in process of time Adam had complete economical power'. I know not what he means by this *complete economical power*, nor how or in what it doth really and essentially differ from political. If Adam did or might exercise in his family the same jurisdiction which a King doth now in a commonweal, then the kinds of power are not distinct. And though they may receive an accidental difference by the amplitude or extent of the bounds of the one beyond the other, yet since the like difference is also found in political estates, it follows that economical and political power differ no otherwise than a little commonweal differs from a great one. Next, saith Suarez, 'community did not begin at the creation of Adam'. It is true, because he had nobody to communicate with. Yet community did presently follow his creation, and that by his will alone, for it was in his power only, who was lord of all, to appoint what his sons should have in proper and what in common. So *propriety* and *community* of goods did follow originally from him, and it is the duty of a Father to provide as well for the common good of his children as for their particular.

Lastly Suarez concludes that: 'By the law of nature alone it is not due unto any progenitor to be also King of his posterity.' This assertion is confuted point blank by Bellarmine, who expressly affirmeth that 'the first parents ought to have been Princes of their posterity'. And until Suarez bring some reason for what he saith, I shall trust more to Bellarmine's proofs than to his bare denials.

XII Aristotle Agrees with the Scripture, Deducing Royal Authority from the Fatherhood[2]

Because the Scripture is not favourable to the liberty of the people, therefore many fly to natural reason and to the authority of Aristotle. I must crave liberty to examine or explain the opinion of this great philosopher.

[1] These two paragraphs to this point are paraphrased from Bodin. Parts of them are quoted again in the Forms.

[2] This chapter is differently placed in the MS. and printed versions. Its arguments are used again by Filmer in his tracts.

I find this sentence in the third of his *Politics, c.* 16: 'It seems *to some* not to be natural for one man to be lord of all the citizens, since a city consists of equals.' Lambin, in his Latin interpretation of this text, hath omitted the translation of this word 'τισιν'. By that means he maketh that to be the opinion of Aristotle which Aristotle allegeth to be the opinion but of some. This negligent, or wilful, escape of Lambin, in not translating a word so material, hath been an occasion to deceive many, who, looking no further than to the Latin translation, have concluded, and made the world now of late believe, that Aristotle here maintains a *natural equality of men.* And not only our English translator of Aristotle's *Politics* is, in this place, misled by following Lambin, but even the learned Monsieur Duvall in his analytical 'Synopsis' bears them company. And yet this version of Lambin's is esteemed the best, and printed at Paris, with Casaubon's corrected Greek copy, though in the rendering of this place the other translations have been more faithful. And he that shall compare the Greek text with the Latin will find that Casaubon had just cause in his preface to Aristotle's works to complain that the best translation of Aristotle did need correction.[1] To prove that in these words, which seem to favour the equality of mankind, Aristotle doth not speak according to his own judgment, but recites only the opinion of others, we find him clearly deliver his own opinion that *the power of government did originally arise from the right of fatherhood,* which cannot possibly consist with that *natural equality* which men dream of. For in the first of his *Politics* he agrees exactly with the Scripture, and lays this foundation of government: 'The first society made of many houses is a village, which seems most naturally to be a colony of families or foster brethren of children and children's children. And therefore, at the beginning, cities were under the government of Kings, for the eldest in every house is King. And so for kindred sake it is in colonies.'[2] And in the fourth of his *Politics, c.* 2, he gives the title of the first and divinest sort of government to the institution of Kings, by defining tyranny to be a digression from the first and divinest.[3]

---

[1] Comparison of the texts of Aristotle quoted by Filmer shows him to be correct in this complaint. See LAMBIN, DENIS, *Aristotelis Opera,* 2 vols. Paris, 1619, with *Synopsis Analytica . . . Authore Guilielmo Du Val,* and Isaac Casaubon's Preface, vol. I, p. 359. The English translation, *Aristotles Politiques . . . translated out of Greeke into French by Loys Le Roy . . . out of French into English,* 1598, omits this phrase (see p. 179), although Le Roy retained it (see *Les Politiques d'Aristote,* 1576, p. 197). This may have been due to Lambin, whose version was first published in 1567. Barker's translation is on p. 145.

[2] ibid., p. 4.

[3] ibid., p. 158.

Whosoever weighs advisedly these passages will find little hope of natural reason in Aristotle to prove *the natural liberty of the multitude.* Also before him the divine Plato concludes 'a commonweal to be nothing else but a large family'. I know that for this position Aristotle quarrels with his master, but most unjustly. For therein he contradicts his own principles, for they both agree to fetch the original of civil .government from the prime government of families. No doubt but Moses' history of the creation guided these two philosophers in finding out of this lineal subjection deduced from the loins of the first parents according to that rule of St. Chrysostom: 'God made all mankind of one man, that he might teach the world to be governed by a King, and not by a multitude.'[1]

The ignorance of the Creation occasioned several errors amongst the heathen philosophers. Polybius, though otherwise a most profound philosopher and judicious historian, yet here he stumbles. For in searching out the original of civil societies he conceited that: 'Multitudes of men after a deluge, a famine or a pestilence, met together like herds of cattle without any dependency, until the strongest bodies and boldest minds got the mastery of their fellows,'* even as it is (saith he) among bulls, boars and cocks.

And Aristotle himself, forgetting his first doctrine, tells us 'the first heroical Kings were chosen by the people for their deserving well of the multitude, either by teaching them some arts, or by warring for them, or for gathering them together, or for dividing land amongst them.'† Also Aristotle had another fancy, that those men 'which prove wise of mind, were by nature intended to be lords and govern, and those which were strong of body were ordained to obey and be servants'.‡ But this is a dangerous and uncertain rule, and not without some folly. For if a man prove both wise and strong, what will Aristotle have done with him? As he was wise, he could be no servant, and as he had strength, he could not be master. Besides, to speak like a philosopher, nature intends all men to be perfect both in wit and strength. The folly or imbecility proceeds from some error in generation or education, for nature aims at perfection in all her works.

---

* *Polybius, lib. 6.*[2]   † *Politics, lib. 3, c. 14.*[3]   ‡ *Politics, lib. 1, c, 2.*[4]

---

[1] This probably refers to Suarez' use of a passage from Chrysostom, op. cit., p. 202.
[2] See GRIMESTON, EDWARD, *The History of Polybius*, 1634, p. 284.
[3] BARKER, p. 139.
[4] ibid., p. 3.

XIII Of Election of Kings by the Major Part of the People, by Proxy, by Silent Acceptation

But let us condescend for a while to the opinion of Bellarmine, Grotius and Suarez, and of all those who place supreme power in the whole people, and ask them if their meaning be that there is but one and the same power in all the people of the world, so that no power can be granted except all men upon the earth meet and agree to choose a governor? An answer is here given by Suarez, that: 'It is scarce possible nor yet expedient that all men in the world should be gathered together into one community. It is likelier that either never, or for a very short time, that this power was in this manner in the whole multitude of men collected, but a little after the Creation men began to be divided into several commonwealths, and this distinct power was in each of them.'[1]

This answer of *scarce possible nor yet expedient*, and *it is likelier* begets a new doubt how this distinct power comes to each particular community when God gave it to the whole multitude only, and not to any particular assembly of men. Can they show or prove that ever the whole multitude met and divided this power which God gave them in gross, by breaking it into parcels and by apportioning a distinct power to each several commonwealth? Without such a compact, I cannot see, according to their own principles, how there can be any election of a magistrate by any commonwealth, but by a mere usurpation upon the privilege of the whole world. If any man think that particular multitudes, at their own discretion, had power to divide themselves into several commonwealths, those that think so have neither reason nor proof for so thinking, and thereby a gap is opened for every petty factious multitude to raise a new commonwealth, and to make more commonweals than there be families in the world.

But let this also be yielded them, that in each particular commonwealth there is a distinct power in the multitude. Was a general meeting of a whole kingdom ever known for the election of a Prince? Was there any example of it ever found in the world? To conceit such a thing is to imagine little less than an impossibility, and so by consequence no one form of government or King was ever established according to this supposed law of nature.

It may be answered by some that, if either the greatest part of a kingdom, or, if a smaller part only by themselves and all the rest by proxy, or, if the part not concurring in the election do after by tacit

---

[1] SUAREZ, op. cit., p. 203.

assent ratify the act of others, that in all these cases it may be said to
be the work of the whole multitude.

1. As to the acts of the *major* part of a multitude. It is true that by
politic human constitutions, it is oft ordained that the voices of the
most shall overrule the rest. And such ordinances bind, because, where
men are assembled by a human power, that power that doth assemble
them can also limit and direct the manner of the execution of that
power. And by such derivative power, made known by law or custom, either the greater part, or two thirds parts, or three parts of five
or the like, have power to oversway the liberty of their opposites.
But in assemblies that take their authority from the law of nature it
cannot be so. For what freedom or liberty is due to any man by the
law of nature, no inferior power can alter, limit or diminish. No one
man, nor a multitude, can give away the natural right of another. The
law of nature is unchangeable, and howsoever one man may hinder
another in the use or exercise of his natural right, yet thereby no man
loseth the right itself. For the right and the use of the right may be
distinguished, as right and possession are oft distinct. Therefore,
unless it can be proved by some law of nature that the major, or some
other part, have power to overrule the rest of the multitude, it must
follow that the acts of multitudes not entire are not binding to all, but
only to such as consent unto them.

2. As to the point of proxy. It cannot be showed or proved that
all those that have been absent from popular elections did ever give
their voices to some of their fellows. I ask but one example out of any
history. Let the commonweal be but named wherever the multitude,
or so much as the greatest part of it, consented either by voice or by
procuration to the election of a Prince. The ambition sometimes of
one man, sometimes of many, or the faction of a city or citizens, or the
mutiny of an army, hath set up or pulled down Princes. But they have
never tarried for this pretended orderly proceeding of the whole
multitude.

3. Lastly. If the silent acceptation of a governor by part of the
people be an argument of their concurring in the election of him, by
the same reason the tacit assent of the whole commonwealth may be
maintained. From whence it follows that every Prince that comes to
a crown, either by succession, conquest or usurpation, may be said
to be elected by the people. Which inference is too ridiculous, for
in such cases the people are so far from the liberty of *specification* that
they want even that of *contradiction*.

XIV   No Example in Scripture of the People's Choosing their King. Mr. Hooker's Judgment therein

But it is vain to argue against the liberty of the people in the election of Kings as long as men are persuaded that examples are to be found of it in Scripture. It is fit, therefore, to discover the grounds of this error. It is plain by an evident text that it is one thing to choose a King, and another thing to set a King over the people. This latter power the children of Israel had, but not the former. This distinction is found most evident in Deuteronomy xvii, 15, where the law of God saith: 'Him shalt thou set King over thee whom the Lord shall choose.' So God must *eligere*, and the people only do *constituere*. Mr. Hooker, in his eighth book of *Ecclesiastical Polity*,* clearly expounds this distinction: his words are worth the citing: 'Heaps of Scripture' (saith he) 'are alleged concerning the solemn coronation or inauguration of Saul, David, Solomon and others, by Nobles, Ancients and People of the commonwealth of Israel; as if the Solemnities were a kind of deed, whereby the right of dominion is given, which strange, untrue and unnatural conceits set abroad by seedmen of Rebellion, only to animate unquiet spirits, and to feed them with possibilities of aspiring unto the thrones, if they can win the hearts of the people, whatsoever hereditary title any other before them may have, I say these unjust and insolent positions I would not mention, were it not thereby to make the countenance of truth more orient. For unless we will openly proclaim defiance unto all law, equity and reason, we must, there is no remedy, acknowledge that, in kingdoms, hereditary birthright giveth right unto sovereign Dominion, and the death of the predecessor putteth the successor by blood in seisin. Those public solemnities before mentioned do either serve for an open testification of the inheritor's right, or belong to the form of inducting of him into possession of that thing he hath right unto.'

This is Mr. Hooker's judgment of the Israelites' power to set a King over themselves. No doubt but if the people of Israel had had power to choose their King, they would never have made their choice of Joas, a child but of seven years old, nor of Manasses, a boy but of twelve, since, as Solomon saith, 'Woe to the land whose King is a

* MS.[1]

---

[1] This marginal reference appears only in the MS. and in the 1685 printing. It has great significance in proving that a manuscript of Hooker's eighth book was in circulation in Kent in the late 1630s, though it was not printed until 1648. The passage appears on p. 174 of HOUK, R. A., *Hooker's Ecclesiastical Polity*, Book VIII, New York, 1931, but the version used by Filmer was evidently different.

child.' Nor is it probable they would have elected Josias, but a very child, and a son of so wicked an idolatrous father as that his own servants murdered him. And yet all the people set up this young Josias and slew all the conspirators of the death of Ammon his father, which justice of the people God rewarded by making this Josias the most religious King that ever that nation enjoyed.

XV God Governed always by Monarchy. Bellarmine's and Aristotle's Judgment of Monarchy

Because it is affirmed that the people have power to choose as well what form of government as what governors they please, of which mind is Bellarmine in those places we cited at first,[1] therefore it is necessary to examine the strength of what is said in defence of popular commonweals against this natural form of kingdoms which I maintain. Here I must first put you in mind of what Bellarmine affirms in cold blood in other places, where he saith: 'God, when he made all mankind of one man, did seem openly to signify that He rather approved the government of one man than of many.' Again, 'God showed His opinion when He endued not only men, but all creatures, with a natural propensity to monarchy. Neither can it be doubted but a natural propensity is to be referred to God, who is author of nature'. And again in a third place, 'what form of government God confirmed by His authority may be gathered by that commonweal which He instituted among the Hebrews, which was not aristocratical (as Calvin saith) but plainly monarchical'.[2]

Now, if God (as Bellarmine saith) have taught us by natural instinct, signified to us by the Creation and confirmed by His own example, the excellency of monarchy, why should Bellarmine or we doubt but that it is natural? Do we not find that in every family the government of one alone is most natural? God did always govern His own people by monarchy only. The Patriarchs, dukes, judges and Kings were all monarchs. There is not in all the Scripture mention and approbation of any other form of government. At the time when the Scripture saith: 'There was no King in Israel, but that every man did that which was right in his own eyes',[3] even then, the Israelites were under the kingly government of the Fathers of particular families. For in the consultation after the Benjamitical war for providing wives for the Benjamites, we find the elders of the congregation bear only sway,

---

[1] See supra, p. 56.   [2] BELLARMINE, op. cit., vol. I, p. 313.   [3] Judges xxi, 25

Judges xxi, 16. To them also were complaints to be made, as appears by verse 22. And though mention be made of 'all the children of Israel', 'all the congregation', and 'all the people', yet by that term of *all* the Scripture means only *all* the Fathers, and not the whole multitude. As the text plainly expounds itself in the 2 Chronicles i, 2, where Solomon speaks unto *all* Israel, to the captains, the judges, and to every governor, the chief of the Fathers, so the elders of Israel are expounded to be the chief of the Fathers of the children of Israel, 1 Kings viii, 1, 2, 2 Chronicles v, 2.

At that time also, when the people of Israel begged a King of Samuel, they were governed by kingly power. God, out of a special care and love to the house of Israel, did choose to be their King Himself, and did govern them at that time by His viceroy Samuel and his sons. And therefore God tells Samuel: 'They have not rejected thee but Me, that I should not reign over them.'[1] It seems they did not like a King by deputation, but desired one by succession like all the nations. All nations belike had Kings then, and those by inheritance, not by election. For we do not find the Israelites prayed that they themselves might choose their own King: they dream of no such liberty, and yet they were the elders of Israel gathered together. If other nations had elected their own Kings, no doubt but they would have been as desirous to have imitated other nations as well in the electing as in the having of a King.

Aristotle, in his books of *Politics*, when he comes to compare the several kinds of government, he is very reserved in discovering what form he thinks best. He disputes subtly to and fro of many points, and judiciously confutes many errors, but concludes nothing himself. In all those books I find little in commendation of monarchy. It was his hap to live in those times when the Grecians abounded with several commonwealths, who had learning enough to make them seditious. Yet in his *Ethics* he hath so much good manners as to confess in right down words that 'monarchy is the best form of government,' and a popular estate the worst'.[2] And though he be not so free in his *Politics*, yet the necessity of truth hath here and there extorted from him that which amounts no less to the dignity of monarchy. He confesseth it to be 'the first, the natural, and the Divinest form of government, and that the gods themselves did live under a monarchy'.[3] What can a heathen say more?

Indeed, the world for a long time knew no other sort of govern-

---

[1] 1 Sam. viii, 7.   [2] Loeb edition, p. 489.
[3] Compare BARKER, p. 158 and p. 4.

ment but only monarchy. The best order, the greatest strength, the most stability and easiest government are to be found in monarchy, and in no other form of government. The new platforms of commonweals were first hatched in a corner of the world, amongst a few cities of Greece, which have been imitated by very few other places. Those very cities were first for many years governed by Kings, until wantonness, ambition or faction made them attempt new kinds of regiment. All which mutations proved most bloody and miserable to the authors of them, happy in nothing but that they continued but a small time.

XVI Imperfections of Democracies.   Rome Began her Empire under Kings and Perfected it under Emperors. The People of Rome in Danger oft Fled to Monarchy

A little to manifest the imperfection of popular government, let us but examine the most flourishing democracy that the world hath ever known. I mean that of Rome.

1. First, for the durability. At the most it lasted but 480 years (for so long it was from the expulsion of Tarquin to Julius Caesar). Whereas both the Assyrian monarchy lasted, without interruption, at the least twelve hundred years, and the Empire of the East continued 1495 years.

2. Secondly, for the order of it. During those 480 years there was not any one settled form of government in Rome. For after they had once lost the natural power of Kings, they could not find upon what form of government to rest:* their fickleness is an evidence that they found things amiss in every change. At the first they choose two annual Consuls instead of Kings. Secondly, those did not please them long but they must have Tribunes of the people to defend their liberty. Thirdly, they leave Tribunes and Consuls, and choose them ten men to make them laws. Fourthly, they call for Consuls and Tribunes again, sometimes they choose Dictators, which were temporary Kings, and sometimes Military Tribunes, who had Consular power. All these shiftings caused such notable alteration in the government, as it poseth both historians and politicians to find out any perfect form of regiment in so much confusion; one while the Senate made laws,

* See BODIN, *De Repub.*, lib. 6, c. 4.[1]

---

[1] BODIN, op. cit. Filmer's account of Roman history seems to have been almost a copy of Bodin.

another while the people. The dissensions which were daily between the nobles and the commons bred those memorable seditions about usury, about marriages and about magistracy. Also the Gracchian, the Apulian and the Drusian seditions filled the market-places, the temples and the Capitol itself with blood of the citizens. The Social War was plainly civil; the wars of the Slaves and the other of the Fencers, the civil wars of Marius and Sulla, of Cataline, of Caesar and Pompey, the Triumvirate of Augustus, Lepidus and Antonius, all shed an ocean of blood within Italy and the streets of Rome.

3. Thirdly, for their government. Let it be allowed that for some part of this time it was popular, yet was it popular as to the city of Rome only, and not as to the dominions, or whole empire of Rome. For no democracy can extend further than to one city. It is impossible to govern a kingdom, much less many kingdoms, by the whole people, or by the greatest part of them.

But, you will say, yet the Roman Empire grew all up under this kind of popular government, and the city became mistress of the world. It is not so. For Rome began her empire under Kings, and did perfect it under Emperors; it did only increase under the popularity.* Her greatest exultation was under Trajan, as her longest peace had been under Augustus. Even at those times when the Roman victories abroad did amaze the world, then the tragical slaughter of citizens at home deserved commiseration from their vanquished enemies. What though in that age of her popularity she bred many admired captains and commanders (each of which was able to lead an army, though many of them were but ill requited by the people) yet all of them were not able to support her in times of danger. But she was forced in her greatest troubles to create a *Dictator* (who was a King for a time), thereby giving this honourable testimony of monarchy, that the last refuge in perils of states is to fly to regal authority. And though Rome's popular estate for a while was miraculously upheld in glory by a greater Providence than her own, yet in a short time, after manifold alterations, she was ruined by her own hands. 'Suis et ipsa Roma viribus ruit', for the arms she had prepared to conquer other nations were turned upon herself, and civil contentions at last settled the government again into a monarchy.

* See BODIN, *De Repub.*, lib. 6, c. 4.[1]

---

[1] ibid., KNOLLES, pp. 715, 716. The same material is used again in the Forms.

XVII   Democracies not Invented to Bridle Tyrants, but Came in
by Stealth

The vulgar opinion is that the first cause why the democratical
government was brought in was to curb the tyranny of monarchs.
But the falsehood of this doth best appear by the first flourishing
popular estate of Athens, which was founded not because of the vices
of their last King, but for that his virtuous deserts were such as the
people thought no man worthy enough to succeed him: a pretty wanton quarrel to monarchy. For when their King Codrus understood by
the oracle that his country could not be saved unless the King were
slain in the battle, he in disguise entered his enemy's camp and provoked
a common soldier to make him a sacrifice for his own kingdom. And
with his death ended the royal government, for after him was never
any more Kings of Athens. As Athens thus for the love of their Codrus
changed their government, so Rome, on the contrary, out of hatred to
their Tarquin, did the like. And though these two famous commonweals did for contrary causes abolish monarchy, yet they both agreed
in this, that neither of them thought it fit to change their state into a
democracy. But the one chose Archontes and the other Consuls to
be their governors, both which did most resemble Kings, and continued
until the people, by lessening the authority of these their magistrates,
did by degrees and stealth bring in their popular government. And I
verily believe never any democratical state showed itself first fairly to
the world by any elective entrance, but they all secretly crept in by the
back door of sedition and faction.

XVIII   Democracies Vilified by their own Historians

If we will listen to the judgment of those who should best know the
nature of popular government, we shall find no reason for good men
to desire or choose it. Xenophon, that brave scholar and soldier, dis-
allowed the Athenian commonweal, for that they followed that form
of government wherein 'the wicked are always in greatest credit, and
virtuous men kept under'.* They expelled Aristides the just; Themis-
tocles died in banishment, Miltiades in prison; Phocion, the most
virtuous and just man of his age, though he had been chosen forty-
five times to be their general, yet was put to death with all his friends,
kindred and servants by the fury of the people, without sentence,

* BODIN, lib. 6, c. 4.[1]

[1] See KNOLLES, pp. 702-5. These two paragraphs are little more than extracts from this
source. It is typical of Filmer to quote Xenophon *via* Bodin.

_accusation or any cause at all. Nor were the people of Rome much more favourable to their worthies. They banished Rutilius, Metellus, Coriolanus, the two Scipios and Tully. The worst men sped best: for as Xenophon saith of Athens, so Rome was a sanctuary for all turbulent, discontented and seditious spirits. The impunity of wicked men was such that upon pain of death it was forbidden all magistrates to condemn to death, or banish any citizen, or to deprive him of his liberty, or so much as to whip him, what offence soever he had committed, either against the gods or men.

The Athenians sold justice as they did other merchandise, which made Plato call a popular estate 'a fair, where everything is to be sold'. The officers, when they entered upon their charge, would brag 'they went to a golden harvest'. The corruption of Rome was such that Marius and Pompey durst carry bushels of silver into the assemblies to purchase the voices of the people. Many citizens under their grave gowns came armed unto the public meetings, as if they went to war. Often contrary factions fell to blows, sometimes with stones, and sometimes swords. The blood hath been sucked up in the market-places with sponges: the river Tiber hath been filled with the dead bodies of citizens, and the common privies stuffed full with them.

If any man think these disorders in popular states were but casual or such as may happen under any kind of government, he must know that such mischiefs are unavoidable and of necessity do follow all democratical regiments. The reason is given: because the nature of all people is to desire liberty without restraint, which cannot be but where the wicked bear rule. And if the people should be so indiscreet as to advance virtuous men, they lose their power, for that good men would favour none but the good, which are always the fewer in number. And the wicked and vicious (which is still the greatest part of the people) should be excluded from all preferment, and in the end, by little and little, wise men should seize upon the state and take it from the people.

I know not how to give a better character of the people than can be gathered from such authors as lived among or near to popular states. Thucydides, Xenophon, Livy, Tacitus, Cicero and Sallust have set them out in their colours. I will borrow some of their sentences.

'There is nothing more uncertain than the people: their opinions are as variable and sudden as tempests: there is neither truth nor judgment in them: they are not led by wisdom to judge of anything, but by violence and by rashness, nor put they any difference between things true and false. After the manner of cattle they follow the herd

G

that goes before: with envious eyes they behold the felicity of others: they have a custom always to favour the worst and weakest: they are most prone to suspicions, and use to condemn men for guilty upon every false suggestion. They are apt to believe all news, especially if it be sorrowful, and, like Fame, they make it more in the believing: when there is no author, they fear those evils which they themselves have feigned: they are most desirous of new stirs and changes, and are enemies to quiet and rest. Whatsoever is giddy or headstrong, they account manly and courageous, but whatsoever is modest or provident seems sluggish: each man hath a care of his particular, and thinks basely of the common good: they look upon approaching mischiefs as they do upon thunder, only every man wisheth it may not touch his own person. It is the nature of them: they must either serve basely or domineer proudly, for they know no mean.' Thus do their own friends paint to the life this beast of many heads. Let me give you the cypher of their form of government. As it is begot by sedition, so it is nourished by arms: it can never stand without wars, either with an enemy abroad, or with friends at home. The only means to preserve it is to have some powerful enemy near, who may serve instead of a King to govern it, that so, though they have not a King among them, yet they may have as good as a King over them, for the common danger of an enemy keeps them in better unity than the laws they make themselves.

XIX   Popular Government more Bloody than a Tyranny

Many have exercised their wits in paralleling the inconveniencies of regal and popular government. But if we will trust experience before speculations philosophical, it cannot be denied but this one mischief of sedition, which necessarily waits upon all popularity, weighs down all the inconveniencies that can be found in monarchy, though they were never so many. It is said: 'Skin for skin, yea, all that a man hath will he give for his life.'* And: 'A man will give his riches for the ransom of his life.'† The way then to examine what proportion the mischiefs of sedition and tyranny have to one another is to inquire in which kind of government most subjects have lost their lives. Let Rome, which is magnified for her popularity and vilified for those tyrannical monsters the emperors, furnish us with examples. Consider whether the cruelty of all the tyrannical emperors which ever ruled in this city, did spill a quarter of that blood that was poured out in the last

* Job ii, 4.   † Prov. xiii, 8.

hundred years of her glorious commonwealth. The murders by
Tiberius, Caligula, Nero, Domitian and Commodus put all together,
cannot match that civil tragedy which was acted in that one sedition
between Marius and Sulla. Nay, even by Sulla's part alone (not to
mention the acts of Marius) were fourscore and ten senators put to
death, fourteen consuls, two thousand and six hundred gentlemen and
a hundred thousand others.

This was the height of the Roman liberty — any man might be killed
that would. A favour not fit to be granted under a royal government.
The misery of these licentious times are briefly touched by Plutarch in
these words. 'Sulla' (saith he) 'fell to the shedding of blood and filled
all Rome with infinite and unspeakable murders. And this was not
only done in Rome, but in all the cities of Italy throughout there was
no temple of any god whatsoever, no altar in anybody's house, no
liberty of hospital, no Father's house, which was not imbrued with
blood and horrible murder. The husbands were slain in the wives'
arms and the children in the mothers' laps, and yet they that were slain
for private malice were nothing in respect of those that were murdered
only for their goods . . . He openly sold their goods by the crier, sitting
so proudly in his chair of state, that it grieved the people more to see
their goods packed up by them to whom he gave or disposed them than
to see them taken away. Sometimes he would give a whole country
or the whole revenues of certain cities unto women for their beauty,
or to pleasant jesters, minstrels or wicked slaves made free. And to
some he would give other men's wives by force, and make them to
be married against their wills.'[1]

Now let Tacitus and Suetonius be searched, and see if all their cruel
emperors can match this popular villain in such an universal slaughter
of citizens or civil butchery. God only was able to match him, and
overmatched him by fitting him with a most remarkable death, just
answerable to his life. For, as he had been the death of many thousands
of his countrymen, so as many thousands of his own kindred in the
flesh were the death of him, for he died of an imposthume 'which
corrupted his flesh in such sort that it turned all to lice. He had many
about him to shift him continually night and day, yet the lice they
wiped from him were nothing to them that multiplied upon him.
There was neither apparel, linen, baths, washings or meat itself, but
was presently filled with swarms of this vile vermin.'[2]

[1] See PLUTARCH, *Lives*, translated by Sir Thomas North, 1603, etc., 1612, ed., pp. 485-6,
word for word.
[2] ibid., p. 487.

I cite not this to extenuate the bloody acts of any tyrannical Princes, nor will I plead in defence of their cruelties. Only in the comparative I maintain the mischiefs to a state to be less universal under a tyrant King. For the cruelty of such tyrants extends ordinarily no further than to some particular men that offend him, and not to the whole kingdom. It is truly said by his late Majesty of blessed memory:[1] 'A King can never be so notoriously vicious but he will generally favour justice, and maintain some order, except in the particulars wherein his inordinate lust carries him away.' Even cruel Domitian, Dionysius the tyrant and many others are commended by historians for great observers of justice. A natural reason is to be rendered for it. It is the multitude of people and the abundance of their riches which are the strength and glory of every Prince. The bodies of his subjects do him service in war, and their goods supply his public wants, therefore, if not out of affection to his people, yet out of natural love to himself, every tyrant desires to preserve the lives and protect the goods of his subjects, which cannot be done but by justice, and if it be not done, the Prince's loss is the greatest.

On the contrary, in a popular state every man knows that the public good doth not depend wholly on his care, but the Commonwealth may be well enough governed by others though he tend only his private benefit. He never takes the public to be his own business. Thus, as in a family, where one office is to be done by many servants, one looks upon another, and every one leaves the business for his fellow until it is quite neglected by all. Nor are they much to be blamed for their negligence, since it is an even wager their ignorance is as great. For the magistrates among the people, being for the most part annual, do always lay down their office before they understand it, so that a Prince of a duller understanding, by use and experience, must needs excel them.

Again, there is no tyrant so barbarously wicked but his own reason and sense will tell him that, though he be a god, yet he must die like a man, and that there is not the meanest of his subjects but may find a means to revenge himself of the injustice that is offered him. Hence it is that great tyrants live continually in base fears, as did Dionysius the elder. And Tiberius, Caligula and Nero are all noted by Suetonius to have been frighted with panic fears. But it is not so where wrong is done to any particular person by a multitude. He knows not who hurt him, or who to complain of, or to whom to address himself for

[1] See JAMES I, *Trew law of free monarchie* . . . in McILWAIN, C. H., *Political Works of James I*, Cambridge, Mass., 1918, p. 66.

reparation. Any man may boldly exercise his malice and cruelty in all popular assemblies. There is no tyranny to be compared to the tyranny of a multitude.

XX Of a Mixed Government of King and People: the People May not Judge or Correct their King

What though the government of the people be a thing not to be endured, much less defended, yet many men please themselves with an opinion that, though the people may not govern, yet they may partake and join with a King in government, and so make a state mixed of popular and regal power, which they take to be the best tempered and equallest form of government. But the vanity of this fancy is too evident. It is a mere impossibility or contradiction. For if a King but once admit the people to be his companions, he leaves to be a King, and the state becomes a democracy. At least, he is but a titular and no real King, that hath not the sovereignty to himself: for the having of this alone, and nothing but this, makes a King to be a King. As for that show of popularity which is found in such kingdoms as have general assemblies for consultation about making public laws, it must be remembered that such meetings do not share or divide the sovereignty with the Prince, but do only deliberate and advise their supreme head, who still reserves the absolute power in himself. For if in such assemblies the King, the nobility and people have equal shares in the sovereignty, then the King hath but one voice, the nobility likewise one, and the people one, and then any two of these voices should have power to overrule the third, thus the nobility and commons together should have power to make a law to bind the King, which was never yet seen in any kingdom, but if it could, the state must needs be popular and not regal.

If it be unnatural for the multitude to choose their governors, or to govern or to partake in the government, what can be thought of that damnable conclusion which is made by too many, that the multitude may correct or depose their Prince if need be? Surely the unnaturalness and injustice of this position cannot sufficiently be expressed. For admit that a King make a contract or paction with his people, either originally in his ancestors, or personally at his coronation (for both these pactions some dream of but cannot offer any proof of either) yet by no law of any nation can: 'A contract be thought broken, except that first a lawful trial be had by the ordinary judge of the breakers thereof, or else every man may be both party and judge in his own case, which is absurd once to be thought. For then it will lie in the hands of the headless multitude when they please to cast off the yoke of government (that God hath laid·upon them) to judge and punish him by whom they should be judged and punished.'* Aristotle can tell us what judges the multitude are in their own case: 'τᾶδε υἱ πλέιστοι φαῦλοι κριται περὶ τῶν οἰκέιων'† — the multitude are ill judges in their own case.

The judgment of the multitude in disposing of the sovereignty may be seen in the Roman history, where we find many good emperors murdered by the people, and many bad elected by them. Nero, Heliogabalus, Otho, Vitellus and such other monsters of nature were the minions of the multitude, and set up by them. Pertinax, Alexander, Severus, Gordianus, Gallus, Emilianus, Quintilius, Aurelianus, Tacitus, Probus and Numerianus, all of them good emperors in the judgment of all historians, yet murdered by the multitude.

XXI No Tyrants in England since the Conquest

Whereas many out of imaginary fear pretend the power of the people to be necessary for the repressing of the insolences of tyrants, herein they propound a remedy far worse than the disease. Neither is the disease so frequent as they would have us think. Let us be judged by the history of our own nation. We have enjoyed a succession of Kings from the Conquest now near about 600 years (a time far longer than ever yet any popular state could continue). We reckon to the number of twenty-five of these Princes of the Norman race, and yet not one of these is taxed by our histories for tyrannical government.[1] It is true, two of these Kings have been deposed by the people and barbarously murdered, but neither of them for tyranny. For, as a learned historian of our age saith: 'Edward II and Richard II were not insupportable either in their nature or rule, and yet the people more upon wantonness than for any want, did take an unbridled course against them. Edward II, by many of our historians is reported to be of a good and virtuous nature, and not unlearned; they impute his defects rather to fortune than either to counsel or carriage of his affairs. The deposition of him was violent fury, led by a wife both cruel and unchaste, and can with no better countenance of right be justified than may his lamentable both indignities and death. Likewise the deposition of King Richard II was a tempestuous rage, neither led or restrained

* True Law of Free Monarchy.[2]   † Politics, lib. 3, c. 9.[3]

---

[1] In the printed versions 'about 600' was altered to 'above 600' and '25' to '26'.
[2] JAMES I, op. cit., pp. 68–9.   [3] cf. BARKER, p. 117.

by any rules of reason or state. Examine his actions without dis-
tempered judgment, and you will not condemn him to be exceeding
either insufficient or evil: weigh the imputations that were objected
against him, and you shall find nothing either of any truth or of great
moment.'* Hollingshed writeth 'That he was most unthankfully used
by his subjects; for, although through the frailty of his youth he de-
meaned himself more dissolutely than was agreeable to the royalty of
his estate, yet in no King's days the commons were in greater wealth,
the nobility more honoured, and the clergy less wronged, who, notwithstanding, in the evil guided strength of their will, took head against
him, to their own headlong destruction afterwards, partly during the
reign of Henry his next successor, whose greatest achievements were
against his own people in executing those who conspired with him
against King Richard, and more especially in succeeding times,
when, upon occasion of this disorder, more English blood was spilt
than was in all the foreign wars together which have been since the
Conquest.'

Twice hath this kingdom been miserably wasted with civil war,
but neither of them occasioned by the tyranny of any Prince. The
cause of the Barons' Wars is by good historians attributed to the
stubbornness of the nobility, as the bloody variance of the houses of
York and Lancaster sprang from the wantonness of the people.
These two[2] unnatural wars have dishonoured our nation among
strangers, so that in the censure of kingdoms of the King of Spain is
said to be the King of men, because of his subjects' willing obedience;
the King of France, King of asses, because of their infinite taxes and
impositions; but the King of England is said to be the King of devils,
because of his subjects' often insurrections against, and depositions of,
their Princes.

XXII Regal Authority not Subject to Human Laws. Kings
Before Laws. The Kings of Judah and Israel not Tied
to Laws

Hitherto I have endeavoured to show the natural institution of regal
authority, and to free it from subjection to an arbitrary election of the

* SIR JOHN HEYWOOD, In Answer to Dolman.[1]

---

[1] See HEYWARD, op. cit., pp. K and K reverse.
[2] The printed versions were altered to add 'and the late rebellion' after the Barons'
Wars and the Wars of the Roses. 'Two unnatural wars' became 'three'. This is in itself
proof that Patriarcha was written before it was realized that the difference between
Charles I and his Parliament constituted a Civil War.

people. It is necessary also to inquire whether human laws have a superiority over Princes, because those that maintain the acquisition of royal jurisdiction from the people do subject the exercise of it to human positive laws. But in this also they err. For as Kingly power is by the law of God, so it hath no inferior law to limit it. The Father of a family governs by no other law than by his own will, not by the laws or wills of his sons or servants. There is no nation that allows children any action or remedy for being unjustly governed. And yet for all this every Father is bound by the law of nature to do his best for the preservation of his family. But much more is a King always tied by the same law of nature to keep this general ground, that the safety of his kingdom be his chief law. He must remember that the profit of every man in particular, and of all together in general, is not always one and the same, that the public is to be preferred before the private and that the force of laws must not be so great as natural equity itself. Which cannot fully be comprised in any laws, but is to be left to the religious arbitrament of those who know how to manage the affairs of state, and wisely to balance the particular profit with the counterpoise of the public, according to the infinite variety of times, places, persons.

A proof unanswerable for the superiority of Princes above laws is this, that there were Kings long before there were any laws. For a long time the word of the King was the only law. 'And if practice' (as saith Sir Walter Raleigh) 'declare the greatness of authority, even the best Kings of Judah and Israel were not tied to any law, but they did whatsoever they pleased in the greatest matters.'*

XXIII Samuel's Description of a King. The Power Ascribed to Kings in the New Testament

The unlimited jurisdiction of Kings is so amply described by Samuel, that it hath given occasion to some to imagine that it was but either a plot or trick of Samuel to keep the government in himself and family by frighting the Israelites with the mischiefs in monarchy, or else a prophetical description only of the future ill-government of Saul. But the vanity of these conjectures are judiciously discovered in that majestical discourse of 'The True Law of Free Monarchy'.[2] Wherein

---

* Lib. 2, Part 1, c. 16.[1]

[1] This is from the History of the World, RALEIGH, op. cit., vol. IV, p. 474.
[2] JAMES I, op. cit., p. 56-.

it is evidently showed that the scope of Samuel was to teach the people a dutiful obedience to their King, even in those things which themselves did esteem mischievous and inconvenient. For, by telling them what a King would do, he instructs them what a subject must suffer. Yet not so that it is right for Kings to do injury, but it is right for them to go unpunished by the people if they do it. So that in this point it is all one whether Samuel describe a King or a tyrant for patient obedience is due to both. No remedy in the text against tyrants, but in crying and praying unto God in that day. But howsoever in a rigorous construction Samuel's description be applied to a tyrant, yet the words by a benign interpretation may agree with the manners of a just King, and the scope and coherence of the text[1] doth best imply the more moderate or qualified sense of the words.

For, as Sir W. Raleigh confesseth: 'All those inconveniences and miseries' (which are reckoned up by Samuel as belonging to kingly government) 'were not intolerable, but such as have been borne, and are still borne, by free consent of subjects towards their Princes.'[2] Nay, at this day, and in this land many tenants, by their tenures and services, are tied to the like subjection to subordinate and inferior lords. To serve the King in his wars and to till his ground is not only agreeable to the nature of subjects but much desired by them, according to their several births and conditions. The like may be said for the offices of women servants, confectioners, cooks and bakers. For we cannot think that the King would use their labours without giving them wages, since the text itself mentions a liberal reward of his servants. As for the 'taking the tenth of their seed, of their vines and of their sheep', it might be a necessary provision for their King's household, and so belong to the right of tribute. For whereas it mentions the taking of the tenth, it cannot well agree to a tyrant, who observes no proportion in fleecing his people.

Lastly, 'the taking of their fields, vineyards and olive trees', if it be by force or fraud, or without just recompense to the damage of private persons only, it is not to be defended. But if it be upon the public charge and by general consent, it might be justified as necessary at the first erection of a kingdom. For those who will have a King are bound to allow him royal maintenance by providing revenues for the crown, since it is both for the honour, profit and safety of the people to have their King glorious, powerful and abounding in riches. Besides, we all know the lands and goods of many subjects may be oft times

---

[1] I Sam. viii.   [2] RALEIGH, loc. cit., p. 472.

legally taken by the King, either by forfeitures, escheats, attainders,
outlawries, confiscation or the like. Thus we see Samuel's character
of a King may literally well bear a mild sense. For greater probability
that Samuel so meant, and the Israelites so understood it, this may be
added. Samuel tells the Israelites: 'This will be the manner of the King
that shall reign over you, and ye shall cry because of your King which
ye shall have chosen you.' That is to say: This shall be the common
custom or fashion or proceeding of *Saul* your King. Or, as the vulgar
Latin renders it: This shall be the right or law of your King — not
meaning, as some expound it, the casual event or act of some *individuum
vagum*, or indefinite King, that might happen one day to tyrannize
over them. So that Saul, and the constant practice of Saul, doth best
agree with the literal sense of the text.

Now that Saul was no tyrant, we may note that the people 'asked
a King, as all nations had'. God answers, and bids Samuel to 'hear the
voice of the people in all things which they spake', and 'appoint them
a King'. They did not ask a tyrant, and to give them a tyrant when
they asked a King had not been 'to hear their voice in all things', but
when they asked an egg to have given them a scorpion, unless we will
say that all nations had tyrants. Besides, we do not find in all scripture
that Saul was punished, or so much as blamed, for committing those
acts which Samuel describes. And if Samuel's drift had been only to
terrify the people, he would not have forgotten to foretell Saul's
bloody cruelty in murdering eighty-five innocent priests, and smiting
with the edge of the sword the city of Nob, both man, woman and
child. Again, the Israelites it seems never shrank at these conditions
proposed by Samuel, but accepted of them, as such as all other nations
were bound unto.* For their conclusion is: 'Nay, but we will have a
King over us, that we also may be like all the nations, and that our
King may judge us, and go out before us to fight our battles.' Meaning
he should earn his privileges by doing their work for them, by judging
them, and fighting for them.

Lastly, whereas the mention of the people's complaints and cries
unto the Lord argues they should be under some tyrannical oppression,
we may remember that the people's complaints and cries are not always
an argument of their living under a tyrant. No man can say King
Solomon was a tyrant, yet all the congregation of Israel complained
that Solomon made their yoke grievous, and therefore their prayer
to Rehoboam is: 'Make thou the grievous service of thy father Solomon, and his heavy yoke which he put upon us, lighter, and we will

* I Sam. xxii.

serve thee.'[1] To conclude: it is true Saul lost his kingdom, but not for being too cruel or tyrannical to his subjects, but for being too merciful to his enemies. His sparing Agag when he should have slain him was the cause why the kingdom was torn from him.

It was objected that when Saul was made King, Samuel gave him a written law by which he was to govern, so that Saul was subject to that law. The answer is, the law which Samuel writ was to instruct the people their duty, not to teach the King his office. For the text saith: 'That Samuel told the people the manner of the kingdom.'* There is no speech of reading to the King what Samuel had formerly told the people when they desired a King. Of the manner of the King and the things they must suffer he now writes it, and leaves it to remain upon record to all posterity, and laid it up before the Lord. Thus saith Josephus, lib. 6, c. 5,[2] who should best know the Jewish records. Those err that think that the law in Deuteronomy xvii concerning the duty of a King was the same law that Samuel writ and laid up. If it had been the same, what need Samuel have writ and laid it up? — since that was writ and laid up long before in the Ark, Deuteronomy xxxi. Secondly, the law in Deuteronomy concerned properly the King, and should have been read to him rather than to the people. Thirdly, the law itself in Deuteronomy xvii was but some few general precepts which did properly concern the particular Kings of the Jews, as the not multiplying of horses or wives, not returning into Egypt. And though there be no question but that God may give laws to all the Kings, though the people may not, yet the laws in Deuteronomy xvii were only laws for the Kings of the particular commonwealth of the Hebrews.

If any desire the direction of the New Testament, he may find our Saviour limiting and distinguishing royal power, 'By giving to Caesar those things that were Caesar's, and to God those things that were God's'. Let St. Basil expound this text: 'Obediendum est in quibus mandatum Dei non impeditur: we must obey Princes in those things wherein the commandment of God is not hindered.' There is no other law but God's law to hinder our obedience. It was the answer of a Christian to the emperor: 'We only worship God, in other things we gladly serve you.' And it seems Tertullian thought that whatsoever was not God's was the emperor's, when he saith: 'Bene opposuit

* 1 Sam. x, 25.

---

[1] 1 Kings xii, 4.
[2] See The . . . works of Josephus, translated . . . by T. Lodge . . ., 1609, p. 133.

Caesari pecuniam, te ipsum Deo, alioqui quid erit Dei, si omnia Caesaris: our Saviour hath well apportioned our money for Caesar, and ourselves for God, for, otherwise, what shall God's share be if all be Caesar's.' The Fathers mention no reservation of any power to the laws of the land, or to the people. St. Ambrose, in his 'Apology for David', expressly saith: 'He was a King, and therefore bound to no laws, because Kings are free from the bonds of any fault.' St. Augustine also resolves: 'Imperator non est subjectus legibus, qui habet in potestate alias leges ferre: the emperor is not subject to laws, who hath power to make other laws.' For, indeed, it is the rule of Solomon that: 'We must keep the King's commandment, and not say to him, what dost thou?, because where the word of a King is, there is power, and what he pleaseth he will do.'*

If any dislike this divinity in England, let him but hearken to Bracton, Chief Justice in King Henry III's days, who lived since the institutions of Parliaments. ·His words are, speaking of the King: 'Omnes sub eo, et ipse sub nullo, nisi tantum sub Deo, etc.: all are under him, and he under none but God only. If he offend, since no writ can go against him, their remedy is by petitioning him to amend his fault. Which, if he shall not do, it will be punishment sufficient for him to expect God as a revenger. Let none presume to search into his deeds, much less to oppose them.'[1]

When the Jews asked our blessed Saviour whether they should pay tribute, He did not first demand what the law of the land was, or whether there was any statute against it, nor inquired whether the tribute were given by Act of Parliament, nor advised them to stay their payment till a Parliament should grant it. He did no more but look upon the superscription, and concluded, 'This image you say is Caesar's, therefore give it to Caesar.' Nor must it here be said that Christ taught this lesson only to the conquered Jews, for in this He gave direction for all nations, who are bound as much in obedience to their lawful Kings as to any conqueror or usurper whatsoever.

Whereas St. Paul bids us: 'Be subject unto the higher powers', some have strained these words of *higher power* to signify the laws of the land, or else to mean the highest power, as well aristocratical or democratical as regal. It seems St. Paul looked for such interpreters, and therefore thought fit to be his own expositor, and let it be known that by power

* Eccles. viii.

---

[1] See BRACTON, *De legibus et consuetudinis Angliae* . . ., 1569, etc., ed. 1597, f. 5, reverse. Same passage quoted in the 'Freeholder'.

he understood a monarch that carried a sword. 'Wilt thou not be afraid of the power?' that is 'the ruler that carrieth the sword', for 'he is the minister of God to thee . . . for he beareth not the sword in vain.' It is not the law that is the *minister of God*, or that *carries the sword*, but the ruler or magistrate. So that they that say the law governs the kingdom, may as well say that the carpenter's rule builds the house and not the carpenter, for the law is but the rule or instrument of the ruler. And St. Paul concludes: 'For this cause pay you tribute also, for they are God's ministers, attending continually upon this very thing. Render therefore tribute to whom tribute is due, custom to whom custom.' He doth not say give tribute as a gift to God's minister, but ἀπόσυτε, render or restore tribute as a due.

Also St. Peter doth most clearly expound this place of St. Paul, where he saith: 'Submit yourselves to every ordinance of man for the Lord's sake, whether it be to the King as supreme or unto governours, as unto them that are sent by him.'[1] Here is the very self same word 'supreme' or 'ὑπερέχοντι' which St. Paul coupleth with power, St. Peter conjoineth with the King, 'Βασιλεῖ ὡς ὑπερέχον', thereby to manifest that King and power are both one. Also St. Peter expounds his own words of *human ordinance* to be the King, who is *lex loquens* — a speaking law. He cannot mean that Kings themselves are an human ordinance, since St. Paul calls the supreme power an ordinance of God, and the 'Wisdom' of God saith: 'By me Kings reign.' But his meaning must be that the commands or laws of Kings are human ordinances. Next, the governors that are sent by him. That is by the King, not by God as some corruptly would wrest the text, to justify popular governors as authorized by God. Whereas, in grammatical construction *him*, the relative, must be referred to the next antecedent, which is *the King*. Besides, the antithesis between *supreme* and *sent* proves plainly that the governors were sent by Kings, for, if the governors were sent by God and the King be an human ordinance, then it follows that the governors were supreme and not the King. Or, if it be said that both King and governors are sent by God, then they are both equal, and so neither of them 'supreme'. Therefore St. Peter's meaning is in short: 'Obey the laws of the King or of his ministers.' By which it is evident that neither St. Peter nor St. Paul intended any other form of government than only monarchical, much less any subjection of Princes to human laws.

That familiar distinction of the schoolmen, whereby they subject

---

[1] 1 Peter ii, 13. The references to St. Paul are all from Romans xiii. These arguments and texts are repeated in the 'Forms'.

Kings to the *directive*, but not to the *co-active*, power of laws,[1] is a confession that Kings are not bound by the positive laws of any nation. Since the compulsory power of laws is that which properly makes laws to be laws, by binding men by rewards or punishment to an obedience; whereas the direction of the law is but like the advice and direction which the King's Council gives the King, which no man says is a law to the King.

XXIV Laws not First Found out to Bridle Tyrants but the People. The Benefit of Laws. Kings Keep the Laws, though not Bound by Them.

There want not those who believe that the first invention of laws was to bridle and moderate the over-great power of Kings, but the truth is the original of laws was for the keeping of the multitude in order. Popular states could not subsist at all without laws, whereas kingdoms were governed many ages without them. The people of Athens, as soon as they gave over Kings, were forced to give power to Draco first, then to Solon, to make them laws, not to bridle Kings, but themselves. And though many of their laws were very severe and bloody, yet for the reverence they bare to their lawmakers they willingly submitted to them. Nor did the people give any limited power to Solon, but an absolute jurisdiction at his pleasure to abrogate and confirm what he thought fit, the people never challenging any such power to themselves. So the people of Rome gave to the Ten Men, who were to choose and correct their laws for the Twelve Tables, an absolute power without any appeal to the people.

The reason why laws have been also made by Kings was this. When Kings were either busied with wars or distracted with public cares, so that every private man could not have access to their persons to learn their wills and pleasure, then of necessity were laws invented. That so every particular subject might find his Prince's pleasure deciphered unto him in the tables of his laws that so there might be no need to resort to the King but either for the interpretation or mitigation of obscure or rigorous laws, or else, in new cases, for a supplement where the law was defective. By this means both King and people were in many things eased.

1. The King, by giving laws, doth free himself of great and intolerable troubles, as Moses did himself by choosing elders.*

---

* Exod. xviii.

[1] Also quoted in the 'Freeholder'.

2. The people have the law as a familiar admonisher and interpreter of the King's pleasure, which being published throughout the kingdom doth represent the presence and majesty of the King.

Also the judges and magistrates (whose help in giving judgment in many causes Kings have need to use) are restrained by the common rules of the law from using their own liberty to the injury of others, since they are to judge according to the King's laws, and not follow their own opinions.

Now albeit Kings who make the laws be (as his late Majesty teacheth us) 'above the laws, yet will they rule their subjects by the law. And a King, governing in a settled kingdom, leaves to be a King and degenerates into a tyrant so soon as he leaves to rule according to his laws. Yet where he sees the laws rigorous or doubtful he may mitigate and interpret. General laws made by Parliament may, upon known respects to the King, by his authority be mitigated or suspended upon causes only known to him. And although a King do frame all his actions to be according to the laws, yet he is not bound thereto, but at his good will and for good example',[1] or so far forth as the general law of the safety of the commonweal doth naturally bind him. For in such sort only positive laws may be said to bind the King, not by being positive but as they are naturally the best or only means for the preservation of the commonwealth. By this means are all Kings, even tyrants and conquerors, bound to preserve the lands, goods, liberties and lives of all their subjects, not by any municipal law of the land, but by the natural law of a Father, which binds them to ratify the acts of their forefathers and predecessors in things necessary for the public good of their subjects.

XXV   Of the Oaths of Kings

Others there be that affirm that, although laws of themselves do not bind Kings, yet the oaths of Kings at their coronation tie them to keep all the laws of their kingdoms. How far this is true, let us but examine the oath of the Kings of England at their coronation, the words whereof are these: 'Art thou pleased to cause to be administered in all thy judgments indifferent and upright justice, and to use discretion with mercy and verity? Art thou pleased that our upright laws and customs be observed, and dost thou promise that those shall be protected and maintained by thee?' These two are the articles of the King's oath which concern the laity or subjects in general, to which the King

[1] cf. JAMES I, *Trew Law* . . ., op. cit., p. 63.

answers affirmatively, being first demanded by the Archbishop of Canterbury: 'Pleaseth it you to confirm and observe the laws and customs of ancient times, granted from God by just and devout Kings unto the English nation, by oath unto the said people, specially the laws, customs and liberties granted unto the clergy and laity by the famous King Edward?'*

We may observe, in these words of the articles of the oath, that the King is required to observe not *all* the laws, but only the *upright laws*, and that with discretion and mercy. The word *upright* cannot mean *all* laws, because in the oath of King Richard II I find 'evil and unjust laws' mentioned, which the King swears to abolish. And in the old 'Abridgement of the Statutes' set out in King Henry VIII's days, the King is to swear wholly to 'put out evil laws', which he cannot do if he be bound to keep all laws. Now what laws are upright and what evil, who shall judge but the King, since he swears to administer upright justice with discretion and mercy, or, as Bracton hath it 'aequitatem praecipiat, et misericordiam'.[1] So that in effect the King doth swear to keep no laws but such as in his judgment are upright, and those not literally always, but according to the equity of his conscience joined with mercy, which is properly the office of a chancellor rather than of a judge. And if a King did strictly swear to observe all the laws, he could not without perjury give his consent to the repealing or abrogating of any statute by Act of Parliament, which would be very mischievous to the state.

Let it be supposed for truth that Kings do swear to observe all the laws of their kingdoms, yet no man can think it reason that Kings should be more bound by their voluntary oaths than common persons are by theirs. If a private person make a contract either with oath or without oath he is no further bound than the equity and justice of the contract ties him. For a man may have relief against an unreasonable and unjust promise, if either deceit, or error, or force or fear induced him thereunto, or if it be hurtful or grievous in the performance. Since the laws in many cases give the King a prerogative above common persons, I see no reason why he should be denied the privilege which the meanest of his subjects doth enjoy.

Here is a fit place to examine a question which some have moved, whether it be a sin for a subject to disobey the King if he command

* MILLS, *Of Nobility.*[2]

---

[1] BRACTON, op. cit., p. 107.
[2] See MILL[E]S, THOMAS, *Nobilitas politica . . .*, 1608, 1610 translation, p. 53. The arguments of this chapter on the coronation oath are repeated in the 'Freeholder'.

anything contrary to his laws? For satisfaction in this point we must resolve that not only in human laws, but even in divine, a thing may be commanded contrary to law, and yet obedience to such a command is necessary. The sanctifying of the Sabbath is a divine law, yet if a master command his servant not to go to Church upon the Lord's day, the best Divines teach us that the servant must obey this command, though it may be sinful and unlawful in the master. Because the servant hath no authority or liberty to examine and judge whether his master sin or no in so commanding, for there may be a just cause for a master to keep his servant from church, as appears in Luke xiv, 5. Yet it is not fit to tie the master to acquaint his servant with his secrets, counsels or present necessity, and in such cases the servant's not going to church becomes the sin of the master, and not of the servant. The like may be said of the King's commanding a man to serve him in the wars. He may not examine whether the war be just or unjust, but must obey, since he hath no commission to judge of the titles of kingdoms or causes of war, nor hath any subject power to condemn his King for breach of his own laws.

XXVI   Of the King's Prerogative over Laws

Many will be ready to say it is a slavish and a dangerous condition to be subject to the will of any one man who is not subject to the laws. But such men consider not:

1. That the prerogative of a King is to be above all laws, for the good only of them that are under the laws, and to defend the people's liberties, as his majesty graciously affirmed in his speech after this last answer to the Petition of Right.[1] Howsoever some are afraid at the name of prerogative, yet they may assure themselves the case of subjects would be desperately miserable without it. The court of Chancery itself is but a branch of the King's prerogative to relieve men against the inexorable rigour of the law, which without it is no better than a tyrant, since *summum jus* is *summa injuria*. General pardons at the coronation and at parliaments are but the bounty of the prerogative.

2. There can be no laws without a supreme power to command or make them. In all aristocracies the nobles are above the laws, and in all democracies the people. By the like reason in a monarchy the King must of necessity be above the laws. There can be no sovereign majesty in him that is under them. That which giveth the very being to a King is the power to give laws, without this power he is but an

[1] See *Lords Journals*, June 7th, 1628.

H

equivocal King. It skills not which way Kings come by their power,
whether by election, donation, succession or by any other means, for
it is still the manner of the government by supreme power that makes
them properly Kings, and not the means of obtaining their crowns.
Neither doth the diversity of laws, nor contrary customs, whereby
each kingdom differs from another, make the forms of commonweal
different, unless the power of making laws be in several subjects.

For confirmation of this point, Aristotle saith that 'a perfect kingdom
is that wherein the King rules all things according to his own will, for
he that is called a King according to the law makes no kind of kingdom
at all'.* This, it seems, also the Romans well understood to be most
necessary in monarchy. For though they were a people most greedy
of liberty, yet the senate did free 'Augustus from all necessity of laws,
that he might be free of his own authority and of absolute power over
himself and over the laws to do what he pleased and leave undone
what he list. And this decree was made while Augustus was yet
absent'.† Accordingly we find that Ulpian, the great lawyer, delivers
it for a rule of the Civil Law: 'Princeps legibus solutus est: the Prince
is not bound by the laws.'[1]

XXVII The King is Author, Interpreter and Corrector of the
       Common Law

If the nature of laws be advisedly weighed, the necessity of the
Prince's being above them may the more manifest itself. We all know
that a law in general is the command of a superior power. Laws are
divided (as Bellarmine divides the word of God) into written and unwritten. 'τῶν νόμων, οἱ μεν ἐγγραφόι, οἱ δε αγραφόι,' saith Ulpian in
the Civil Law, 'The Common Law unwritten, the statute law written.'[2]
The Common Law is called unwritten, not for that it is not written
at all, but because it was not written by the first devisers or makers of
it. The Common Law (as the Lord Chancellor Egerton teacheth us)[3]
is the *common custom of the realm*. Now concerning customs, this must
be considered, that for every custom there was a time when it was no
custom, and the first precedent we now have had no precedent when

* *Politics, lib.* 3, *c.* 16.[4]   † *Dio. lib.* 53.

[1] MOMMSEN, op. cit., p. 13.   [2] See MOMMSEN, op. cit., p. 2.
[3] See, 'The speech of the Lord Chancellor [Egerton] . . . Post Nati', 1609, p. 35.
[4] cf. BARKER, p. 145.

it began. When every custom began, there was something else than custom that made it lawful, or else the beginning of all customs were unlawful. Customs at first became lawful only by some superior power which did either command or consent unto their beginning. And the first power which we find (as is confessed by all men) is Kingly power, which was both in this and in all other nations of the world long before any laws or any other kind of government was thought of. From whence we must necessarily infer that the Common Law itself, or common customs of this land, were originally the laws and commands of Kings at first unwritten.

Nor must we think that the common customs (which are the principles of the Common Law, and are but few) to be such or so many as are able to give special rules to determine every particular cause. Diversity of cases are infinite, and impossible to be regulated by any law. And therefore we find even in the divine laws which were delivered by Moses, there be only certain principal laws which did not determine but only direct the high priest or magistrate, whose judgment in special cases did determine what the general law intended. It is so with the Common Law, for when there is no perfect rule judges do resort to those principle or Common Law axioms whereupon former judgments in cases somewhat like have been delivered by former judges, who all receive authority from the King in his right and name to give sentence according to the rules and precedents of ancient times. And where precedents have failed the judges have resorted to the general law of reason, and accordingly given judgment without any Common Law to direct them. Nay, many times where there have been precedents to direct, they upon better reason only have changed the law both in causes criminal and civil, and have not insisted so much on the examples of former judges as examined and corrected their reasons. Hence it is that some laws are now obsolete and out of use, and the practice quite to what it was in former times, as the Lord Chancellor Egerton proves by several instances.[1]

Nor is this spoken to derogate from the Common Law, for the case standeth so with laws of all nations, although some of them have their laws and principles written and established. For witness in this we have Aristotle his testimony in his *Ethics*, and in several places in his *Politics*. I will cite some of them.* 'Every law' (saith he) 'is in the general, but of some things there can be no general law ... When therefore the

---

* *Ethics, lib. 5, c. 14.*

[1] EGERTON, op. cit., p. 48.

law speaks in general, and some things fall out after besides the general rule, then it is fit that what the lawmaker hath omitted, or where he hath erred by speaking generally, it should be corrected or supplied, as if the lawmaker himself were present to ordain it. The governor, whether it be one man or more, ought to be lord over all those things whereof it was impossible the law should exactly speak, because it is not easy to comprehend all things under general rules. Whatsoever the law cannot determine, it leaves to the governors to give judgment therein, and permits them to rectify whatsoever upon trial they find to be better than the written laws.*'

And the Civil Law agrees with Aristotle, for it saith: 'Jura constitui oportet (ut dixit Theophrastes) in his quae ἐπὶ τὸ πλεῖστον accidunt, non quae ἐκ παραλόγου': they are the words of Pomponius. Again: 'Ex his quae forte uno aliquo casu accidere possunt jura non constituuntur . . . nam ad ea potius debet aptari jus quae et frequenter et facile, . . . quam quae perraro eveniunt', saith Celsus. 'quae semel aut bis accidunt praetereunt legislatores. Neque leges ita scribi possunt, ut omnes casus qui quandoque inciderint comprehendantur, sed sufficit et ea quae plerumque accidunt contineri', saith Julianus. 'Cum in aliqua causa sententia eorum est manifesta, is qui jurisdictione praeest, ad similia procedere atque ita jus dicere debet.'[1]

Besides, all laws are of themselves dumb, and some or others must be trusted with the application of them to particulars, who, by examining all circumstances, are to pronounce when they are broken or by whom. This work of right application of laws is not a thing easy or obvious for ordinary capacities, but requires profound abilities of nature for the beating out of the truth. Witness the diversity and sometimes the contrariety of opinions of the learned judges in some difficult points.

---

* *Politics, lib.* 3, *c.* 11.[2]

---

[1] MOMMSEN, op. cit., p. 12. 'Laws ought to be laid down, as Theophrastes said, in respect of things which happen for the most part, not which happen against reasonable expectation.' 'Rules of Law are not founded upon possibilities which may chance to come to pass on some one occasion . . . since law ought to be framed to meet cases which occur frequently, and easily, rather than such as very seldom happen.' 'What occurs once or twice . . . law-givers pass by.' 'Neither can statutes . . . possibly be drawn in such terms as to comprehend every case which will ever arise; it is enough if they embrace such as occur very often.' 'If in any case that arises, the meaning of the enactment is clear, the presiding magistrate ought to extend the rule to analogous cases and lay down the law accordingly.' (Trans. C. H. MUNRO, *The Digest of Justinian*, 1904.)

[2] cf. BARKER, p. 127.

XXVIII The King is Judge in all Causes. The King and his Council Anciently Determined Causes

Since this is the common condition of Laws, it is most reasonable that the lawmaker should be trusted with the application or interpretation of the laws. For this cause anciently the Kings of this land have sitten personally in courts of judicature and are still representatively present in all courts. The judges are but substituted and called the King's justices, and their power ceaseth when the King is in place. To this purpose Bracton, that learned Chief Justice in the reign of King Henry III, saith in express terms: 'In doubtful and obscure points the interpretation and will of the lord our King is to be expected, since it is his part to interpret who made the law.' For, as he hath it in another place, 'Rex et non alius debet judicare si solus ad id sufficere possit, etc: the King and nobody else ought to give judgment if he were able, since by virtue of his oath he is bound to it. Therefore the King ought to exercise power as the vicar or minister of God. But if our lord the King be not able to determine every cause, to ease part of his pains by distributing the burden to moe persons, he ought to choose wise men, fearing God, etc., and make justices of them.'[1]

Much to the same purpose are the words of King Edward I in the beginning of the book of laws written by his appointment by John Briton, Bishop of Hereford. 'We will' (saith the King) 'that our own jurisdiction be above all the jurisdictions of our realm, so as in all manner of felonies, trespasses, contracts and in all other actions, personal or real, we have power to yield such judgments as do appertain without other process wheresoever we know the right truth as judges.'[2] Neither may this be taken of an imaginary presence of the King's person in his courts, because he doth immediately after in the same place severally set forth by themselves the jurisdictions of his ordinary courts, but must necessarily be understood of a jurisdiction remaining in the King's royal person. And that this then was no new made law, or first brought in by the Norman Conquest, appears by a Saxon law made by King Edgar in these words, as I find them in Mr. Lambert:[3] 'Nemo in lite regem appellato, nisi quidem domi justitiam consequi, aut impetrare non poterit, sin summo jure domi urgeatur, ad regem, ut is onus aliqua ex parte allevet, provocato. Let no man in

---

[1] BRACTON, op. cit., p. 108. These passages are also quoted in 'Freeholder'.
[2] See BRITTON, 2nd ed., 1640, page A, reverse. Also quoted in 'Freeholder'.
[3] i.e. LAMBARD, WILLIAM. The work quoted is *Archionomia*, London, 1568, fol. 79, and the translation is a paraphrase of Lambard's own translation in *Archion*, London 1635. The same passage is quoted in 'Freeholder'.

suit appeal to the King unless he may not get right at home. But if the right be too heavy for him, then let him go to the King to have it eased.'

As the judicial power of Kings was exercised before the Conquest, so in those settled times after the Conquest wherein parliaments were much in use, there was a high court following the King, which was the place of sovereign justice both for matter of law and conscience. As may appear by a parliament in King Edward I's time taking order: 'that the Chancellor and the Justices of the Bench should follow the King, to the end that he might have always at hand able men for his direction in suits that came before him'.[1] And this was after the time that the Court of Common Pleas was made stationary, which is an evidence the King reserved a sovereign power by which he did supply the want or correct the rigour of the Common Law. Because the positive law, being grounded upon that which happens for the most part, cannot foresee every particular which time and experience bring forth.

Therefore, though the Common Law be generally good and just, yet in some special case it may need correction by reason of some considerable circumstance falling out which at the time of the law-making was not thought of. Also sundry things do fall out both in war and peace that require extraordinary help, and cannot wait for the usual care of the Common Law, the which is not performed but altogether after one sort, and that not without delay of help and expense of time. So that, although most causes are, and ought to be, referred to the ordinary process of Common Law, yet rare matters from time to time do grow up meet, for just reasons, to be referred to the aid of the absolute and infinite authority of the Prince. And the statute of Magna Charta hath and must be understood of the institution then made of the ordinary jurisdiction in common causes, and not for restraint of the absolute authority which serves in rare and singular cases. For though the subjects were put to great damage by false accusations and malicious suggestions made to the King and his council, especially during the time of King Edward III whilst he was absent in the wars in France, insomuch as in his reign divers statutes were made that provided none should be put to answer before the King and his council without due process, yet it is apparent the necessity of such proceedings was so great that both before Edward III's days and in his time and after his death several statutes were made to help and order the proceedings of the King and his council.

[1] See LAMBARD, *Archion*, pp. 47, 48.

As the parliament in 28 *Edw. I, c.* 5, did provide that the Chancellor and Justices of the King's Bench should follow the King, 'so that he may have near unto·him some that be learned in the laws, which be able to order all such matters as shall come unto the court at all times when need shall require'.[1] By the statute of 37 *Edw. III, c.* 18, taliation was ordained in case the suggestion to the King proved untrue.[2] Then 38 *Edw. III, c.* 9, takes away taliation and appoints imprisonment till the King and party grieved be satisfied.[3] In the statutes of 17 *Ric. II, c.* 6, and 15 *Hen. VI, c.* 4, damages and expenses are awarded in such cases. In all these statutes it is necessarily implied that complaints upon just causes might be moved before the King and his council.

At a parliament at Gloucester, 2 King Richard II, when the Commons made petition that none might be forced by writ out of Chancery or by Privy Seal to appear before the King and his council to answer touching freehold, the King's answer was he thought it not reasonable that he should be restrained to send for his lieges upon causes·reasonable. And albeit he did not purpose that such as were sent for should answer *finalment*, peremptorily, touching their free-hold, but should be remanded for trial thereof as law required, 'Pro-vided always' (saith he) 'that at the suit of the party where the King and his council shall be credibly informed that, because of maintenance, oppression or other outrages, the Common Law cannot have duly her course, in such case the council may send for the party.'[4]

Also, in the thirteenth year of his reign, when the Commons did pray that, upon pain of forfeits, the Chancellor or Council of the King should not after the end of parliament make any ordinance against the Common Law, the King answered: 'Let it be used as it hath been used before this time, so as the regality of the King be saved; for the King will save his regalities as his progenitors have done.'[5]

Again, in the fourth year of King Henry IV, when the Commons complained against subpoenas and other writs grounded upon false suggestions, the King answered: 'That he would give in charge to his officers that they should abstain more than before time they had to send for his subjects in that manner. But yet', saith he, 'it is not our intention that our officers shall so abstain that they may not send for our subjects in matters and causes necessary, as it hath been used in the time of our good progenitors.'[6]

[1] See *The statutes at large*, 1618, p. 51. Also quoted in 'Freeholder'.
[2] ditto, p. 122.   [3] ditto, p. 123. All these quotations appear also in *Archion*.
[4] Taken from LAMBARD's *Archion*, p. 137 [really p. 149].
[5] Paragraph copied from *Archion*, pp. 150-1.
[6] ditto, pp. 151-3, copied almost verbatim.

Likewise, when for the same cause complaint was made by the Commons anno 3, King Henry V, the King's answer was: 'Le roi s'advisera: the King will be advised', which amounts to a denial for the present, by a phrase peculiar for the King's denying to pass any act that hath passed the Lords and Commons.[1]

These complaints of the Commons, and the answers of the Kings, discover that such moderation should be used that the course of the Common Law be ordinarily maintained [lest subjects be convented before the King and his council without just cause, that the proceedings of the council table be not upon every slight suggestion, nor to determine finally concerning freehold of inheritance]. And yet that, for causes reasonable upon credible information in matters of weight, the King's regality or prerogative in sending for his subjects be maintained, as of right it ought and in former times hath been constantly used.[2]

King Edward I, finding that Bogo de Clare was discharged of an accusation brought against him in parliament, for that some formal imperfections were found in that complaint, commanded him nevertheless to appear before him and his council, 'ad faciendum et recipiendum quod per regem et ejus consilium fuerit faciendum', and so proceeded to an examination of the whole cause.*

King Edward III in the Star Chamber (which was the ancient Council Chamber at Westminster) upon the complaint of Elizabeth Audley, commanded James Audley to appear before him and his Council, and determined a controversy between them touching lands contained in the covenants of her jointure.†

King Henry V, in a suit before him and his Council for the titles of the manors of Serre and St. Lawrence in the Isle of Thanet in Kent, took order for the sequestering the profits till the right were tried, as well for the avoiding the breach of the peace as for the prevention of waste and spoil.‡

King Henry VI commanded the justices of the bench to stay the arraignment of one Verney in London till they had other commandment from him and his Council. Because Verney, being indebted to the King and others, practised to be indicted of felony, wherein he might have his clergy, and make his purgation of intent to defraud his creditors.§

* An. 18 Edw. I.   † Rot. claus. de an. 41 Edw. III.   ‡ Rot. pat. an. 6: Hen. 5.
§ 34 Hen. VI, rot. 37 in Banco Regis.

---

[1] Paragraph copied from Archion, pp. 153-4.
[2] ditto, p. 155. Sentence in brackets interpolated by Filmer, but omitted from the 1680 printed version. It was re-inserted by Bohun in the 1685 edition.

King Edward IV and his Council in the Star Chamber heard the cause of the master and poor brethren of St. Leonards in York, complaining that Sir Hugh Hastings and others withdrew from them a great part of their living, which consisted chiefly upon the having of a thrave of corn of every plough land within the counties of York, Westmoreland, Cumberland and Lancashire.*

King Henry VII and his Council, in the Star Chamber, decreed that Margery and Florence Becket should sue no further in their cause against Alice Radley, widow, for lands in Woolwich and Plumstead in Kent, forasmuch as the matter had been heard, first before the council of King Edward IV, after that before the President of the Requests of that King Henry VII, and then lastly before the council of the said King.†

What is hitherto affirmed of the dependency and subjection of the Common Law to the sovereign Prince, the same may be said as well of all Statute Laws. For the King is the sole immediate author, corrector and moderator of them also. So that neither of these two kinds of laws are, or can be, any diminution of that natural power which Kings have over their people by right of fatherhood, but are an argument to strengthen the truth of it. For evidence whereof we may in some points consider the nature of parliaments, because by them only all statutes are enacted.

XXIX   Of Parliaments

Though the name of 'Parliament', as Mr. Camden saith,[1] 'be of no great antiquity', but brought in out of France, yet our ancestors the English Saxons had a meeting which they called 'the assembly of the wise', termed in Latin 'Conventum Magnatum, or praesentia regis, procerumque, prelaterumque collectorum; the meeting of the nobility; or the presence of the King, prelates and peers assembled': or, in general, Magnum Concilium, or Commune Concilium. And many of our Kings in elder times made use of such great assemblies for to consult of important affairs of state, all which meetings in a general sense may be termed 'Parliaments'.

Great are the advantages which both the King and people may

* Rot. pat. de an. 8 Edw. IV, part 3, membr. 14.   † 1 Hen. VII.[2]

[1] CAMDEN, WILLIAM, Britannia. Hollands translation into English, 1637, p. 177. The same passage is quoted in the 'Freeholder'.
[2] The whole of these six paragraphs is lifted word for word from LAMBARD'S Archion, pp. 156-64. Five of them also appear verbatim in 'Freeholder'

receive by a well ordered parliament. There is nothing more expresseth the majesty and supreme power of a King than such an assembly, wherein all his people acknowledge him for sovereign lord, and make all their addresses to him by humble petition and supplication, and by their consent and approbation do strengthen all the laws which the King at their request, and by their advice and ministry, shall ordain. Thus they facilitate the government of the King by making the laws unquestionable, either to the subordinate magistrates or refractory multitude. Then the benefit which accrues to the subject by parliaments is, that by their prayers and petitions Kings are drawn many times to redress their just grievances, and are overcome by their importunity to grant many things which otherwise they would not yield unto: for the voice of a multitude is easier heard. Many vexations of the people are without the knowledge of the King, who in parliament seeth and heareth his people himself, whereas at other times he commonly useth the eyes and ears of other men.

XXX　The People, when first Called to Parliament. The Liberties of Parliaments not from Nature, but from the Grace of Princes

Against the antiquity of parliaments we need not dispute, since the more ancient they be, the more they make for the honour of monarchy. Yet there be certain circumstances touching the forms of[1] parliaments which are fit to be considered.

1. First, we are to remember that until about the time of the Conquest there could be no parliaments assembled of the general states of the whole kingdom of England, because till those days we cannot find it was entirely united into one kingdom, but it was either divided into several kingdoms, or governed by several laws. When Julius Caesar landed he found four Kings in Kent, and the British names of Danmonii, Durotriges, Belgae, Attrebatii, Trinobantes, Iceni, Silures and the rest[2] are plentiful testimonies of the several kingdoms of the Britons when the Romans became our lords. As soon as ever the Romans left us the Saxons divided us into seven kingdoms. When these were united into a monarchy, they had always the Danes their companions or masters in the empire till Edward the Confessor's days, since whose time the kingdom of England hath continued united as now it doth. But for a thousand years before we cannot find it was entirely settled during the time of any one King's reign. As for laws,

---

[1] 'The forms of' not in MS.

[2] These are the first six ethnic divisions used by Camden in *Britannia*,

we find the middle part of the kingdom under the Mercian law, the West Saxons were confined to the Saxon laws, Essex, Norfolk, Suffolk and some other places were vexed with Danish laws. The Northumbrians also had their laws apart, and until Edward the Confessor's reign, who was the next but one before the Conqueror, the laws of the kingdom were so several and uncertain that he was forced to cull a few of the most indifferent and best of them, which were from him called St. Edward's laws. Yet some say that Edgar made those laws, and that the Confessor did but restore and mend them. King Alfred also gathered out of Mulmutius laws such as he translated into the Saxon tongue. Thus during the time of the Saxons the laws were so variable that there is little or no likelihood to find any constant form of parliaments of the whole kingdom.

2.   A second point considerable is, whether in such parliaments as was in the Saxons' times, the nobility, clergy and the King's Council only were of those assemblies, or whether the Commons were also called.* Some are of the opinion that, though none of the Saxon laws do expressly mention the Commons, yet it may be gathered by the word 'witena', 'wisemen', that the Commons are intended to be of those assemblies. And they bring (as they conceive) probable arguments to prove it from the antiquity of some boroughs that were decayed before the Conquest and yet send burgesses, and from the proscription of those in *ancient demesne* not to send any burgesses to parliament or pay knights' wages.

By the word *witena* it is very likely the thanes were meant, who were the same in the Saxon times that the barons were in the times of the Normans, as the Saxon ealdormen were those that were afterwards Norman earls. As for those ancient boroughs that might be decayed at the time of the Conquest, it is possible that for their antiquity or some other reason they might receive the privileges of sending burgesses after the Conquest. The like may be said for the contrary privileges for lands in ancient demesne. [If it be true that the West Saxons had a custom to assemble burgesses out of some of their towns, yet it may be doubted whether other kingdoms had the same usage, but sure it is that during the Heptarchy the people could not elect any knights of the shire, because England was not then divided into shires.]

On the contrary there be historians who do affirm that King Henry I

* MR. LAMBERT, *Archion.*[1]

---

[1] op. cit., p. 257, etc. This and the next paragraph do not appear complete in any version, and the sentence in brackets is not in the MS. Nevertheless, it evidently belongs, and is another indication of a different manuscript source.

'caused the commons first to be assembled by knights and burgesses of their appointment, for before this time only certain of the nobility and prelates of the realm were called to consultation about the most important affairs of state'.[1] What the ancientest usage of the Normans were may best appear by such testimonies as Mr. Selden produceth in his *Titles of Honour*.[2] King William the Conqueror in the fourth year of his reign by the consent of his Barons, had twelve men out of every county who showed what the customs of the kingdom were. And by the assent of the barons these customs were confirmed for laws. Which appears also by the laws of King Henry I, where it is said: 'I restore you the laws of King Edward with those amendments by which my father amended them by the counsel of his barons.' It is probable, if there had been any custom in the Saxon times to have summoned knights and burgesses, that the Conqueror (who was so desirous to know and confirm the ancient customs) would rather have called such knights and burgesses than twelve men out of every county. Mr. Selden citeth proofs for other parliaments in King William I's reign, but in none of them any mention of any other but *comites et primates et principum conventus*, which was only earls and barons.

In the second year of King William II there was a parliament by *cunctis regni principibus*, and another which had *quosque regni proceres*. At the coronation of King Henry I all the people of the kingdom were called, and laws then made per *commune consilium baronum*. 3 *Hen. I proceres regni* were called, and another Parliament a while after *consensu comitum et Baronum* and in his tenth year of *comites* and *proceres*. In the eleventh year, at a parliament at Northampton, were summoned: *omnes qui tenebant de rege in capite*. In the twenty-third year, *earls and barons*. The year following the same King held a parliament or Great Council with his *barons spiritual and temporal*.

. In the fifth year of King John: *Rex et magnates convenerunt* and the roll of that year hath *commune consilium baronum meorum ad Winchester*. The Grand Charter made in the last year of King John mentions *Maiores barones regni, et qui in capite tenent de nobis*. King Henry III, anno 1223, called *omnes clericos et laicos totius regni*. King Edward I in his third year summoned the *comunaltie* of the land. King Edward II in his fourteenth year had *tout le cominaltie de son royaume*.[3]

---

[1] This is a quotation from POLYDORE VERGIL, *Anglicae historia*, 1570 ed., p. 188. The next sentence introduces a passage which is omitted from all the published versions except that of 1685.

[2] See SELDEN, JOHN, *Titles of Honour*, 1614, 2nd ed., 1631.

[3] These three paragraphs are quoted in detail from Selden's book: Filmer sometimes misrepresents him. The last quotation is from LAMBARD, *Archion*, p. 265.

By these testimonies it appears that the ancientest and most usual summons was of earls and barons and that Kings did vary their summons at their pleasure. Which may be further confirmed out of Mr. Camden, who, speaking of barons, saith that: 'King Henry III out of a great multitude which was seditious and turbulent called out the best of them by his writ to Parliament.[1] And the prudent King Edward I summoned always those barons of ancientest families that were most wise to his parliaments, but omitted their sons after their death if they were not answerable to their parents in understanding.'

King Henry III commanded 'duos milites gladio cinctos magis discretos et idoneos' to be chosen to serve for knights of the shire. And it is the acknowledgment of Mr. Selden that the 'first writs we find accompanied with the other circumstances of a summons to parliament as well for the Commons as Lords is in the 49th year of King Henry III'. Amongst all those proofs which I can find produced for the antiquity of Parliaments, I see nothing for the choosing of knights and burgesses by popular elections before the times of this King Henry III, although King Henry I were the first that summoned all the people. And it had been more for the honour of parliaments if a King whose title to the crown had been better than that of King Henry I had been author of the first calling the people to parliament, because he made use of it for his unjust ends.[2] For thereby he secured himself against his competitor and elder brother, by taking the oaths of the nobility in parliament and got the crown to be settled upon his children.

And as the King made use of the people, so they, by colour of a parliament, served their own turns. For after the establishment of parliaments by strong hand and by the sword, they drew from him the Great Charter, which he granted the rather to flatter the nobility and people, as Sir Walter Raleigh in his *Dialogue of Parliaments* doth affirm in these words. 'The Great Charter was not originally granted regally and freely, for King Henry I did but usurp the kingdom, and therefore the better to assure himself against Robert his elder brother, flattered the nobility and people with these charters. Yea, King John that confirmed them had the like respect, for Arthur Duke of Britaine was the undoubted heir of the crown, upon whom King John usurped. And so to conclude these charters had their original from Kings *de facto* but not *de jure* ... The Great Charter had first an obscure birth by usurpation, and was secondly fostered and showed to the world by rebellion.[3]

---

[1] CAMDEN, op. cit., p. 169. Also quoted in the 'Freeholder'.

[2] End of passage omitted in all but 1685 printings.

[3] RALEIGH, SIR WALTER, 'The Prerogative of Parliament', 1628, in *Works*, vol. VII. The quotation is on pp. 159 and 161 and is also used in the 'Freeholder'.

3.   A third consideration must be, that in the form of parliaments instituted and continued since King Henry I's and King Henry III's times is not to be found the usage of any natural liberty of the people. For all those liberties that are claimed in parliaments are the liberties of grace from the King, and not the liberties of nature to the people. For if the liberty were natural it would give power to the multitude to assemble themselves *when* and *where* they please, to bestow sovereignty and by pactions to limit and direct the exercise of it, whereas the liberties of favour and grace which are claimed in parliament are restrained both for time, place, persons and other circumstances, to the sole pleasure of the King. The people cannot assemble themselves, but the King, by his writs, calls them to what place he pleases, and then again scatters them with his breath at an instant, without any other cause shown them than his will. Neither is the whole summoned, but only so many as the King's writs appoint, nor have the whole people voices in the election of Knights of the Shire or Burgesses, but only freeholders in the counties and freemen in the cities and boroughs, yet in the City of Westminster all the householders though they be neither freemen nor freeholders have voices in their election of Burgesses.

Also during the time of parliament those privileges of the House of Commons, of freedom of speech, power to punish their own members, to examine the proceedings and demeanour of courts of justice and officers, to have access to the King's person and the like, are not due by any natural right, but are derived from the bounty or indulgence of the King, as appears by a solemn recognition of the House. For at the opening of parliament when the Speaker is presented to the King, he, in the behalf and name of the whole House of Commons, humbly craves of his majesty that he would be pleased to grant them their accustomed liberties of freedom of speech, of access to his person and the rest. These privileges are granted with a condition implied that they keep themselves within the bounds and limits of loyalty and obedience, for else why do the House of Commons inflict punishment themselves upon their own members for transgressing in some of these points? And the King as head hath many times punished the members for the like offences.

The power which the King giveth in all his courts to his judges or others to punish doth not exclude him from doing the like by way of prevention, concurrence or evocation, even in the same points which he hath given in charge by a delegated power. For they who give authority by commission do always retain more than they grant.

Neither of the two houses claim ihfallibility of not erring, no more than a general council can. It is not impossible but that the greatest part may be in fault, or at least interested or engaged in the delinquency of one particular member. In such cases it is most proper for the head to correct, and not to expect the consent of the members, or for the parties peccant to be their own judges. Nor is it needful to confine the King in such cases within the circle of any one court of justice, who is supreme judge in all courts. And in rare and new cases rare and new remedies must be sought out, for it is a rule of the Common Law in 'novo casu, novum remedium est apponendum', and the Statute of Westminster, 2, c. 24, giveth power even to the clerks of the Chancery to make new forms of writ in new cases, lest any man that came to the King's Court of Chancery for help should be sent away without remedy.[1] A precedent cannot be found for every case, and of things that happen seldom and are not common there cannot be a common custom. Though crimes exorbitant do pose the King and council in finding a precedent for a condign punishment, yet they must not therefore pass unpunished.

I have not heard that the people by whose voices the Knights and Burgesses are chosen did ever call to an account those whom they had elected. They neither give them instructions or directions what to say or what to do in parliament, therefore they cannot punish them when they come home for doing amiss. If the people had any such power over their burgesses then we might have some colour to call it the natural liberty of the people. But they are so far from punishing that they may be punished themselves for intermeddling with parliamentary business. They must only choose, and trust those whom they choose to do what they list, and that is as much liberty as many of us deserve for our irregular elections of burgesses.

XXXI   The King alone Makes Laws in Parliament

A fourth point to be considered is, that in parliament all statutes are made properly by the King alone at the rogation of the people, as his late majesty of happy memory affirms in his *Law of Free Monarchy*,[2] and as Mr. Hooker teacheth us that 'Laws do not take their constraining force from the quality of such as devise them, but from the power that doth give them the strength of laws'. 'Le roi le veult: the King will have it so' is the imperative phrase pronounced at the King's passing of every Act of Parliament. And it was the ancient custom for a long

---

[1] Statutes, op. cit., p. 34.   [2] JAMES I, op. cit., p. 62.

time till the days of King Henry IV that the Kings, when any bill was brought unto them that had passed both houses, to take and pick out as much or as little thereof as they pleased and to leave out what they liked not or to alter it, and so much as they chose or set down was enacted for a law. Which seems to prove that in ancient times the assent of the Commons was not always requisite, for though their assent may seem to ratify, yet it doth not follow that therefore their dissent must nullify an Act of Parliament. Those may have deliberative voices which have not always a negative.

Mr. Fuller in his arguments against the proceedings of the High Commission Court affirms that the statute of 2 *Hen. IV, c.* 15, which giveth power to ordinaries to imprison and set fines on subjects, was made without the assent of the Commons because they are not mentioned in the Act.[1] We find very many ancient statutes of the same kind, for the assent of the Commons was seldom mentioned in the elder parliaments. [The most usual title of parliaments in King Edward III, King Richard II, the three Henries, IV, V, VI, in King Edward IV and King Richard III's days was: 'The King and his parliament, with the assent of the Prelates Earls and Barons, and at the petition, or at the special instance, of the Commons, doth ordain.']* The same Mr. Fuller saith that the statute made against Lollards was without the assent of the Commons, as appears by their petition in these words: 'The Commons beseech that whereas a statute was made in the last Parliament etc., which was never assented to nor granted by the Commons, but that which was done therein was done without their assent.'[2]

XXXII The King Hath Governed Both Houses, either by Himself or by His Council, or by His Judges

The parliament is the King's court, for so all the oldest statutes call it, 'The King in his Parliament'. But neither of the two houses are that supreme court, nor yet both of them together. They are only members and a part of the body, whereof the King is the head and ruler. The King's governing of this body of the Parliament we may find most significantly proved, both by the statutes themselves, as also by such

* 5 *Ric. II, c.* 5.[3]

---

[1] See *The argument of Mr. Nicholas Fuller in the case of . . . the Ecclesiastical Commission . . .*, 1607, p. 7. This paragraph differently placed in the printed version.
[2] FULLER, op. cit., p. 8.
[3] This passage between brackets only summarized in the MS.

precedents as expressly show us how the King sometimes by himself, sometimes by his Council, and at other times by his judges, have over-ruled and directed the judgments of the Houses of Parliament. For the King we find that Magna Charta and the Charter of the Forests and many other statutes about those times had only the form of the King's letters-patents, or grants under the Great Seal, testifying those great liberties to be the sole act and bounty of the King. The words of Magna Charta begin thus: 'Edward, by the Grace of God, etc. To all our Archbishops, etc., and our faithful subjects, greeting. Know ye that We, out of our *mere freewill* have granted to all freemen these liberties.'

In the same style goeth the Charter of Forests and other statutes. Statutum Hiberniae, made at Westminster, February 9th, 14 *Hen. III*, is but a letter of the King to Gerard son of Maurice, Justiciar of Ireland. The statute 'de anno bisextili' begins thus: 'The King to his Justices of the Bench, greeting, etc.'* Explanationes statuti Glocestriae, made by the King and his justices only, were received always as statutes, and are still printed among them.

The statute made for correction of the twelfth chapter of the Statute of Gloucester was signed under the Great Seal, and sent to the Justices of the Bench after the manner of a writ-patent, with a certain writ closed, dated by the King's hand at Westminster 'that they should do and execute all and everything contained in it', although the same do not accord with the Statute of Gloucester in all things.

The Statute of Rutland is the King's letters to his treasurer and Barons of his Exchequer and to his Chamberlain. The Statute of Circumspecte Agatis saith: 'The King to his judges sendeth greeting.'

There are many other statutes of the same form and some of them which run only in the majestic form of 'The King commands', or 'The King wills', or 'Our Lord the King hath established', or 'Our Lord the King hath ordained', or 'Of his special grace hath granted', without mention of consent of the Commons or people, insomuch that some statutes rather resemble proclamations than Acts of Parliament. And indeed some of them were no other than mere proclamations, as the Provisions of Merton, made by the King at an assembly of the prelates and nobility for the coronation of the King and his Queen Eleanor, which begins: 'Provisum est in Curia domini Regis apud Merton'. Also a provision was made: 19 *Hen. III*, 'De assisa ultimae prae-sentionis',† which was continued and allowed for law until Westminster 2, *an.* 13 *Edw. I, c.* 5, which provides the contrary by express

---

* 6 *Edw. I.*   † 20 *Hen. III.*

I

words. This provision begins: 'Provisum fuit coram domino Rege, archiepiscopis, episcopis et baronibus. Quod', etc.[1]

It seems originally the difference was not great between a Proclamation and a Statute. This latter the King made by common council of the kingdom. In the former he had but the advice only of his Great Council of the peers, or of his Privy Council only. That the King had a Great Council besides his parliament appears by a record of 5 *Hen. IV* about an exchange between the King and the Earl of Northumberland, whereby the King promiseth to deliver to the earl lands to the value, etc., by the 'advice of parliament, or otherwise by the advice of his Grand Council and other estates of the realm, which the King will assemble in case the parliament do not meet'.

We may find what judgment of later times parliaments have had of Proclamations by the statute of 31 *Hen. VIII*, c. 8, in these words. 'Forasmuch as the King, by the advice of his Council, hath set forth Proclamations which obstinate persons have contemned, not considering what a King by his royal power may do, considering that sudden cases fortune many times which do require speedy remedies, and that by abiding for a parliament in the meantime might happen great prejudice to ensue to the realm, and weighing also that His Majesty, which by the kingly power and regal power given him by God may do many things in such cases, should not be driven to entend the liberties and supremacy of his regal power and dignity by wilfulness of froward subjects: It is therefore thought fit that the King with the advice of his honourable Council should set forth Proclamations for the good of the people and defence of his regal dignity, as necessity shall require.'

This opinion of a House of Parliament was confirmed afterwards by a second Parliament, and the statute made Proclamations of as great validity as if they had been made by Parliament.* This law continued until the government of the state came to be under a Protector during the minority of King Edward VI, and in his first year it was repealed.†

I find also that a parliament in the eleventh year of King Henry VII did so great reverence to the actions or Ordinances of the King, that by statute they provided a remedy or means to levy a benevolence granted to the King, although by a statute made not long before all benevolences were damned and annulled for ever.

* 34 *Hen. VIII*, c. 23.   † 1 *Edw. VI*.

---

[1] These quotations are all from the Statute Book: three of them are used again in the 'Freeholder'. One is cribbed from EGERTON, op. cit.

How far the King's Council hath directed and swayed in Parliament hath in part appeared by what hath been already produced. For further evidence we may add the Statute of Westminster the First, which saith: 'These be the Acts of King Edward I, made at his first parliament general by his council, and by the assent of Bishops, Abbots, Priors, Earls, Barons and all the Commonalty of the Realm, etc.'* The Statute of Bigamy saith: 'In the presence of certain Reverend Fathers, Bishops of England and others of the King's Council, the constitutions underwritten were recited and after published before the King and his Council. Forasmuch as all the King's Council, as well Justices as others, did agree that they should be put in writing and observed.'† The Statute of Acton Burnel saith: 'The King, for himself and his Council, hath ordained and established.'‡

In 'Articuli super Chartas', when the Great Charter was confirmed 'at the request of his Prelates, Earls and Barons', we find these passages. § '1. Nevertheless the King and his Council do not intend by reason of this Estatute to diminish the King's right, etc.|| 2. And notwithstanding all these before-mentioned or any part of them, both the King and his Council and all they that were present at the making of the Ordinance, will and intend that the right and prerogative of the Crown shall be saved to him in all things.'¶ Here we may see in the same parliament the charter of the liberties of the subjects confirmed, and a saving of the King's prerogative. Those times neither stumbled at the name, nor conceived any such antipathy between the terms as should make them incompatible.

The Statute of Escheators hath this title: 'At the Parliament of our Sovereign Lord the King, by his Council it was agreed, and also by the King himself commanded.'** And the Ordinance of Inquest goeth thus: 'It is agreed and ordained by the King and all his Council.'††

The Statute made at York saith: 'Whereas the Knights, Citizens and Burgesses desired our Sovereign Lord the King in his Parliament by their petition, that for his profit and the commodity of his Prelates, Earls, Barons and Commons, it may please him to provide remedy, Our Sovereign Lord the King desiring the profit of his people by the assent of his Prelates, Earls, Barons and other nobles of this realm,

---

* 3 Edw. I. † 4 Edw. I. ‡ 13 Edw. I.[1] § 28 Edw. I. || Cap. 2.
¶ Cap. 20. ** 29 Edw. I. †† 33 Edw. I.

[1] All the quotations in this passage are also from the Statute Book. Three are also used in the 'Freeholder'. There is a difference in arrangement in this passage from that of the published version.

'summoned at this Parliament, and by the advise of his Council being there, hath ordained.'*

In the parliament primo King Edward III, where Magna Charta was confirmed, I find this preamble: 'At the request of the Commonalty · by their petition made before the King and his Council in Parliament, by the assent of the Prelates, Earls, Barons and other great men assembled, it was granted.'

The Commons presenting a petition unto the King which the King's Council did mislike, were content thereupon to mend and explain their petition; the form of which petition is in these words: 'To their most redoubted Sovereign Lord the King, praying the said Commons. That whereas they have prayed him to be discharged of all manner of Articles of the Eyre, etc. Which petition seemeth to his Council to be prejudicial unto him and in disherison of his crown if it were so generally granted. His said Commons, not willing nor desiring to demand things of him which should fall in disherison of him or his Crown perpetually, as of Escheats, etc., But of trespasses, misprisions, negligences and ignorances, etc. . . . .'†[1]

In the time of King Henry III an Order or Provision was made by the King's Council, and it was pleaded at the Common Law to a writ of dower.‡ The plaintiff's attorney could not deny it and thereupon the judgment was *ideo sine die*. It seems in those days an Order of the Council board was either parcel of the Common Law or above it.§

The reverend Judges have had regard in their proceedings that before would resolve or give judgment in new cases they consulted with the King's Privy Council. In the cause of Adam Brabson, who was assaulted by R.W. in the presence of the Justices of Assize at Winchester, the judges would have advice of the King's Council. For in a like case, because R.C. did strike a juror at Westminster, which passed in an inquest against one of his friends, it was adjudged by all the Council that his right hand should be cut off and all his lands and goods forfeited to the King.[2]

Green and Thorpe were sent by the Judges to the King's Council to demand of them whether by the statute of 14 *Edw. III, c. 6*, 'a

* 9 *Edw. III.*   † 27 *Edw. III.*   ‡ 4 *Hen. III.*   § FITZHERBERT, *Dower*,[3] 179.

---

[1] These paragraphs are similarly mainly verbatim extracts from the Statute Book. Nearly all of the quotations are repeated in the 'Freeholder'.

[2] Taken from EGERTON, op. cit., pp. 50-1 and reproduced in 'Freeholder'.

[3] This appears to be quoted not from Fitzherbert direct but from EGERTON, op. cit., p. 13. Egerton's reference is to 'Fitz. 197' and his text in Latin. The identical passage is quoted in 'Freeholder'.

word may be amended in a writ'. And it was answered that 'a word may well be amended', although the statute speak but of a letter or a syllable.[1]

In the case of Sir Thomas Oghtred, knight, who brought a formedon against a poor man and his wife, they came and yielded to the demandant, which seemed suspicious to the Court, whereupon judgment was stayed.* And Thorpe said that in the like case of Giles Blacket it was spoken of in parliament, and we were commanded that when any like case should come we should not go to judgment without good advice. Therefore the judges' conclusion was: 'Sues au conseil et comment ils voilent que nous devomus faire, nous volomus faire, et auterment nient en cest case.' 'Sue to the Council, and as they will have us to do, we will; and otherwise not in this case.'[2]

In the last place we may consider how much hath been attributed to the opinions of the King's Judges by parliaments, and so find that the King's Council hath guided and ruled the Judges, and the Judges guided the parliament.

In the parliament of 28 King Henry VI, the Commons made suit: 'That William de la Pole, Duke of Suffolk, should be committed to prison for many treasons and other crimes. The lords of the higher house were doubtful what answer to give: the opinion of the Judges was demanded. Their opinion was that he ought not to be committed, for that the Commons did not charge him with any particular offence, but with general reports and slanders.'[3] This opinion was allowed.

In another parliament (which was prorogued) in the vacation the Speaker of the House of Commons was condemned in a thousand pounds damages in an action of trespass, and was committed to prison in execution of the same.† When the parliament was reassembled the Commons made suit to the King and Lords to have their Speaker delivered. The Lords demanded the opinions of the Judges whether he might be delivered out of prison by privilege of parliament. Upon the Judges' answer it was concluded that the Speaker should still remain in prison according to the law, notwithstanding the privilege of Parliament and that he was the Speaker. Which resolution was declared to the Commons by Moyle, the King's Serjeant at Law, and the Commons were commanded in the King's name by the Bishop of

* 39 Edw. III   † 31 Hen. VI.

---

[1] Also taken from EGERTON, p. 52, and reproduced in 'Freeholder'.
[2] Verbatim from EGERTON, loc. cit., and reproduced in 'Freeholder'.
[3] EGERTON, op. cit., p. 19. Also quoted in the 'Freeholder'.

Lincoln (in the absence of the Archbishop of Canterbury, then Chancellor) to choose another Speaker.[1]

In 7 King Henry VIII a question was moved in Parliament: whether spiritual persons might be convented before temporal judges for criminal cases?* There Sir John Fineux and the other judges delivered their opinion: 'That they might and ought to be.' And their opinion was allowed and maintained by the King and Lords, and Dr. Standish, who before had holden the same opinion. The same opinion was delivered from the bishops.

If a writ of error be sued in Parliament upon a judgment given in the King's Bench, the lords of the Higher House alone (without the Commons) are to examine the errors.† The Lords are to proceed according to the law, and for their judgment therein they are to be informed by the advice and counsel of the judges, who are to inform them what the law is, and so to direct them in their judgment. For the Lords are not to follow their own opinions or discretions otherwise. So it was in a writ of error brought by the Dean and Chapter of Lichfield against the Prior and Convent of Newton-Panel, as appeareth by record. See Flower Dew's case, page 1, H. vii, fol. 19.[2]

---

* *Post Nati*, p. 22.[3] † ibidem.

---

[1] EGERTON, op. cit., pp. 20-1. Also in 'Freeholder'.

[2] From EGERTON, pp. 22-3. The last sentence does not appear in the MS.

[3] This is the only mention by Filmer of Egerton's work by name. The passage is reproduced word for word in the 'Freeholder' but the last sentence is apparently misprinted. Comparison of the way in which identical passages are quoted in the *Patriarcha* MS. and the 'Freeholder' shows that the 'Freeholder' was based on a different MS. original.

THE

FREEHOLDER'S

GRAND INQUEST

TOUCHING

Our Soveraigne LORD *the* KING

AND

His PARLIAMENT

Printed in the three and twentieth year of the Reign of our
Soveraign Lord King CHARLES

(Copy in Trinity College Library, Cambridge, dated January 31st, 1647 (1648 new style). Very probably published by Royston. Almost universally attributed to Sir Robert Holborne (d. 1647), by both contemporaries and modern scholars. Nevertheless it was published in the collected editions later in the century, 1679, 1680, 1684 and 1696. It gave its title to all of these collections except that of 1696; it is omitted from the title of the problematic 1695 collection.

This tract is an expansion and completion of the last five chapters (xxviii-xxxii) of *Patriarcha*. The texts of these two are very closely parallel, there are numerous direct repetitions and the same quotations from other authorities are frequently used in both works: attention is drawn to most of the instances in the footnotes to *Patriarcha*. It represents Filmer's idea of how *Patriarcha* itself, or that part of it which referred to the constitution of Great Britain, would have had to be edited for publication. It seems to have been directly aimed at Prynne's interpretation of the constitution, but it cites, and in most cases reproves, nearly all the important writers in this field who were influential in the 1640s.

The 'Freeholder' is the prime source for Filmer's constitutional doctrines and is of great interest as a statement of Royalist absolutism. It seemed to attract little attention from the Whig critics of Filmer, and Locke makes no reference to the work, although it is possible that the continuation of Locke's First Treatise, which he never published, may have contained a refutation of it. It is the most finished, the most scholarly and the most courteous and moderate of the works of this mild and well-mannered author.

The contents of this tract are of interest to the constitutional historian for two reasons. First, it illustrates the great importance of the work of the scholars of the period to the constitutional controversies. Secondly, it shows that Royalist absolutism was worked out in detail before the Civil War — remembering that the 'Freeholder' is simply an expansion of part of *Patriarcha*. The conclusions it puts forward are interesting in their comparative accuracy: they are certainly closer to the conclusions of modern scholarship than the case made by the Parliamentary writers, which later developed into the Whig interpretation and informed the scholarship of the nineteenth century.)

THE ARGUMENT

A presentment of divers statutes, records and other precedents, explaining the Writs of Summons to Parliament: showing:

I. That the Commons, by their Writ, are only to perform and consent to the Ordinances of Parliament.

II. That the Lords or Common Council by their Writ are only to treat, and give counsel in Parliament.

III. That the King himself only ordains and makes laws, and is supreme judge in Parliament.

With the suffrages of

Hen. de Bracton	Hen. Spelman
Jo. Britton	Jo. Glanvil
Tho. Egerton	Will. Lambard
Edw. Coke	Rich. Crompton
Walter Raleigh	William Campden, and
Rob. Cotton	Jo. Selden

THERE is a general belief that the Parliament of England was at first an imitation of the Assembly of the Three Estates in France: therefore, in order to prepare the understanding in the *recherche* we have in hand, it is proper to give a brief account of the mode of France in those Assemblies: Scotland and Ireland being also under the dominion of the King of England; a touch of the manner of their Parliaments shall be by way of preface.

1. In France, the King's Writ goeth to the Bailiffs, Seneschals or Stewards of Liberties, who issue out warrants to all such as have fees and lands within their liberties, and to all towns, requiring all such as have any complaints, to meet in the principal city, there to choose two or three delegates, in the name of that province, to be present at the General Assembly.

At the day appointed, they meet at the Principal city of the bailiwick. The King's Writ is read, and every man called by name, and sworn to choose honest men, for the good of the King and Commonwealth, to be present at the General Assembly, as delegates, faithfully to deliver their grievances, and demands of the province. Then they choose their delegates and swear them. Next they consult what is necessary to be complained of, or what is to be desired of the King: and of these things they make a catalogue or index. And because every man should freely propound his complaint or demands, there is a chest placed in the town hall, into which every man may cast his writing. After the catalogue is made and signed, it is delivered to the delegates to carry to the General Assembly.

All the bailiwicks are divided into twelve classes. To avoid confusion, and to the end there may not be too great delay in the Assembly, by the gathering of all the votes, every classis compiles a catalogue or book of the grievances and demands of all the bailiwicks within that classis, then these classes at the Assembly compose one book of the grievances and demands of the whole kingdom. This being the order of the proceedings of the third estate; the like order is observed by the clergy and nobility. When the three books for the three estates are perfected, then they present them to the King by their presidents. First, the president for the clergy begins his oration on his knees, and the King commanding, he stands up bare-headed, and proceeds. And so the next president for the nobility doth the like. But the president for the Commons begins and ends his oration on his knees. Whilst the president for the clergy speaks, the rest of that order rise up, and stand bare, till they are bid by the King to sit down, and be covered, and so the like for the nobility. But whilst the president of the Commons speaks, the rest are neither bidden to sit, or be covered. Thus the grievances and demands being delivered, and left to the King and his council, the General Assembly of the three estates endeth, *Atque ita totus actus concluditur.*

Thus it appears, the General Assembly was but an orderly way of presenting the public grievances and demands of the whole kingdom, to the consideration of the King: not much unlike the ancient usage of this kingdom for a long time, when all laws were nothing else but the King's answers to the petitions presented to him in Parliament, as is apparent by very many statutes, Parliament-Rolls, and the confession of Sir Edward Coke.

2. In Scotland, about twenty days before the Parliament begins, proclamation is made throughout the kingdom, to deliver in to the King's Clerk, or Master of the Rolls, all bills to be exhibited that sessions, before a certain day: then are they brought to the King, and perused by him: and only such as he allows are put into the Chancellor's hand, to be propounded in Parliament, and none others: and if any man in Parliament speak of another matter than is allowed by the King, the Chancellor tells him, there is no such bill allowed by the King. When they have passed them for laws, they are presented to the King, who, with his sceptre put into his hand by the Chancellor, ratifies them, and if there be anything the King dislikes they raze it out before.

3. In Ireland, the Parliament, as appears by a statute made in the tenth year of Henry VIII, c. 4, is to be after this manner: No Parliament is to be holden but at such season as the King's Lieutenant and council there, do first certify the King, under the Great Seal of that land, the causes and considerations, and all such acts as they think fit should pass in the said Parliament. And such causes and considerations, and acts affirmed by the King and his council to be good and expedient for that land: and his licence thereupon as well in affirmation of the said causes and acts, as to summon the Parliament under his Great Seal of England had and obtained. That done, a Parliament to be had and holden after the form and effect afore-rehearsed, and if any Parliament be holden in that land contrary to the form and provision aforesaid, it is deemed void, and of none effect in law. It is provided, that all such bills as shall be offered to the Parliament there; shall be

first transmitted hither under the Great Seal of that kingdom, and having received allowance and approbation here, shall be put under the Great Seal of this kingdom, and so returned thither to be preferred to the Parliament. By a statute of 3 and 4 Philip and Mary, for the expounding of Poynings Act, it is ordered, for the King's passing of the said acts in such form and tenor as they should be sent into England, or else for the change of them, or any part of them.

After this shorter narrative of the usage of Parliaments in our neighbour and fellow kingdoms, it is time the *inquisitio magna* of our own be offered to the verdict or judgment of a moderate and intelligent reader.

ROBERT FILMER

THE FREEHOLDER'S GRAND INQUEST TOUCHING OUR SOVEREIGN LORD THE KING, AND HIS· PARLIAMENT

·Every freeholder that hath a voice in the election of Knights, Citizens or Burgesses for the parliament ought to know with what power he trusts those whom he chooseth, because such trust is the foundation of the power of the House of Commons.

A writ from the King to the Sheriff of the county is that which gives authority and commission for the freeholders to make their election at the next County Court day after the receipt of the writ; and in the writ there is also expressed the duty and power of the Knights, Citizens and Burgesses that are there elected.

The means to know what trust or authority the country or free-holders confer, or bestow by their election, is in this, as in other like cases, to have an eye to the words of the commission or writ itself: thereby it may be seen whether that which the House of Commons doth act be within the limit of their commission: greater or other trust than is comprised in the body of the writ, the freeholders do not or cannot give if they obey the writ: the writ being Latin and not extant in English, few freeholders understand it, and fewer observe it; I have rendered it in Latin and English.

Rex Vicecomiti salut', etc.

Quia de Advisamento et Assensu Concilii nostri pro quibusdam arduis et urgentibus Negotiis, Nos, statum et defensionem regni nostri Angliae, et Ecclesiae Anglicanae concernen', quoddam Parliamentum nostrum apud Civitatem nostram West. duodecimo die Novembris prox' futur' teneri ordinavimus, et ibid' cum Praelatis, Magnatibus et Proceribus dicti regni nostri colloquium habere et tract': Tibi praecipimus firmiter injungentes quod facta proclam' in prox' comitat' tuo post receptionem hujus brevis nostri tenend' die et loco praedict' duos milit' gladiis cinct' magis idoneos et discretos comit' praedicti, et de qualib' civitate com' illius duos Cives, et de quolibet Burgo duos Burgenses de discretior' et magis sufficientibus libere et indifferenter per illos qui proclam' hujusmodi interfuerint juxta formam statutorum inde edit' et provis' eligi, et nomina eorundem milit', civium et Burgensium, sic electorum in quibusdam indentur' inter te et illos qui hujusmodi election' interfuerint, inde conficiend' sive hujusmodi electi

133

praesentes fuerint vel absentes, inferi: eosque ad dict' diem et locum venire fac'. Ita quod iidem milites plenam et sufficientem potestatem pro se et communitate comit' praedicti, ac dict' Cives et Burgenses pro se et communitat' Civitatum et Burgorum praedictorum divisim ab ipsis habeant, ad faciendum et consentiendum his quae tunc ibid' de communi Consilio dicti reg. nostri (favente Deo) contigerint ordinari super negotiis ante dictis: Ita quod pro defectu potestatis hujusmodi, seu propter improvidam electionem milit' Civium aut Burgensium praedictorum, dicta negotia infecta non remaneant quovismodo. Nolumus autem quod tu nec aliquis alius vic' dicti reg. nostri aliqualiter sit electus. Et electionem illam in pleno comitatu factam, distincte et aperte sub sigillo tuo et sigillis eorum qui electioni illi interfuerint, nobis in cancellar' nostram ad dict' diem et locum certifices indilate, remittens nobis alteram partem indenturarum praedictarum praesentibus consut' una cum hoc breve. Teste meipso apud Westmon'.

The King to the Sheriff of   Greeting.

'Whereas, by the advice and consent of our Council, for certain difficult and urgent businesses concerning us, the State and defence of our Kingdom of England and the English Church: We have ordained a certain Parliament of ours, to be held at Our City of the   day of   next ensuing, and there to have Conference, and to treat with the Prelates, great men, and Peers of our said kingdom. We command and straitly enjoin you, that making Proclamation at the next County Court after the receipt of this our writ, to be holden the day, and place aforesaid: You cause two Knights, girt with swords, the most fit and discreet of the county aforesaid: and of every City of that County two citizens; of every Borough, two Burgesses of the discreeter and most sufficient; to be freely, and indifferently chosen by them who shall be present at such Proclamation, according to the tenor of the statutes in that case made and provided: and the names of the said Knights, Citizens and Burgesses so chosen, to be inserted in certain Indentures to be then made between you, and those that shall be present at such Election, whether the parties so elected be present, or absent: and shall make them to come at the said day, and place: so that the said Knights for themselves, and for the county aforesaid; and the said Citizens, and Burgesses for themselves, and the commonalty of the aforesaid cities and boroughs, may have severally from them, full and sufficient power to *perform:* and to *consent* to those things which then by the favour of God shall there happen to be ordained by the Common Council of our said Kingdom, concerning the businesses aforesaid: So that the business may not by any means remain undone for want of such power or by reason of the improvident election of the aforesaid Knights, Citizens and Burgesses. But we will not in any case you or any other Sheriff of our said Kingdom shall be elected; and at the day and place aforesaid, the said election made in the full County Court, you shall certify without delay to us in our chancery, under your seal, and the seals of them which shall be present at that election, sending back unto us the other part of the indenture aforesaid affiled to these presents, together with this writ. Witness our self at Westmin'.

By this writ we do not find that the Commons are called to be any part of the Common Council of the kingdom, or of the Supreme Court of Judicature, or to have any part of the legislative power, or to consult de arduis regni negotiis, of the difficult businesses of the kingdom. The writ only says, the King would have conference and treat with the Prelates, great men, and Peers: but not a word of treating or conference with the Commons; the House of Commons, which does not minister an oath, nor fine, nor imprison any, but their own members (and that but of late in some cases) cannot properly be said to be a court at all; much less to be a part of the Supreme Court, or highest judicature of the kingdom. The constant custom, even to this day, for the members of the House of Commons to stand bare, with their hats in their hands in the presence of the Lords, while the Lords sit covered at all conferences, is a visible argument, that the Lords and Commons are not fellow-commissioners, or fellow-counsellors of the kingdom.

The duty of Knights, Citizens and Burgesses, mentioned in the writ, is only ad Faciendum, et Consentiendum, to perform and to consent to such things as should be ordained by the common council of the kingdom; there is not so much mentioned in the writ as a power in the Commons to dissent. When a man is bound to appear in a court of justice, the words are, 'ad Faciendum et Recipiendum quod ei per curiam injungetur': which shows that this word 'Faciendum' is used as a term in law, to signify 'to give obedience': for this we meet with a precedent even as ancient as the Parliament-writ itself, and it is concerning proceedings in Parliament, 33 *Edw. I*, 'Dominus Rex mandavit vicecom' quod, etc. summon' Nicolaum de Segrave, et ex parte Domini Regis firmiter ei injungeret, quod esset coram Domino Rege in proximo Parl. etc. ad audiendum voluntatem ipsius Domini Regis, etc. Et ad faciendum et recipiendum ulterius quod curia Domini Regis consideraret in Praemissis.' (Our Lord the King commands the Sheriff to summon Nicholas Segrave to appear before our Lord the King in the next parliament, to hear the will of the Lord our King himself, and to perform and receive what the King's Court shall further consider of the premises.)

Sir Edward Coke, to prove the clergy hath no voice in Parliament, saith, that by the words of their writ, their consent was only to such things as were ordained by the common council of the realm. If this argument of his be good, it will deny also voices to the Commons in Parliament; for in their writ are the selfsame words, viz. to consent to such things as were ordained by the common council of the kingdom. Sir Edward Coke concludes, that the Procuratores Cleri have many times appeared in Parliament, as spiritual assistants, to consider, consult and to consent; but never had voice there; how they could consult and consent without voices he doth not show: though the clergy (as he saith) oft appeared in Parliament, yet was it only *ad consentiendum*, as I take it, and not *ad faciendum*, for the word *faciendum* is omitted in their writ; the cause, as I conceive, is, the clergy, though they were to assent, yet by reason of clerical exemptions, they were not required to perform all the ordinances or Acts of Parliament.

But some may think, though the writ doth not express a calling of the Knights, Citizens and Burgesses to be part of the common council of the kingdom; yet it supposeth it a thing granted, and not to be questioned, but that they are a part of the common council.

Indeed if their writ had not mentioned the calling of Prelates, great men and Peers to council, there might have been a little better colour for such a supposition: but the truth is, such a supposition doth make the writ itself vain and idle; for it is a senseless thing to bid men assent to that which they have already ordained: since ordaining is an assenting, and more than an assenting.

For clearing the meaning and sense of the writ, and satisfaction of such as think it impossible, but that the Commons of England have always been a part of the common council of the kingdom, I shall insist upon these points: 1. That anciently the Barons of England were the common council of the kingdom. 2. That until the time of Henry I, the Commons were not called to Parliament. 3. Though the Commons were called by Henry I, yet they were not constantly called, nor yet regularly elected by writ until Henry III's time.

For the first point, Mr. Cambden in his *Britannia*, doth teach us, that in the time of the English Saxons, and in the ensuing age, a Parliament was called *Commune Concilium*, which was (saith he) 'Praesentia Regis, Praelatorum, Procerumque collectorum' (The presence of the King, Prelates and Peers assembled.) No mention of the Commons: the Prelates and Peers were all Barons.

The author of the chronicle of the church of Lichfield, cited by Mr. Selden,* saith, 'Postquam Rex Edvardus, etc. Concilio Baronum Angliae, etc.' After King Edward was King, by the council of the Barons of England, he revived a law which had lain asleep threescore and seven years: and this law was called the Law of St. Edward the King.

In the same chronicle it is said, that William the Conqueror, anno regni sui quarto apud Londin', had Concilium Baronum suorum, a council of his Barons. And it is of this Parliament, that his son Henry I speaks, saying, 'I restore you the laws of King Edward the Confessor, with those amendments wherewith my father amended them by the council of his Barons.'

In the fifth year, as Mr. Selden thinks, of the Conqueror, was a Parliament, or *Principum conventus*, an assembly of Earls and Barons at Pinenden Heath in Kent, in the cause between Lanfrank the Archbishop of Canterbury and Odo, Earl of Kent. The King gave commission to Godfrid, then Bishop of Constance in Normandy, to represent his own person for hearing the controversy (as saith M. Lambard); and caused Egelrick, the Bishop of Chichester (an aged man, singularly commended for skill in the laws and customs of the realm), to be brought thither in a wagon for his assistance in council: commanded Haymo, the Sheriff of Kent, to summon the whole county to give in evidence: three whole days spent in debate: in the end Lanfrank and the Bishop of Rochester were restored to the possession of Detling and other lands which Odo had withheld.

21 *Edw. III. fol.* 60. There is mention of a Parliament held under the same King William the Conqueror, wherein all the Bishops of the land, Earls and Barons, made an ordinance touching the exemption of the Abbey of Bury from the Bishops of Norwich.

In the tenth year of the Conqueror, 'Episcopi, Comites, et Barones regni regia potestate ad universalem Synodum pro causis audiendis et tractandis convocati', saith the Book of Westminster.

In the second year of William II, there was a Parliament de cunctis regni Principibus; another which had quosq; regni Proceres: All the Peers of the kingdom.†

In the seventh year was a Parliament at Rockingham Castle in

* *Apud* Selden.   † Selden.

Northamptonshire. Episcopis, Abbatibus cunctisque regni Principibus una coecuntibus.

A year or two after, the same King, de statu regni acturus, etc. called thither, by the command of his writ, the Bishops, Abbots and all the Peers of the kingdom.

At the coronation of Henry I all the people of the kingdom of England were called, and laws were then made; but it was Per Commune Concilium Baronum meorum, by the common council of my Barons.

In his third year, the Peers of the kingdom were called without any mention of the Commons: and another, a while after, consensu Comitum et Baronum, by the consent of the Earls and Barons.*

Florentius Wigorniensis saith, these are statutes which Anselme and all the other Bishops in the presence of King Henry, by the assent of his Barons ordained: and in his tenth year, of Earls and Peers; and in his twenty-third of Earls and Barons. In the year following, the same King held a Parliament, or great council, with his Barons Spiritual and Temporal.

King Henry II in his tenth year, had a great council or Parliament at Clarendon, which was an assembly of Prelates and Peers.

22 Henry II, saith Hovenden, was a great council at Nottingham, and by the common council of the Archbishops, Bishops, Earls and Barons, the kingdom was divided into six parts. And again, Hovenden saith, that the same King at Windsor (apud Windeshores) Communi Concilio of Bishops, Earls and Barons, divided England into four parts. And in his twenty-first year a Parliament at Windsor of Bishops, Earls and Barons. And another of like persons at Northampton.

King Richard I had a Parliament at Nottingham, in his fifth year, of Bishops, Earls and Barons: this Parliament lasted but four days, yet much was done in it: the first day the King disseiseth Gerard de Canvil of the Sherifwick of Lincoln, and Hugh Bardolph of the castle and Sherifwick of York. The second day he required judgment against his brother John, who was afterwards King: and Hugh de Novant, Bishop of Coventry. The third day was granted to the King of every plough-land in England 2s. He required also the third part of the service of every Knight's fee for his attendance into Normandy, and all the wool that year of the Monks Cisteaux, which, for that it was grievous and unsupportable, they fine for money. The last day was for hearing of grievances: and so the Parliament broke up; and the same year held another at Northampton of the nobles of the realm.

King John, in his fifth year, he and his great men met, Rex et mag-

* Selden.

nates convenerunt: and the roll of that year hath Commune Concilium Baronum Meorum, the common council of my Barons at Winchester.

In the sixth year of King Henry III the Nobles granted to the King, of every Knight's Fee, two marks in silver.

In the seventh year he had a Parliament at London, an assembly of Barons. In his thirteenth year an assembly of the Lords at Westminster. In his fifteenth year, of Nobles, both Spiritual and Temporal.

M. Par saith, that 20 Henry III 'Congregati sunt Magnates ad colloquium de negotiis regni tractaturi' (The great men were called to confer and treat of the business of the kingdom.) And at Merton, Our Lord the King granted, by the consent of his great men, that hereafter usury should not run against a ward from the death of his ancestor.

21 Henry III. The King sent his royal writs, commanding all belonging to his kingdom, that is to say, Archbishops, Bishops, Abbots and Priors installed, Earls and Barons, that they should all meet at London, to treat of the King's business touching the whole kingdom: and at the day prefixed, the whole multitude of the Nobles of the kingdom met at London, saith Matt. Westminster.

In his twenty-first year, at the request, and by the council of the Lords, the charters were confirmed.

22 Henry III. At Winchester, the King sent his royal writs to Archbishops, Bishops, Priors, Earls and Barons, to treat of business concerning the whole kingdom.

32 Henry III. The King commanded all the nobility of the whole kingdom to be called to treat of the state of his kingdom. Matt. Westminster.

49 Henry III. The King had a treaty at Oxford with the Peers of the kingdom. Matt. Westminster.

At a Parliament at Marlborough, 55 Henry III, statutes were made by the assent of Earls and Barons.

Here the place of Bracton, Chief Justice in this King's time, is worth the observing; and the rather for that it is much insisted on of late, to make for Parliaments being above the King. The words in Bracton are, 'The King hath a superior, God; also the law by which he is made King; also his court, viz. the Earls and Barons'. The court that was said in those days to be above the King, was a court of Earls and Barons, not a word of the Commons, or the representative body of the kingdom being any part of the superior court. Now for the true sense of Bracton's words, how the law and the court of Earls and Barons, are the King's superiors; they must of necessity be understood to be superiors, so far only as to advise, and direct the King out of his own grace and good will only: which appears plainly by the words of Bracton himself, where, speaking of the King, he resolves thus, 'Nec potest ei necessitatem aliquis imponere quod injuriam suam corrigat et emendat, cum superiorem non habeat nisi Deum; et satis ei erat ad poenam, quod Dominum expectat ultorem. Nor can any man put a necessity upon him to correct and amend his injury unless he will himself, since he hath no superior but God; it will be sufficient punishment for him, to expect the Lord an avenger.' Here the same man, who speaking according to some men's opinion, saith, the law and court of Earls and Barons are superior to the King; in this place tells us himself, the King hath no superior but God: the difference is easily reconciled; according to the distinction of the school-men, the King is free from the co-active power of laws or counsellors: but may be subject to their directive power, according to his own will: that is, God can only compel, but the law and his courts may advise him.

Rot. Parliament. 1 *Hen. IV, nu.* 79 The Commons expressly affirm, judgment in Parliament belongs to the King and Lords.

These precedents show, that from the Conquest until a great part of Henry III's reign (in whose days it is thought the writ for election of Knights was framed) which is about two hundred years, and above a third part of the time since the Conquest, to our days, the Barons made the Parliament or common council of the kingdom; under the name of Barons, not only the Earls, but the Bishops also were comprehended, for the Conqueror made the Bishops Barons. Therefore it is no such great wonder, that in the writ we find the Lords only to be the counsellors, and the Commons called only to perform and consent to the ordinances.

Those there be who seem to believe, that under the words Barons anciently the Lords of Court-Barons were comprehended, and that they were called to Parliament as Barons; but if this could be proved to have been at any time true, yet those Lords of Court-Barons were not the representative body of the Commons of England, except it can be also proved, that the Commons or freeholders of the kingdom, chose such Lords of Court-Barons to be present in Parliament. The Lords of Manors came not at first by election of the people, as Sir Edward Coke, treating of the institution of Court-Barons, resolves us in these words: By the laws and ordinances of ancient Kings, and especially of King Alfred, it appeareth, that the first Kings of this realm had all the lands of England in demean; and the grand manors and royalties they reserved to themselves, and of the remnant they, for the defence of the realm, enfeoffed the Barons of the realm with such jurisdiction as the Court-Baron now hath. Coke's *Institutes*, Part I, fol. 58.

Here, by the way, I cannot but note, that if the first Kings had all the lands of England in demean, as Sir Edward Coke saith they had; and if the first Kings were chosen by the people (as many think they were) then surely our forefathers were a very bountiful (if not a prodigal) people, to give all the lands of the whole kingdom to their Kings, with liberty for them to keep what they pleased, and to give the remainder to their subjects, clogged and encumbered with a condition to defend the realm: this is but an ill sign of a limited monarchy by original constitution or contract. But, to conclude the former point, Sir Edward Coke's opinion is, that in the ancient laws, under the name of Barons, were comprised all the Nobility.

This doctrine of the Barons being the common council doth displease many, and is denied, as tending to the disparagement of the Commons, and to the discredit and confutation of their opinion, who teach that the Commons are assigned counsellors to the King by the people; therefore I will call in Mr. Pryn to help us with his testimony: he in his book of *Treachery and Disloyalty, etc.*, proves, that before the Conquest, by the laws of Edward the Confessor, c. 17: The King by his oath was to do justice by the council of the Nobles of his realm. He also resolves, that the Earls and Barons in Parliament are above the King, and ought to bridle him, when he exorbitates from the laws. He further tells us, the Peers and Prelates have often translated the crown from the right heir.

1. Electing and crowning Edward, who was illegitimate; and putting by Ethelred, the right heir, after Edgar's decease.

2. Electing and crowning Canutus, a mere foreigner, in opposition to Edmund, the right heir to King Ethelred.

3. Harold and Hardiknute, both elected Kings successively without title; Edmund and Alfred the right heirs being dispossessed.

4. The English nobility, upon the death of Harold, enacted, that none of the Danish blood should any more reign over them.

5. Edgar Etheling, who had best title, was rejected; and Harold elected and crowned King.

6. In the second and third years of Edward II the Peers and Nobles of the land, seeing themselves contemned, entreated the King to manage the affairs of the kingdom by the council of his Barons. He gave his assent, and swore to ratify what the Nobles ordained; and

one of their articles was, that he would thenceforward order all the affairs of the kingdom by the council of his clergy and Lords.

7. William Rufus, finding the greatest part of the Nobles against him, swore to Lanfrank, that if they would choose him for King, he would abrogate their overhard laws.

8. The beginning, saith Mr. Pryn, of the charter of Henry I is observable; Henry by the Grace of God, of England, etc., know ye, that by the Mercy of God and common council of the Barons of the kingdom, I am crowned King.

9. Maud the Empress, the right heir, was put-by the crown, by the Prelates and Barons, and Stephen Earl of Mortain, who had no good title, assembling the Bishop and Peers, promising the amendment of the laws according to all their pleasures and liking, was by them all proclaimed King.

10. Lewis of France crowned King by the Barons, instead of King John.

All these testimonies from Mr. Pryn may satisfy, that anciently the Barons were the common council, or Parliament of England. And if Mr. Pryn could have found so much antiquity, and proof for the Knights, Citizens and Burgesses, being of the common council: I make no doubt but we should have heard from him in capital characters; but alas! he meets not with so much as these names in those elder ages. He dares not say, the Barons were assigned by the people, counsellors to the King; for he tells us, every Baron in Parliament doth represent his own person, and speaketh in behalf of himself alone; but in the Knights, Citizens and Burgesses, are represented the Commons of the whole realm: therefore every one of the Commons hath a greater voice in Parliament than the greatest Earl in England. Nevertheless Master Pryn will be very well content if we will admit and swallow these Parliaments of Barons, for the representative body of the kingdom; and to that purpose he cites them, or to no purpose at all. But to prove the treachery and disloyalty of Popish Parliaments, Prelates, and Peers, to their Kings: which is the main point, that Master Pryn, by the title of his book is to make good, and to prove.

As to the second point; which is, that until the time of Henry I the Commons were not called to Parliament: besides, the general silence of antiquity which never makes mention of the Commons coming to Parliament until that time; our histories say, before his time only certain of the nobility were called to consultation about the most important affairs of the state: he caused the Commons also to be assembled by Knights, Citizens and Burgesses of their own appointment: much to the same purpose writes Sir Walter Raleigh, saying, it is held that the Kings of England had no formal Parliaments till about the eighteenth year of King Henry I. For in his third year, for the marriage of his daughter, the King raised a tax upon every hide of land, by the advice of his privy council alone. And the subjects (saith he) soon after this Parliament was established, began to stand upon terms with their King, and drew from him by strong hand, and their swords, their great charter; it was after the establishment of the Parliament, by colour of it, that they had so great daring. If any desire to know the cause why Henry I called the people to Parliament, it was upon no very good occasion, if we believe Sir Walter Raleigh; the grand charter (saith he) was not originally granted regally and freely, for King Henry I did but usurp the kingdom, and therefore the better to secure himself against Robert his elder brother, he flattered the people with those charters: yea, King John that confirmed them, had the like respect: for Arthur D. of Britain was the undoubted heir of the crown, upon whom John usurped: so these charters had their original from Kings, *de facto*, but not *de jure*: and then afterwards his conclusion is, that the great charter had first an obscure birth by usurpation, and was fostered, and showed to the world by rebellion: in brief, the King called the people to Parliament, and granted them Magna Charta, that they might confirm to him the crown.

The third point consists of two parts; first, that the Commons were not called to Parliament until the days of Henry III, this appears by divers of the precedents formerly cited, to prove that the Barons were the common council. For though Henry I called all the people of the land to his coronation, and again in the fifteenth or eighteenth year of his reign; yet always he did not so; neither many of those Kings that did succeed him, as appeareth before.

Secondly, for calling the Commons by writ, I find it acknowledged in a book entitled *The Privilege and Practice of Parliaments*, in these words, 'In ancient times, after the King had summoned his Parliament, innumerable multitudes of people did make their access thereunto, pretending that privilege of right to belong to them. But King Henry III having experience of the mischief, and inconveniences by occasion of such popular confusion, did take order that none might come to his Parliament but those who were specially summoned. To this purpose it is observed by Master Selden, that the first writs we find accompanied with other circumstances of a summons to Parliament, as well for the Commons as Lords, is in the forty-ninth year of

Henry III. In the like manner Master Cambden speaking of the dignity of Barons, hath these words: 'King Henry III out of a great multitude which were seditious and turbulent, called the very best by writ or summons to Parliament; for he, after many troubles and vexations between the King himself, and Simon de Montfort, with other Barons; and after appeased: did decree and ordain, that all those Earls and Barons unto whom the King himself vouchsafed to direct his writs of summons should come to his Parliament, and no others: but that which he began a little before his death, Edward I and his successors constantly observed and continued. The said prudent King Edward summoned always those of ancient families, that were most wise, to his Parliament; and omitted their sons after their death if they were not answerable to their parents in understanding.' Also Mr. Cambden* in another place saith, that in the time of Edward I select men for wisdom and worth among the gentry were called to Parliament, and their posterity omitted, if they were defective therein.

As the power of sending writs of summons for elections, was first exercised by Henry III so succeeding Kings did regulate the elections upon such writs, as doth appear by several statutes, which all speak in the name and power of the Kings themselves; for such was the language of our forefathers.

In 5 *Ric. II, c.* 4, these be the words, 'The King willeth and commandeth all persons which shall have summons to come to Parliament: and every person that doth absent himself (except he may reasonably and honestly excuse him to Our Lord the King) shall be amerced, and otherwise punished.'

7 *Hen. IV, c.* 15. Our Lord the King, at the grievous complaint of his Commons, of the undue election of the Knights of Counties, sometimes made of affection of Sheriffs, and otherwise against the form of the writs, to the great slander of the counties, etc. Our Lord the King, willing therein to provide remedy, by the assent of the Lords and Commons, hath ordained, that election shall be made in the full County Court, and that all that be there present, as well suitors as others, shall proceed to the election freely, notwithstanding any request, or command to the contrary.

11 *Hen. IV, c.* 1. Our Lord the King ordained, that a Sheriff that maketh an undue return, etc. shall incur the penalty of a £100 to be paid to Our Lord the King.

1 *Hen. V, c.* 1. Our Lord the King, by the advice and assent of the Lords, and the special instance and request of the Commons, ordained

* Cambden.

that the Knights of the Shire be not chosen, unless they be resiant within the shire the day of the date of the writ: and that Citizens and Burgesses be resiant, dwelling, and free in the same cities and boroughs, and no others, in any wise.

6 *Hen. VI, c.* 4. Our Lord the King, willing to provide remedy for knights chosen for Parliament, and sheriffs, hath ordained, that they shall have their answer, and traverse to inquest of office found against them.

8 *Hen. VI, c.* 7. Whereas elections of Knights have been made by great outrages, and excessive number of people, of which most part was of people of no value, whereof every one of them pretend a voice equivalent to worthy Knights and Esquires, whereby manslaughters, riots and divisions among gentlemen shall likely be: Our Lord the King had ordained that Knights of Shires be chosen by people dwelling in the counties, every one of them having lands or tenements to the value of £2 the year at the least, and that he that shall be chosen, shall be dwelling and resiant within the counties.

10 *Hen. VI.* Our Lord the King ordained, that knights be chosen by people dwelling, and having £2 by the year within the same county.

11 *Hen. VI, c.* 11. The King, willing to provide for the ease of them that come to the Parliaments and councils of the King by his commandment, hath ordained, that if any assault or fray be made on them that come to Parliament, or other council of the King; the party which made any such affray or assault, shall pay double damages, and make fine and ransom at the King's will.

23 *Hen. VI, c.* 15. The King, considering the statutes of 1 *Hen. V, c.* 1 and 8 *Hen. VI, c.* 7 and the defaults of Sheriffs in returning Knights, Citizens and Burgesses, ordained:

1. That the said statutes should be duly kept.

2. That the Sheriffs shall deliver precepts to Mayors and Bailiffs to choose Citizens and Burgesses.

3. The penalty of £100 for a Sheriff making an untrue return concerning the election of Knights, Citizens and Burgesses.

4. The penalty of £40 for Mayors or Bailiffs, making untrue returns.

5. Due election of Knights must be in the full County Court, between the hours of eight and eleven before noon.

6. The party must begin his suit within three months after the Parliament began.

7. Knights of the Shire shall be notable Knights of the county, or

such notable esquires, or gentlemen born, of the said counties, as shall be able to be Knights, and no man to be such Knight which standeth in the degree of a Yeoman, and under.

The last thing I observe in the writ for election of Members of Parliament is, that by the express words of the writ, Citizens and Burgesses for the Parliament were eligible at the County Court, as well as Knights of the Shire; and that not only freeholders, but all others, whosoever were present at the County Court, had voices in such elections: see the Statute 7 *Hen. IV, c.* 15.

I have the longer insisted on the examination of the writ, being the power and actions of the House of Commons are principally justified by the trust which the freeholders commit unto them by virtue of this writ.

I would not be understood to determine what power the House of Commons doth; or may exercise if the King please: I confine myself only to the power in the writ. I am not ignorant that King Henry VII in the cause of the Duke of Britain, and King James in the business of the Palatinate, asked the council of the House of Commons; and not only in the House of Commons, but every subject in particular by duty and allegiance, is bound to give his best advice to his sovereign, when he is thought worthy to have his council asked.

13 *Edw. III, nu.* 10. All the merchants of England were summoned by writ to appear at Westminster, in proper person, to confer upon great business concerning the King's honour, the salvation of the realm, and of themselves.

In passages of public council it is observable (saith Sir Robert Cotton)* that in ancient times the Kings of England did entertain the Commons with weighty causes, thereby to apt and bind them to a readiness of charge; and the Commons to shun expense have warily avoided to give advice.

13 *Edw. III.* The Lords and Commons were called to consult how the domestic quiet may be preserved, the marches of Scotland defended, and the sea secured from enemies. The Peers and Commons having apart consulted, the Commons desired not to be charged to council of things of which they had no cognizance; de queux ils n'ont pas de cognisance.

21 *Edw. III.* Justice Thorp declaring to the Peers and Commons, that the French war began by their advice: the truce after by their assent accepted, and now ended: the King's pleasure was, to have their counsel in the prosecution: the Commons, being commanded to

* Cotton.

assemble themselves, and when they were agreed, to give notice to the King, and the Lords of the council; after four days' consultation, humbly desire of the King that he would be advised therein by the Lords and others of more experience than themselves in such affairs.

6 *Ric. II.* The Parliament was called to consult whether the King should go in person to rescue Gaunt, or send an army. The Commons, after two days' debate, crave a conference with the Lords, and Sir Thomas Puckering (their Speaker) protests, that councils for war did aptly belong to the King and His Lords; yet since the Commons were commanded to give their advice, they humbly wished a voyage by the King.

7 *Ric. II.* At the second session, the Commons are willed to advise upon view of articles of peace with the French; whether war or such amity should be accepted; they modestly excuse themselves, as too weak to counsel in so weighty causes. But charged again, as they did tender their honour and the right of the King; they make their answer, giving their opinions, rather for peace than war.

For fuller manifestation of what hath been said touching the calling, election and power of the Commons in Parliament, it is behoveful to observe some points delivered by Sir Edward Coke in his treatise of the Jurisdiction of Parliaments; where,

First, he fairly begins, and lays his foundation, that the High Court of Parliament consisteth of the King's Majesty sitting there, and of the three estates:

1. The Lords Spiritual
2. The Lords Temporal
3. And the Commons

Hence it is to be gathered, that truly and properly it cannot be called the High Court of Parliament, but whilst the King is sitting there in person: so that the question nowadays, whether the Parliament be above the King, is either false or idle: false, if you exclude, and idle if you include the King's person in the word Parliament: the case truly put, and as it is meant, is, whether the three estates (or, which is all one, the Lords and Commons) assembled in Parliament be above the King: and not whether the King with the three estates be above the King: it appears also that they are much mistaken, who reckon the King one of the three estates, as Mr. Pryn, page 20, and many others do; for the three estates make the body, and the King is *Caput, Principium, et Finis Parliamentor'*, as confesseth Sir Edward Coke.

Secondly, Sir Edward Coke delivers, that certain it is, both Houses at first sat together, and that it appears in Edward III's time, the Lords and Commons sat together, and the Commons had no continual Speaker. If he mean, the Lords and Commons did sit, and vote together in one body, few there be that will believe it; because the Commons never were wont to lose, or forgo any of their liberties, or privileges; and for them to stand now with their hats in their hands (which is no magistratical posture) there, where they were wont to sit and vote, is an alteration not imaginable to be endured by the Commons. It may be, in former times, when the Commons had no constant Speaker, they were oft, and perhaps for the most part, in the same chamber, and in the presence of the Lords, to hear the debates and consultations of the great council, but not to sit and vote with them: for when the Commons were to advise among themselves, the chapter-house of the Abbey of Westminster was oft-times their place to meet in, before they had a settled House, and their meetings not being very frequent, may be the reason, I conceive, why the name of the House of Commons is not of such great antiquity, or taken notice of; but the House of Lords was only called the Parliament House: and the treatise called, *Modus tenendi Parliamentum*, speaks of the Parliament as but of one House only. The House, where now the Commons sit in Westminster, is but of late use, or institution: for in Edward VI's days it was a chapel of the College of St. Stephen, and had a dean, secular canons and chorists, who were the King's choir at his palace at Westminster, and at the dissolution were translated to the King's chapel at Whitehall.

Also I read, that Westminster Hall being out of repair, Richard II caused a large house to be builded betwixt the clock tower and the gate of the great old hall in the midst of the palace court: the house was long and large, made of timber, covered with tiles, open on both sides, that all might see and hear what was both said and done: four thousand archers of Cheshire, which were the King's own guard, attended on that house, and had *bouche a Court*, and sixpence by the day.

Thirdly, he saith, The Commons are to choose their Speaker, but seeing after their choice the King may refuse him, the use is (as in the *conge d'eslire* of a Bishop) that the King doth name a discreet, learned man, whom the Commons elect: when the Commons have chosen, the King may allow of his excuse, and disallow him, as Sir John Popham was (saith his margin).

Fourthly, he informs us, That the first day of the Parliament four justices' assistants, and two civilians (masters of the chancery) are appointed receivers of petitions, which are to be delivered within six days following: and six of the nobility, and two Bishops, calling to them the King's learned council, when need should be, to be tryers of the said petitions, whether they were reasonable, good, and necessary to be offered and propounded to the Lords. He doth not say, that any of the Commons were either receivers, or tryers of petitions: nor that the petitions were to be propounded to them, but to the Lords.

Fifthly, he teacheth us, that a Knight, Citizen or Burgess, cannot make a proxy, because he is elected, and trusted by multitudes of people: here a question may be, whether a committee, if it be trusted to act anything, be not a proxy? since he saith, the high power of Parliament to be committed to a few, is holden to be against the dignity of Parliaments; and that no such commission ought to be granted.

Sixthly, he saith, The King cannot take notice of anything said, or done in the House of Commons, but by the report of the House. Surely, if the Commons sat with the Lords, and the King were present, he might take notice what was done in his presence. And I read in *Vowel*, that the old usage was, that all the degrees of Parliament sat together, and every man that had there to speak, did it openly, before the King and his whole Parliament.

In the 35 Elizabeth there was a report, that the Commons was against the subsidies, which was told the Queen: whereupon, Sir Henry Knivet said, It should be a thing answerable at the bar for any man to report anything of speeches, or matters done in the House. Sir John Woolley liked the motion of secrecy; except only the Queen, from whom, he said, there is no reason to keep anything: and Sir Robert Cecil did allow, that the council of the House should be secretly kept, and nothing reported in *malam partem*. But, if the meaning be, that they might not report anything done here to the Queen, he was altogether against it.

Seventhly, he voucheth an inditement or information in the King's Bench against thirty-nine of the Commons, for departing without licence from Parliament, contrary to the King's inhibition; whereof six submitted to their fines, and Edmund Ployden pleaded, he remained continually from the beginning to the end of the Parliament: note, he did not plead to the jurisdiction of the court of King's Bench, but pleaded his constant attendance in Parliament, which was an acknowledgment, and submitting to the jurisdiction of that court: and had been an unpardonable betraying of the privileges of Parliament by so learned a lawyer, if his case ought only to be tried in Parliament.

Eighthly, he resolves, that the House of Lords in their House have power of judicature, and the Commons in their House: and both

Houses together. He brings records to prove the power of judicature of both Houses together, but not of either of them by itself. He cites the 33 *Edw. I* for the judicature of both Houses together: where Nicholas de Segrave was adjudged *per Praelatos, Comites, et Barones, et alios de Concilio*, by the Prelates, Earls and Barons, and others of the council. Here is no mention of the judgment of the Commons. Others of the council, may mean, the King's Privy Council, or his council learned in the laws, which are called by their writs to give counsel; but so are not the Commons. The judgment itself saith, 'Nicholas de Segrave confessed his fault in Parliament, and submitted himself to the King's will: thereupon the King, willing to have the advice of the Earls, Barons, great men, and others of his council, enjoined them by the homage, fealty and allegiance which they owed, that they should faithfully counsel him what punishment should be inflicted for such a fact: who all, advising diligently, say, that such a fact deserves loss of life and members.' Thus the Lords (we see) did but advise the King what judgment to give against him that deserted the King's camp, to fight a duel in France.

Ninthly, he saith, Of later times, see divers notable judgments at the prosecution of the Commons, by the Lords: where the Commons were prosecutors, they were no judges, but (as he terms them) general inquisitors, or the grand inquest of the kingdom. The judgments he cites are but in King James's days, and no elder.

Tenthly, also he tells us, of the judicature in the House of Commons alone; his most ancient precedent is but in Queen Elizabeth's reign, of one Thomas Long, who gave the Mayor of Westbury £10 to be elected Burgess.

Eleventhly, he hath a section entitled 'The House of Commons (to many purposes) a distinct court': and saith, '*Nota*, the House of Commons to many purposes, a distinct court'; of those many purposes he tells but one, that is, it uses to adjourn itself. Commissioners that be but to examine witnesses, may adjourn themselves, yet are no court.

Twelfthly, he handles the privileges of Parliament, where the great wonder is, that this great master of the law, who hath been oft a Parliament-man, could find no other, nor more privileges of Parliament but one, and that is, freedom from arrests; which, he saith, holds, unless in three cases, treason, felony and the peace. And for this freedom from arrests, he cites ancient precedents for all those in the House of Lords, but he brings not one precedent at all for the Commons freedom from arrests.

It is behoveful for a freeholder to consider what power is in the House of Peers; for although the freeholder have no voice in the election of the Lords, yet if the power of that House extend to make ordinances that bind the freeholders, it is necessary for him to inquire what and whence that power is, and how far it reacheth. The chief writ of summon to the Peers was in these words:

Carolus Dei Gratia, etc. Reverendissimo in Christo patri G. eadem gratia Archiepiscopo Cantuariensi totius Angliae Primati et Metropolitano, salutem. Quia de advisamento et assensu Concilii nostri, pro quibusdam arduis et urgentibus negotiis, Nos et statum et defensionem regni nostri Angliae, et ecclesiae Anglicanae concernentibus, quoddam Parliamentum nostrum apud W. etc. teneri ordinavimus, et ibidem vobiscum, et cum caeteris Praelatis, Magnatibus et Proceribus dicti regni nostri Angliae colloquium habere, et tractatum: Vobis in fide, et dilectione quibus nobis te nemini firmiter injungendo mandamus, quod consideratis dictorum negotiorum arduitate, et periculis imminentibus, cessante quacunque excusatione dictis die et loco personaliter intersitis. Nobiscum et cum caeteris Praelatis, Magnatibus, et Proceribus praedictis, super dictis negotiis tractaturi, vestrumque concilium impensuri, et hoc sicut Nos et Honorem nostrum ac salvationem regni praedicti, ac ecclesiae sanctae, expeditionemque dictorum negotiorum diligitis, nullatenus omittatis; Praemonentes Decanum et Capitulum ecclesiae vestrae Cantuariensis, ac Archidiaconos, totumque Clerum vestrae Diocesis, quod idem Decanus et Archidiaconi in propriis personis suis, ac dictum Capitulum per unum, idemque Clerus per duos Procuratores idoneos, plenam et sufficientem potestatem ab ipsis Capitulo et Clero habentes, praedictis die et loco personaliter intersint, ad consentiendum hiis quae tunc ibidem de Commune Concilio ipsius Regni Nostri, divina favente Clementia, contigerint ordinari. Teste Meipso apud Westm', etc.

Charles by the Grace of God, etc. To the most Reverend Father in Christ W., by the same grace Archbishop of Canterbury, Primate and Metropolitan of all England, health. Whereas by the advice and assent of our council, for certain difficult and urgent businesses concerning us, the state, and defence of our kingdom of England, and of the English Church. We have ordained a certain Parliament of ours to be holden at W. etc., and there to have conference, and to treat with you the Prelates, great men and Peers of our said kingdom. We straitly charge and command, by the faith and love by which you are bound to us, that considering the difficulties of the businesses aforesaid, and the imminent dangers, and setting aside all excuses, you be personally present at the day and place aforesaid, to treat and give your counsel concerning the said businesses: and this, as you love us and our honour, and the safeguard of the aforesaid kingdom and Church, and the expedition of the said businesses, you must no way omit. Forewarning the dean and chapter of your Church of Canterbury, and the Archdeacons and all the Clergy of your diocese, that the same dean, and the Archdeacon in their proper persons, and the said chapter by one, and the said clergy by two fit proctors, having full and sufficient power from them the chapter and clergy, be personally present at the foresaid day and place, to consent to those things, which then and there shall happen by the favour of God, to be ordained by the common council of our kingdom. Witness ourself at Westminster.

The same form of writ, *mutatis mutandis*, concluding with, 'you must no way omit. Witness, etc.', is to the temporal Barons: but whereas the spiritual Barons are required by the faith and love; the temporal are required by their allegiance or homage.

The difference between the two writs is, that the Lords are to treat and to give counsel; the Commons are to perform and consent to what is ordained.

By this writ the Lords have a deliberative or a consultative power to treat, and give counsel in difficult businesses: and so likewise have the Judges, Barons of the exchequer, the Kings council, and the masters of the chancery, by their writs. But over and besides this power, the Lords do exercise a decisive or judicial power, which is not mentioned or found in their writ.

For the better understanding of these two different powers, we must carefully note the distinction between a judge and a counsellor in a monarchy: the ordinary duty, or office of a judge is to give judgment, and to command in the place of the King; but the ordinary duty of a counsellor is to advise the King what he himself shall do, or cause to be done: The judge represents the King's person in his absence, the counsellor in the King's presence gives his advice: judges by their commission or institution are limited their charge and power, and in such things they may judge, and cause their judgments to be put in execution: but counsellors have no power to command their consultations to be executed, for that were to take away the sovereignty from their Prince, who by his wisdom is to weigh the advice of his council, and at liberty to resolve according to the judgment of the wiser part of his council, and not always of the greater: in a word, regularly a councillor hath no power but in the King's presence, and a judge no power but out of his presence; these two powers thus distinguished, have yet such correspondency, and there is so near affinity between the acts of judging and counselling; that although the ordinary power of the judge is to give judgment: yet by their oath they are bound in causes extra-ordinary, when the King pleaseth to call them, to be his counsellors; and on the other side, although the proper work of a counsellor be only to make report of his advice to his sovereign, yet many times for the ease only, and by the permission of the King, councillors are allowed to judge and command in points wherein ordinarily they know the mind of the Prince; and what they do is the act of the royal power itself: for the council is always presupposed to be united to the person of the King, and therefore the decrees of the council are styled, by the King in his Privy Council.

To apply this distinction to the House of Peers: we find originally they are called as counsellors to the King, and so have only a delibera-tive power specified in their writ, and therefore the lords do only then properly perform the duty for which they are called, when they are in the King's presence, that he may have conference and treat with them: the very words of the writ are, Nobiscum ac cum Praelatis, Magnatibus et Proceribus praedictis super dictis negotiis tractaturi vestrumque concilium impensuri, with us and with the prelates, great men and Peers, to treat and give your counsel: the word 'Nobiscum' implieth plainly the King's presence. It is a thing in reason most absurd, to make the King assent to the judgments in Parliament, and allow him no part in the consultation; this were to make the King a subject. Council loseth the name of counsel, and becomes a command, if it put a necessity upon the King to follow it: such imperious counsels, make those that are but counsellors in name to be Kings in fact: and Kings themselves to be but subjects. We read in Sir Robert Cotton, that towards the end of the Saxons, and the first times of the Norman Kings, Parliaments stood in custom-grace fixed to Easter, Whitsuntide and Christmas; and that at the King's court, or palace, Parliaments sat in the presence, or privy chamber: from whence he infers an improba-bility to believe the King excluded his own presence; and unmannerly for guests to bar him their company who gave them their entertain-ment. And although nowadays the parliament sit not in the court where the King's household remains, yet still even to this day, to show that Parliaments are the King's guests, the lord steward of the King's household keeps a standing table to entertain the Peers during the

L

sitting of Parliament; and he alone, or some from, or under him, as the treasurer, or comptroller of the King's household takes the oaths of the members of the House of Commons the first day of the Parliament.

Sir Richard Scroop, steward of the household of our Sovereign Lord the King, by the commandment of the Lords sitting in full Parliament in the great chamber, put J. Lord Gomeniz and William Weston to answer severally to accusations brought against them (Selden).

The necessity of the King's presence in Parliament, appears by the desire of Parliaments themselves in former times; and the practice of it Sir Robert Cotton proves by several precedents: whence he concludes that in the consultations of state, and decisions of private plaints, it is clear from all times, the King was not only present to advise, but to determine also. Whensoever the King is present, all power of judging, which is derived from his, ceaseth: The votes of the Lords may serve for matter of advice, the final judgment is only the King's. Indeed, of late years, Queen Mary and Queen Elizabeth, by reason of their sex, being not so fit for public assemblies, have brought it out of use, by which means it is come to pass, that many things which were in former times acted by Kings themselves, have of late been left to the judgment of the peers; who, in quality of judges extraordinary, are permitted for the ease of the King, and in his absence, to determine such matters as are properly brought before the King himself sitting in person, attended with his great council of Prelates and Peers. And the ordinances that are made there, receive their establishment either from the King's presence in Parliament, where his chair of state is commonly placed; or at least from the confirmation of him, who in all courts, and in all causes is supreme judge. All judgment is by, or under him; it cannot be without, much less against his approbation. The King only and none but he, if he were able, should judge all causes; saith Bracton, that ancient chief justice in Henry III's time.

An ancient precedent I meet with cited by Master Selden, of a judicious proceeding in a criminal cause of the Barons before the conquest, wherein I observe the King's Will was, that the Lords should be judges, in the cause wherein himself was a party; and he ratified their proceeding: The case was thus, Earl Godwin having had a trial before the lords under King Hardicanute, touching the death of Alfred (son to King Ethelbert, and brother to him who was afterwards Edward the Confessor) had fled out of England; and upon his return, with hope of Edward the Confessor's favour, he solicited the Lords to intercede for him with the King; who (consulting together) brought Godwin with them before the King to obtain his grace and favour: but the King presently, as soon as he beheld him, said, Thou traitor Godwin, I do appeal thee of the death of my brother Alfred whom thou hast most traitorously slain; then Godwin, excusing it, answered, My Lord the King, may it please your Grace, I neither betrayed nor killed your brother, whereof I put myself upon the judgment of your court: then the King said, You noble Lords, Earls and Barons of the land, who are my liege men now gathered here together, and have heard my appeal, and Godwin's answer, I will that in this appeal between us, ye decree right judgment, and do true justice. The Earls and Barons treating of this among themselves were of differing judgments; some said, that Godwin was never bound to the King, either by homage, service or fealty, and therefore could not be his traitor, and that he had not slain Alfred with his own hands: others said, that neither Earl nor Baron, nor any other subject of the King, could wage his war by law against the King in his appeal; but must wholly put himself into the King's mercy, and offer competent amends. Then Leofric Consul of Chester, a good man before God and the world, said, Earl Godwin, next to the King, is a man of the best parentage of all England, and he cannot deny, but that by his counsel Alfred the King's brother was slain, therefore for my part I consider, that he and his son, and all we twelve Earls who are his friends and kinsmen, do go humbly before the King, laden with so much gold and silver as each of us can carry in our arms, offering him that for his offence, and humbly praying for pardon; and he will pardon the Earl, and taking his homage and fealty, will restore him all his lands. All they in this form lading themselves with treasure, and coming to the King, did show the manner and order of their consideration, to which, the King not willing to contradict, did ratify all that they had judged.

23 *Hen.* II. In Lent there was an assembly of all the spiritual and temporal Barons at Westminster, for the determination of that great contention between Alfonso, King of Castile, and Sancho, King of Navarre, touching divers castles and territories in Spain, which was by compromise submitted to the judgment of the King of England. And the King, consulting with his Bishops, Earls and Barons determined it (as he saith) himself in the first person, in the exemplification of the judgment.

2. Of King John also, that great controversy touching the barony that William of Moubray claimed against William of Stutvil, which had depended from the time of King Henry II was ended by the council of the kingdom and will of the King: Concilio Regni, et Voluntate Regis.

The Lords in Parliament adjudge William de Weston to death for surrendering Barwick Castle, but for that our Lord the King was not informed of the manner of the judgment, the constable of the tower, Allen Bruxal, was commanded safely to keep the said William until he had other commandment from our Lord the King. *4 Ric. II* (Selden).

Also the Lords adjudged John Lord of Gomeniz for surrendering the towns and castles of Ardee: and for that he was a gentleman and bannaret, and had served the late King, he should be beheaded, and. for that our Lord the King was not informed of the manner of the judgment, the execution thereof shall be respited until our Lord the King shall be informed. It is commanded to the constable of the tower, safely to keep the said John, until he hath other commandment from our Lord the King.

In the case of Henry Spencer, Bishop of Norwich, *7 Ric. II* who was accused for complying with the French, and other failings; the Bishop complained, what was done against him, did not pass by the assent and knowledge of the Peers; whereupon it was said in Parliament, that the cognisance and punishment of his offence did, of common right, and ancient custom of the realm of England, solely and wholly belong to our Lord the King, and no other: Le Cognisance et Punissement de commune droit et auntienne custome de Royalme de Engleterre, seul et per tout apperteine au Roy nostre Seigneir, et a nul autre.

In the case of the Lord de la Ware, the judgment of the Lords was, that he should have place next after the Lord Willoughby of Erisby, by consent of all, except the Lord Windsor: and the Lord Keeper was required to acquaint her Majesty with the Determination of the Peers, and to know her pleasure concerning the same.

The inference from these precedents, is, that the decisive or judicial power exercised in the chamber of Peers, is merely derivative, and subservient to the supreme power, which resides in the King, and is grounded solely upon his grace and favour; for howsoever the House of Commons do allege their power to be founded on the principles of nature, in that they are the representative body of the kingdom (as they say) and so being the whole, may take care, and have power by nature to preserve themselves: yet the House of Peers do not, nor cannot make any such the least pretence, since there is no reason in nature, why amongst a company of men who are all equal, some few should be picked out to be exalted above their fellows, and have power to govern those who by nature are their companions. The difference between a Peer and a Commoner, is not by nature, but by the grace of the Prince: who creates honours, and makes those honours to be hereditary (whereas he might have given them for life only, or during pleasure, or good behaviour) and also annexeth to those honours the power of having votes in Parliament, as hereditary councillors, furnished with ampler privileges than the commons: All these graces conferred upon the Peers, are so far from being derived from the law of nature, that they are contradictory and destructive of that natural equality and freedom of mankind, which many conceive to be the foundation of the privileges and liberties of the House of Commons; there is so strong an opposition between the liberties of grace and nature, that it had never been possible for the two houses of Parliament to. have stood together without mortal enmity,. and eternal jarring, had they been raised upon such opposite foundations: but the truth is, the liberties and privileges of both houses have but one, and the self-same foundation, which is nothing else but the mere and sole grace of Kings.

Thus much may serve to show the nature and original of the deliberative and decisive power of the Peers of the kingdom.

The matter about which the deliberative power is conversant, is generally the consulting and advising upon any urgent business which concerns the King, or defence of the kingdom: and more especially sometimes in preparing new laws; and this power is grounded upon the writ.

The decisive power is exercised in giving judgment in some difficult cases; but for this power of the Peers, I find no warrant in their writ.

Whereas the Parliament is styled the supreme court, it must be understood properly of the King sitting in the House of Peers in person; and but improperly of the Lords without him: every supreme court must have the supreme power, and the supreme power is always arbitrary; for that is arbitrary which hath no superior on earth to control it. The last appeal in all government, must still be to an arbitrary power, or else appeals will be in infinitum, never at an end. The legislative power is an arbitrary power, for they are *termini convertibiles*.

The main question in these our days, is, where this power legislative remains? or is placed; upon conference of the writs of summons for both houses, with the bodies and titles of our ancient acts of Parliament, we shall find the power of making laws rests solely in the King. Some affirm, that a part of the legislative power is in either of the houses; but besides invincible reason from the nature of monarchy itself, which must have the supreme power alone; the constant ancient declaration of this kingdom is against it. For howsoever of later years in the titles and bodies of our Acts of Parliament it be not so particularly expressed who is the author and maker of our laws, yet in almost all our elder statutes it is precisely expressed, that they are made by the King himself: the general words used of later times, that laws are made by authority of Parliament, are particularly explained in former statutes, to mean, that the King ordains, the Lords advise, the Commons consent, as by comparing the writs with the Statutes that expound the writs, will evidently appear.

Magna Charta begins thus, Henry by the Grace of God, know ye, that we of our mere and free will have given these liberties.

In the self-same style runs Charta de Foresta, and tells us the author of it.

The Statute de Scaccario 41 *Hen. III* begins in these words, the King commandeth, that all Bailiffs, Sheriffs and other Officers, etc. And concerning the justices of Chester, the King willeth, etc., and again, he commandeth the Treasurer and Barons of the Exchequer upon their allegiance.

The Statute of Marlborough, 52 *Hen. III*, goeth thus: The King hath made these Acts, Ordinances and Statutes, which he willeth to be observed of all his subjects, high and low.

3 *Edw. I.* The title of this statute is, These are the acts of King Edward; and after it follows, The King hath ordained these acts; and in the first chapter, the King forbiddeth and commandeth, that none do hurt, damage, or grievance to any religious man, or person of the Church: and in the thirteenth chapter, the King prohibiteth that none do ravish or take away by force, any maid within age.

6 *Edw. I.* It is said, our Sovereign Lord the King hath established these acts, commanding they be observed within his realm: and in the fourteenth chapter the words are, the King of his special grace granteth, that the City of London shall recover in an assize, damage with the land.

The Statute of Westminster 2. saith, Our Lord the King hath ordained, that the will of the giver be observed: and in chap. 3., Our Lord the King hath ordained, that a woman after the death of her husband shall recover by a Writ of Entry.

The Statute of *Quo Warranto* saith, Our Lord the King at his Parliament, of his special grace, and for affection which he beareth to his Prelates, Earls and Barons, and others, hath granted, that they that have Liberties by Prescription shall enjoy them.

In the Statute *de finibus Levatis*, the King's words are, We intending to provide remedy in our Parliament, have ordained, etc.

28 *Edw. I, c. 5.* The King wills, that the Chancellor, and the Justices of the Bench shall follow him, so that he may have at all times some

near unto him that be learned in the laws: and in chapter 24 the words are, Our Lord the King, after full conference and debate had with his Earls, Barons, Nobles, and other great men, by their whole consent, hath ordained, etc.

The Statute de Tallagio (if any such statute there be) speaks in the King's person, no officer of ours; no tallage shall be taken by us; we will and grant.

1 Edw. II begins thus, Our Lord the King willeth and commandeth.

The Statute of 9 the same King, saith, Our Lord the King, by the assent of the Prelates, Earls, and other great states, hath ordained.

10 Edw. II. It is provided by Our Lord the King and his Justices.

The Statute of Carlyle saith, We have sent our command in writing firmly to be observed.

1 Edw. III begins thus, King Edward III at his Parliament at the request of the Commonalty by their Petition before him, and his Council in Parliament, hath granted, etc. And in chapter 5, The King willeth, that no man be charged to arm himself otherwise than he was wont.

5 Edw. III. Our Lord the King, at the request of his people, hath established these things, which he wills to be kept.

9 Of the same King there is this title, Our Lord the King by the assent, etc., and by the advice of his Council being there, hath ordained, etc.

In his tenth year it is said, Because Our Lord King Edward III hath received by the complaint of the Prelates, Earls, Barons, also at the showing of the Knights of the Shires, and his Commons by their Petition put in his Parliament, etc. Hath ordained, by the assent, etc., at the request of the said Knights and Commons, etc.

The same year in another Parliament you may find, These be the Articles accorded by Our Lord the King, with the assent, etc., at the request of the Knights of the Shires, and the Commons by their Petition put in the said Parliament.

In the year-book 22 Edw. III, 3. pl. 25, it is said, the King makes the laws by the assent of the Peers and Commons; and not the Peers and Commons.

The Statute of 1 Ric. II hath this beginning: Richard II, by the assent of the Prelates, Dukes, Earls and Barons, and at the instance and special request of the Commons, ordained.

There being a statute made 5 Ric. II, c. 5, against Lollards, in the next year the Commons petition him, 'Supplient les Commons que come un estatute fuit fait, etc.' (The Commons beseech, that whereas a statute was made in the last Parliament, etc. which was never assented to, or granted by the Commons, but that which was done therein was done without their assent.) In this Petition the Commons acknowledge it a statute, and so call it, though they assented not to it.

17 *Ric. II, nu.* 44. The Commons desire, some pursuing to make a law which they conceive hurtful to the commonwealth; that His Majesty will not pass it.

As for the Parliaments in Henry IV's, Henry V's, Henry VI's, Edward IV's and Richard III's reigns, the most of them do agree in this one title, Our Lord the King, by the advice and assent of his Lords, and at the special instance and request of the Commons, hath ordained. The precedents in this point are so numerous, that it were endless to cite them.

The statutes in Henry VII's days do for the most part agree, both in the titles and bodies of the Acts, in these words: Our Lord the King by the assent of the Lords Spiritual and Temporal, and the Commons in Parliament assembled, and by the authority of the same hath ordained.

Unto this King's time we find the Commons very often petitioning, but not petitioned unto. The first petition made to the Commons that I meet with among the statutes, is but in the middle of this King Henry VII's reign, which was so well approved, that the petition itself is turned into a statute: It begins thus, To the Right Worshipful Commons in this present Parliament assembled: Showeth to your discreet wisdoms the wardens of the Fellowship of the Craft of Upholsterers within London, etc. This petition, though it be directed to the Commons in the title; yet the prayer of the petition is turned to the King, and not to the Commons; for it concludes, Therefore it may please the King's Highness, by the advice of the Lords Spiritual and Temporal, and his Commons, in Parliament, etc.

Next for the Statutes of Henry VIII, they do most part agree both in their titles, and the bodies of the Acts, with those of his father King Henry VII.

Lastly, in the Statutes of Edward VI, Queen Mary, Queen Elizabeth, King James, and of our Sovereign Lord the King that now is, there is no mention made in their titles of any assent of Lords and Commons, or of any ordaining by the King, but only in general terms it is said, Acts made in Parliament: or thus, At the Parliament were enacted: yet in the bodies of many of these Acts of these last Princes, there is sometimes mention made of consent of Lords and Commons, in these or the like words: It is enacted by the King, with the assent of the

Lords and Commons; Except only in the Statutes of our Lord King Charles, wherein there is no mention, that I can find, of any consent of the Lords and Commons; or ordaining by the King. But the words are, Be it enacted by authority of Parliament; or else, Be it enacted by the King, the Lords Spiritual and Temporal and Commons; as if they were all fellow-commissioners.

Thus it appears, that even till the time of King Edward VI, who lived but in our father's days, it was punctually expressed in every King's Laws, that the Statutes and Ordinances were made by the King. And withal we may see by what degrees the styles and titles of Acts of Parliament had been varied, and to whose disadvantage. The higher we look, the more absolute we find the power of Kings in ordaining laws; nor do we meet with at first so much as the assent or advice of the Lords mentioned. Nay, if we cast our eye upon many Statutes of those that be of most antiquity, they will appear as if they were no laws at all; but as if they had been made only to teach us, that the punishments of many offences were left to the mere pleasure of Kings. The punitive part of the law, which gives all the vigour and binding part to the law, we find committed by the Statutes to the King's mere will and pleasure, as if there were no law at all. I will offer a few precedents to the point.

3 *Edw. I. c.* 9. saith, That Sheriffs, Coroners and Bailiffs, for concealing of felonies shall make grievous fines at the King's pleasure.

Chap. 13. Ordains, That such as be found culpable of ravishing of women, shall fine at the King's pleasure.

Chap. 15. saith, The penalty for detaining a prisoner that is mainpernable, is a fine at the King's pleasure, or a grievous amercement to the King; and, he that shall take reward for deliverance of such, shall be at the great mercy of the King.

Chap. 20. Offenders in parks or ponds shall make fines at the King's pleasure.

Chap. 25. Committers of champerty, and extortioners are to be punished at the King's pleasure.

Chap. 31. Purveyors, not paying for what they take, shall be grievously punished at the King's pleasure.

Chap. 32. The King shall punish grievously the Sheriff, and him that doth maintain quarrels.

Chap. 37. The King shall grant attaint in plea of land where it shall seem to him necessary.

7 *Edw. I* saith, Whereas of late, before certain persons deputed to treat upon debates between us and certain great men, it was accorded

that in our next Parliament provision shall be made by us, and the common assent of the Prelates, Earls and Barons, that in all Parliaments for ever, every man shall come without force and armour. And now in our next Parliament the Prelates, Earls, Barons and Commonalty have said, That to us it belongeth, through our royal signory, straitly to defend force of armour at all times, when it shall please us, and to punish them which shall do otherwise, and hereunto they are bound to aid us their Sovereign Lord at all seasons when need shall be.

13 *Edw. I.* Takers away of nuns from religious houses, fined at the King's will.

If by the default of the Lord that will not avoid the dyke, underwoods and bushes in highways, murder be done, the Lord shall make fine at the King's pleasure.

28 *Edw. I.* If a goldsmith be attainted for not assaying, touching and working vessels of gold, he shall be punished by a ransom at the King's pleasure.

2 *Hen. IV.* The Commons desire they may have answer of their petitions before the gift of any subsidy; to which the King answers, He would confer with the Lords, and do what should be best according to their advice; and the last day of Parliament he gave this answer, That that manner of doing had not been seen, nor used in no time of his progenitors or predecessors, that they should have any answer of their petitions, or knowledge of it before they have showed, and finished all their other business of Parliament, be it of any grant, business, or otherwise, and therefore the King would not in any ways change the good customs and usages made and used of ancient times.

5 *Hen. IV, c.* 6. Whereas one Savage did beat and maim one Richard Chedder, Esquire, menial servant to Thomas Brook, Knight of the Shire for Somersetshire, the Statute saith, Savage shall make fine and ransom at the King's pleasure.

8 *Hen. IV.* It is said, 'Potestas Principis non est inclusa legibus' (the power of the Prince is not included in the laws).

13 *Hen. IV, nu.* 20. We read of a Restitution in Blood, and Lands of William Lasenby, by the King, by the assent of the Lords Spiritual, and Commons; omitting the Lords Temporal.

2 *Hen. V.* In a law made, there is a clause, That it is the King's Regality to grant or deny such of their petitions as pleaseth himself.

6 *Hen. VI, c.* 6. An Ordinance was made for to endure as long as it shall please the King.

11 *Hen. VII, c.* 1 hath this Law, 'The King our Sovereign Lord, calling to his remembrance the duty of allegiance of his subjects of this

his realm, and that by reason of the same they are bound to serve their Prince and Sovereign Lord for the time being in his wars, for the defence of him, and the land, against every rebellion, power and might reared against him, and with him to enter and abide in service in battle, if case so require; and that for the same service, what fortune ever fall by chance in the same battle, against the mind and will of the Prince (as in this land some time past hath been seen) that it is not reasonable, but against all laws, reason and good conscience, that the said subjects, going with their Sovereign Lord in wars, attending upon him in his person, or being in other places by his commandment within the land, or without, any thing should lose or forfeit, for doing their true duty and service of allegiance; be it therefore enacted, that no person that shall attend upon the King, and do him true service, shall be attainted therefore of treason, or any other offence by Act of Parliament or otherwise.'

Also chapter 18 of the same year saith, 'Where every subject by the duty of his Allegiance, is bounden to serve and assist his Prince and Sovereign Lord at all seasons, when need shall require, and bound to give attendance upon his royal person, to defend the same when he shall fortune to go in person in war for defence of the realm, or against his rebels and enemies, for the subduing and repressing of them and their malicious purpose.'

Christopher Wray, Serjeant at Law, chosen Speaker, 13 *Eliz.*, in his speech to Her Majesty, said, that for the orderly Government of the Commonwealth three things were necessary:

1. Religion
2. Authority
3. Law

'By the first, we are taught not only our duty to God, but to obey the Queen, and that not only in temporals but in spirituals, in which her power is absolute.'

Mr. Grivel in the 35 *Eliz.* said in Parliament, He wished not the making of many laws; since the more we make, the less liberty we have ourselves; Her Majesty not being bound by them.

For further proof that the legislative power is proper to the King, we may take notice, that in ancient time, as Sir Edward Coke saith, All Acts of Parliament were in form of Petitions: if the petitions were from the Commons, and the answer of them the King's, it is easy thereby to judge who made the Act of Parliament: Also Sir Jo. Glanvil affirms, that in former times the course of Petitioning the King was this, The

Lords and Speaker, either by words or writing, preferr'd their Petition to the King; this then was called the Bill of Commons, which being received by the King, part he received, part he put out, and part he ratified; for as it came from him, it was drawn into a Law.

Also it appears* that Provisions, Ordinances, and Proclamations, made heretofore out of Parliament, have been always acknowledged for Laws and Statutes: We have amongst the printed Statutes, one called the Statute of Ireland, dated at Westminster, 9 Feb. 14 *Hen. III*, which is nothing but a letter of the King to Gerard son of Maurice, Justicer of Ireland.

The explanations of the Statute of Gloucester made by the King and His Justices only, were received always for Statutes, and are still printed with them.

Also the statute made for the correction of the twelfth chapter of the Statute of Gloucester, was signed under the Great Seal, and sent to the Justices of the Bench after the manner of a Writ Patent, with a certain Writ closed, dated by the King's hand at Westminster, 2 *Maii*, 9 *Edw. I*, requiring that they should do and execute all and everything contained in it, though the same do not accord with the Statute of Gloucester in all things.

The Provisions of Merton, made by the King at an Assembly of Prelates, and the greater part of the Earls and Barons, for the coronation of the King, and his Queen Elenor, are in the form of a Proclamation, and begin, Provisum est in Curia Domini Regis apud Merton.

19 *Hen. III*, a Provision was made, *de assisa ultimae praesentationis*, which was continued and allowed for a Law until the Statute of Westminster 2, which provides the contrary in express words.

In the old statutes it is hard to distinguish what Laws were made by Kings in Parliament, and what out of Parliament: when Kings called Peers only to Parliament, and of those how many, or whom they pleased (as it appears anciently they did) it was no easy matter to put a difference between a council table and a Parliament: or between a Proclamation and a Statute: yet it is most evident, that in old times there was a distinction between the King's especial or Privy Council, and his Common Council of the Kingdom, and his special Council did sit with the Peers in Parliament, and were of great and extraordinary authority there.

In the Statute of Westminster 1, it is said, These are the Acts of King Edward I made at his first Parliament by his Council, and by the Assent

* Chanc. Egerton.

of Bishops, Abbots, Priors, Earls, Barons, and all the Commonalty of the Realm.

The Statute of Acton Burnell hath these words: The King for himself, and by his Council, hath ordained and established.

In articulis super Chartas, when the Great Charter was confirmed at the request of the Prelates, Earls and Barons, are found these two provisions:

1. Nevertheless the King and his Council do not intend by reason of this statute to diminish the King's right.

2. Notwithstanding all these things before-mentioned, or any part of them, both the King and his Council, and all they that were present, will and intend, that the right and Prerogative of his Crown shall be saved to him in all things.

The Statute of Escheators hath this title: At the Parliament of our Sovereign Lord the King, by his Council it was agreed, and also by the King himself commanded.

1 *Edw. III* where Magna Charta was confirmed, this preamble is found, 'At the request of the Commonalty, by their petition made before the King and his Council in Parliament, by the assent of the Prelates, Earls and Barons, etc.'

The statute made at York, 9 *Edw. III*, goeth thus: 'Whereas the Knights, Citizens and Burgesses desired Our Sovereign Lord the King in His Parliament by their petition, etc. Our Sovereign Lord the King, desiring the profit of his people, by the assent of his Prelates, Earls, Barons and other nobles of his realm, and by the advice of his Council being there, hath ordained.'

25 *Edw. III.* In the Statute of Purveyors, where the King, at the request of the Lords and Commons, made a declaration what offences should be adjudged treason: it is there further said, if per-case any man ride armed with men of arms against any other to slay him, or rob him, it is not the mind of the King or of his Council, that in such cases it shall be adjudged treason. By this statute it appears, that even in the case of treason, which is the King's own cause, as, whereas a man doth compass or imagine the death of our Lord the King, or a man do wage war against our Lord the King in his realm, or be adherent to the King's enemies in his realm, giving to them aid or comfort in the realm, or elsewhere; in all these cases it is the King's declaration only that makes it to be treason: and though it be said, that difficult points of treason shall be brought and shown to the King, and his Parliament, yet it is said, it is the mind of the King and his Council that determines what shall be adjudged treason, and what felony, or trespass.

27 *Edw. III.* The Commons presenting a petition to the King, which the King's Council did mislike, were content thereupon to amend and explain their petition: the petition hath these words, 'To their most redoubted Sovereign Lord the King, praying your said Commons, that whereas they have prayed him to be discharged of all manner of articles of the eyre, etc., which petition seemeth to his Council to be prejudicial unto him, and in disinherison of his Crown if it were so generally granted. His said Commons not willing nor desiring to demand things of him, or of his Crown perpetually, as of escheats, etc. But of trespasses, misprisons, negligences, ignorances, etc.'

And as in Parliaments the King's Council were of super-eminent power, so out of Parliament Kings made great use of them.

King Edward I finding that Bogo de Clare was discharged of an accusation brought against him in Parliament, commanded him nevertheless to appear before him and his Council, *ad faciendum et recipiendum quod per Regem et ejus Concilium fuerit faciendam*, and so proceeded to the examination of the whole cause, 8 *Edw. I.*

Edward III. In the Star-chamber (which was the ancient council-table at Westminster) upon the complaint of Eliz. Audley, commanded James Audley to appear before him and his Council; and determined a controversy between them, touching land contained in her jointure, *Rot. claus. de An.* 41 *Edw. III.*

Henry V. In a suit before him and his Council, for the titles of the manors of Serre and St. Lawrence in the Isle of Thanet in Kent, took order for the sequestering the profits till the right were tried.

Henry VI commanded the justices of the bench to stay the arraignment of one Verney in London, till they had other commandment from him and his Council, 34 *Hen. VI, rot.* 37 *in Banco.*

Edward IV and his Council, in the Star-chamber heard the cause of the master and poor brethren of Saint Leonards in York, complaining that Sir Hugh Hastings, and others, withdrew from them a great part of their living, which consisted chiefly upon the having of a thrave of corn of every plough-land within the counties of York, Westmorland, Cumberland and Lancashire, *Rot. pat. de an.* 8 *Edw. IV, part* 3, *memb.* 14.

Henry VII and his Council, in the Star-chamber, decreed that Margery and Florence Becket should sue no further in their cause against Alice Radley, widow, for lands in Woolwich and Plumstead in Kent, forasmuch as the matter had been heard first before the Council of Edward IV, after that before the President of the Requests of that King Henry VII and then lastly before the Council of the said King, 1 *Hen. VII.*

In the time of Henry III an order or provision was made by the King's Council, and it was pleaded at the common law in bar to a writ of dower; the plaintiffs attorney could not deny it, and thereupon the judgment was *ideo sine die.* It seems in those days an Order of the King's Council was either parcel of the common law, or above it.

Also we may find, the judges have had regard, that before they would resolve or give judgment in new cases, they consulted with the King's Privy Council.

In the case of Adam Brabson who was assaulted by R.W. in the presence of the justices of assize at Westminster, the judges would have the advice of the King's Council: for in a like case, because R.C. did strike a juror at Westminster which passed against one of his friends, it was adjudged by all the Council that his right hand should be cut off, and his lands and goods forfeited to the King.

Green and Thorp were sent by the judges to the King's Council, to demand of them whether by the Statute of 14 *Edw. III*, 16, a word may be amended in a writ; and it was answered that a word may be well amended, although the statute speaks but of a letter or syllable.

In the case of Sir Thomas Ogthred, who brought a Formedon against a poor man and his wife; they came and yielded to the demandant, which seemed suspicious to the court; whereupon judgment was staid, and Thorp said that in the like case of Giles Blacket it was spoken of in Parliament, and we were commanded that when any like should come we should not go to judgment without good advice; therefore the judges conclusion was, 'Sues au counseil et comment ils voilent que nous devomus faire, nous volums faire, et autrement nient en cest case'; sue to the Council, and as they will have us to do, we will do; and otherwise not in this case, 39 *Edw. III.*

Thus we see the judges themselves were guided by the King's Council, and yet the opinions of judges have guided the Lords in Parliament in point of law.

All the Judges of the realm, Barons of exchequer, of the quoif, the King's learned Council, and the civilians, masters of chancery, are called temporal assistants by Sir Edward Coke, and though he deny them voices in Parliament, yet he confesseth, that by their writ they have power both to treat, and to give council. I cannot find that the Lords have any other power by their writ: the words of the Lord's writ are, that you be present with us, the Prelates, great men and Peers, to treat and give your counsel. The words of the judges writ are, That you be present with us, and others of the Council (and sometimes with us only) to treat and give your Council.

The judges usually joined in committees with the Lords in all Parliaments, even in Queen Elizabeth's reign, until her thirty-ninth year; and then upon November 7th the judges were appointed to attend the Lords. And whereas the judges have liberty in the upper House itself, upon leave given them by the Lord's Keeper, to cover themselves, now at committees they sit always uncovered.

The power of judges in Parliament is best understood, if we consider how the judicial power of peers hath been exercised in matter of judicature: we may find it hath been the practice, that though the Lords in the King's absence give judgment in point of law, yet they are to be directed and regulated by the King's judges, who are best able to give direction in the difficult points of the law; which ordinarily are unknown to the Lords. And therefore, if any error be committed in the King's Bench, which is the highest ordinary court of common law in the kingdom, that error must be redressed in Parliament. And the manner is, saith the Lord Chancellor Egerton, if a writ of error be sued in Parliament upon a judgment given by the judges in the King's Bench, the Lords of the higher House alone (without the Commons) are to examine the errors. The Lords are to proceed according to the law, and for their judgments therein they are to be informed by the advice and counsel of the judges, who are to inform them what the law is, and to direct them in their judgment; for the Lords are not to follow their own discretion or opinion otherwise.

28 *Hen. VI.* The Commons made suit that W. de la Pool, Duke of Suffolk, should be committed to prison for many treasons, and other crimes; the Lords of the higher House were doubtful what answer to give; the opinion of the judges was demanded, their opinion was, that he ought not to be committed, for that the Commons did not charge him with any particular offence, but with general reports and slanders: this opinion was allowed.

31 *Hen. VI.* A Parliament being prorogued, in the vacation the Speaker of the House of Commons was condemned in a thousand pounds damages in an action of trespass, and committed to prison in execution for the same: when the Parliament was re-assembled, the Commons made suit to the King and Lords, to have their Speaker delivered. The Lords demanded the opinion of the judges, whether he might be delivered out of prison by privilege of Parliament; upon the judges' answer it was concluded, that the Speaker should remain in prison according to the law, notwithstanding the privilege of Parliament, and that he was Speaker; which resolution was declared to the Commons by Moyle the King's Serjeant at Law, and the Commons

were commanded in the King's name by the Bishop of Lincoln (in the absence of the Archbishop of Canterbury, then Chancellor) to choose another Speaker.

7 *Hen. VIII.* A question was moved in Parliament, whether spiritual persons might be convented before temporal judges for criminal causes? There Sir John Fineux, and the other judges delivered their opinion, that they might and ought to be; and their opinion allowed and maintained by the King and Lords, and Dr. Standish, who before had holden the same opinion, was delivered from the bishops.

I find it affirmed, that in causes which receive determination in the House of Lords, the King hath no vote at all, no more than in other courts of ministerial jurisdiction. True it is, the King hath no vote at all, if we understand by vote a voice among others: for he hath no partners with him in giving judgment. But if by no vote is meant he hath no power to judge; we despoil him of his sovereignty: it is the chief mark of supremacy to judge in the highest causes, and last appeals. This the Children of Israel full well understood, when they petitioned for a King to judge them; if the *dernier resort* be to the Lords alone, then they have the supremacy. But as Moses by choosing elders to judge in small causes, did not thereby lose his authority to be judge himself when he pleased, even in the smallest matters; much less in the greatest, which he reserved to himself: so Kings by delegating others to judge under them, do not hereby denude themselves of a power to judge when they think good.

There is a distinction of these times, that Kings themselves may not judge, but they may see and look to the judges, that they give judgment according to law; and for this purpose only (as some say) Kings may sometimes sit in the courts of justice. But it is not possible for Kings to see the laws executed, except there be a power in Kings both to judge when the laws are duly executed, and when not; as also to compel the judges if they do not their duty. Without such power a King sitting in courts is but a mockery, and a scorn to the judges. And if this power be allowed to Kings, then their judgments are supreme in all courts. And indeed our common law to this purpose doth presume that the King hath all laws within the cabinet of his breast, in *Scrinio pectoris*, saith Crompton's Jurisdiction, 108.

When several of our statutes leave many things to the pleasure of the King, for us to interpret all those statutes of the will and pleasure of the King's Justices only, is to give an absolute arbitrary power to the justices in those cases wherein we deny it to the King.

The Statute of 5 *Hen. IV, c.* 2 makes a difference between the King,

M

and the King's Justices, in these words, 'Divers notorious felons be indicted of divers felonies, murders, rapes: and as well before the King's Justices, as before the King himself, arraigned of the same felonies.'

I read that in 1256 Henry III sat in the Exchequer, and there set down order for the appearance of Sheriffs, and bringing in their accounts; there was five marks set on every Sheriff's head for a fine, because they had not distrained every person that might dispend fifteen pounds lands by the year, to receive the order of knighthood, according as the same Sheriff's were commanded.

In Michaelmas Term, 1462, Edward IV sat three days together in open court in the King's Bench.

For this point there needs no further proofs, because Mr. Pryn doth confess that Kings themselves have sat in person in the King's Bench, and other courts, and there given judgment, p. 32. Treachery and Disloyalty, etc.

Notwithstanding all that hath been said for the legislative and judicial power of Kings, Mr. Pryn is so far from yielding the King a power to make laws, that he will not grant the King a power to hinder a law from being made; that is, he allows him not a negative voice in most cases, which is due to every other, even to the meanest member of the House of Commons in his judgment.

To prove the King hath not a negative voice, his main, and in truth, his only argument insisted on, is a Coronation Oath, which is said anciently some of our Kings of England have taken, wherein they grant to defend and protect the just laws and customs, which the vulgar hath, or shall choose: *justas Leges et Consuetudines quas Vulgus elegerit*: hence Mr. Pryn concludes, that the King cannot deny any law which the Lords and Commons shall make choice of; for so he will have *vulgus* to signifie.

Though neither our King, nor many of his predecessors ever took this oath, nor were bound to take it, for ought appears; yet we may admit that our King hath taken it; and answer, we may be confident, that neither the Bishops, nor Privy Council, nor Parliament, nor any other, whosoever they were, that framed or penned this oath, ever intended in this word *Vulgus*, the Commons in Parliament, much less the Lords: they would never so much disparage the Members of Parliament, as to disgrace them with a title both base and false: it had been enough, if not too much, to have called them *Populus*, the people; but *Vulgus* the vulgar, the rude multitude (which hath the epithet of *Ignobile Vulgus*) is a word as dishonorable to the composers of the oath to give, or for the King to use, as for the Members of the Parliament to receive; it being most false: for the Peers cannot be *Vulgus*, because they are the prime persons of the kingdom: next, the Knights of the Shires are, or ought to be notable knights, or notable esquires, or gentlemen born in the counties, as shall be able to be Knights: then the Citizens and Burgesses are to be most sufficient, none of these can be *Vulgus*: even those freeholders that choose Knights, are the best and ablest men of their counties; there being for every freeholder, above ten of the common people to be found to be termed the vulgar. Therefore it rests that *Vulgus* must signify the vulgar or common people, and not the Lords and Commons.

But now the doubt will be, what the common people, or *Vulgus*, out of Parliament, have to do to choose laws? The answer is easy and ready; there goeth before *quas vulgus*, the antecedent *Consuetudines*, that is, the customs which the vulgar hath, or shall choose. Do but observe the nature of custom, and it is the *Vulgus* or common people only who choose customs: common usage time out of mind creates a custom; and the commoner a usage is, the stronger and the better is the custom: nowhere can so common a usage be found, as among the vulgar, who are still the far greatest part of every multitude: if a custom be common through the whole kingdom, it is all one with the common law in England, which is said to be common custom. Thus in plain terms, to protect the customs which the vulgar choose, is to swear to protect the common laws of England.

But grant that *Vulgus* in the oath, signifies Lords and Commons, and that *Consuetudines* doth not signify customs, but statutes (as Mr. Pryn, for a desperate shift affirms) and let *elegerit* be the future, or preter-perfect tense, even which Mr. Pryn please, yet it cannot exclude the King's negative voice; for as *Consuetudines* goeth before *quas vulgus*, so doth *justas* stand before *leges et consuetudines*: so that not all laws, but only all just laws are meant. If the sole choice of the Lords and Commons did oblige the King to protect their choice, without power of denial, what need, or why is the word *justas* put in, to raise a scruple that some laws may be unjust? Mr. Pryn will not say that a decree of a general council or of a Pope is infallible, nor (I think) a Bill of the Lords and Commons is infallibly just, and impossible to err; if he do, Sir Edward Coke will tell him, that Parliaments have been utterly deceived, and that in cases of greatest moment, even in case of high treason: and he calls the Statute of 11 *Hen. VII* an unjust and strange act. But it may be Mr. Pryn will confess, that laws chosen by the Lords and Commons may be unjust, so that the Lords and Commons themselves may be the judges of what is just or unjust. But where the King by oath binds his conscience to protect just laws, it concerns him to be satisfied in his own conscience, that they be just, and not by an implicit faith, or blind obedience: no man can be so proper a judge of the justness of laws, as he whose soul must lie at the stake for the defence and safeguard of them.

Besides, in this very oath the King doth swear, to do equal and right justice and discretion in mercy and truth in all his judgments: facies fieri in omnibus judiciis tuis aequam et rectam justitiam et discretionem in Misericordia et Veritate: if we allow the King discretion and mercy in his judgments, of necessity he must judge of the justness of the laws.

Again, the clause of the oath, *quas vulgus elegerit,* doth not mention the assenting unto, or granting any new laws, but of holding, protecting, and strengthening with all his might, the just laws that were already in being: there were no need of might or strength, if assenting to new laws were there meant.

Some may wonder why there should be such labouring to deny the King a negative voice, since a negative voice is in itself so poor a thing, that if a man had all the negative voices in the kingdom, it would not make him a King; nor give him power to make one law: a negative voice is but a privative power, that is, no power at all to do or act anything; but a power only to hinder the power of another. Negatives are of such a malignant or destructive nature, that if they have nothing else to destroy, they will, when they meet, destroy one another, which is the reason why two negatives make an affirmative, by destroying the negation which did hinder the affirmation. A king with a negative voice only, is but like a syllogism of pure negative propositions, which can conclude nothing. It must be an affirmative voice that makes both a King, and a law, and without it there can be no imaginable government.

The reason is plain why the King's negative voice is so eagerly opposed; for though it gives the King no power to do anything; yet it gives him a power to hinder others: though it cannot make him a King, yet it can help him to keep others from being Kings.

For conclusion of this discourse of the negative voice of the King, I shall oppose the judgment of a Chief Justice of England; to the opinion of him that calls himself an utter Barrister of Lincolns Inn, and let others judge who is the better lawyer of the two: the words are Bracton's, but concern Mr. Pryn to lay them to heart. 'Concerning the charters and deeds of Kings, the justices nor private men neither ought, nor can dispute; nor yet if there rise a doubt in the King's

Charter, can they interpret it; and in doubtful and obscure points, or if a word contain two senses, the interpretation, and will of our Lord the King is to be expected, seeing it is his part to interpret, who makes the charter.' Full well Mr. Pryn knows, that when Bracton wrote, the laws that were then made, and strived for, were called the King's charters, as Magna Charta, Charta de Foresta, and others: so that in Bracton's judgment the King hath not only a negative voice to hinder, but an affirmative, to make a law, which is a great deal more than Master Pryn will allow him.

Not only the law-maker, but also the sole judge of the people is the King, in the judgment of Bracton; these are his words: Rex et non alius debet judicare, si solus ad id sufficere possit, the King and no other ought to judge, if he alone were able. Much like the words of Bracton, speaketh Briton, where, after that he had showed that the King is the Viceroy of God, and that he hath distributed his charge into sundry portions, because he alone is not sufficient to hear all complaints of his people, then he addeth these words, in the person of the King: Nous volons que nostre jurisdiction soit sur touts Jurisdictions, etc. We will that our jurisdiction be above all the jurisdictions of our realm, so as in all manner of felonies, trespasses, contracts, and in all other actions personal or real, we have power to yield, or cause to be yielded, such judgments as do appertain without other process, wheresoever we know the right truth as judges.

Neither was this to be taken, saith Mr. Lambard, to be meant of the King's Bench, where there is only an imaginary presence of his person, but it must necessarily be understood of a jurisdiction remaining and left in the King's royal body and breast, distinct from that of his bench, and other ordinary courts; because he doth immediately after, severally set forth by themselves, as well the authority of the King's Bench, as of the other courts.

And that this was no new made law, Mr. Lambard puts us in mind of a Saxon law of King Edgar. Nemo in lite Regem appellato, etc. Let no man in suit appeal unto the King, unless he cannot get right at home, but if that right be too heavy for him, then let him go to the King to have it eased. By which it may evidently appear, that even so many years ago there might be appellation made to the King's person, whensoever the cause should enforce it.

The very like law in effect is to be seen in the laws of Canutus the Dane, sometimes King of this realm, out of which law Master Lambard gathers, that the King himself had a High Court of Justice, wherein it seemeth he sat in person; for the words be, 'Let him not seek to the

King', and the same court of the King did judge not only according to mere right and law, but also after equity and good conscience.

For the close, I shall end with the suffrage of our late antiquary Sir Henry Spelman. In his *Glossary* he saith, 'Omnis Regni Justitia solius Regis est,' etc. All justice of the kingdom is only the King's, and he alone, if he were able, should administer it; but that being impossible, he is forced to delegate it to ministers, whom he bounds by the limits of the laws; the positive laws are only about generals; in particular cases, they are sometimes too strict, sometimes too remiss; and so, oft wrong instead of right will be done, if we stand to strict law: also causes hard and difficult daily arise, which are comprehended in no law-books, in those there is a necessity of running back to the King, the fountain of justice, and the vicegerent of God himself, who in the commonwealth of the Jews took such causes to his own cognisance, and left to Kings not only the example of such jurisdiction, but the prerogative also.

OF PRIVILEGE OF PARLIAMENTS

WHAT need all this ado, will some say, to sift out what is comprised in the writ for the election of the Commons to Parliament, since it is certain, though the writ doth not, yet privilege of Parliament gives sufficient power for all proceedings of the two Houses? It is answered, that what slight esteem soever be made of the writ, yet in all other cases the original writ is the foundation of the whole business, or action: and to vary in substance from the writ, makes a nullity in the cause, and the proceedings thereupon: and where a commissioner exerciseth more power than is warranted by his commission, every such act is void, and in many cases punishable: yet we will lay aside the writ, and apply ourselves to consider the nature of privilege of Parliament. The task is the more difficult, for that we are not told what the number of privileges are, or which they be; some do think that as there be dormant articles of faith in the Roman Church, which are not yet declared; so there be likewise privileges dormant in the House of Commons, not yet revealed, we must therefore be content in a generality to discourse of the quality or condition of privilege of Parliament, and to confine ourselves to these three points:

1. The privilege of Parliament gives no power; but only helps to the execution of the power given by the writ.

2. That the freeholders by their elections give no privilege.

3. That privilege of Parliament is the gift of the King.

First, the end or scope of privilege of Parliament is not to give any power to do any public act, not warranted by the writ: but they are intended as helps only to enable to the performance of the duty enjoined, and so are subservient to the power comprised in the writ: for instance, the grand privilege of freedom from arrests doth not give any power at all to the House of Commons to do any act; but by taking away from the freeholders and other subjects the power of arrests, the Commons are the better enabled to attend the service to which they are called by the King.

In many other cases the servants, or ministers of the King are privileged, and protected much in the same nature. The servants in household to the King may not be arrested without special licence: also the officers of the Kings Courts of Justice, having a privilege not to be sued in any other court but where they serve and attend; and to this purpose they are allowed a writ of privilege. Likewise all such as serve the King in his wars, as are employed on foreign affairs for him, are protected from actions and suits. Nay the King's protection descends to the privileging even of laundresses, nurses and midwives, if they attend upon the camp, as Sir Edward Coke saith, *quia Lotrix, seu Nutrix, seu obstetrix.* Besides the King protects his debtors from arrests of the subject till his own debts be paid.

These sorts of protections are privileges the common law takes notice of, and allows: and hath several distinctions of them; and some are protections, *quia profecturus,* and others are, *quia moraturus:* some are with a clause of *Volumus* for stay of suits: others with a clause of *Nolumus* for the safety of men's persons, servants and goods: and the King's writs do vary herein according to the nature of the business.

But none of these privileges or protections do give any power; they are not positive, but privative: they take away and deprive the subject of the power, or liberty to arrest, or sue, in some cases only; no protection or privilege doth defend in point of treason, felony or breach of the peace: privileges are directly contrary to the law, for otherwise they should not be privileges, and they are to be interpreted in the strictest manner, as being odious and contrary to law: we see the use of privileges; they do but serve as a dispensation against law, intended originally, and principally for the expediting of the King's business; though secondarily, and by accident there do sometimes redound a benefit by them to the parties themselves that are protected. Strictly and properly every privilege must be against a public or common law, for there is no use or need of a private law to protect, where there is no public law to the contrary: favours and graces which are only besides, and not against the law, do not properly go under the name of privileges, though common use do not distinguish them: I know no other privilege that can be truly so called, and to belong to the House of Commons, which is so vast and great, as this privilege of their persons, servants and goods: this being indeed against the common law, and doth concern the whole kingdom to take notice of it, if they must be bound by it.

Touching this grand privilege of freedom from arrests, I read, that in 33 *Hen. VIII*, the Commons did not proceed to the punishment of offenders for the breach of it, until the Lords referred the punishment thereof to the Lower House. The case is thus reported, George Ferrers, gentleman, servant to the King, and Burgess for Plymouth, going to the Parliament House was arrested in London, by process out of the King's Bench for debt, wherein he had before been condemned as surety for one Welden, at the suit of one White: which arrest, signified to Sir Thomas Moyl, Speaker, and to the rest; the Serjeant (called Saint-Johns) was sent to the Counter in Bread Street to demand Ferrers: the officer of the counter refused to deliver him, and gave the Serjeant such ill language, that they fall to an affray: the Sheriff coming, taketh the officer's part, the Serjeant returned without the prisoner. This being related to the Speaker and Burgesses, they would sit no more without their Burgess; and rising, repaired to the Upper House, where the case was declared by the Speaker before Sir Thomas Audley, Chancellor, and the Lords and judges there assembled, who judging the contempt to be very great, referred the punishment thereof to the House of Commons itself.

This privilege of freedom from arrests is the only privilege which Sir Edward Coke finds to belong to the House of Commons; he cannot, or at least he doth not, so much as name any other in his section of the privileges of Parliament: neither doth he bring so much as one precedent for the proof of this one privilege for the House of Commons; which may cause a doubt that this sole privilege is not so clear as many do imagine. For in a Parliament in the 27 Elizabeth, Richard Coke, a member, being served with a Subpoena of Chancery, the Lord Chancellor thought the House had no such privilege for subpoenas as they pretended; neither would he allow of any precedents of the House committed unto them, formerly used in that behalf, unless the House of Commons could also prove the same to have been likewise thereupon allowed, and ratified also by precedents in the Court of Chancery.

In the 39 Elizabeth, Sir Edward Hobby, and Mr. Brograve, Attorney of the Duchy, were sent by the House to the Lord Keeper, in the name of the whole House, to require his lordship to revoke two writs of subpoenas, which were served upon Mr. Thomas Knevit, a Member of the House since the beginning of Parliament. The Lord Keeper demanded of them whether they were appointed by any advised consideration of the House, to deliver this message unto him with the word required, in such manner as they had done, or no: they answered his lordship, yea: his lordship then said, as he thought reverently and honourably of the House, and of their liberties, and privileges of the same, so to revoke the said subpoenas in that sort, was to restrain Her Majesty in her greatest power, which is, justice in the place wherein he serveth under her, and therefore he concluded, as they required him to revoke his writ, so he did require to deliberate.

Upon February 22nd, being Wednesday, 18 Elizabeth, report was made by Mr. Attorney of the Duchy, upon the committee, for the delivering of one Mr. Hall's man; that the committee found no precedent for setting at large by the Mace any person in arrest but only by writ, and that by divers precedents of records perused by the said committee, it appeareth that every Knight, Citizen or Burgess, which doth require privilege, hath used in that case to take a corporal oath before the Lord Chancellor, or Lord Keeper, that the party for whom such writ is prayed, came up with him, and was his servant at the time of the arrest made. Thereupon Mr. Hall was moved by the House to repair to the Lord Keeper, and make oath, and then take a warrant for a writ of privilege for his servant.

It is accounted by some to be a privilege of Parliament to have power to examine misdemeanours of courts of justice, and officers of state: yet there is not the meanest subject but hath liberty, upon just cause, to question the misdemeanour of any court or officer, if he suffer by them; there is no law against him for so doing; so that this cannot properly be called a privilege, because it is not against any public law: it hath been esteemed a great favour of princes to permit such examinations: for, when the Lords were displeased with the greatness of Pierce Gaveston, it is said, that in the next Parliament, the whole assembly obtain of the King to draw articles of their grievances, which they did. Two of which articles were, first, that all strangers should be banished the court and kingdom: of which Gaveston was one. Secondly, that the business of the state should be treated of by the council of the clergy and nobles.

In the reign of King Henry VI, one Mortimer, an instrument of the Duke of York, by promising the Kentish men a reformation, and freedom from taxations, wrought with the people, that they drew to a head, and made this Mortimer (otherwise Jack Cade) their leader: who styled himself Captain Mend-all: he presents to the Parliament the complaints of the Commons, and he petitions that the Duke of York and some other lords might be received by the King into favour, by the undue practices of Suffolk and his complices, commanded from his presence; and that all their opposites might be banished the court, and put from their offices, and that there might be a general amotion of corrupt officers: these petitions are sent from the Lower House to the Upper, and from thence committed to the Lords of the King's Privy Council, who, having examined the particulars, explode them as frivolous, and the authors of them to be presumptuous rebels.

Concerning liberty, or freedom of speech, I find that at a Parliament at Black Friars in the 14 Henry VIII, Sir Thomas More being chosen Speaker of the House of Commons: he first disabled himself, and then petitioned the King, that if in communication and reasoning, any man in the Commons House should speak more largely than of duty they ought to do, that all such offences should be pardoned, and to be entered of record; which was granted. It is observable in this petition that liberty or freedom of speech is not a power for men to speak what they will, or please, in Parliament; but a privilege not to be punished, but pardoned for the offence of speaking more largely than in duty ought to be; which in an equitable construction must be understood of rash, unadvised, ignorant, or negligent escapes, and slips in speech; and not for wilful, malicious offences in that kind; and then the pardon of the King was desired to be upon record, that it might be pleaded in bar to all actions. And it seemeth that Richard Strood and his complices, were not thought sufficiently protected for their free speech in Parliament, unless their pardon were confirmed by the King in Parliament; for there is a printed statute to that purpose in Henry VIII's time.

Touching the freedom of speech, the Commons were warned in Queen Elizabeth's days not to meddle with the Queen's Person, the State, or Church-government. In her time the discipline of the Church was so strict, that the Litany was read every morning in the House of Commons, during the Parliament, and when the Commons first ordered to have a fast in the Temple, upon a Sunday, the Queen hindered it.

Saturday, January 21st, 23 Elizabeth, the case is thus reported: Mr. Peter Wentworth moveth for a public set fast, and for a preaching every morning at seven of the clock, before the House sat: the House was divided about the fast, 115 were for it, and 100 against it; it was ordered, that as many of the House as conveniently could, should on Sunday fortnight after, assemble, and meet together in the Temple· Church, there to hear preaching, and to join together in prayer, with humiliation and fasting, for the assistance of God's Spirit in all their consultations, during this Parliament, and for the preservation of the Queen's Majesty and her realms: and the preachers to be appointed by the Privy Council that were of the House, that they may be discreet, not meddling with innovation or unquietness. This order was followed by a message from Her Majesty to the House, declared by Mr. Vice-chamberlain, that Her Highness had a great admiration of the rashness of this House, in committing such an apparent contempt of her express command, as to put in execution such an innovation, without her privity, or pleasure first known. Thereupon Mr. Vice-chamberlain moved the House to make humble submission to Her Majesty, acknow-ledging the said offence and contempt, craving a remission of the same, with a full purpose to forbear the committing of the like hereafter: and by the consent of the whole House, Mr. Vice-chamberlain carried their submission to her Majesty.

35 Elizabeth, Mr. Peter Wentworth and Sir Henry Bromley de-livered a petition to the Lord Keeper, desiring the Lords of the Upper House to be suppliants with them of the Lower House, unto her Majesty, for entailing the succession of the Crown. Whereof a Bill was ready drawn by them. Her Majesty was highly displeased here-with, as contrary to her former strait command, and charged the Council to call the parties before them: Sir Thomas Henage sent for them, and after speech with them, commanded them to forbear the Parliament, and not to go out of their several lodgings; after, they were called before the Lord Treasurer, the Lord Buckhurst and Sir Thomas Henage; Mr. Wentworth was committed by them to the Tower, Sir Henry Bromley, with Mr. Richard Stephens, to whom Sir Henry Bromley had imparted the matter, were sent to the Fleet, as also Mr. Welch, the other Knight for Worcestershire.

In the same Parliament, Mr. Morrice, Attorney of the Court of Wards, moved against the hard courses of the Bishops, ordinaries and other ecclesiastical judges in their courts, used towards sundry learned, and godly ministers and preachers; and spake against subscriptions and oaths; and offered a Bill to be read against imprisonment for refusal of oaths: Mr. Dalton opposed the reading of it, as a thing expressly against Her Majesty's command, to meddle in: Doctor Lewin showed, that subscription was used even at Geneva: at two of the clock the same day, the Speaker, Mr. Coke (afterwards Sir Edward Coke), was sent for to the court, where the Queen herself gave him in command a message to the House: she told him, it being wholly in her power to call, to determine, to assent, or dissent to anything done in Parliament: that the calling of this was only, that the majesty of God might be more religiously observed, by compelling, by some sharp laws, such as neglect that service: and that the safety of Her Majesty's person, and the realm might be provided for: it was not meant they should meddle with matters of state, or causes ecclesiastical (for so Her Majesty termed them) she wondered that any could be of so high command-ment, to attempt (they were Her own words) a thing so expressly contrary to that which she had commanded: wherefore with this she was highly offended: and because the words spoken by my Lord Keeper are not now perhaps well remembered, or some be now here that were not then present. Her Majesty's present charge and express command is, that no Bill touching the said matter of state, or reformation in causes ecclesiastical, be exhibited; and upon my allegiance (saith Mr. Coke) I am charged, if any such Bill be exhibited, not to read it. I have been credibly informed, that the Queen sent a messenger or serjeant-at-arms, into the House of Commons, and took out Mr. Morrice, and committed him to prison: within few days after, I find Mr. Wroth moved in the House, that they might be humble suitors to Her Majesty, that she would be pleased to set at liberty those Members of the House that were restrained. To this it was answered by the Privy Councillors, that Her Majesty had committed them for causes best known to herself, and to press Her Highness with this suit, would but hinder them whose good is sought: that the House must not call the Queen to account for what she doth of Her Royal Authority: that the causes for which they are restrained may be high and dangerous: that Her Majesty liketh no such questions; neither doth it become the House to search into such matters.

In the 39 Elizabeth, the Commons were told their privilege was Yea and No: and that Her Majesty's pleasure was, that if the Speaker perceived any idle heads which would not stick to hazard their own estates; which will meddle with reforming the Church, and transform-ing the commonweal, and do exhibit Bills to that purpose; the Speaker should not receive them till they were viewed and considered by those, whom it is fitter should consider of such things, and can better judge of them: and at the end of this Parliament, the Queen refused to pass forty-eight Bills which had passed both Houses.

In the 28 Elizabeth, the Queen said, 'She was sorry the Commons meddled with choosing and returning Knights of the Shire for Norfolk, a thing impertinent for the House to deal with, and only belonging to the office and charge of the Lord Chancellor, from whom the writs issue and are returned'.

4 *Hen. IV.* October 10th, the Chancellor before the King declared, the Commons had sent to the King, praying him that they might have advice and communication with certain Lords about matters of business in Parliament, for the common good of the realm: which prayer Our Lord the King graciously granted, making protestation, he would not do it of duty, nor of custom, but of his special grace at this time: and therefore Our Lord the King charged the Clerk of the Parliament, that this protestation should be entered on record upon the Parliament-Roll: which the King made known to them by the Lord Say, and his secretary; how that neither of due nor of custom, our Lord the King ought to grant any Lords to enter into communication with them, of matters touching the Parliament; but by his special grace at this time he hath granted their request in this particular: upon which matter, the said steward and secretary made report to the King in Parliament; that the said Commons knew well that they could not have any such Lords to commune with them, of any business of Parliament, without special grace and command of the King himself.

It hath heretofore been a question, whether it be not an infringing and prejudice to the liberties and privileges of the House of Commons, for them to join in conference with the Lords in cases of benevolence, or contribution, without a Bill.

In 35 Elizabeth, on Tuesday, March 1st, Mr. Egerton, Attorney General, and Doctor Cary came with a message from the Lords; their Lordships desired to put the House in remembrance of the speech delivered by the Lord Keeper, the first day, for consultation and provision of treasure, to be had against the great and imminent dangers of the realm; thereupon their Lordships did look to have something from the Houses, touching those causes before this time (and yet the Parliament had sat but three days, for it began February 26th), and therefore their Lordships had hitherto omitted to do anything therein themselves. And thereupon their Lordships desired, that according to former laudable usages between both Houses in such like cases, a committee of Commons may have conference with a committee of Lords, touching provision of treasure against the great dangers of the realm, which was presently resolved by the whole House, and they signified to their Lordships the willing, and ready assent of the whole House. At the meeting, the Lords negatively affirm, not to assent to less than three subsidies, and do insist for a second conference. Mr. Francis Bacon yielded to the subsidy, but opposed the joining with the Lords, as contrary to the privileges of the House of Commons; thereupon the House resolved to have no conference with the Lords, but to give their Lordships most humble and dutiful thanks with all reverence for their favourable and courteous offer of conference, and to signify, that the Commons cannot in those cases of benevolence, or contribution join in conference with their Lordships, without prejudice to the liberties and privileges of the House: and to request their Lordships to hold the members of this House excused in their not assenting to their Lordships, said motion for conference, for that so to have assented without a Bill, had been contrary to the liberties and privileges of this House, and also contrary to the former precedents of the same House in like cases had. This answer delivered to the Lords by the Chancellor of the Exchequer, their Lordships said, they well hoped to have had a conference according to their former request, and desired to see those precedents by which the Commons seem to refuse the said conference. But in conclusion it was agreed unto, upon the motion of Sir Walter Raleigh; who moved, that without naming a subsidy, it might be propounded in general words, to have a conference touching the dangers of the realm, and the necessary supply of treasure to be provided speedily for the same, according to the proportion of the necessity.

In 43 Elizabeth Serjeant Heal said in Parliament, he marvelled the House stood either at the granting of a subsidy or time of payment, when all we have is her Majesty's, and she may lawfully at her pleasure take it from us; and that she had as much right to all our lands and goods, as to any revenue of the crown; and he said he could prove it by precedents in the time of Henry III, King John and King Stephen. The ground upon which this serjeant-at-law went, may be thought the same Sir Edward Coke delivers in his *Institutes*, where he saith, 'the first Kings of this realm had all the lands of England in demesne, and the great manors and royalties they reserved to themselves, and of the remnant for the defence of the kingdom, enfeoffed the Barons': from whence it appears, that no man holds any lands but under a condition to defend the realm; and upon the self-same ground also the King's prerogative is raised, as being a pre-eminence, in cases of necessity, above, and before the law of property, or inheritance. Certain it is, before the Commons were ever chosen to come to Parliament, taxes or subsidies were raised and paid without their gift. The great and long continued subsidy of Dane-gelt was without any gift of the Commons, or of any Parliament at all, that can be proved. In 8 *Hen. III* a subsidy of 2 marks in silver upon every Knight's fee was granted to the King by the Nobles, without any Commons. At the passing of a Bill of Subsidies, the words of the King are, 'the King thanks his loyal subjects, accepts their good will, and also will have it so: le Roy remercie ses loyaux Subjects, accept leur benevolence, et ausi ainsi le veult': which last words of *ainsi le veult*, 'the King wills it to be so', are the only words that makes the Act of Subsidy a law to bind every man to the payment of it.

In 39 Elizabeth, the Commons, by their Speaker, complaining of monopolies, the Queen spake in private to the Lord Keeper, who then made answer touching monopolies, that Her Majesty hoped her dutiful and loving subjects would not take away her prerogative, which is the chiefest flower in her garland, and the principal and head pearl in her crown and diadem; but that they will rather leave that to her disposition.

The second point is, that the freeholders, or counties do not, nor cannot give privilege to the Commons in Parliament. They that are under the law cannot protect against it, they have no such privilege themselves, as to be free from arrests and actions: for if they had, then it had been no privilege, but it would be the common law: and what they have not, they cannot give; *Nemo dat quod non habet*, neither do the freeholders pretend to give any such privilege, either at their election, or by any subsequent act; there is no mention of any such thing in the return of the writ; nor in the indentures between the Sheriff, and the freeholders.

The third point remains: That privilege of Parliament is granted by the King. It is a known rule, that which gives the form, give the consequences of the form; the King by his writ gives the very essence and form to the Parliament: therefore privileges, which are but consequences of the form, must necessarily flow from Kings.

All other privileges and protections are the acts of the King; and by the King's writ. Sir Edward Coke saith, that the 'Protection of men's persons, servants and goods, is done by a writ of grace from the King'. At the presentment of the Speaker of the House of Commons to the King upon the first day of Parliament, the Speaker in the name and behoof of the Commons, humbly craveth that his Majesty would be graciously pleased to grant them their accustomed liberties and privileges; which petition of theirs, is a fair recognition of the primitive grace and favour of Kings in bestowing of privilege, and it is a shrewd argument against any other title: for our ancestors were not so ceremonious nor so full of complement, as to beg that by grace, which they might claim by right. And the renewing of this petition every Parliament, argues the grant to be but temporary, during only the present Parliament; and that they have been accustomed, when they have been accustomably sued, or petitioned for. I will close this point with the judgment of King James, who in his declaration touching his proceedings in Parliament, 1621, resolves, that most privileges of Parliament grew from precedents, which rather show a toleration than an inheritance; therefore he could not allow of the style, calling it their ancient and undoubted right and inheritance, but could rather have wished that they had said, their privileges were derived from the grace and permission of his ancestors and him: and thereupon he concludes, he cannot with patience endure his subjects to use such antimonarchical words concerning their liberties, except they had subjoined, that they were granted unto them by the grace and favours of his predecessors: yet he promiseth to be careful of whatsoever privileges they enjoy by long custom and uncontrolled and lawful precedents.

OBSERVATIONS

UPON

Aristotles Politiques

TOUCHING

Forms of Government

Together with

DIRECTIONS

FOR

OBEDIENCE to GOVERNOURS

in dangerous and doubtfull Times

LONDON

Printed for R. Royston, at the *Angel*
in Ivie Lane, 1652.

(Bought by Thomason May 25th, entered by Royston in the Stationers' Register May 27th, 1652. Reprinted in all the collected editions — 1679, 1680, 1684, 1685(?), 1696. Always printed first in order of Filmer's tracts — after the *Freeholder* — although it was probably the last written. The *Forms* and the *Directions* always appeared together, but they are distinct essays.

The *Forms* is an elaboration of the remarks on Aristotle in *Patriarcha* (See Chapters IX, XI, XV and especially Chapter XII). There are numerous instances of parallel passages and several direct quotations. Nevertheless the tract adds considerably to the general theory of *Patriarcha* and modifies it in many respects. Locke and Filmer's other opponents evidently regarded it as the most important of the tracts and Locke refers repeatedly to the Preface.

Although the *Directions* was published with the *Forms* it is entirely independent. It is a separate recapitulation of the patriarchal case, a broadside applying Sir Robert's doctrines to the political position of 1652. It is also derivative from *Patriarcha* and quotes from it. Locke made extensive use of this tract.)

THE PREFACE

In every alteration of government there is something new, which none can either divine or judge of, till time hath tried it: we read of many several ways of government; but they have all, or most of them, been of particular cities, with none, or very small territories at first belonging to them. At this present the government of the Low Countries, and of Switzerland, are not appropriated either of them to any one city, for they are compounded of several petty principalities, which have special and different laws and privileges each of them; insomuch that the united provinces, and united cantons are but confederacies and leaguers, and not two entire commonweals; associates only for mutual defence. Nay, the cantons of Switzerland are not only several republics, but reputed to have different forms of commonweals; some being said to be aristocratically governed, and others democratically, as the mountaineers: and some of the cantons are papists, and some Protestants, and some mixed of both: we do not find that any large or great dominion or kingdom united in one government, and under the same laws, was ever reduced at once to any kind of popular government, and not confined to the subjection of one city. This being a thing not yet done, requires the abler men to settle such a peaceable government as is to be desired: there being no precedent in the case; all that can be done in it, is, at first to inquire into such other governments, as have been existent in the world. As a preface to such an inquiry, the sacred scripture (if it be but for the antiquity of it) would be consulted; and then Aristotle, the grand master of politiques; and after him the Greek and Latin historians that lived in popular times, would be diligently examined. To excite others of greater abilities to an exacter disquisition, I presume to offer a taste of some doctrines of Aristotle, which are ushered in with a briefer touch of the holy scriptures.

It is not probable that any sure direction of the beginning of government can be found either in Plato, Aristotle, Cicero, Polybius, or in any other of the heathen authors; who were ignorant of the manner of the creation of the world: we must not neglect the scriptures, and search in philosophers for the grounds of dominion and property, which are the main principles of government and justice. The first government in the world was monarchical, in the father of all flesh. Adam being commanded to multiply, and people the earth, and to subdue it, and having dominion given him over all creatures, was

thereby the monarch of the whole world; none of his posterity had
any right to possess anything, but by his grant or permission, or by
succession from him: the earth (saith the Psalmist) hath he given to the
children of men: which shows, the title comes from the fatherhood.
There never was any such thing as an independent multitude, who at
first had a natural right to a community: this is but a fiction, or fancy
of too many in these days, who please themselves in running after the
opinions of philosophers and poets, to find out such an original of
government, as might promise them some title to liberty, to the great
scandal of Christianity, and bringing in of Atheism, since a natural
freedom of mankind cannot be supposed without the denial of the
creation of Adam. And yet this conceit of original freedom is the only
ground upon which not only the heathen philosophers, but also the
authors of the principles of the civil law; and Grotius, Selden, Hobbes,
Ascham and others, raise and build their doctrines of government, and
of the several sorts or kinds, as they call them, of commonwealths.

  Adam was the Father, King and Lord over his family: a son, a subject and a servant or a slave, were one and the same thing at first; the
Father had power to dispose, or sell his children or servants; whence we
find, that at the first reckoning up of goods in scripture, the manservant, and the maidservant are numbered among the possessions and
substance of the owner, as other goods were. As for the names of
subject, slave, and tyrant, they are not found in scripture, but what
we now call a subject or a slave, is there named no other than a servant:
I cannot learn that either the Hebrew, Greek or Latin have any proper
and original word for a tyrant or a slave, it seems these are names of
later invention, and taken up in disgrace of monarchical government.

  I cannot find any one place, or text in the Bible, where any power
or commission is given to a people either to govern themselves, or to
choose themselves governors, or to alter the manner of government
at their pleasure; the power of government is settled and fixed by the
commandment of 'honour thy Father'; if there were a higher power
than the fatherly, then this commandment could not stand, and be
observed: whereas we read in scripture, of some actions of the people
in setting up of Kings, further than to a naked declaration by a part of
the people of their obedience, such actions could not amount, since
we find no commission they have, to bestow any right; a true representation of the people to be made, is as impossible, as for the whole
people to govern; the names of an aristocracy, a democracy, a commonweal, a state, or any other of like signification, are not to be met either
in the law or gospel.

That there is a ground in nature for monarchy, Aristotle himself affirmeth, saying, the first Kings were fathers of families; as for any ground of any other form of government, there hath been none yet alleged, but a supposed natural freedom of mankind; the proof whereof I find none do undertake, but only beg it to be granted. We find the government of God's own people varied under the several titles of Patriarchs, Captains, Judges and Kings; but in all these the supreme power rested still in one person only. We nowhere find any supreme power given to the people, or to a multitude in scripture, or ever exercised by them. The people were never the Lords anointed, nor called gods, nor crowned, nor had the title of nursing fathers, Genesis xxxv, 11. The supreme power being an indivisible beam of majesty, cannot be divided among, or settled upon a multitude. God would have it fixed in one person, not sometimes in one part of the people, and sometimes in another; and sometimes, and that for the most part, nowhere, as when the assembly is dissolved, it must rest in the air, or in the walls of the chamber where they were assembled.

If there were anything like a popular government among God's people, it was about the time of the Judges, when there was no King in Israel; for they had then some small show of government, such as it was, but it was so poor and beggarly, that the scripture brands it with this note, that every man did what was right in his own eyes, because there was no King in Israel; it is not said, because there was no government, but because there was no King; it seems no government, but the government of a King, in the judgment of the scriptures, could restrain men from doing what they listed; where every man doth what he pleaseth, it may be truly said, there is no government; for the end of Government is, that every man should not do what he pleaseth, or be his own judge in his own case; for the scripture to say there was no King, is to say, there was no form of government in Israel.

And what the Old Testament teacheth us, we have confirmed in the New: If Saint Paul had only said, let every soul be subject to the higher powers, and said no more: then men might have disputed, whether Saint Paul, by higher powers, had not meant as well other governors as Kings; or other forms of government, as monarchy; but the good luck is, Saint Paul hath been his own interpreter or comment: for, after the general doctrine of obedience, to be given by all men to the higher powers, he proceeds next to charge it home, and lay it to the conscience under pain of damnation, and applies it to each particular man's conscience; saying, wilt thou not be afraid of the power? which power he expounds in the singular number, restraining it to one person, saying, he is the minister of God to thee; it is not, they are the ministers to thee; and then again, he beareth not the sword in vain; and then a third time in the same verse, lest thou shouldest forget it, he saith, for he is the minister of God, a revenger to wrath, etc., upon thee: if Saint Paul had said, they are the ministers of God, or they bear not the sword in vain, it might be doubted, whether 'they' were meant of Kings only, or of other governors also; but this scruple is taken away by the apostle himself. And as Saint Paul hath expounded what he means by higher powers, so Saint Peter also doth the like: for the self-same word that Saint Paul useth for higher, in Saint Peter is translated supreme; so that though in our English Bibles the words differ, yet in the original they are both the same; so that Saint Paul might have been Englished, let every soul be subject to the supreme power; or Saint Peter might have been translated, whether to the King as to the higher; yet there is this difference, that whereas Saint Paul useth the word in the plural number, Saint Peter hath it in the singular, and with application to the King.

It will be said, though Saint Peter make the King supreme, yet he tells us the King is a humane ordinance, or a creature of the peoples. But it is answered, Kings may be called a humane ordinance, for being made of one of the people, and not by the people; and so are humane in regard of their material cause, not of their efficient. If Saint Peter had meant that Kings had been made by the people, he must also have meant that Governors had been made by the people, for he calls the governors as well an ordinance of man, as the King; for his words are, submit yourselves to every ordinance of man for the Lord's sake, whether it be to the King as supreme, or whether it be to governors: but Saint Peter showeth, that governors are not made by the people; for he saith, they that are sent by him (not by them) for the punishment of evil doers: so that governors are sent by the King, and not by the people: some would have sent by him, to be sent by God; but the relative must be referred to the next antecedent, which is the King, and not God. Besides, if governors be sent by God, and Kings by the people, then governors would be supreme, which is contrary to Saint Peter's doctrine; and it will follow, that the people have not the power of choosing representers to govern, if governors must be sent of God.

The safest sense of Saint Peter's words is, submit yourselves to all humane laws, whether made by the King, or by his subordinate governors. So the King may be called a humane ordinance, as being all one with a speaking law: the word in the original is, be subject to every humane creation; it is more proper to call a law made by a King a creation of an ordinance, than the peoples choosing or declaring of a King, a creation of him.

But take the words in what sense soever you will, it is most evident, that Saint Peter in this place, takes no notice of any government or governors, but of a King, and governors sent by him, but not by the people. And it is to be noted that Saint Peter and Saint Paul, the two chief of the Apostles, wrote their epistles at such a time, when the name of a popular Government, or of the power of the people of Rome, was at least so much in show and in name, that many do believe that notwithstanding the emperors by strong hand usurped a military power; yet the government was for a long time in most things then in the senate and people of Rome; but for all this, neither of the two apostles take any notice of any such popular government; no, nor our saviour himself, who divides all between God and Caesar, and allows nothing that we can find for the people.

OBSERVATIONS UPON ARISTOTLE'S POLITICS TOUCHING FORMS OF GOVERNMENT

WHAT cannot be found in scripture, many do look for in Aristotle; for if there be any other form of government besides monarchy, he is the man best able to tell what it is, and to let us know by what name to call it, since the Greek tongue is most happy in compounding names most significant to express the nature of most things: the usual terms in this age of aristocracy and democracy are taken up from him to express forms of government most different from monarchy: we must therefore make inquiry into Aristotle touching these two terms.

True it is, Aristotle seems to make three sorts of government, which he distinguishes by* the sovereignty of one man, or of a few, or of many, for the common good. These (he saith) are right or perfect governments, but those that are for the private good of one, or of a few, or of a multitude, are transgressions. The government of a monarchy for the common good, he calls a kingdom. The government of a few more than one, an aristocracy; either because the best men govern, or because it is for the best of the governed; when a multitude governs for the common good, it is called by the common name of all governments, a polity. It is possible that one or a few may excel in virtue, but it is difficult for many to excel in all virtue, except in warlike affairs, for this is natural in a multitude, therefore, in this sort of government their principal use is to war one for another, and to possess the arms or ammunition. The transgressions of government before spoken of, are these: tyranny is the transgression of the kingdom; and democracy is the transgression of the polity. For tyranny is a monarchy for the benefit of the monarch, the oligarchy for the profit of the rich; the democracy for the benefit of the poor. None of these are for the common good.

Here Aristotle, if he had stood to his own principles, should have said an oligarchy should be for the benefit of a few, and those the best; and not for the benefit of the rich; and a democracy for the benefit of many, and not of the poor only; for so the opposition lieth; but then Aristotle saw his democracy would prove to be no transgression, but a

---

* 'Ανάγκη δ' εἶναι κύριον ἢ ἕνα, ἢ ὀλίγους, ἢ τοὺς πολλούς ... πρὸς τὸ κοινὸν συμφέρον, (Lib. 3, c. 7). Ταύτας μὲν ὀρθὰς εἶναι πολιτείας, τὰς δὲ πρὸς τὸ ἴδιον ἢ τοῦ ἑνὸς ἢ τῶν ὀλίγων, ἢ τοῦ πλήθους παρεκβάσεις. Τῶν μὲν μοναρχιῶν τὴν πρὸς τὸ κοινὸν ἀποβλέπουσαν συμφέρον βασιλείαν ...

perfect polity, and his oligarchy would not be for the benefit of a few, and those the best men; for they cannot be the best men, that seek only their private profit. In this chapter, the mind of Aristotle about the several kinds of government, is clearliest delivered, as being the foundation of all his books of politics, it is the more necessary to make a curious observation of these his doctrines. In the first place, he acknowledgeth the government of one man, or of a monarchy, and that it is a perfect form of government.

Concerning monarchy, Aristotle teacheth us the beginning of it; for, saith he, the *first society made of many houses is a colony, which seems most naturally to be a colony of families, or foster-brethren of children and children's children. And therefore at the beginning cities were under the government of Kings; the Eldest in every house is King, and so for kindred sake it is in colonies.

Thus he deduced the original of government from the power of the fatherhood, not from the election of the people. This it seems he learnt of his master Plato, who in his third book of laws affirms, that the true and first reason of authority is that the father and mother, and simply those that beget and ingender, do command and rule over all their children. Aristotle also tells us from Homer, †that every man gives laws to his wife and children.

In the fourth book of his *Politics*, chap. 2, he gives to monarchy the title of the ‡first and divinest sort of government, defining tyranny to be a transgression from the first, and divinest.

Again, Aristotle in the eighth book of his *Ethics*, in chap. 12 saith: That of §the right kinds of government, a monarchy was the best, and a popular estate the worst.

Lastly, in the third book of his *Politics*, chap. 16 concerning monarchy, he saith, that ‖A perfect kingdom is that wherein the King rules all things according to his own will; for he that is called a King according to the law makes no kind of government.

Secondly, he saith there is a government of a few men, but doth not tell us how many those few men may, or must be, only he saith

---

* Μάλιστα δ' ἔοικε κατὰ φύσιν ἡ κώμη ἀποικία οἰκίας εἶναι, οὓς καλοῦσί τινες ὁμογάλακτας παῖδάς τε καὶ παίδων παῖδας, διὸ καὶ τὸ πρῶτον ἐβασιλεύοντο αἱ πόλεις, καὶ νῦν ἔτι τὰ ἔθνη. (*Lib.* 1, *c.* 2). πᾶσα γὰρ οἰκία βασιλεύεται ὑπὸ τοῦ πρεσβυτάτου, ὥστε καὶ αἱ ἀποικίαι διὰ τὴν συγγένειαν.

† Θεμιστεύει δὲ ἕκαστος παίδων ἠδ' ἀλόχων.

‡ Ἀνάγκη γὰρ τὴν μὲν τῆς πρώτης καὶ θειοτάτης παρέκβασιν εἶναι χειρίστην.

§ Τούτων δὲ βελτίστη ἡ βασιλεία, χειρίστη δὲ τιμοκρατία.

‖ Περὶ δὲ τῆς παμβασιλείας καλουμένης, αὕτη δ' ἐστὶ καθ' ἣν ἄρχει πάντων κατὰ τὴν ἑαυτοῦ βούλησιν ὁ βασιλεύς ... ὁ μὲν γὰρ κατὰ νόμον λεγόμενος βασιλεύς, οὐκ ἔστιν εἶδος, καθάπερ εἴπομεν, πολιτείας.

they must be more than one man, but how many, that he leaves uncertain.

This perfect government of a few, any man would think Aristotle should have called an oligarchy, for that this word properly signifies so much; but instead of the government of a few, Aristotle gives it quite another name, and terms it an aristocracy, which signifies the power of the best; the reason why it is called an aristocracy, saith Aristotle, is for that there the best men govern, or (because that is not always true) for that it is for the best of the governed; by this latter reason any government, and most especially a monarchy, may be called an aristocracy, because the end of monarchy is for the best of the governed, as well as the end of an aristocracy; so that of these two reasons for calling the government of a few an aristocracy, the first is seldom true; and the latter is never sufficient to frame a distinction. This Aristotle himself confesseth in his next chapter, saying *that the causes aforesaid do not make a difference, and that it is poverty and riches, and not few, and many, that makes the difference between an oligarchy and democracy; there must be an oligarchy where rich men rule, whether they be few or many: and wheresoever the poor have the sovereignty, there must be a democracy.

Now if Aristotle will allow riches and poverty to make a difference between an oligarchy and a democracy: these two must likewise make the difference between an aristocracy and a polity: for the only difference Aristotle makes between them, is, in their ends, and not in their matter; for the same few men may make an aristocracy, if their end be the common good; and they may be an oligarchy, if they aim only at their private benefit.

Thus is Aristotle distracted and perplexed how to distinguish his aristocracy, whether by the smallness of their number, or by the greatness of their estates. Nay, if we look into Aristotle's *Rhetorics*† we shall find a new conceit, not only about aristocracy, but also about the sorts of government: for whereas he has taught us in his *Politics*, that there be three sorts of right or perfect government, and as many sorts of wrong, which he calls transgressions or corruptions, he comes in his *Rhetorics*, and teacheth us that there be four sorts of government.

1. ‡A democracy, where magistracies are distributed by lots.
2. In an oligarchy by their wealth.

---

* Διὸ καὶ οὐ συμβαίνει διὰ τὰς ῥηθείσας αἰτίας γίνεσθαι διαφοράς, ᾧ δὲ διαφέρουσιν ἥ τε δημοκρατία καὶ ἡ ὀλιγαρχία ἀλλήλων, πενία καὶ πλοῦτός ἐστιν, etc., *Lib.* 3, *c.* 8.
† *Lib.* 2, *c.* 8.
‡ Ἔστι δὲ δημοκρατία πολιτεία ἐν ᾗ κλήρῳ διανέμονται τὰς ἀρχάς· ὀλιγαρχία δὲ ἐν ᾗ οἱ ἀπὸ τιμημάτων· ἀριστοκρατία δὲ ἐν ᾗ οἱ κατὰ παιδείαν.

3. In an aristocracy by their instructions in the law. It is necessary for these to appear the best from whence they have their name.

4. *A monarchy according to the name, wherein one is Lord over all.

Here we see aristocracy is not distinguished by smallness of numbers, nor by riches, but by skill in the laws; for he saith those that are instructed in the laws govern in an aristocracy; οἱ γὰρ ἐμμεμενηκότες ἐν τοῖς νομίμοις ἐν τῇ Ἀριστοκρατίᾳ ἄρχωσιν· a point not dreamt of in his *Politics*; by which it seems Aristotle himself did not know well what he would have to be an aristocracy. And as he cannot teach us truly what an aristocracy is, so he is to seek to tell us where any aristocracy ever was; even himself seems to doubt, whether there be any such form of government, where he saith in his third book of *Politics*, chap. 5.

†It is impossible for any mechanical man to be a citizen in an aristocracy, if there be any such government as they call aristocratical.

His 'if' makes him seem to doubt of it: yet I find him affirm that the Commonwealth of Carthage was aristocratical; he doth not say it was an aristocracy, for he confesseth it had many of the transgressions which other commonwealths had, and did incline either to a democracy or an oligarchy.

‡The government of Carthage did transgress from an aristocracy to an oligarchy.

And he concludes, that if by misfortune there should happen any discord among the Carthaginians themselves, there would be no medicine by law found out to give it rest; wherein methinks Aristotle was a kind of prophet, for the discords between the citizens of Carthage, were the main cause that Hannibal lost not only Italy, but Carthage itself.

By these few collections we may find how uncertain Aristotle is in determining what an aristocracy is, or where, or when any such government was; it may justly be doubted whether there ever was, or can be any such government.

Let us pass from his aristocracy to his third sort of perfect or right government; for which he finds no particular name, but only the common name of all government, politia: it seems the Greeks were wonderfully to seek, that they of all men should not be able to compound a name for such a perfect form of government; unless we should believe that they esteemed this kind of commonwealth so superlatively

* Μοναρχία δέ ἐστι κατὰ τοὔνομα ἐν ᾗ εἷς ἁπάντων κύριός ἐστι.

† Εἰ τις ἐστίν ἣν καλοῦσιν ἀριστοκρατικήν.

‡ Παρεκβαίνει δὲ τῆς ἀριστοκρατίας ἡ τάξις τῶν Καρχηδονίων μάλιστα πρὸς τὴν ὀλιγαρχίαν. *Lib.* 2, *c.* 11.

excellent, as to be called, κατ' ἐξοχὴν, the government of governments, or polity of polities.

But, howsoever, Aristotle in his books of *Politics* vouchsafe us not a name, yet in his books of *Ethics* he affirmeth it may very properly be called *a Timocratical government, where magistrates are chosen by their wealth: but why Aristotle should give it such a name I can find no reason; for a polity by his doctrine is the government of many, or of a multitude, and the multitude he will have to be the poorer sort, insomuch that except they be poor, he will not allow it to be the government of a multitude, though they be never so many; for he makes poverty the truest note of a popular estate; and as if to be poor and to be free were all one, he makes liberty likewise to be a mark of a popular estate, for in his fourth book, and fourth chapter, he resolves, that †a popular state is where free men govern, and an oligarchy where rich men rule; as if rich men could not be free men: now how magistrates should be chosen for their wealth, ἀπὸ τιμημάτων, among all poor men, is to me a riddle.

Here I cannot but wonder why all our modern politicians, who pretend themselves Aristotelians, should forsake their great master, and account a democracy a right or perfect form of government, when Aristotle brands it for a transgression, or a depraved, or corrupted manner of government. They had done better to have followed Aristotle, who (though other Grecians could not, yet he) could find out the name of a timocracy for a right popular government. But, it may be, our politicians forbear to use the word timocracy, because he affords an ill character of it, saying, that of all the right kinds of government a monarchy was the best, and a timocracy the worst; βελτίστη ἡ βασιλεία, χειρίστη ἡ τιμοκρατία. Yet afterwards Aristotle in the same chapter makes amends for it, in saying, a democracy is the least vicious, because it doth but a little transgress from a timocracy.

But not to insist longer on the name of this nameless form of government, let inquiry be made into the thing itself, that we may know what Aristotle saith is the government of many, or of a multitude, for the common good.

This many, or multitude is not the whole people, nor the major part of the people, or any chosen by the people to be their representors. No, Aristotle never saith, or meaneth any such thing; for he tells us ‡the best city doth not make any artificer, or handicraftsman a citizen.

---

* Τρίτη δ' ἡ ἀπὸ τιμημάτων, ἣν τιμοκρατικὴν λέγειν οἰκεῖον φαίνεται. *Lib.* 8, *c.* 12.

† Ὅτι δῆμος ἐστὶν ὅταν ἐλεύθεροι κύριοι ὦσιν, ὀλιγαρχία δ' ὅταν οἱ πλούσιοι.

‡ Ἡ δὲ βελτίστη πόλις οὐ ποιήσει βάναυσον πολίτην. *Lib.* 31, *c.* 5.

And if these be excluded out of the number of citizens, there will be but a few left in every city to make his timocratical government, since artificers or mercenary men make far the greatest part of a city; or to say *a city is a community of free men, and yet to exclude the greatest part of the inhabitants from being citizens, is but a mockery of freedom; for any man would think that a city being a society of men assembled to the end to live well, that such men without whom a city cannot subsist, and who perform necessary works, and minister to all in public, should not be barred from being citizens, yet says Aristotle, †all those are not to be deemed citizens without whom a city cannot subsist, except they abstain from necessary works; for he resolves it ‡impossible for him to exercise the work of virtue, that useth a mechanical or mercenary trade.

And he makes it one of his conclusions, that §in ancient times among some men, no public workman did partake of the government, until the worst of democracies were brought in.

Again, Aristotle will have his best popular government consist of free men, and accounts the poorer sort of people to be free men; how then will he exclude poor artificers, who work for the public, from participating of the government?

Further, it is observable in Aristotle, that, quite contrary to the signification of the Greek names, the government of a multitude may be termed an oligarchy if they be rich, and the rule of a few a democracy if they be poor and free.

After much uncertainty of the nature of this politic government, which wants a name; Aristotle at last resolves that this general commonweal, or politia is compounded of a democracy and oligarchy; for, ‖ to speak plainly, a polity is a mixture of a democracy and an oligarchy.

That is, one perfect form is made of two imperfect ones; this is rather a confounding than compounding of government, to patch it up of two corrupt ones, by appointing an oligarchical penalty for the rich magistrates that are chosen by election, and a democratical fee for the poor magistrates that are chosen by lot.

Lastly, it is to be noted, that Aristotle doth not offer to name any one city or commonweal in the world, where ever there was any such government as he calls a polity: for him to reckon it for a perfect form

---

* Ἡ δὲ πόλις κοινωνία τῶν ἐλευθέρων ἐστί. Lib. 3, c. 7.

† Ὂυ πάντας θετέον πολίτας ὧν ἄνευ οὐκ ἂν εἴη πόλις. Lib. 3, c. 5.

‡ Ὂυ γὰρ οἶόν τ᾽ ἐπιτηδεῦσαι τὰ τῆς ἀρετῆς ζῶντα βίον βάναυσον ἢ θητικόν.

§ Διὸ παρ᾽ ἐνίοις οὐ μετεῖχον οἱ δημιουργοὶ τὸ παλαιὸν ἀρχῶν πρὶν δῆμον γενέσθαι τὸν ἔσχατον. Lib. 3, c. 4.

‖ Ἔστι γὰρ ἡ πολιτεία, ὡς ἁπλῶς εἰπεῖν, μίξις ὀλιγαρχίας καὶ δημοκρατίας. Lib. 4, c. 8.

of government, and of such excellency as to carry the name from all other, and yet never to have been extant in the world, may seem a wonder, and a man may be excused for doubting, or for denying any such form to be possible in nature, if it cannot be made manifest what it is, nor when, nor where it ever was.

In conclusion, since Aristotle reckons but three kinds of perfect government, which are; first, a monarchy of one; secondly, an aristocracy of a few; thirdly, a polity of a multitude; and if these two latter cannot be made good by him: there will remain but one right form of government only which is monarchy: and it seems to me, that Aristotle in a manner doth confess as much, ·where he informs us, *that the first commonweal among the Grecians, after kingdoms, was made of those that waged war: meaning that the Grecians, when they left to be governed by kings, fell to be governed by an army: their monarchy was changed into a stratocracy, and not into an aristocracy or democracy: for if unity in government, which is only found in monarchy, be once broken, there is no stay or bound, until it come to a constant standing army, for the people or multitude, as Aristotle teacheth us, can excel in no virtue but military, and that that is natural to them, and therefore in a popular estate, †the sovereign power is in the sword, and those that are possessed of the arms. So that any nation or kingdom that is not charged with the keeping of a King, must perpetually be at the charge of paying and keeping of an army.

These brief observations upon Aristotle's perfect forms of government, may direct what to judge of those corrupted or imperfect forms which he mentions; for *rectum est index sui et obliqui*, and he reckons them to be all one in matter and form, and to differ only in their end: the end of the perfect forms being for the good of the governed; and of the imperfect, for the benefit only of the governors. Now since Aristotle could not tell how to define or describe his right or perfect forms of government, it cannot be expected he can satisfy us concerning those he calls imperfect: yet he labours and bestirs himself mainly in the business, though to little purpose; for howsoever the title of his book be Πολιτικῶν, of *Politics*, and that he mentions πολιτεία for a special form of government, which hath the common name of a polity: yet when he comes to dispute in particular of government, he argues

---

* Καὶ ἡ πρώτη δὲ πολιτεία ἐν τοῖς Ἕλλησιν ἐγένετο, μετὰ τὰς βασιλείας, ἐκ τῶν πολεμούντων. *Lib.* 3, *c.* 13.

† Πλείους δ' ἤδη χαλεπὸν ἠκριβῶσθαι πρὸς πᾶσαν ἀρετὴν, ἀλλὰ μάλιστα τὴν πολεμικήν· αὕτη γὰρ ἐν πλήθει γίγνεται. διόπερ κατὰ ταύτην τὴν πολιτείαν κυριώτατον τὸ προπολεμοῦν, καὶ μετέχουσιν αὐτῆς οἱ κεκτημένοι τὰ ὅπλα. *Lib.* 3, *c.* 7.

only about democracies and oligarchies, and therein he is copious,
because only those which he calls corrupt forms of governments were
common in Greece in his days. As for an aristocracy, or a polity which
he mentions, they are only speculative notions, or airy names, invented
to delude the world, and to persuade the people, that under those
quaint terms, there might be found some subtle government, which
might at least equal, if not excel, monarchy: and the inventors of those
fine names were all but rebels to monarchy, by Aristotle's confession,
where he saith, the first commonweals of Greece after Kings were
left, were made of those that waged war, *Lib.* 4, *c.* 13.

As Aristotle is irresolute to determine what are truly perfect aristocracies and polities, so he is to seek in describing his imperfect forms
of government, as well oligarchies as democracies, and therefore he is
driven to invent several sorts of them, and to confound himself with
subdivisions: we will allege some of his words. 'The cause why there
be many kinds of commonweals is, for that there are many parts of
every city. Sometimes all these parts are in a commonweal, sometimes
more of them, sometimes fewer: whence it is manifest, that there are
many commonweals differing from each other in kind: because the
parts of them differ after the same manner. For a commonweal is
the order of magistrates distributed, either according to the power of
them that are partakers of it, or according to some other common
equality belonging to poor and rich, or some other thing common to
both. It is therefore necessary, that there be so many commonweals
as there are orders, according to the excellencies and differences of
parts. But it seemeth principally there are but two chief kinds of
commonweals; the democracy and the oligarchy: for they make the
aristocracy a branch of oligarchy, as if it were a kind of oligarchy; and
that other which is properly a polity, to be a branch of democracy.
So they are wont to esteem of commonweals; but it is both truer and
better; that there being two right forms, or one, that all the other be
transgressions.' Here we find Aristotle of several minds, sometimes he
is for many commonweals, sometimes for two, or sometimes for one.
As for his many commonweals, if he allow them according to the
several parts of a city, he may as well make three thousand kinds of
commonweals, as three: if two artificers and three soldiers should
govern, that should be one kind of commonweal: if four husbandmen,
and five merchants, that would be a second sort; or six tailors, and ten
carpenters, a third sort; or a dozen sailors and a dozen porters, a fourth,
and so *in infinitum*, for Aristotle is not resolved how many parts to
make of a city, or how many combinations of those parts; and there-

fore in his reckoning of them, he differs from himself, sometimes makes more, sometimes fewer parts: and oft concluding at the end of his account with *etceteras*: and confessing that one and the same man may act several parts; as he that is a soldier, may be a husbandman and an artificer, and in his fourth book and fourth chapter, he seems to reckon up eight parts of a city, but in the tail of them, he misses or forgets the sixth. 1. He names the ploughman. 2. The artificer. 3. The tradesman or merchant. 4. The mercenary hireling. 5. The soldier. (Here Aristotle falls foul upon Plato, for making but four parts of a city. 1. The weaver. 2. The ploughman. 3. The tailor. 4. The carpenter. Afterwards, as if these were not sufficient, he addeth the smith, and the feeder of necessary cattle, the merchant, and the ingrosser or retailer.) Whilst Aristotle was busy in this reprehension of Plato, he forgets himself, and skips over his sixth part of a city, and names 7. the rich men, 8. the magistrates. In the same chapter, he offers at another division of the parts of a city or commonweal, first dividing it into a populacy, and nobility. The people he divides first into husbandmen. 2. Into artificers. 3. Into merchants, or those that use buying or selling. 4. Into those that frequent the seas, of whom some follow the war, others seek for gain, some are carriers or transporters, others fishermen. 5. Handicraftsmen that possess so little goods, that they cannot be idle. 6. Those that are not free on both sides, and any other such like multitude of people. The kinds of noblemen are distinguished by riches, by lineage, by virtue, by learning and other such like things.

That there may be more parts of a commonweal than are here numbered, Aristotle confesseth or supposeth; and of a multitude of parts, and of a multitude of mixtures of such parts may be made a world of forms of oligarchies and democracies.

This confusion of the parts and kinds of commonweals drove Aristotle rather to rest upon the division of rich and poor, for the main parts of a commonweal, than any other. The distinction of a few and of a multitude, or the whole people, might seem more proper to distinguish between an oligarchy and a democracy; but the truth is, Aristotle looking upon the cities of Greece, and finding that in every one of them, even in Athens itself, there were many of the people that were not allowed to be citizens, and to participate in the government, and that many times he was a citizen in one sort of government, who was not a citizen in another, and that citizens differed according to every commonweal; he considered that if he should place a right in the whole people, either to govern, or to choose their form of government, or the parties that should govern: he should hereby condemn

o

the government of all the cities in Greece, and especially of aristocracy, . which, as he saith, allows no artificer to be a citizen, and besides, he should thereby confute a main principle of his own *Politics*, which is, that some men are born slaves by nature; which quite contradicts the position, that all men are born equal and free; and therefore Aristotle thought it fitter to allow all imaginable forms of government, that so he might not disparage any one city, than to propound such a form as might condemn and destroy all the rest.

Though Aristotle allows so many several forms of corrupted governments; yet he insists upon no one form of all those that he can define or describe, in such sort, that he is able to say that any one city in all Greece was governed just according to such a form; his diligence is only to make as many forms as the giddy or inconstant humour of a city could happen upon; he freely gives the people liberty to invent as many kinds of government as they please, provided he may have liberty to find fault with every one of them; it proved an easier work for him to find fault with every form, than to tell how to amend any one of them; he found so many imperfections in all sorts of commonweals, that he could not hold from reproving them before ever he tells us what a commonweal is, or how many sorts there are, and to this purpose he spends his whole second book in setting out, and correcting the chief commonweals of Greece, and among others the Lacedemonian, the Cretan and Carthaginian commonweals; which three he esteems to be much alike, and better than any other, yet he spares not to lay open their imperfections, and doth the like to the Athenian; wherein he breaks the rule of method, by delivering the faults of commonweals, before he teach us what a commonweal is; for in his first book, he speaks only of the parts, of which a city, or a commonweal is made, but tells us not what a city or commonweal is, until he come to his third book, and there in handling the sorts of government, he observes no method at all, but in a disorderly way, flies backward and forward from one sort to another: and howsoever there may be observed in him many rules of policy touching government in general, yet without doubt where he comes to discourse of particular forms, he is full of contradiction, or confusion, or both: it is true, he is brief and difficult, the best right a man can do him, is to confess he understands him not; yet a diligent reader may readily discern so many irregularities and breaches in Aristotle's books of *Politics*, as tend to such distraction or confusion, that none of our new politicians can make advantage of his principles, for the confirmation of an original power by nature in the people, which is the only theme now in fashion: for Aristotle's discourse is of such commonweals as were founded by particular persons, as the Chalcedonian by Phaleas, the Milesian by Hippodamas, the Lacedemonian by Lycurgus, the Cretan by Minos, the Athenian by Solon, and the like: but the natural right of the people to found, or elect, their kind of government is not once disputed by him: it seems the underived majesty of the people, was such a metaphysical piece of speculation as our grand philosopher was not acquainted with; he speaks very contemptuously of the multitude in several places, he affirms that the people are base or wicked judges in their own cases, οἱ πλεῖστοι φαῦλοι κριταὶ περὶ τῶν οἰκείων·* and that many of them differ nothing from beasts; τί διαφέρουσιν ἔνιοι τῶν θηρίων;† and again he saith, the common people or freemen are such as are neither rich, nor in reputation for virtue; and it is not safe to commit to them great governments; for, by reason of their injustice and unskilfulness, they would do much injustice, and commit many errors and it is pleasanter to the multitude to live disorderly, than soberly, ἥδιον γὰρ τοῖς πολλοῖς τὸ 3ῆν ἀτάκτως ἢ τὸ σωφρόνως.‡ If Aristotle had believed a public interest to have been in the people, to the enabling them to be their own carvers in point of government, he would never have entangled himself with such intricate and ambiguous forms of commonweals, as himself cannot tell how to explain, nor any of his commentators how to understand, or make use of.

This one benefit I have found by reading Aristotle, that his books of *Politics* serve for an admirable commentary upon that text of scripture, which saith, 'In those days there was no King in Israel; every man did that which was right in his own eyes'. For he grants a liberty in every city, for any man, or multitude of men, either by cunning, or force to set up what government they please; and he will allow some name or other of a commonweal, which in effect is to allow every man to do what he lists, if he be able; hence it is, that by the confession of Aristotle, the first commonweals in Greece, after Kings were given over, were made of those that waged war; those several kinds of commonweals were all summed up into the government of an army; for §it is, saith Aristotle, in their power, who manage arms to continue, or not continue the form of government, whereby the estate is governed, which is nothing else but a stratocracy, or military government. We cannot much blame Aristotle for the uncertainty and contrariety in him about the sorts of government, if we consider him as a heathen; for it is not possible for the wit of man to search out the first

* *Lib.* 3, *c.* 9.   † *Lib.* 3, *c.* 11.   ‡ *Lib.* 6, *c.* 4.
§ Οἱ γὰρ τῶν ὅπλων κύριοι, καὶ μένειν καὶ μὴ μένειν κύριοι τὴν πολιτείαν. *Lib.* 7, *c.* 9.

grounds or principles of government (which necessarily depend upon the original of property) except he know that at the creation one man alone was made, to whom the dominion of all things was given, and from whom all men derive their title. This point can be learnt only from the scriptures: as for the imaginary contract of people, it is a fancy not improbable only, but impossible, except a multitude of men at first had sprung out, and were engendered of the earth, which Aristotle knows not whether he may believe, or no:* if justice (which is to give every man his due) be the end of government, there must necessarily be a rule to know how any man at first came to have a right to anything to have it truly called his. This is a point Aristotle disputes not; nor so much as ever dreamt of an original contract among people: he looked no further in every city, than to a scrambling among the citizens, whereby every one snatched what he could get: so that a violent possession was the first, and best title that he knew.

The main distinction of Aristotle touching perfect or right forms of government from those that are imperfect or corrupt, consists solely in this point, that where the profit of the governed is respected, there is a right government, but where the profit of the governors is regarded, there is a corruption or transgression of government. By this it is supposed by Aristotle, that there may be a government only for the benefit of the governors; this supposition to be false, may be proved from Aristotle himself; I will instance about the point of tyranny.

Tyranny, saith Aristotle, †is a despotical or masterly monarchy; now he confesseth, that ‡in truth the masterly government is profitable both to the servant by nature, and the master by nature, and he yields a solid reason for it, saying, §'It is not possible, if the servant be destroyed, that the mastership can be saved'; whence it may be inferred, that if the masterly government of tyrants cannot be safe without the preservation of them whom they govern, it will follow that a tyrant cannot govern for his own profit only: and thus his main definition of tyranny fails, as being grounded upon an impossible supposition by his own confession. No example can be shown of any such government that ever was in the world, as Aristotle describes a tyranny to be; for under the worst of Kings, though many particular men have unjustly suffered, yet the multitude, or the people in general have found benefit and profit by the government.

It being apparent that the different kinds of government in Aristotle arise only from the difference of the number of governors, whether one, a few, or many, there may be as many several forms of govern-

---

* _Lib._ 2, _c._ 8.   † _Lib._ 3, _c._ 7.   ‡ _Lib._ 4, _c._ 10.   § _Lib._ 3, _c._ 6.

ments as there be several numbers, which are infinite; so that not only the several parts of a city or commonweal, but also the several numbers of such parts may cause multiplicity of forms of government by Aristotle's principles.

It is further observable in assemblies, that it is not the whole assembly, but the major part only of the assembly that hath the government; for that which pleaseth the most, is always ratified, saith Aristotle, *Lib. 4, c. 4*, by this means one and the same assembly may make, at one sitting, several forms of commonweals, for in several debates and votes the same number of men, or all the self-same men do not ordinarily agree in their votes; and the least disagreement, either in the persons of the men, or in their number, alters the form of government. Thus in a commonweal, one part of the public affairs shall be ordered by one form of government, and another part by another form, and a third part by a third form, and so *in infinitum*. How can that have the denomination of a form of government, which lasts but for a moment only, about one fraction of business? for in the very instant, as it were in the twinkling of an eye, while their vote lasteth, the government must begin and end.

To be governed, is nothing else but to be obedient and subject to the will or command of another; it is the will in a man that governs; ordinarily men's wills are divided according to their several ends or interests; which most times are different, and many times contrary the one to the other, and in such cases where the wills of the major part of the assembly do unite and agree in one will, there is a monarchy of many wills in one, though it be called an aristocracy or democracy in regard of the several persons; it is not the many bodies, but the one will or soul of the multitude that governs. *Where one is set up out of many, the people becometh a monarch, because many are Lords, not separately, but altogether as one; therefore such a people as if it were a monarch, seeks to bear rule alone, *Lib. 4, c. 4*.

It is a false and improper speech to say that a whole multitude, senate, council, or any multitude whatsoever doth govern where the major part only rules; because many of the multitude that are so assembled, are so far from having any part in the government, that they themselves are governed against and contrary to their wills; there being in all government various and different debates and consultations, it comes to pass oft-times, that the major part in every assembly, differs according to the several humours or fancies of men; those who agree

* Μόναρχος γὰρ ὁ δῆμος γίνεται, σύνθετος εἷς ἐκ πολλῶν· οἱ γὰρ πολλοὶ κύριοι εἰσὶν οὐχ ὡς ἕκαστος, ἀλλὰ πάντες· ὁ δὲ οὖν τοιοῦτος δῆμος ἅτε μόναρχος ὢν ζητεῖ μοναρχεῖν.

in one mind, in one point, are of different opinions in another; every
change of business, or new matter begets a new major part, and is a
change both of the government and governors; the difference in the
number, or in the qualities of the persons that govern, is the only thing
that causes different governments, according to Aristotle, who divides
his kinds of government to the number of one, a few, or many. As
amongst the Romans their tribunitial laws had several titles, according
to the names of those tribunes of the people, that preferred and made
them. So in other governments, the body of their acts and ordinances
is composed of a multitude of momentary monarchs, who by the
strength and power of their parties or factions are still under a kind of
a civil war, fighting and scratching for the legislative miscellany, or
medley of several governments. If we consider each government
according to the nobler part of which it is composed, it is nothing else
but a monarchy of monothelites, or of many men of one will, most
commonly in one point only: but if we regard only the baser part, or
bodies of such persons as govern, there is an interrupted succession of
a multitude of short-lived governments, with as many intervals of
anarchy; so that no man can say at any time, that he is under any form
of government; for in a shorter time than the word can be spoken,
every government is begun and ended. Furthermore in all assemblies,
of what quality soever they be, whether aristocratical or democratical,
as they call them, they all agree in this one point, to give that honourable regard to monarchy, that they do interpret the major, or prevailing
part in every assembly to be but as one man, and so do feign to themselves a kind of monarchy.

Though there be neither precept nor practice in scripture, nor yet
any reason alleged by Aristotle for any form of government, but only
monarchy; yet it is said that it is evident to common sense, that of old
time Rome, and in this present age Venice, and the Low Countries,
enjoy a form of government different from monarchy: hereunto it
may be answered, that a people may live together in society, and help
one another; and yet not be under any form of government; as we
see herds of cattle do, and yet we may not say they live under government. For government is not a society only to live, but to live well
and virtuously. This is acknowledged by Aristotle, who teacheth that
*the end of a city, is to live blessedly and honestly. Political communities
are ordained for honest actions, but not for living together only.

Now there be two things principally required to a blessed and

* Τέλος πόλεως τὸ εὖ ζῆν εὐδαιμόνως καὶ καλῶς· τῶν καλῶν πράξεων χάριν θετέον εἶναι
τὴν πολιτικὴν κοινωνίαν, ἀλλὰ οὐ τὸ συζῆν.

·honest life: religion towards God and peace towards men: that is, a quiet and peaceable life in all godliness and honesty, 1 Timothy ii, 2. Here then will be the question: whether godliness and peace can be found under any government but monarchy, or whether Rome, Venice, or the Low Countries did enjoy these under any popular government. In these two points, let us first briefly examine the Roman government, which is thought to have been the most glorious.

For religion, we find presently after the building of the city by Romulus, the next King, Numa most devoutly established a religion, and began his kingdom with the service of the Gods; he forbade the Romans to make any images of God, which law lasted and was observed 170 years, there being in all that time no image or picture of God in any temple or chapel of Rome; also he erected the Pontifical College, and was himself the first Bishop or Pontifex; these Bishops were to render no account either to the Senate or Commonalty. They determined all questions concerning religion, as well between priests as between private men: they punished inferior priests, if they either added or detracted from the established rites, or ceremonies, or brought in any new thing into religion. The chief Bishop, Pontifex Maximus, taught every man how to honour and serve the gods. This care had monarchy of religion.

But after the expulsion of Kings, we do not find during the power of the people, any one law made for the benefit or exercise of religion: there be two tribunitian laws concerning religion, but they are merely for the benefit of the power of the people, and not of religion. L. Papirius, a tribune, made a law, called *Lex Papiria*, that it should not be lawful for any to consecrate either houses, grounds, altars, or any other things without the determination of the people. Domitius Ænobarbus, another tribune, enacted a law called *Domitia Lex*, that the Pontifical College should not, as they were wont, admit whom they would into the order of priesthood, but it should be in the power of the people; and because it was contrary to their religion, that church-dignitaries should be bestowed by the common people; hence for very shame he ordained, that the lesser part of the people, namely seventeen tribes, should elect whom they thought fit, and afterwards the party elected should have his confirmation or admission from the college: thus by a committee of seventeen tribes taken out of thirty-five, the ancient form of religion was altered and reduced to the power of the lesser part of the people. This was the great care of the people to bring ordination and consecration to the laity.

The religion in Venice and the Low Countries is sufficiently known,

much need not be said of them: they admirably agree under a seeming
contrariety; it is commonly said, that one of them hath all religions,
and the other no religion; the atheist of Venice may shake hands
with the sectary of Amsterdam. This is the liberty that a popular
estate can brag of, every man may be of any religion, or no religion,
if he please; their main devotion is exercised only in opposing and sup-
pressing monarchy. They both agree to exclude the clergy from
meddling in government, whereas in all monarchies both before the
law of Moses, and under it, and ever since; all barbarians, Grecians,
Romans, Infidels, Turks and Indians, have with one consent given such
respect and reverence to their priests, as to trust them with their laws;
and in this our nation, the first priests we read of before Christianity,
were the Druids, who, as Caesar saith, decided and determined controversies, in murder, in case of inheritance, of bounds of lands, as they
in their discretion judged meet; they grant rewards and punishments.
It is a wonder to see what high respect even the great Turk giveth to
his Mufti, or Chief Bishop, so necessary is religion to strengthen and
direct laws.

To consider of the point of peace: it is well known, that no people
ever enjoyed it without monarchy. Aristotle saith, the Lacedemonians
preserved themselves by warring; and after they had gotten to themselves the empire, then were they presently undone, for that they could
not live at rest, nor do any better exercise, than the exercise of war,
Lib. 2, *c*. 7. After Rome had expelled Kings, it was in perpetual war,
till the time of the emperors: once only was the temple of Janus shut,
after the end of the first Punic War, but not so long as for one year, but
for some months. It is true, as Orosius saith, that for almost 700 years,
that is, from Tullus Hostilius to Augustus Caesar, only for one summer,
the bowels of Rome did not sweat blood. On the behalf of the Romans
it may be said, that though the bowels of Rome did always sweat blood,
yet they did obtain most glorious victories abroad. But it may be
truly answered, if all the Roman conquests had no other foundation
but injustice; this alone soils all the glory of her warlike actions. The
most glorious war that ever Rome had, was with Carthage; the beginning of which war, Sir Walter Raleigh proves to have been most
unjustly undertaken by the Romans, in confederating with the Mamer-
tines, and aiding of rebels, under the title of protecting their con-
federates; whereas Kings many times may have just cause of war, for
recovering and preserving their rights to such dominions as fall to
them by inheritance or marriage, a popular estate, that can neither
marry, nor be heir to another, can have no such title to a war in a

foreign kingdom; and to speak the truth, if it be rightly considered; the whole time of the popularity of Rome, the Romans were no other than the only prosperous and glorious thieves and robbers of the world.

If we look more narrowly into the Roman government, it will appear, that in that very age, wherein Rome was most victorious, and seemed to be most popular; she owed most of her glory to an apparent kind of monarchy. For it was the kingly power of the Consuls, who (as Livy saith) had the same royal jurisdiction, or absolute power that the Kings had, not any whit diminished or abated, and held all the same regal ensigns of supreme dignity, which helped Rome to all her conquests: whilst the tribunes of the people were struggling at home with the Senate about election of magistrates, enacting of laws, and calling to account, or such other popular affairs, the kingly Consuls gained all the victories abroad: thus Rome at one and the same time was broken and distracted into two shows of government; the popular, which served only to raise seditions and discords within the walls, whilst the regal achieved the conquests of foreign nations and kingdoms. Rome was so sensible of the benefit and necessity of monarchy, that in her most desperate condition and danger, when all other hopes failed her, she had still resort to the creation of a dictator, who for the time was an absolute King; and from whom no appeal to the people was granted, which is the royallest evidence for monarchy in the world; for they who were drawn to swear, they would suffer no King of Rome, found no security but in perjury, and breaking their oath by admitting the kingly power in spite of their teeth, under a new name of a Dictator or Consul: a just reward for their wanton expelling their King for no other crime they could pretend but pride, which is most tolerable in a King of all men: and yet we find no particular point of pride charged upon him, but that he enjoined the Romans to labour in cleansing and casting of ditches, and paving their sinks: an act both for the benefit and ornament of the city, and therefore commendable in the King: but the citizens of Rome, who had been conquerors of all nations round about them, could not endure of warriors to become quarriers and day-labourers. Whereas it is said, that Tarquin was expelled for the rape committed by his son on Lucrece; it is unjust to condemn the Father for the crime of his son; it had been fit to have petitioned the Father for the punishment of the offender: the fact of young Tarquin cannot be excused, yet without wrong to the reputation of so chaste a lady as Lucrece is reputed to be, it may be said, she had a greater desire to be thought chaste, than to be chaste; she might have died untouched, and unspotted in her body, if she had not been afraid to be slandered for inchastity; both Dionysius Halicarnasseus and Livy, who both are her friends, so tell the tale of her, as if she had chosen rather to be a whore, than to be thought a whore. To say truth, we find no other cause of the expulsion of Tarquin, than the wantonness and licentiousness of the people of Rome.

This is further to be considered in the Roman government, that all the time between their Kings, and their Emperors, there lasted a continued strife, between the nobility and Commons, wherein by degrees the Commons prevailed at last, so to weaken the authority of the Consuls and Senate, that even the last sparks of monarchy were in a manner extinguished, and then instantly began the civil war, which lasted till the regal power was quickly brought home, and settled in monarchy. So long as the power of the Senate stood good for the election of Consuls, the regal power was preserved in them, for the Senate had their first institution from monarchy: it is worth the noting, that in all those places that have seemed to be most popular, that weak degree of government, that hath been exercised among them, hath been founded upon, and been beholden unto monarchical principles, both for the power of assembling, and manner of consulting: for the entire and gross body of any people, is such an unwieldy and diffused thing as is not capable of uniting, or congregating, or deliberating in an entire lump, but in broken parts, which at first were regulated by monarchy.

Furthermore, it is observable that Rome in her chief popularity, was oft beholden for her preservation to the monarchical power of the Father over the children: by means of this fatherly power, saith Bodin, the Romans flourished in all honour and virtue, and oftentimes was their commonweal thereby delivered from most imminent destruction, when the Fathers drew out of the consistory, their sons being tribunes publishing laws tending to sedition. Amongst others Cassius threw his son headlong out of the consistory, publishing the law Agraria (for the division of lands) in the behoof of the people, and after by his own private judgment put him to death, the magistrates, serjeants and people standing thereat astonished, and not daring to withstand his fatherly authority, although they would with all their power have had that law for division of lands; which is sufficient proof, this power of the father not only to have been sacred and inviolable, but also to have been lawful for him, either by right or wrong to dispose of the life and death of his children, even contrary to the will of the magistrates and people.

It is generally believed that the government of Rome, after the expulsion of Kings, was popular; Bodin endeavours to prove it, but I am not satisfied with his arguments, and though it will be thought a paradox, yet I must maintain, it was never truly popular.

First, it is difficult to agree, what a popular government is. Aristotle saith, it is where many or a multitude do rule; he doth not say where the people, or the major part of the people, or the representers of the people govern.

Bodin affirms, if all the people be interested in the government, it is a popular estate, *Lib.* 2, *c.* 1, but after in the same chapter he resolves, that it is a popular estate, when all the people, or the greater part thereof hath the sovereignty, and he puts the case, that if there be three-score thousand citizens, and forty thousand of them have the sovereignty, and twenty thousand be excluded, it shall be called a popular estate: but I must tell him, though fifty-nine thousand, nine hundred and ninety-nine of them govern, yet it is no popular estate; for if but one man be excluded, the same reason that excludes that one man, may exclude many hundreds, and many thousands, yea, and the major part itself; if it be admitted, that the people are or ever were free by nature, and not to be governed, but by their own consent, it is most unjust to exclude any one man from his right in government; and to suppose the people so unnatural, as at the first to have all consented to give away their right to a major part (as if they had liberty given them only to give away, and not to use it themselves) is not only improbable, but impossible; for the whole people is a thing so uncertain and change-able, that it alters every moment, so that it is necessary to ask of every infant so soon as it is born its consent to government, if you will ever have the consent of the whole people.

Moreover, if the arbitrary trial by a jury of twelve men, be a thing of that admirable perfection and justice, as is commonly believed, wherein the negative voice of every single person is preserved, so that the dissent of any of the twelve frustrates the whole judgment: how much more ought the natural freedom of each man be preserved, by allowing him his negative voice, which is but a continuing him in that estate, wherein, it is confessed, nature at first placed him? Justice requires that no one law should bind all, except all consent to it, there is nothing more violent and contrary to nature, than to allow a major part, or any other greater part less than the whole to bind all the people.

The next difficulty to discovering what a popular estate is, is to find out where the supreme power in the Roman government rested; it is Bodin's opinion, that in the Roman state the government was in the magistrates, the authority and council in the Senate, but the sovereign power and majesty in the people, *Lib.* 2, *c.* 1. So in his first book his doctrine is, that the ancient Romans said, 'Imperium in Magistratibus, authoritatem in Senatu, Potestatem in plebe, Majestatem in Populo jure esse dicebant'. These four words, command, authority, power and majesty, signify ordinarily one and the same thing, to wit, the sovereignty, or supreme power. I cannot find that Bodin knows how to distinguish them; for they were not distinct faculties placed in several subjects, but one and the same thing diversely qualified, for Impèrium, Authoritas, Potestas and Majestas were all originally in the Consuls; although for the greater show the Consuls would have the opinion and consent of the Senate who were never called together, nor had their advice asked, but when and in what points only it pleased the Consuls to propound: so that properly Senatusconsultum was only a decree of the Consuls, with the advice of the Senators: and so likewise the Consuls, when they had a mind to have the countenance of an ampler council, they assembled the Centuries, who were reckoned as the whole people, and were never to be assembled, but when the Consuls thought fit to propound some business of great weight unto them; so that *jussus populi*, the command of the people which Bodin so much magnifies, was properly *jussus consulum*, the command of the Consuls, by the advice or consent of the assembly of the Centuries, who were a body composed of the Senators, and the rest of the Patricians, Knights and Gentlemen, or whole nobility together with the Commons: for the same men who had voices in Senate, had also their votes allowed in the assembly of the Centuries, according to their several capacities.

It may further appear, that the Roman government was never truly popular, for that in her greatest show of popularity, there were to be found above ten servants for every citizen or freeman, and of those servants, not one of them was allowed any place, or voice in government: if it be said that the Roman servants were slaves taken in war, and therefore not fit to be freemen; to this it may be answered, that if the opinion of our modern politicians be good, which holds that all men are born free by nature, or if but the opinion of Aristotle be sound, who saith that by nature some men are servants, and some are masters, then it may be unnatural, or unjust to make all prisoners in war servants, or (as they are now called) slaves, a term not used in the popular governments, either of Rome or Greece; for in both languages, the usual word that doth answer to our late term of slave, is but *servus* in Latin, and δοῦλος in Greek. Besides, if the wars of the Romans, by which they gained so many servants, were unjust, as I take all offensive war to be without a special commission from God, and as I believe all the

Roman wars were that were made for the enlargement of their empire, then we may conclude that the Romans were the notablest plagiaries, or men-stealers in the world.

But to allow the lesser part of the people of Rome, who called them-selves citizens, to have had a just right to exclude all servants from being a part of the people of Rome, let us inquire whether the major part of those, whom they allowed to be citizens, had the government of Rome; whereby we may discover easily how notoriously the poorer and greater part of the citizens were gulled of their share in government; there were two famous manners of their assembling the people of Rome: the first was by classes, as they called them, which were divided into Centuries; the second was by tribes, or wards; the former of these was a ranking of the people, according to their abilities or wealth; the latter according to the place or ward, wherein every citizen dwelt. In the assemblies of neither of these had the major part of the people the power of government, as may thus be made appear.

First, for the assembly of the Centuries, there were six degrees or classes of men according to their wealths; the first class was of the richest men in Rome, none whereof were under £200 in value: the valuation of the second classes was not under fourscore pounds; and so the third, the fourth, and the fifth classes were each a degree one under another. The sixth class contained the poorer sort, and all the rabble. These six classes were subdivided into Hundreds or Centuries.

The first class had	98	
The second class had	22	
The third class had	20	
The fourth class had	22	Centuries
The fifth class had	30	
The sixth class had	1	

193

The classes, and Centuries being thus ordered, when the assembly came to give their votes, they did not give their voices by the poll, which is the true popular way: but each Century voted by itself, each Century having one voice, the major part of the Centuries carried the business: now there being fourscore and eighteen Centuries in the first class, in which all the Patricians, Senators, Noblemen, Knights and Gentlemen of Rome were enrolled, being more in number, and above half the Centuries, must needs have the government, if they agreed all together in their votes, because they voted first, for when ninety-seven

Centuries had agreed in their votes, the other Centuries of the inferior class were never called to vote; thus the nobles and richer men who were but few in comparison of the common people did bear the chief sway, because all the poorer sort, or proletarian rabble, were clapped into the sixth class, which in reckoning were allowed but the single voice of one Century, which never came to voting: whereas in number they did far exceed all the five other classes or Centuries, and if they had been allowed the liberty of other citizens, they might have been justly numbered for a thousand Centuries, or voices in the assembly; this device of packing so many thousands into one Century, did exclude far the greatest part of the people from having a part in the government.

Next, for the assembly of the people of Rome by tribes, it must be considered, that the tribes did not give their voices by the poll all together, which is the true way of popular voting, but each tribe or ward did vote by itself, and the votes of the major part (not of the people but) of the tribes did sway the government, the tribes being unequal, as all divisions by wards usually are, because the number of the people of one tribe, is not just the same with the number of the people of each other tribe; whence it followed, that the major number of the tribes might possibly be the minor number of the people, which is a destroying of the power of the major part of the people.

Add thereunto, that the nobility of Rome were excluded from being present at the assembly of the tribes; and so the most considerable part of the people was wanting, therefore it could not be the voices of the major part of the people, where a great part of the people were allowed no voices at all, for it must be the major part of the whole, and not of a part of the people, that must denominate a popular government.

Moreover, it must be noted, that the assembly of the tribes was not originally the power of the people of Rome, for it was almost forty years after the rejection of Kings before an assembly of tribes were thought on, or spoken of; for it was the assembly of the people by Centuries, that agreed to the expulsion of Kings, and creating of Consuls in their room, also the famous laws of the twelve tables were ratified by the assembly of the Centuries. This assembly by Centuries, as it was more ancient, than that by tribes; so it was more truly popular, because all the nobility, as well as the Commons, had voices in it. The assembly by tribes, was pretended at first, only to elect tribunes of the people, and other inferior magistrates, to determine of lesser crimes that were not capital, but only fineable; and to decree that peace should be made; but they did not meddle with denouncing war to be made; for that high point did belong only to the assembly of the Centuries; and so also did the judging of treason, and other capital crimes. The difference between the assembly of the tribes, and of the Centuries, is very material; for though it be commonly thought, that either of these two assemblies were esteemed to be the people, yet in reality it was not so, for the assembly of the Centuries only could be said to be the people, because all the nobility were included in it as well as the Commons, whereas they were excluded out of the assembly of the tribes; and yet in effect, the assembly of the Centuries was but as the assembly of the Lords or Nobles only, because the lesser, and richer part of the people had the sovereignty, as the assembly of the tribes was but the Commons only.

In maintenance of the popular government of Rome, Bodin objects, that there could be no regal power in the two Consuls, who could neither make law, nor peace, nor war. The answer is, though there were two Consuls, yet but one of them had the regality; for they governed by turns, one Consul one month, and the other Consul another month; or the first one day, and the second another day. That the Consuls could make no laws is false, it is plain by Livy, that they had the power to make laws, or war, and did execute that power, though they were often hindered by the tribunes of the people; not for that the power of making laws or war, was ever taken away from the Consuls, or communicated to the tribunes, but only the exercise of the consular power was suspended by a seeming humble way of inter-cession of the tribunes; the Consuls by their first institution had a lawful right to do those things, which yet they would not do by reason of the shortness of their reigns, but chose rather to countenance their actions with the title of a decree of the Senate (who were their private council) yea, and sometimes with the decree of the assembly of the Centuries (who were their public council) for both the assembling of the Senate, and of the Centuries, was at the pleasure of the Consuls, and nothing was to be propounded in either of them, but at the will of the Consuls: which argues a sovereignty in them over the Senate and Centuries; the Senate of Rome was like the House of Lords, the assembly of the tribes resembled the House of Commons, but the assembling of the Centuries was a body composed of Lords and Commons united to vote together.

The tribunes of the people bore all the sway among the tribes, they called them together when they pleased, without any order, whereas the Centuries were never assembled without ceremony, and religious observation of the birds by the augurs, and by the approbation of the Senate, and therefore were said to be *auspicata*, and *ex authoritate Patrum*.

These things considered, it appears, that the assembly of the Centuries was the only legitimate, and great meeting of the people of Rome: as for any assembling, or electing of any trustees, or representers of the people of Rome, in nature of the modern Parliaments, it was not in use, or ever known in Rome.

Above two hundred and twenty years after the expulsion of Kings, a sullen humour took the Commons of Rome, that they would needs depart the city to Janiculum, on the other side of Tiber, they would not be brought back into the city, until a law was made, that a *plebiscitum*, or a decree of the Commons might be observed for a law; this law was made by the Dictator Hortensius, to quiet the sedition by giving a part of the legislative power to the Commons in such inferior matters only, as by toleration and usurpation had been practised by the Commons. I find not that they desired an enlargement of the points which were the object of their power, but of the persons, or nobility that should be subject to their decrees: the great power of making war, of creating the greater magistrates, of judging in capital crimes, remained in the Consuls, with the Senate and assembly of the Centuries.

For further manifestation of the broken and distracted government of Rome, it is fit to consider the original power of the Consuls, and of the tribunes of the Commons, who are ordinarily called the tribunes of the people.

First, it is undeniable, that upon the expulsion of Kings, kingly power was not taken away, but only made annual and changeable between two Consuls; who in their turns, and by course had the sovereignty, and all regal power; this appears plainly in Livy, who tells us that Valerius Publicola being Consul, he himself alone ordained a law, and then assembled a general session.

Turentillus Arsa inveighed and complained against the Consul's government, as being so absolute, and in name only less odious than that of Kings, but in fact more cruel; for instead of one Lord the city had received twain, having authority beyond all measure, unlimited and infinite. Sextius and Licinus complain, that there would never be any indifferent course, so long as the nobles kept the sovereign place of command, and the sword to strike, whilst the poor Commons have only the buckler; their conclusion was, that it remains, that the Commons bear the office of Consuls too, for that were a fortress of their liberty; from that day forward shall the Commons be partakers of those things, wherein the nobles now surpass them, namely sovereign rule and authority.

The law of the twelve tribes affirm, 'Regio imperio duo sunto, iique consules appellantur'. Let two have regal power, and let them be called Consuls: also the judgment of Livy is, that the sovereign power was translated from Consuls to Decemvirs, as before from Kings to Consuls. These are proofs sufficient to show the royal power of the Consuls.

About sixteen years after the first creation of Consuls, the Commons finding themselves much run into debt, by wasting their estates in following the wars; and so becoming, as they thought, oppressed by usury, and cast into prison by the judgment, and sentence of the Consuls, they grievously complained of usury, and of the power of the Consuls, and by sedition prevailed, and obtained leave to choose among themselves magistrates called tribunes of the people, who by their intercession might preserve the Commons from being oppressed, and suffering wrong from the Consuls: and it was further agreed, that the persons of those tribunes should be sacred, and not to be touched by any. By means of this immunity of the bodies of the tribunes from all arrests or other violence, they grew in time by degrees to such boldness, that by stopping the legal proceedings of the Consuls (when they pleased to intercede) they raised such an anarchy oft times in government, that they themselves might act, and take upon them, what power so ever they pleased (though it belonged not to them). This gallantry of the tribunes was the cause, that the Commons of Rome, who were diligent pretenders to liberty, and the great masters of this part of politics, were thought the only famous preservers, and keepers of the liberty of Rome. And to do them right, it must be confessed, they were the only men that truly understood the rights of a negative voice; if we will allow every man to be naturally free till they give their consent to be bound, we must allow every particular person a negative voice; so that when as all have equal power, and are as it were fellow-magistrates or officers, each man may impeach, or stop his fellow-officers in their proceedings. This is grounded upon the general reason of all them, which have anything in common, where he which forbiddeth, or denieth, hath most right; because his condition in that case is better than his which commandeth, or moveth to proceed; for every law or command, is in itself an innovation, and a diminution of some part of popular liberty; for it is no law except it restrain liberty; he that by his negative voice doth forbid or hinder the proceeding of a new law, doth but preserve himself in that condition of liberty, wherein nature hath placed him, and whereof he is in present possession; the condition of him thus in possession being the better, the stronger is his prohibition, any single man hath a juster title to his negative voice, than any multitude can have to their affirmative; to say the people are free, and not to be governed, but by their own consent, and yet to allow a major part to rule the whole, is a plain contradiction, or a destruction of natural freedom. This the Commons of Rome rightly understood, and therefore the transcendent power of the negative voice of any one tribune, being able of itself to stay all the proceedings, not of the Consuls and Senate only, and other magistrates, but also of the rest of his fellow-tribunes, made them seem the powerfullest men in all Rome; and yet in truth they had no power or jurisdiction at all, nor were they any magistrates, nor could they lawfully call any man before them, for they were not appointed for administration of justice, but only to oppose the violence and abuse of magistrates, by inter-ceding for such as appealed, being unjustly oppressed; for which purpose at first they sat only without the door of the Senate, and were not permitted to come within the doors: this negative power of theirs was of force only to hinder, but not to help the proceedings in courts of justice; to ungovern, and not to govern the people. And though they had no power to make laws, yet they took upon them to propound laws, and flattered and humoured the Commons by the Agrarian and Frumentarian Laws, by the first they divided the common fields and conquered lands among the common people; and by the latter, they afforded them corn at a cheaper or lower price: by these means these demagogues or tribunes of the Commons led the vulgar by the noses, to allow whatsoever usurpations they pleased to make in government.

The royal power of the Consuls was never taken away from them by any law that I hear of, but continued in them all the time of their pretended popular government, to the very last, though repined at, and opposed in some particulars by the Commons.

The no-power, or negative power of the tribunes, did not long give content to the Commons, and therefore they desired, that one of the Consuls might be chosen out of the Commonalty: the eager propounding of this point for the Commons, and the diligent opposing of it by the nobility or Senate, argues how much both parties regarded the sovereign power of a Consul; the dispute lasted fourscore years within two: the tribunes pressing it upon all advantages of opportunity, never gave over till they carried it by strong hand, or stubbornness, hindering all elections of the *Curule*, or greater magistrates, for five years together, whereby the nobles were forced to yield the Commons a Consul's place, or else an anarchy was ready to destroy them all, and yet the nobility had for a good while allowed the Commons military tribunes with consular power, which, in effect or substance, was all one with having one of the Consuls a commoner, so that it was the bare name of a Consul which the Commons so long strived for with the nobility. In this contention, some years Consuls were chosen, some years military tribunes in such confusion, that the Roman historians cannot agree among themselves, what Consuls to assign, or name for each year, although they have capitoline tables, Sicilian and Greek registers, and calenders, fragments of Capitoline marbles, linen books or records to help them: a good while the Commons were content with the liberty of having one of the Consuls a commoner; but about four score years after they enjoyed this privilege, a desire took them to have it enacted, that a decree of the Commons called a *Plebiscitum* might be observed for a law, Hortensius the dictator yielded to enact it, thereby to bring back the seditious Commons, who departed to Janiculum on the other side of Tiber, because they were deeply engaged in debt in regard of long seditions and dissensions. The eleventh book of Livy, where this sedition is set down, is lost; we have only a touch of it in Florus his epitome, and Saint Augustine mentions the plundering of many houses by the Commons at their departing: this sedition was above 220 years after the expulsion of Kings, in all which time the people of Rome got the spoil of almost all Italy, and the wealth of very many rich cities: and yet the Commons were in so great penury, and overwhelmed with debts, that they fell to plunder the rich houses of the citizens, which sounds not much for the honour of a popular government. This communicating of a legislative power to the Commons, touching power of enfranchising allies, judgments penal, and fines, and those ordinances that concerned the good of the Commons called *Plebiscita*, was a dividing of the supreme power, and the giving a share of it to others, as well as to the Consuls, and was in effect to destroy the legislative power, for to have two supremes is to have none, because the one may destroy the other, and is quite contrary to the indivisible nature of sovereignty. The truth is, the Consuls, having but annual sovereignty, were glad for their own safety, and ease in matters of great importance, and weight, to call together sometimes the Senate, who were their ordinary council, and many times the Centuries of the people, who were their council extraordinary, that by their advice they might countenance, and strengthen such actions as were full of danger and envy: and thus the Consuls by weakening their original power brought the government to confusion, civil dissension, and utter ruin: so dangerous a thing it is to show favour to common people, who interpret all graces and favours for their rights, and just liberties: the Consuls following the advice of the senate or people, did not take away their right of governing no more than Kings lose their supremacy by taking advice in Parliaments.

Not only the Consuls, but also the praetors and censors (two great offices, ordained only for the ease of the Consuls, from whom an appeal lay to the Consuls) did in many things exercise an arbitrary or legislative power in the absence of the Consuls, they had no laws to limit them: for many years after the creation of Consuls, ten men were sent into Greece to choose laws; and after the twelve tables were confirmed, whatsoever the praetors, who were but the Consuls' substitutes, did command, was called *jus honorarium*; and they were wont at their entrance into their office to collect and hang up for public view, a form of administration of justice which they would observe, and though the *edictum Praetoris* expired with the praetors office, yet it was called *Edictum perpetuum*.

What peace the Low Countries have found since their revolt is visible; it is near about a hundred years since they set up for themselves, of all which time only twelve years they had a truce with the Spaniard, yet in the next year, after the truce was agreed upon, the war of Julers broke forth, which engaged both parties; so that upon the matter, they have lived in a continual war, for almost a hundred years; had it not been for the aid of their neighbours, they had been long ago swallowed up, when they were glad humbly to offer their new hatched commonweal, and themselves vassals to the Queen of England, after that the French King, Henry III, had refused to accept them as his subjects; that little truce they had, was almost as costly as a war; they being forced to keep about thirty thousand soldiers continually in garrison. Two things they say they first fought about, religion and taxes, and they have prevailed it seems in both, for they have gotten all the religions in christendom, and pay the greatest taxes in the world; they pay tribute half in half for food, and most necessary things, paying as much for tribute as the price of the thing sold; excise is paid by all retailers of wine, and other commodities; for each tun of beer six shillings, for each cow for the pail two stivers every week; for oxen, horses, sheep and other beasts sold in the market the twelfth part at least; be they never so oft sold by the year to and fro, the new master still pays as much; they pay five stivers for every bushel of their own wheat, which they use to grind in public mills. These are the fruits of the Low Country war.

It will be said that Venice is a commonwealth that enjoys peace. She indeed of all other states hath enjoyed of late the greatest peace; but she owes it not to her kind of government, but to the natural situation of the city, having such a bank in the sea of near three score miles, and such marshes towards the land, as make her unapproachable by land, or sea; to these she is indebted for her peace at home, and what peace she hath abroad she buys at a dear rate; and yet her peace is little better than a continued war; the city always is in such perpetual fears, that many besieged cities are in more security; a Senator or gentleman dares not converse with any stranger in Venice, shuns acquaintance, or dares not own it; they are no better than banditos to all human society. Nay, no people in the world live in such jealousy one of another; hence are their intricate solemnities, or rather lotteries in election of their magistrates, which in any other place, would be ridiculous and useless. The Senators or gentlemen are not only jealous of the common people, whom they keep disarmed, but of one another, they dare not trust any of their own citizens to be a leader of their army, but are forced to hire, and entertain foreign princes for their generals, excepting their citizens from their wars, and hiring others in their places; it cannot be said that people live in peace, which are in such miserable fears continually.

The Venetians at first were subject to the Roman Emperor; and for fear of the invasion of the Huns forsook Padua, and other places in Italy; and retired with all their substance to those islands where now Venice stands: I do not read they had any leave to desert the defence of their prince and country, where they had got their wealth, much less to set up a government of their own; it was no better than a rebellion, or revolting from the Roman empire. At first they lived under a kind of oligarchy; for several islands had each a tribune, who all met and governed in common; but the dangerous seditions of their tribunes, put a necessity upon them to choose a duke for life, who, for many hundreds of years had an absolute power; under whose government Venice flourished most, and got great victories, and rich possessions. But by insensible degress, the great council of the gentlemen have for many years been lessening the power of their Dukes, and have at last quite taken it away. It is a strange error for any man to believe, that the government of Venice hath been always the same that it is now: he that reads but the history of Venice, may find for a long time a sovereign power in their Dukes: and that for these last two hundred years, since the diminishing of that power, there have been no great victories and conquests obtained by that estate.

That which exceeds admiration, is that Contarene hath the confidence to affirm the present government of Venice to be a mixed form of monarchy, democracy and aristocracy: for, whereas he makes the Duke to have the person and show of a King; he after confesseth, that the

Duke can do nothing at all alone, and being joined with other magistrates, he hath no more authority than any of them: also the power of
the magistrates is so small, that no one of them, how ever great so he
be, can determine of anything of moment, without the allowance of
the council. So that this duke is but a man dressed up in purple, a King
only in pomp and ornament, in power but a Senator, within the city
a captive, without a traitor, if he go without leave. As little reason is
there to think a popular estate is to be found in the great council of
Venice, or S.P.Q.V. for it doth not consist of the fortieth part of the
people, but only of those they call patricians or gentlemen; for the
Commons, neither by themselves, nor by any chosen by them for
their representers, are admitted to be any part of the great council: and
if the gentlemen of Venice have any right to keep the government in
their own hands, and to exclude the Commons, they never had it
given them by the people, but at first were beholding to monarchy for
their nobility. This may further be noted, that though Venice of late
enjoyed peace abroad, yet it had been with that charge, either for
fortification·and defence, or in bribery so excessive, whereby of late
upon any terms they purchased their peace, that it is said their taxes
are such, that christians generally live better under the Turk, than under
the Venetians, for there is not a grain of corn, a spoonful of wine, salt,
eggs, birds, beasts, fowl, or fish sold, that payeth not a certain custom:
upon occasions the labourers and craftsmen pay a rate by the poll
monthly, they receive incredible gains by usury of the Jews; for in
every city they keep open shops of interest, taking pawns after fifteen
in the hundred, and if at the year's end it be not redeemed, it is forfeited,
or at the least, sold at great loss. The revenues which the very
courtesans pay for toleration, maintains no less than a dozen of galleys.

By what hath been said, it may be judged how unagreeable the
popular government of Rome heretofore, and of Venice, and the
United Provinces at present are, either for religion or peace (which two
are the principal ingredients of government) and so consequently not
fit to be reckoned for forms, since whatsoever is either good or tolerable in either of their governments, is borrowed or patched up of a
broken and distracted monarchy. Lastly, though Venice and the Low
Countries are the only remarkable places in this age that reject monarchy; yet neither of them pretend their government to be founded
upon any original right of the people, or have the common people
any power amongst them, or any chosen by them. Never was any
popular estate in the world famous for keeping themselves in peace;
all their glory hath been for quarrelling and fighting.

Those that are willing to be persuaded, that the power of government is originally in the people, finding how impossible it is for any people to exercise such power, do surmise, that though the people cannot govern, yet they may choose representers or trustees, that may manage this power for the people, and such representers must be surmised to be the people. And since such representers cannot truly be chosen by the people, they are fain to divide the people into several parts, as of provinces, cities, and borough-towns, and to allow to every one of those parts to choose one representer or more of their own: and such representers, though not any of them be chosen by the whole, or major part of the people, yet still must be surmised to be the people; nay, though not one of them be chosen either by the people, or the major part of the people of any province, city, or borough, for which they serve, but only a smaller part, still it must be said to be the people. Now when such representers of the people do assemble or meet, it is never seen that all of them can at one time meet together; and so there never appears a true, or full representation of the whole people of the nation, the representers of one part or other being absent, but still they must be imagined to be the people. And when such imperfect assemblies be met, though not half be present, they proceed: and though their number be never so small, yet it is so big, that in the debate of any business of moment, they know not how to handle it, without referring it to a fewer number than themselves, though themselves are not so many as they should be. Thus those that are chosen to represent the people, are necessitated to choose others, to represent the representers themselves; a trustee of the north doth delegate his power to a trustee of the south; and one of the east may substitute one of the west for his proxy: hereby it comes to pass, that public debates which are imagined to be referred to a general assembly of a kingdom, are contracted into a particular or private assembly, than which nothing can be more destructive, or contrary to the nature of public assemblies. Each company of such trustees hath a prolocutor, or speaker; who, by the help of three or four of his fellows that are most active, may easily comply in gratifying one the other, so that each of them in their turn may sway the trustees, whilst one man, for himself or his friend, may rule in one business, and another man for himself or his friend prevail in another cause, till such a number of trustees be reduced to so many petty monarchs as there be men of it. So in all popularities, where a general council, or great assembly of the people meet, they find it impossible to dispatch any great action, either with expedition or secrecy, if a public free debate be admitted; and therefore are constrained to epitomize and sub-epitomize themselves so long, till at last they crumble away into the atoms of monarchy, which is the next degree to anarchy; for anarchy is nothing else but a broken monarchy, where every man is his own monarch, or governor.

Whereas the power of the people in choosing both their government and governors is of late highly magnified, as if they were able to choose the best and excellentest men for that purpose. We shall find it true what Aristotle hath affirmed, that to choose well is the office of him that hath knowledge; none can choose a geometrician but he that hath skill in geometry, *Lib.* 3, *c.* 11, for, saith he, all men esteem not excellency to be one and the same, *Lib.* 3, *c.* 17.

A great deal of talk there is in the world of the freedom and liberty that they say is to be found in popular commonweals; it is worth the inquiry how far, and in what sense this speech of liberty is true. True liberty is for every man to do what he list, or to live as he please, and not to be tied to any laws. But such liberty is not to be found in any commonweal; for there are more laws in popular estates than anywhere else; and so consequently less liberty: and government many say was invented to take away liberty, and not to give it to every man; such liberty cannot be; if it should, there would be no government at all: therefore, Aristotle, *Lib.* 6, *c.* 4, 'It is profitable not to be lawful to do everything that we will, for power to do what one will, cannot restrain that evil that is in every man'; so that true liberty cannot, nor should not be in any estate. But the only liberty that the talkers of liberty can mean, is a liberty for some men to rule and to be ruled, for so Aristotle expounds it; one while to govern, another while to be governed; to be a King in the forenoon, and a subject in the afternoon; this is the only liberty that a popular estate can brag of, that where a monarchy hath but one King, their government hath the liberty to have many Kings by turns. If the common people look for any other liberty, either of their persons or their purses, they are pitifully deceived, for a perpetual army and taxes are the principal materials of all popular regiments: never yet any stood without them, and very seldom continued with them; many popular estates have started up, but few have lasted; it is no hard matter for any kind of government to last one, or two, or three days, *Lib.* 6, *c.* 5. For all such as out of hope of liberty, attempt to erect new forms of government, he gives this prudent lesson. We must look well into the continuance of time, and remembrance of many years, wherein the means tending to establish community had not lain hid, if they had been good and useful; for almost all things have been found out, albeit some have not been received, and other some have been rejected, after men have had experience of them, *Lib.* 2, *c.* 5.

It is believed by many, that at the very first assembling of the people, it was unanimously agreed in the first place, that the consent of the major part should bind the whole; and that though this first agreement cannot possibly be proved, either how, or by whom it could be made; yet it must necessarily be believed or supposed, because otherwise there could be no lawful government at all. That there could be no lawful government, except a general consent of the whole people be first surmised, is no sound proposition; yet true it is, that there could be no popular government without it. But if there were at first a government without being beholden to the people for their consent, as all men confess there was, I find no reason but that there may be so still, without asking leave of the multitude.

If it be true, that men are by nature free-born, and not to be governed without their own consents, and that self-preservation is to be regarded in the first place, it is not lawful for any government but self-government to be in the world, it were sin in the people to desire, or attempt to consent to any other government: if the Fathers will promise for themselves to be slaves, yet for their children they cannot, who have always the same right to set themselves at liberty, which their Fathers had to enslave themselves.

To pretend that a major part, or the silent consent of any part, may be interpreted to bind the whole people, is both unreasonable and unnatural; it is against all reason for men to bind others, where it is against nature for men to bind themselves. Men that boast so much of natural freedom, are not willing to consider how contradictory and destructive the power of a major part is to the natural liberty of the whole people; the two grand favourites of the subjects, liberty and property (for which most men pretend to strive) are as contrary as fire to water, and cannot stand together. Though by humane laws in voluntary actions, a major part may be tolerated to bind the whole multitude, yet in necessary actions, such as those of nature are, it cannot be so. Besides, if it were possible for the whole people to choose their representers, then either every, each one of these representers ought to be particularly chosen by the whole people, and not one representer by one part, and another representer by another part of the people, or else it is necessary, that continually the entire number of the representers be present, because otherwise the whole people is never represented.

Again, it is impossible for the people, though they might and would choose a government, or governors, ever to be able to do it: for the people, to speak truly and properly, is a thing or body in continual alteration and change, it never continues one minute the same, being composed of a multitude of parts, whereof divers continually decay and perish, and others renew and succeed in their places, they which are the people this minute, are not the people the next minute. If it be answered, that it is impossible to stand so strictly, as to have the consent of the whole people; and therefore that which cannot be, must be supposed to be the act of the whole people; this is a strange answer, first to affirm a necessity of having the peoples' consent, then to confess an impossibility of having it. If but once that liberty, which is esteemed so sacred, be broken, or taken away but from one of the meanest or basest of all the people; a wide gap is thereby opened for any multitude whatsoever, that is able to call themselves, or whomsoever they please, the people.

Howsoever men are naturally willing to be persuaded, that all sovereignty flows from the consent of the people, and that without it no true title can be made to any supremacy; and that it is so current an axiom of late, that it will certainly pass without contradiction as a late exercitator tells us: yet there are many and great difficulties in the point never yet determined, not so much as disputed, all which the exercitator waives and declines, professing he will not insist upon the distinctions, touching the manner of the peoples passing their consent, nor determine which of them is sufficient, and which not to make the right or title; whether it must be antecedent to possession, or may be consequent: express, or tacite: collective, or representative: absolute, or conditionated: free, or enforced: revocable, or irrevocable. All these are material doubts concerning the peoples' title, and though the exercitator will not himself determine what consent is sufficient, and what not, to make a right or title, yet he might have been so courteous, as to have directed us, to whom we might go for resolution in these cases. But the truth is, that amongst all them that plead the necessity of the consent of the people, none of them hath ever touched upon these so necessary doctrines; it is a task it seems too difficult, otherwise surely it would not have been neglected, considering how necessary it is to resolve the conscience, touching the manner of the peoples passing their consent; and what is sufficient, and what not, to make, or derive a right, or title from the people.

No multitude or great assembly of any nation, though they be all of them never so good and virtuous, can possibly govern; this may be evidently discovered by considering the actions of great and numerous assemblies, how they are necessitated to relinquish that supreme power, which they think they exercise, and to delegate it to a few. There are two parts of the supreme power, the legislative, and the executive, neither of these can a great assembly truly act. If a new law be to be made it may in the general receive the proposal of it from one or more of the general assembly, but the forming, penning, or framing it into a law, is committed to a few, because a great number of persons cannot without tedious, and dilatory debates, examine the benefits and mischiefs of a law. Thus in the very first beginning the intention of a general assembly is frustrated; then after a law is penned or framed, when it comes to be questioned, whether it shall pass or nay; though it be voted in a full assembly, yet by the rules of the assembly, they are all so tied up, and barred from a free and full debate; that when any man hath given the reasons of his opinion; if those reasons be argued against, he is not permitted to reply in justification or explanation of them, but when he hath once spoken, he must be heard no more: which is a main denial of that freedom of debate, for which the great assembly is alleged to be ordained in the high point of legislative power.

The same may be said, touching the executive power. If a cause be brought before a great assembly, the first thing done is to refer, or commit it to some few of the assembly, who are trusted with the examining the proofs, and witnesses, and to make report to the general assembly; who upon the report proceed to give their judgments without any public hearing, or interrogating the witnesses, upon whose testimonies diligently examined every man that will pass a conscientious judgment is to rely. Thus the legislative and executive power are never truly practised in a great assembly; the true reason whereof is, if freedom be given to debate, never anything could be agreed upon without endless disputes; mere necessity compels to refer main transactions of business to particular congregations and committees.

Those governments that seem to be popular are kinds of petty monarchies, which may thus appear: government is a relation between the governors, and the governed, the one cannot be without the other, *mutuo se ponunt et auferunt*; where a command or law proceeds from a major part, there those individual persons that concurred in the vote, are the governors, because the law is only their will in particular: the power of a major part being a contingent, or casual thing, expires in the very act itself of voting, which power of a major part is grounded upon a supposition, that they are the stronger part; when the vote is passed, these voters, which are the major part, return again, and are incorporated into the whole assembly, and are buried as it were in that lump, and not otherwise considered; the act or law ordained by such a vote, loseth the makers of it, before it comes to be obeyed; for when it comes to be put in execution, it becomes the will of those who enjoin it, and force obedience to it, not by virtue of any power derived from the makers of the law. No man can say, that during the reign of the late Queen Elizabeth, that King Henry VIII, or Edward VI did govern, although that many of the laws that were made in those two former princes' times, were observed, and executed under her government; but those laws, though made by her predecessors, yet became the laws of her present government; who willed and commanded the execution of them, and had the same power to correct, interpret, or mitigate them, which the first makers of them had; every law must always have some present known person in being, whose will it must be to make it a law for the present; this cannot be said of the major part of any assembly, because that major part instantly ceaseth, as soon as ever it hath voted: an infallible argument whereof is this, that the same major part after the vote given, hath no power to correct, alter, or mitigate it, or to cause it to be put in execution; so that he that shall act, or cause that law to be executed, makes himself the commander, or willer of it, which was originally the will of others: it is said by Mr. Hobbes in his *Leviathan*, page 141: 'Nothing is law, where the legislator cannot be known, for there must be manifest signs, that it proceedeth from the will of the sovereign, there is requisite, not only a declaration of the law, but also sufficient signs of the author and the authority.'

That senate or great council, wherein it is conceived the supreme, or legislative power doth rest, consists of those persons who are actually subjects at the very same time, wherein they exercise their legislative power, and at the same instant may be guilty of breaking one law, whilst they are making another law; for it is not the whole and entire will of every particular person in the assembly, but that part only of his will, which accidentally falls out to concur with the will of the greater part: so that the sharers of the legislative power have each of them, perhaps not a hundredth part of the legislative power (which in itself is indivisible) and that not in act, but in possibility, only in one particular point for that moment, whilst they give their vote. To close this point which may seem strange and new to some, I will produce the judgment of Bodin, in his sixth book of a commonweal, and the fourth chapter; his words are, 'The chief point of a commonweal, which is the right of sovereignty, cannot be, nor subsist, to speak properly, but in monarchy; for none can be sovereign in a commonweal, but one alone; if they be two, or three, or more, no one is sovereign, for that no one of them can give or take a law from his companion: and although we imagine a body of many Lords or of a whole people to hold the sovereignty, yet hath it no true ground nor support, if there be not a head with absolute power to unite them together, which a simple magistrate without sovereign authority cannot do. And if it chance that the Lords, or tribes of the people be divided (as it often falls out) then must they fall to arms one against another; and although the greatest part be of one opinion, yet may it so happen, as the lesser part, having many legions, and making a head, may oppose itself against the greater number, and get the victory. We see the difficulties which are, and always have been in popular estates, whereas they hold contrary parts, and for divers magistrates, some demand peace, others war; some will have this law, others that; some will have one commander, others another; some will treat a league with the King of France, others with the King of Spain, corrupted or drawn, some one way, some another, making open war, as hath been seen in our age amongst the Grisons, etc.'

Upon these texts of Aristotle fore-cited, and from the mutability of the Roman popularity, which Aristotle lived not to see, I leave the learned to consider, whether it be not probable that these, or the like paradoxes may be inferred to be the plain mind of Aristotle, viz. 1. That there is no form of government, but monarchy only. 2. That there is no monarchy, but paternal. 3. That there is no paternal monarchy, but absolute, or arbitrary. 4. That there is no such thing as an aristocracy or democracy. 5. That there is no such form of government as a tyranny. 6. That the people are not born free by nature.

DIRECTIONS FOR OBEDIENCE TO GOVERN-
MENT IN DANGEROUS OR DOUBTFUL TIMES

ALL those who so eagerly strive for an original power to be in the people, do with one consent acknowledge, that originally the supreme power was in the fatherhood; and that the first Kings were Fathers of families: this is not only evident, and affirmed by Aristotle; but yielded unto by Grotius, Mr. Selden, Mr. Hobbes, Mr. Ascham; and all others of that party, not one excepted, that I know of.

Now for those that confess an original subjection in children,. to be governed by their parents, to dream of an original freedom in man-kind, is to contradict themselves; and to make subjects to be free, and Kings to be limited; to imagine such pactions and contracts between Kings and people, as cannot be proved ever to have been made, or can ever be described or fancied, how it is possible for such contracts ever to have been, is a boldness to be wondered at.

Mr. Selden confesseth, that Adam, by donation from God, was made the general Lord of all things, not without such a private dominion to himself, as (without his grant) did exclude his children. And by donation, or assignation, or some kind of concession (before he was dead, or left any heir to succeed him) his children had their distinct territories, by right of private dominion. Abel had his flocks and pastures for them, Cain had his fields for corn and the land of Nod, where he built himself a city.

It is confessed, that in the infancy of the world, the paternal govern-ment was monarchical; but when the world was replenished with multitude of people, then the paternal government ceased, and was lost; and an elective kind of government by the people, was brought into the world. To this it may be answered, that the paternal power cannot be lost; it may either be transferred or usurped; but never lost, or ceaseth. God, who is the giver of power, may transfer it from the Father to some other; he gave to Saul a fatherly power over his Father Kish, God also hath given to the Father a right or liberty to alien his power over his children, to any other; whence we find the sale and gift of children, to have been much in use in the beginning of the world, when men had their servants for a possession and an inheritance as well as other goods: whereupon we find the power of castrating, and making eunuchs much in use in old times. As the power of the Father may be lawfully transferred or aliened, so it may be unjustly usurped:

and in usurpation, the title of a usurper is before, and better than the title of any other than of him that had a former right: for he hath a possession by the permissive will of God, which permission, how long it may endure, no man ordinarily knows. Every man is to preserve his own life for the service of God, and of his King or Father, and is so far to obey a usurper, as may tend not only to the preservation of his King and Father, but sometimes even to the preservation of the usurper himself, when probably he may thereby be reserved to the correction, or mercy of his true superior; though by humane laws, a long prescription may take away right, yet divine right never dies, nor can be lost, or taken away.

Every man that is born, is so far from being free-born, that by his very birth he becomes a subject to him that begets him: under which subjection he is always to live, unless by immediate appointment from God, or by the grant or death of his Father, he become possessed of that power to which he was subject.

The right of fatherly-government was ordained by God, for the preservation of mankind; if it be usurped, the usurper may be so far obeyed, as may tend to the preservation of the subjects, who may thereby be enabled to perform their duty to their true and right sovereign, when time shall serve: in such cases to obey a usurper, is properly to obey the first and right governor, who must be presumed to desire the safety of his subjects: the command of a usurper is not to be obeyed in anything tending to the destruction of the person of the governor; whose being in the first place is to be looked after.

It hath been said, that there have been so many usurpations by conquest in all kingdoms, that all kings are usurpers, or the heirs or successors of usurpers; and therefore any usurper, if he can but get the possession of a kingdom, hath as good a title as any other.

Answer. The first usurper hath the best title, being, as was said, in possession by the permission of God; and where a usurper hath continued so long, that the knowledge of the right heir be lost by all the subjects, in such a case a usurper in possession is to be taken and reputed by such subjects for the true heir, and is to be obeyed by them as their Father. As no man hath an infallible certitude, but only a moral knowledge, which is no other than a probable persuasion grounded upon a peaceable possession, which is a warrant for subjection to parents and governors; for we may not say, because children have no infallible, or necessary certainty who are their true parents, that therefore they need not obey, because they are uncertain: it is sufficient, and as much as humane nature is capable of, for children to rely upon a credible persuasion; for otherwise the commandment of 'Honour thy Father', would be a vain commandment, and not possible to be observed.

By human positive laws, a possession time out of mind takes away, or bars a former right, to avoid a general mischief, of bringing all right into a disputation not decidable by proof, and consequently to the overthrow of all civil government, in grants, gifts and contracts between man and man: but in grants and gifts that have their original from God or nature, as the power of the Father hath, no inferior power of man can limit, nor make any law of prescription against them: upon this ground is built that common maxim, that *Nullum tempus occurrit regi*, no time bars a King.

All power on earth is either derived or usurped from the fatherly power, there being no other original to be found of any power whatsoever; for if there should be granted two sorts of power without any subordination of one to the other, they would be in perpetual strife which should be supreme, for two supremes cannot agree; if the fatherly power be supreme, then the power of the people must be subordinate, and depend on it; if the power of the people be supreme, then the fatherly power must submit to it, and cannot be exercised without the licence of the people, which must quite destroy the frame and course of nature. Even the power which God himself exerciseth over mankind is by right of fatherhood; he is both the King and Father of us all; as God hath exalted the dignity of earthly Kings, by communicating to them his own title, by saying they are gods; so on the other side, he hath been pleased as it were to humble himself, by assuming the title of a King to express his power, and not the title of any popular government; we find it is a punishment to have no King, Hosea, iii, 4, and promised, as a blessing to Abraham, Genesis xvii, 6, that Kings shall come out of thee.

Every man hath a part or share in the preservation of mankind in general, he that usurps the power of a superior, thereby puts upon himself a necessity of acting the duty of a superior in the preservation of them over whom he hath usurped, unless he will aggravate one heinous crime, by committing another more horrid; he that takes upon him the power of a superior sins sufficiently, and to the purpose; but he that proceeds to destroy both his superior, and those under the superior's protection, goeth a strain higher, by adding murder to robbery; if government be hindered, mankind perisheth, a usurper by hindering the government of another, brings a necessity upon himself to govern, his duty before usurpation was only to be ministerial, or instrumental in the preservation of others by his obedience; but when he denies his own, and hinders the obedience of others, he doth not only not help, but is the cause of the distraction in hindering his superior to perform his duty, he makes the duty his own: if a superior cannot protect, it is his part to desire to be able to do it, which he cannot do in the future if in the present they be destroyed for want of government: therefore it is to be presumed, that the superior desires the preservation of them that should be subject to him; and so likewise it may be presumed, that a usurper in general doth the will of his superior, by preserving the people by government, and it is not improper to say, that in obeying a usurper, we may obey primarily the true superior, so long as our obedience aims at the preservation of those in subjection, and not at the destruction of the true governor. Not only the usurper, but those also over whom power is usurped, may join in the preservation of themselves, yea, and in the preservation sometimes of the usurper himself.

Thus there may be a conditional duty, or right in a usurper to govern; that is to say, supposing him to be so wicked as to usurp, and not willing to surrender or forgo his usurpation, he is then bound to protect by government, or else he increaseth and multiplieth his sin.

Though a usurper can never gain a right from the true superior, yet from those that are subjects he may; for if they know no other that hath a better title than the usurper, then as to them the usurper in possession hath a true right.

Such a qualified right is found at first in all usurpers, as is in thieves who have stolen goods, and during the time they are possessed of them, have a title in law against all others but the true owners, and such usurpers to divers intents and purposes may be obeyed.

Neither is he only a usurper who obtains the government, but all they are partakers in the usurpation, who have either failed to give assistance to their lawful sovereign, or have given aid either by their persons, estates or counsels for the destroying of that governor, under whose protection they have been born and preserved; for although it should be granted, that protection and subjection are reciprocal, so that where the first fails, the latter ceaseth; yet it must be remembered, that where a man hath been born under the protection of a long and peaceable government, he owes an assistance for the preservation of that government that hath protected him, and is the author of his own disobedience.

It is said by some, that a usurped power may be obeyed in things that are lawful: but it may not be obeyed not only in lawful things, but also in things indifferent: obedience in things indifferent, is necessary;

not indifferent. For in things necessarily good God is immediately obeyed, superiors only by consequence: if men command things evil, obedience is due only by tolerating what they inflict: not by performing what they require: in the first they declare what God commands to be done, in the latter what to be suffered, so it remains, that things indifferent only are the proper object of humane laws. Actions are to be considered simply and alone, and so are good as being motions, depending on the first mover; or jointly with circumstances: and that in a double manner. 1. In regard of the ability or possibility, whilst they may be done. 2. In the act when they be performed: before they be done they be indifferent; but once breaking out into act, they become distinctly good or evil according to the circumstances which determine the same. Now an action commanded, is supposed as not yet done (whereupon the Hebrews call the imperative mood the first future) and so remaineth many times indifferent.

Some may be of opinion, that if obedience may be given to a usurper in things indifferent, as well as to a lawful power; that then there is as much obedience due to a usurped power, as to a lawful. But it is a mistake; for though it be granted that in things indifferent, a usurper may be obeyed, as well as a lawful governor; yet herein lieth a main difference, that some things are indifferent for a lawful superior, which are not indifferent, but unlawful to a usurper to enjoin. Usurpation is the resisting, and taking away the power from him, who hath such a former right to govern the usurper, as cannot be lawfully taken away: so that it cannot be just for a usurper, to take advantage of his own unlawful act, or create himself a title by continuation of his own injustice, which aggravates, and never extenuates his crime: and if it never can be an act indifferent for the usurper himself to disobey his lawful sovereign, much less can it be indifferent for him to command another to do that to which he hath no right himself. It is only then a matter indifferent for a usurper to command, when the actions enjoined are such; as the lawful superior is commanded by the law of God, to provide for the benefit of his subjects, by the same, or other like restriction of such indifferent things; and it is to be presumed, if he had not been hindered, would have commanded the same, or the like laws.

OBSERVATIONS

CONCERNING

THE ORIGINALL

OF

GOVERNMENT,

Upon $\left\{\begin{array}{l}\textit{Mr. HOBS Leviathan} \\ \textit{Mr. MILTON against Salmasius} \\ \textit{H. GROTIUS De Jure Belli}\end{array}\right.$

LONDON

Printed for R. ROYSTON, at the *Angel*
in Ivie Lane.   1652.

(Bought by Thomason February 18th, 1652, i.e. 3 months before the *Forms*. These tracts were reprinted later in 1652, and the *Anarchy* bound in at the end. The new title page was identical except that 'Mr. Hunton's *Treatise of Monarchy*' was added within the bracket. There is a manuscript source in Harleian, vol. 6867, No. 17 (presumably from East Sutton) of the first 6½ pages of the *Observations on Hobbes*. All three tracts were reprinted in all the collected editions, 1679, 1680, 1684, 1695(?) and 1696, and come after the *Forms*. The section on Milton was photostatically reproduced in W. R. Parker, *Milton's Contemporary Reputation*, Columbus, Ohio, 1940.

All three essays are based on *Patriarcha*, and there are parallel passages throughout. Page 209, line 31, to page 225, line 6, of the 1684 reprint of the *Observation on Grotius* comprises the passage which was embodied from the *Patriarcha* MS., and is printed above pp. 63–73. Locke made use of all the essays in his refutation, but it is significant that his most extensive quotations come from this passage which really belongs to *Patriarcha*. This section of the work is obviously at least as early as *Patriarcha* itself (*De Jure Belli* first appeared in 1625), but Milton's *Defensio* did not appear until April 1650 and *Leviathan* in mid 1651, so that the other two sections must be much later.

This work does not add a great deal to the theories already set out in *Patriarcha* and the *Anarchy* (published 1648). Its chief interest is in the views Filmer expresses on three of the important political writers of his day, and especially in his frank confession of his agreement with Hobbes. It was the first critique of the *Leviathan* to appear. W. R. Parker in the work referred to above appreciates the *Observations on Milton* as the only dispassionate analysis of Milton's political arguments written by an Englishman.)

THE PREFACE

With no small content I read Mr. Hobbes's book *De Cive*, and his *Leviathan*, about the rights of sovereignty, which no man, that I know, hath so amply and judiciously handled: I consent with him about the rights of exercising government, but I cannot agree to his means of acquiring it. It may seem strange I should praise his building, and yet mislike his foundation; but so it is, his *Jus Naturae*, and his *Regnum Institutivum*, will not down with me: they appear full of contradiction and impossibilities; a few short notes about them, I here offer, wishing he would consider whether his building would not stand firmer upon the principles of *Regnum Patrimoniale* (as he calls it) both according to scripture and reason. Since he confesseth the 'Father being before the institution of a commonwealth was originally an absolute sovereign with power of life and death', and that 'a great family, as to the rights of sovereignty is a little monarchy'. If according to the order of nature he had handled paternal government before that by institution, there would have been little liberty left in the subjects of the family to consent to institution of government.

In his pleading the cause of the people, he arms them with a very large commission of array; which is, a right in nature for every man, to war against every man when he please: and also a right for all the people to govern. This latter point, although he affirm in words, yet by consequence he denies, as to me it seemeth.

He saith a representative may be of all, or but of a part of the people. If it be of all he terms it a democracy, which is the government of the people. But how can such a commonwealth be generated? for if every man covenant with every man, who shall be left to be the representative? if all must be representatives, who will remain to covenant? for he that is sovereign makes no covenant by his doctrine. It is not all that will come together, that makes the democracy, but all that have power by covenant; thus his democracy by institution fails.

The same may be said of a democracy by acquisition; for if all be conquerors, who shall covenant for life and liberty? and if all be not conquerors, how can it be a democracy by conquest?

A paternal democracy I am confident he will not affirm, so that in conclusion the poor people are deprived of their government, if there can be no democracy by his principles.

Next, if a representative aristocratical of a part of the people be free from covenanting, then that whole assembly (call it what you will) though it be never so great, is in the state of nature, and every one of that assembly hath a right not only to kill any of the subjects that they meet with in the streets, but also they all have a natural right to cut one another's throats, even while they sit together in council by his principles. In this miserable condition of war is his representative aristocratical by institution.

A commonwealth by conquest he teacheth, is, then acquired, when the vanquished to avoid present death covenanteth that so long as his life, and the liberty of his body is allowed him, the victor shall have the use of it, at his pleasure: here I would know how the liberty of the vanquished can be allowed, if the victor have the use of it at pleasure, or how is it possible for the victor to perform his covenant, except he could always stand by every particular man to protect his life and liberty?

In his review and conclusion he resolves, that an ordinary subject hath liberty to submit, when the means of his life is within the guards and garrisons of the enemy. It seems hereby that the rights of sovereignty by institution may be forfeited, for the subject cannot be at liberty to submit to a conqueror, except his former subjection be forfeited for want of protection.

If his conqueror be in the state of nature, when he conquers he hath a right without any covenant made with the conquered: if conquest be defined to be the acquiring of right of sovereignty by victory, why is it said the right is acquired in the peoples' submission, by which they contract with the victor, promising obedience for life and liberty? hath not every one in the state of nature a right to sovereignty, before conquest, which only puts him in possession of his right?

If his conqueror be not in the state of nature, but a subject by covenant, how can he get a right of sovereignty by conquest when neither he himself hath right to conquer, nor subjects a liberty to submit? since a former contract lawfully made cannot lawfully be broken by them.

I wish the title of the book had not been of a commonwealth, but of a weal public, or commonweal, which is the true word carefully observed by our translator of *Bodin de Republica* into English: many ignorant men are apt by the name of commonwealth to understand a popular government, wherein wealth and all things shall be common, tending to the levelling community in the state of pure nature.

OBSERVATIONS ON MR. HOBBES'S *LEVIATHAN*: OR HIS ARTIFICIAL MAN—A COMMONWEALTH

I

If God created only Adam, and of a piece of him made the woman; and if by generation from them two as parts of them all mankind be propagated: if also God gave to Adam not only the dominion over the woman and the children that should issue from them, but also over the whole earth to subdue it, and over all the creatures on it, so that as long as Adam lived no man could claim or enjoy anything but by donation, assignation, or permission from him; I wonder how the right of nature can be imagined by Mr. Hobbes, which he saith, page 64, is a liberty for each man to use his own power as he will himself for preservation of his own life; a condition of war of everyone against everyone; a right of every man to everything, even to one another's body, especially since himself affirms, page 178, that originally the Father of every man was also his Sovereign Lord with power over him of life and death.

II

Mr. Hobbes confesseth and believes it was never generally so, that there was such a *jus naturae*; and if not generally, then not at all, for one exception bars all if he mark it well; whereas he imagines such a right of nature may be now practised in America, he confesseth a government there of families, which government how small or brutish soever (as he calls it) is sufficient to destroy his *jus naturale*.

III

I cannot understand how this right of nature can be conceived without imagining a company of men at the very first to have been all created together without any dependency one of another, or as mushrooms (*fungorum more*) they all on a sudden were sprung out of the earth without any obligation one to another, as Mr. Hobbes's words are in his book *De Cive*, chapter 8, section 3: the scripture teacheth us otherwise, that all men came by succession, and generation from one man: we must not deny the truth of the history of the creation.

IV

It is not to be thought that God would create man in a condition worse than any beasts, as if he made men to no other end by nature but to destroy one another, a right for the Father to destroy or eat his

children, and for children to do the like by their parents, is worse than
cannibals.* This horrid condition of pure nature when Mr. Hobbes was
charged with, his refuge was to answer, that no son can be understood
to be in this state of nature: which is all one with denying his own
principle, for if men be not free-born, it is not possible for him to
assign and prove any other time for them to claim a right of nature to
liberty, if not at their birth.

V

But if it be allowed (which is yet most false) that a company of men
were at first without a common power to keep them in awe; I do not
see why such a condition must be called a state of war of all men against
all men: indeed if such a multitude of men should be created as the
earth could not well nourish, there might be cause for men to destroy
one another rather than perish for want of food; but God was no such
niggard in the creation, and there being plenty of sustenance and room
for all men, there is no cause or use of war till men be hindered in the
preservation of life, so that there is no absolute necessity of war in the
state of pure nature; it is the right of nature for every man to live in
peace, that so he may tend the preservation of his life, which whilst he
is in actual war he cannot do. War of itself as it is war preserves no man's
life, it only helps us to preserve and obtain the means to live: if every
man tend the right of preserving life, which may be done in peace,
there is no cause of war.

VI

But admit the state of nature were the state of war; let us see what
help Mr. Hobbes hath for it. It is a principle of his, that 'the law of nature
is a rule found out by reason' (I do think it is given by God), page 64,
'forbidding a man to do that which is destructive to his life, and to
omit that by which he thinks it may be best preserved': If the right of
nature be a liberty for a man to do anything he thinks fit to preserve
his life, then in the first place nature must teach him that life is to be
preserved, and so consequently forbids to do that which may destroy
or take away the means of life, or to omit that by which it may be
preserved: and thus the right of nature and the law of nature will be
all one: for I think Mr. Hobbes will not say the right of nature is a liberty
for a man to destroy his own life. The law of nature might better
have been said to consist in a command to preserve or not to omit the
means of preserving life, than in a prohibition to destroy, or to
omit it.

* De Cive, cap. 1, sect. 10.

VII

Another principle I meet with, page 65. 'If other men will not lay down their right as well as he, then there is no reason for any to divest himself of his': hence it follows that if all the men in the world do not agree, no commonwealth can be established, it is a thing impossible for all the men in the world every man with every man to covenant to lay down their right. Nay it is not possible to be done in the smallest kingdom, though all men should spend their whole lives in nothing else but in running up and down to covenant.

VIII

Right may be laid aside but not transferred, for page 65, 'he that renounceth or passeth away his right, giveth not to any other man a right which he had not before, and reserves a right in himself against all those with whom he doth not covenant'.

IX

Page 87. 'The only way to erect a common power or a commonwealth, is for men to confer all their power and strength upon one man, or one assembly of men, that may reduce all their wills by plurality of voices to one will; which is to appoint one man or an assembly of men to bear their person, to submit their wills to his will: this is a real unity of them all in one person, made by covenant of every man with every man, as if every man should say to every man, I authorize, and give up my right of governing myself to this man, or this assembly of men, on this condition, that thou give up thy right to him, and authorize all his actions. This done, the multitude so united in one person, is called a commonwealth.'

To authorize and give up his right of governing himself, to confer all his power and strength, and to submit his will to another, is to lay down his right of resisting: for if right of nature be a liberty to use power for preservation of life, laying down of that power must be a relinquishing of power to preserve or defend life, otherwise a man relinquisheth nothing.

To reduce all the wills of an assembly by plurality of voices to one will, is not a proper speech, for it is not a plurality but a totality of voices which makes an assembly be of one will, otherwise it is but the one will of a major part of the assembly, the negative voice of any one hinders the being of the one will of the assembly, there is nothing more destructive to the true nature of a lawful assembly, than to allow a major part to prevail when the whole only hath right. For a man to give up his right to one that never covenants to protect, is a great folly, since it is neither 'in consideration of some right reciprocally transferred to himself, nor can he hope for any other good, by standing out of the way, that the other may enjoy his own original right without hindrance from him by reason of so much diminution of impediments'; page 66.

X

The liberty, saith Mr. Hobbes, whereof there is so frequent and honourable mention in the histories and philosophy of the ancient Greeks and Romans, and in the writings and discourse of those that from them have received all their learning in the politics, is not the liberty of particular men, but the liberty of the commonwealth. Whether a commonwealth be monarchical or popular, the freedom is still the same. Here I find Mr. Hobbes is much mistaken: for the liberty of the Athenians and Romans was a liberty only to be found in popular estates, and not in monarchies. This is clear by Aristotle, who calls a city a community of freemen, meaning every particular citizen to be free. Not that every particular man had a liberty to resist his governor or do what he list, but a liberty only for particular men, to govern and to be governed by turns, ἄρχειν and ἄρχεσθαι are Aristotle's words: this was a liberty not to be found in hereditary monarchies: so Tacitus mentioning the several governments of Rome, joins the consulship and liberty to be brought in by Brutus, because by the annual election of Consuls, particular citizens came in their course to govern and to be governed. This may be confirmed by the complaint of our author, which followeth: 'It is an easy thing for men to be deceived by the specious name of liberty: and for want of judgment to distinguish, mistake that for their private inheritance or birthright which is the right of the public only: and when the same error is confirmed by the authority of men in reputation for their writings on this subject, it is no wonder if it produce sedition and change of government. In the western parts of the world, we are made to receive our opinions concerning the institution and right of commonwealths from Aristotle and Cicero, and other men, Greeks and Romans, that living under popular estates, derived those rights not from the principles of nature, but transcribed them into their books out of the practice of their own commonwealths, which were popular. And because the Athenians were taught (to keep them from desire of changing their government) that they were freemen, and all that lived under monarchy slaves: therefore Aristotle puts it down in his *Politics*. In democracy liberty is to be supposed, for it is commonly held that no man is free in any other government. So Cicero and other writers grounded their civil doctrine on the opinions of the Romans, who were taught to hate monarchy, at first, by them that having deposed their sovereign, shared amongst them the sovereignty of Rome. And by reading of these Greek and Latin authors, men from their childhood have gotten a habit (under a false show of liberty) of favouring tumults, and of licentious controlling the actions of their sovereigns.'

XI

Page 102. 'Dominion paternal not attained by generation but by contract', which is 'the child's consent, either express or by other sufficient arguments declared'. How a child can express consent, or by other sufficient arguments declare it before it comes to the age of discretion I understand not, yet all men grant it is due before consent can be given: and I take it Mr. Hobbes is of the same mind, page 249, where he teacheth that 'Abraham's children were bound to obey what Abraham should declare to them for God's law: which they could not be but in virtue of the obedience they owed to their parents'; they owed, not that they covenanted to give. Also where he saith, page 121, the 'Father and master being before the institution of commonweals absolute sovereigns in their own families', how can it be said that either children or servants were in the state of *jus naturae* till the institutions of commonweals? It is said by Mr. Hobbes in his book *De Cive*, chapter 9, section 7, 'the mother originally hath the government of her children, and from her the Father derives his right, because she brings forth and first nourisheth them'. But we know that God at the creation gave the sovereignty to the man over the woman, as being the nobler and principal agent in generation. As to the objection, that 'it is not known who is the Father to the son but by the discovery of the mother, and that he is his son whom the mother will, and therefore he is the mother's'. The answer is, that it is not at the will of the mother to make whom she will the Father, for if the mother be not in possession of a husband, the child is not reckoned to have any Father at all; but if she be in the possession of a man, the child notwithstanding whatsoever the woman discovereth to the contrary is still reputed to be his in whose possession she is. No child naturally and infallibly knows who are his true parents, yet he must obey those that in common reputation are so, otherwise the commandment of honour thy Father and thy mother were in vain, and no child bound to the obedience of it.

XII

If the government of one man, page 94, and the government of two men, make two several kinds of government, why may not the government of two, and the government of three, do the like, and make a third? and so every differing number a differing kind of commonwealth. If an assembly of all (as Mr. Hobbes saith) that will come together be a democracy, and an assembly of a part only an aristocracy, then if all that will come together be but a part only, a democracy and aristocracy are all one; and why must an assembly of part be called an aristocracy and not a merocracy?

It seems Mr. Hobbes is of the mind that there is but one kind of government, and that is monarchy, for he defines a commonwealth to be one person, and an assembly of men, or real unity of them all in one and the same person, the multitude so united he calls a commonwealth: this his moulding of a multitude into one person, is the generation of his great *Leviathan*, the King of the children of pride page 167. Thus he concludes the person of a commonwealth to be a monarch.

XIII

I cannot but wonder Master Hobbes should say, page 112, the consent of a subject to sovereign power is contained in these words, I authorize and do take upon me all his actions, in which there is no restriction at all of his own former natural liberty. Surely here Master Hobbes forgot himself, for before he makes the resignation to go in these words also, 'I give up my right of governing myself to this man': this is a restriction certainly of his own former natural liberty when he gives it away: and if a man allow his sovereign to kill him which Mr. Hobbes seems to confess, how can he reserve a right to defend himself? And if a man have a power and right to kill himself, he doth not authorize and give up his right to his sovereign, if he do not obey him when he commands him to kill himself.

XIV

Mr. Hobbes saith, page 112, 'No man is bound by the words of his submission to kill himself, or any other man: and consequently that the obligation a man may sometimes have upon the command of the sovereign to execute any dangerous or dishonourable office, dependeth not on the words of our submission, but on the intention which is to be understood by the end thereof. When therefore our refusal to obey, frustrates the end for which the sovereignty was ordained, then there is no liberty to refuse: otherwise there is'. If no man be bound by the words of his subjection to kill any other man, then a sovereign may be denied the benefit of war, and be rendered unable to defend his people, and so the end of government frustrated. If the obligation upon the commands of a sovereign to execute a dangerous or dishonourable office, dependeth not on the words of our submission, but on the intention, which is to be understood by the end thereof; no man, by Mr. Hobbes's rules, is bound but by the words of his submission, the intention of the command binds not, if the words do not: if the intention should bind, it is necessary the sovereign must discover it, and the people must dispute and judge it; which how well it may consist with the rights of sovereignty, Mr. Hobbes may consider: whereas Master Hobbes saith the intention is to be understood by the ends, I take it he means the end by effect, for the end and the intention are one and the same thing; and if he mean the effect, the obedience must go before, and not depend on the understanding of the effect, which can never be, if the obedience do not precede it: in fine, he resolves refusal to obey, may depend upon the judging of what frustrates the end of sovereignty, and what not, of which he cannot mean any other judge but the people.

XV

Mr. Hobbes puts a case by way of question, page 112: 'A great many men together have already resisted the sovereign power unjustly, or committed some capital crime, for which every one of them expecteth death: whether have they not the liberty then to join together and assist and defend one another? Certainly they have, for they but defend their lives, which the guilty man may as well do as the innocent: there was indeed injustice in the first breach of their duty, their bearing of arms subsequent to it, though it be to maintain what they have done, is no new unjust act, and if it be only to defend their persons it is not unjust at all.' The only reason here alleged for the bearing of arms is this: that it is no new unjust act, as if the beginning only of a rebellion were an unjust act, and the continuance of it none at all: no better answer can be given to this case than what the author himself hath delivered in the beginning of the same paragraph in these words: To resist the sword of the commonwealth in defence of another man, guilty or innocent, no man hath liberty: because such liberty takes away from the sovereign the means of protecting us, and is therefore destructive of the very essence of government. Thus he first answers the question, and then afterwards makes it, and gives it a contrary answer; other passages I meet with to the like purpose. He saith, page 66, A man cannot lay down the right of resisting them that assault him by force to take away his life: the same be said of wounds, chains and imprisonment. Page 69. A covenant to defend myself from force by force is void. Page 68. Right of defending life and means of living can never be abandoned.

These last doctrines are destructive to all government whatsoever, and even to the *Leviathan* itself: hereby any rogue or villain may murder his sovereign, if the sovereign but offer by force to whip or lay him in the stocks, since whipping may be said to be a wounding, and putting in the stocks an imprisonment: so likewise every man's goods being means of living, if a man cannot abandon them, no contract among men, be it never so just, can be observed: thus we are at least in as miserable a condition of war as Mr. Hobbes at first by nature found us.

XVI

The kingdom of God signifies, saith Master Hobbes, page 216, a kingdom constituted by the votes of the people of Israel in a peculiar manner, wherein they choose God for their King, by covenant made with him, upon God's promising them Canaan. If we look upon Master Hobbes's text for this, it will be found that the people did not constitute by votes, and choose God for their King; but by the appointment first of God himself the covenant was to be a God to them: they did not contract with God, that if he would give them Canaan they would be his subjects, and he should be their King: it was not in their power to choose whether God should be their God, yea, or nay: for it is confessed He reigned naturally over all by his might. If God reigned naturally He had a kingdom, and sovereign power over His subjects, not acquired by their own consent. This kingdom, said to be constituted by the votes of the people of Israel, is but the vote of Abraham only, his single voice carried it, he was the representative of the people. For at this vote, it is confessed, that the name of King is not given to God, nor of kingdom to Abraham, yet the thing, if we will believe Master Hobbes is all one. If a contract be the mutual transferring of right, I would know what right a people can have to transfer to God by contract. Had the people of Israel at Mount Sinai a right not to obey God's voice? If they had not such a right, what had they to transfer?

The covenant mentioned at Mount Sinai was but a conditional contract, and God but a conditional King, and though the people promised to obey God's word, yet it was more than they were able to perform, for they often disobeyed God's voice, which being a breach of the condition the covenant was void, and God not their King by contract.

It is complained by God, they have rejected me that I should not reign over them: but it is not said according to their contract; for I do not find that the desiring of a King was a breach of their contract or covenant, or disobedience to the voice of God: there is no such law extant.

The people did not totally reject the Lord, but in part only, out of timorousness, when they saw Nahash King of the Children of Ammon come against them, they distrusted that God would not suddenly provide for their deliverance, as if they had had always a King in readiness to go up presently to fight for them: this despair in them who had found so many miraculous deliverances under God's government, was that which offended the Lord so highly: they did not desire an alteration of government, and to cast off God's laws, but hoped for a certainer and speedier deliverance from danger in time of war. They did not petition that they might choose their King themselves, that had been a greater sin, and yet if they had, it had not been a total rejection of God's reigning over them, as long as they desired not to depart from the worship of God their King, and from the obedience of his laws. I see not that the kingdom of God was cast off by the election of Saul, since Saul was chosen by God himself, and governed according to God's laws. The government from Abraham to Saul is nowhere called the kingdom of God, nor is it said, that the kingdom of God was cast off at the election of Saul.

Mr. Hobbes allows, that Moses alone had next under God the sovereignty over the Israelites, page 252, but he doth not allow it to Joshua, but will have it descend to Eleazar the high priest, Aaron's son. His proof is, God expressly saith concerning Joshua, he shall stand before Eleazar, who shall ask counsel for him before the Lord, (after the judgment of Urim is omitted by Mr. Hobbes) at his word they shall go out, etc., therefore the supreme power of making peace and war was in the priest.

Answer. The work of the high priest was only ministerial not magisterial; he had no power to command in war; or to judge in peace; only when the sovereign or governor did go up to war, he inquired of the Lord by the ministry of the high priest, and, as the Hebrews say, the inquirer with a soft voice as one that prayeth for himself, asked: and forthwith the Holy Ghost came upon the priest,

R

and he beheld the breast-plate, and saw therein by the vision of pro-
phecy, go up, or go not up, in the letters that showed forth themselves
upon the breast-plate before his face: then the priest answered him,
go up, or go not up. If this answer gave the priest the sovereignty,
then neither King Saul nor King David had the sovereignty, who both
asked counsel of the Lord by the priest.

OBSERVATIONS ON MR. MILTON AGAINST SALMASIUS

I

AMONG the many printed books, and several discourses touching the right of Kings, and the liberty of the people, I cannot find that as yet the first and chief point is agreed upon, or indeed so much as once disputed. The word King and the word people are familiar, one would think every simple man could tell what they signified; but upon examination it will be found that the learnedest cannot agree of their meaning.

Ask Salmasius what a King is, and he will teach us that a King is he who hath the supreme power of the kingdom, and is accountable to none but God, and may do what he please, and is free from the laws. This definition J. M. abominates as being the definition of a tyrant: and I should be of his mind, if he would have vouchsafed us a better, or any other definition at all, that would tell us how any King can have a supreme power, without being freed from humane laws: to find fault with it, without producing any other is to leave us in the dark: but though Mr. Milton brings us neither definition nor description of a King, yet we may pick out of several passages of him, something like a definition, if we lay them together. He teacheth us that 'power was therefore given to a King by the people, that he might see by the authority to him committed that nothing be done against law: and that he keeps our laws, and not impose upon us his own: therefore there is no regal power but in the courts of the kingdom, and by them', page 155.

And again he affirmeth, the King cannot imprison, fine, or punish any man, except he be first cited into some court; where not the King, but the usual judges give sentence, page 168, and before we are told not the King, but the authority of Parliament doth set up and take away all courts, page 167.

Lo, here the description of a King, he is one to whom the people give power, to see that nothing be done against law: and yet he saith there is no regal power but in the courts of justice, and by them, where not the King, but the usual judges give sentence. This description not only strips the King of all power whatsoever, but puts him in a condition below the meanest of his subjects.

Thus much may show that all men are not agreed what a King is. Next, what the word people means is not agreed upon: ask Aristotle what the people is, and he will not allow any power to be in any but in free citizens. If we demand who be free citizens? That he cannot resolve us, for he confesseth that he that is a free citizen in one city, is not so in another city. And he is of opinion that no artificer should be a free citizen, or have voice in a well ordered commonwealth; he accounts a democracy (which word signifies the government of the people) to be a corrupted sort of government; he thinks many men by nature born to be servants, and not fit to govern as any part of the people. Thus doth Aristotle curtail the people, and can give us no certain rule to know who be the people: come to our modern politicians, and ask them who the people is, though they talk big of the people, yet they take up and are content with a few representors (as they call them) of the whole people; a point Aristotle was to seek in, neither are these representors stood upon to be the whole people, but the major part of these representors must be reckoned for the whole people; nay J. M. will not allow the major part of the representors to be the people, but the sounder and better part only of them, page 126, and in right down terms he tells us to determine who is a tyrant, he leaves to magistrates at least to the uprighter sort of them and of the people, though in number less by many to judge as they find cause, page 7. If the sounder, the better, and the uprighter part have the power of the people, how shall we know, or who shall judge who they be?

II

One text is urged by Mr. Milton, for the peoples power: Deuteronomy xvii, 14. When thou art come into the land which thy Lord thy God giveth thee, and shalt say I will set a King over me, like as all the nations about me. It is said by the *Tenure of Kings* 'these words confirm us that the right of choosing, yea, of changing their own government is by the grant of God himself in the people'. But can the foretelling or forewarning of the Israelites of a wanton, and wicked desire of theirs, which God himself condemned, be made an argument that God gave or granted them a right to do such a wicked thing? or can the narration and reproving of a future fact be a donation and approving of a present right, or the permission of a sin be made a commission for the doing of it? The author in his book against Salmasius, falls from making God the donor or grantor, that he cites him only for a witness, 'Teste ipso Deo penes populos arbitrium semper fuisse, vel ea, quae placeret forma reipub. utendi, vel hanc in aliam mutandi, de Hebraeis de hoc diserte dicit Deus: de reliquis non abnuit'.

That here in this text 'God himself being witness, there was always a power in the people, either to use what form of government they pleased, or of changing it into another: God saith this expressly of the Hebrews, and denies it not of others'. Can any man find that God in this text expressly saith, that there was always a right in the people, to use what form of government they please? The text not warranting this right of the people, the foundation of the *Defence of the People* is quite taken away; there being no other grant, or proof of it pretended.

2. Where it is said that the Israelites desired a King, though then under another form of government, in the next line but one it is confessed they had a King at the time when they desired a King, which was God himself, and his viceroy Samuel, and so saith God: They have not rejected thee; but they have rejected me, that I should not reign over them; yet in the next verse God saith, As they have forsaken me, so do they also unto thee. Here is no show of any other form of government but monarchy: God by the mediation of Samuel reigned, who made his sons judges over Israel; when one man constitutes judges we may call him a King, or if the having of judges do alter the government then the government of every kingdom is altered from monarchy, where judges are appointed by Kings: it is now reckoned one of the duties of Kings to judge by their judges only.

3. Where it is said, he shall not multiply to himself horses, nor wives, nor riches, that he might understand that he had no power over others, who could decree nothing of himself, *extra Legem*, if it had said, *contra legem Dei*, it had been true, but if it meant *extra legem humanam*, it is false.

4. If there had been any right given to the people, it seems it was to the elders only, for it is said it was the elders of Israel gathered together, petitioned for a King, it is not said it was all the people, nor that the people did choose the elders, who were the fathers and heads of families authorized by the judges.

5. Where it is said, I will set a King over me like as all the nations about me. To set a King, is not to choose a King, but by some solemn public act of coronation, or otherwise to acknowledge their allegiance to the King chosen; it is said, thou shalt set him King whom the Lord thy God shall choose. The elders did not desire to choose a King like other nations, but they say now make us a King to judge us like all the nations.

III

As for David's covenant with the elders when he was anointed, it was not to observe any laws or conditions made by the people for aught appears; but to keep God's laws and serve Him, and to seek the good of the people as they were to protect him.

6. The Reubenites and Gadites promise their obedience, not according to their laws or conditions agreed upon, but in these words. All that thou commandest us we will do, and whithersoever thou sendest us we will go, as we harkened to Moses in all things, so will we harken unto thee: only the Lord thy God be with thee as he was with Moses. Where is there any condition of any humane law expressed? Though the rebellious tribes offered conditions to Rehoboam, where can we find, that for like conditions not performed, all Israel deposed Samuel? I wonder Mr. Milton should say this, when within a few lines after he professeth that Samuel had governed them uprightly.

IV

Jus regni is much stumbled at, and the definition of a King which saith his power is supreme in the kingdom, and he is accountable to none but to God, and that he may do what he please, and is not bound by laws; it is said if this definition be good, no man is or ever was, who may be said to be a tyrant, page 14, 'for when he hath violated all divine and humane laws, nevertheless he is a King, and guiltless *jure regio*'. To this may be answered, that the definition confesseth he is accountable to God, and therefore not guiltless if he violate divine laws: humane laws must not be shuffled in with divine, they are not of the same authority: if humane laws bind a King, it is impossible for him to have supreme power amongst men. If any man can find us out such a kind of government, wherein the supreme power can be, without being freed from humane laws, they should first teach us that; but if all sorts of popular government that can be invented, cannot be one minute, without an arbitrary power freed from all humane laws: what reason can be given why a royal government should not have the like freedom? if it be tyranny for one man to govern arbitrarily, why should it not be far greater tyranny for a multitude of men to govern without being accountable or bound by laws? It would be further inquired how it is possible for any government at all to be in the world without an arbitrary power; it is not power except it be arbitrary: a legislative power cannot be without being absolved from humane laws, it cannot be showed how a King can have any power at all but an arbitrary power. We are taught that 'power was therefore given to a King by the people, that he might see by the authority to him committed, that nothing be done against law, and that he keep our laws, and not impose upon us his own: therefore there is no royal power, but in the courts of the kingdom, and by them', page 155. And again it is said, the King cannot imprison, fine or punish any man except he be first cited into some court, where not the King but the usual judges give sentence, page 168, and before we are told not the King, but the authority of Parliament doth set up and take away all courts, page 167.

Lo here we have Mr. Milton's perfect definition of a King: He is one to whom the people gave power to see that nothing be done against law, and that he keep our laws, and not impose his own. Whereas all other men have the faculty of seeing by nature, the King only hath it by the gift of the people, other power he hath none; he may see the judges keep the laws if they will; he cannot compel them, for he may not imprison, fine, nor punish any man; the courts of justice may, and they are set up and put down by the Parliament; yet in this very definition of a King, we may spy an arbitrary power in the King; for he may wink if he will: and no other power doth this description of a King give, but only a power to see. Whereas it is said 'Aristotle doth mention an absolute kingdom, for no other cause, but to show how absurd, unjust and most tyrannical it is', there is no such thing said by Aristotle, but the contrary, where he saith, that a King according to law makes no sort of government; and after he had reckoned up five sorts of Kings, he concludes that there were in a manner but two sorts, the Lacedemonian King, and the absolute King; whereof the first was but as general in an army, and therefore no King at all, and then fixes and rests upon the absolute King, who ruleth according to his own will.

V

If it be demanded what is meant by the word people? 1. Sometimes it is *populus universus*, and then every child must have his consent asked, which is impossible. 2. Sometimes it is *pars major*, and sometimes it is *pars potior et sanior*; how the major part, where all are alike free, can bind the minor part, is not yet proved.

But it seems the major part will not carry it, nor be allowed except they be the better part and the sounder part. We are told, 'the sounder part implored the help of the army, when it saw itself and the commonwealth betrayed', and that 'the soldiers judged better than the great council, and by arms saved the commonwealth, which the great council had almost damned by their votes', page 7.

Here we see what the people is; to wit the sounder part of which the army is the judge: thus upon the matter the soldiers are the people: which being so, we may discern where the liberty of the people lieth, which we are taught to consist all for the most part in the power of the peoples choosing what form of government they please, page 61. A miserable liberty, which is only to choose to whom we will give our liberty, which we may not keep. See more concerning the people in a book entitled *The Anarchy*, pages 8, 9, 10, 11, 12, 13, 14.

VI

We are taught that a Father and a King are things most diverse. The Father begets us, but not the King; but we create the King: Nature gives a Father to the people, the people give themselves a King; if the Father kill his son he loseth his life, why should not the King also? page 34.

Answer. Father and King are not so diverse, it is confessed that at first they were all one, for there is confessed *paternum imperium et haereditarium*, page 141, and this fatherly empire, as it was of itself hereditary, so it was *alienable* by the parent, and *seizable* by a usurper as other goods are: and thus every King that now is hath a paternal empire, either by inheritance, or by translation or usurpation, so a Father and a King may be all one.

A Father may die for the murder of his son, where there is a superior Father to them both, or the right of such a supreme Father; but where there are only Father and sons, no sons can question the Father for the death of their brother: the reason why a King cannot be punished is not because he is excepted from punishment, or doth not deserve it, but because there is no superior to judge him, but God only to whom he is reserved.

VII

It is said thus, He that takes away from the people the power of choosing for themselves, what form of government they please; he doth take away that wherein all civil liberty almost consists, page 65. If almost all liberty be in choosing of the kind of government, the people have but a poor bargain of it, who cannot exercise their liberty, but in chopping and changing their government, and have liberty only to give away their liberty, than which there is not a greater mischief, as being the cause of endless sedition.

VIII

'If there be any statute in our law, by which thou can find that tyrannical power is given to a King, that statute being contrary to God's will, to nature and reason, understand that by that general and primary law of ours, that statute to be repealed, and not of force with us', page 153. Here if any man may be judge, what law is contrary to God's will, or to nature, or to reason, it will soon bring in confusion: most men that offend, if they be to be punished, or fined, will think that statute that gives all fines and forfeitures to a King, to be a tyrannical law, thus most statutes would be judged void, and all our forefathers taken for fools or madmen, to make all our laws to give all penalties to the King.

IX

The sin of the children of Israel did lie, not in desiring a King, but in desiring such a King, like as the nations round about had; they distrusted God Almighty that governed them by the monarchical power of Samuel, in the time of oppression, when God provided a judge for them; but they desired a perpetual and an hereditary King, that they might never want; in desiring a King they could not sin, for it was but desiring what they enjoyed, by God's special providence.

X

Men are persuaded, that in the making of a covenant, something is to be performed on both parts by mutual stipulation, which is not always true: for we find God made a covenant with Noah and his seed, with all the fowl and the cattle, not to destroy the earth any more by a flood. This covenant was to be kept on God's part, neither Noah, nor the fowl, nor the cattle, were to perform anything by this covenant. On the other side, Genesis xvii, 9, 10, God covenants with Abraham, saying, Thou shalt keep my covenant . . . every male child among you shall be circumcised. Here it is called God's covenant, though it be to be performed only by Abraham; so a covenant may be called the King's covenant, because it is made to him, and yet to be performed only by the people. So also, 2 Kings xi, 17, Jehojada made a covenant between the Lord, and the King, and the people, that they should be the Lord's people. Between the King also and the people, which might well be, that the people should be the King's servants: and not for the King's covenanting to keep any humane laws, for it is not likely the King should either covenant, or take any oath to the people when he

was but seven years of age, and that never any King of Israel took a
coronation oath that can be shown: when Jehojada showed the King
to the rulers in the house of the Lord, he took an oath of the people:
he did not article with them, but saith the next verse, commanded them
to keep a watch of the King's house, and that they should compass the
King round about, every man with his weapons in his hand, and he
that cometh within the ranges, let him be slain.

XI

To the text, Where the word of a King is, there is power, and who
may say unto him, what dost thou? J. M. gives this answer: 'It is apparent
enough, that the preacher in this place gives precepts to every private
man, not to the great Sanhedrin, nor to the Senate . . . shall not the
Nobles, shall not all the other magistrates, shall not the whole people
dare to mutter, so oft as the King pleaseth to dote?' We must here note,
that the great council, and all other magistrates or Nobles, or the whole
people, compared to the King, are all but private men, if they derive
their power from him: they are magistrates under him, and out of his
presence, for when he is in place, they are but so many private men.
J. M. asks, 'Who swears to a King, unless the King on the other side be
sworn to keep God's laws, and the laws of the country?' We find that
the rulers of Israel took an oath at the coronation of Jehoash: but we
find no oath taken by that King, no not so much as to God's laws, much
less to the laws of the country.

XII

'A tyrant is he, who regarding neither law, nor the common good,
reigns only for himself and his faction', page 19. In his *Defence* he expresseth himself thus, he is a tyrant who looks after only his own, and
not his people's profit. *Eth.*, l. 10, p. 189.

1. If it be tyranny not to regard the law, then all courts of equity,
and pardons for any offences must be taken away: there are far more
suits for relief against the laws, than there be for the observation of
the laws: there can be no such tyranny in the world as the law, if there
were no equity to abate the rigour of it. *Summum jus* is *summa injuria*,
if the penalties and forfeitures of all laws should still be exacted by all
Kings, it would be found, that the greatest tyranny would be, for a
King to govern according to law; the fines, penalties and forfeitures
of all laws are due to the supreme power only, and were they duly
paid, they would far exceed the taxes in all places. It is the chief happi-

ness of a kingdom, and their chief liberty, not to be governed by the laws only.

2. Not to regard the common good, but to reign only for himself, is the supposition of an impossibility in the judgment of Aristotle, who teacheth us, that the despotical power cannot be preserved, except the servant, or he in subjection, be also preserved. The truth of this strongly proves, that it is in nature impossible to have a form of government that can be for the destruction of a people, as tyranny is supposed; if we will allow people to be governed, we must grant, they must in the first place be preserved, or else they cannot be governed.

Kings have been, and may be vicious men, and the government of one, not so good as the government of another, yet it doth not follow that the form of government is, or can be in its own nature ill, because the governor is so: it is anarchy, or want of government, that can totally destroy a nation. We cannot find any such government as tyranny mentioned or named in scripture, or any word in the Hebrew tongue to express it. After such time as the cities of Greece practised to shake off monarchy, then, and not till then (which was after Homer's time) the name of Tyrant was taken up for a word of disgrace, for such men as by craft or force wrested the power of a city, from a multitude to one man only; and not for the exercising, but for the ill-obtaining of the government: but now every man that is but thought to govern ill, or to be an ill man, is presently termed a tyrant, and so judged by his subjects. Few remember the prohibition, Exodus xxii, 28. Thou shalt not revile the Gods, nor curse the ruler of thy people: and fewer understand the reason of it. Though we may not judge one another, yet we may speak evil or revile one another, in that which hath been lawfully judged, and upon a trial wherein they have been heard and condemned: this is not to judge, but only to relate the judgment of the ruler. To speak evil, or to revile a supreme judge, cannot be without judging him who hath no superior on earth to judge him, and in that regard must always be presumed innocent, though never so ill, if he cannot lawfully be heard.

J. M. that will have it tyranny in a King not to regard the laws, doth himself give as little regard to them as any man, where he reckons, that contesting for privileges, customs, forms and that old entanglement of iniquity, their gibberish laws, are the badges of ancient slavery. *Tenure*, page; 3 a disputing presidents, forms and circumstances, page 5.

J. M. is also of opinion, that, 'if at any time our forefathers, out of baseness, have lost anything of their right, that ought not hurt us, they might if they would promise slavery for themselves, for us certainly they could not, who have always the same right to free ourselves, that they had to give themselves to any man in slavery'. This doctrine well practised, layeth all open to constant anarchy.

Lastly, if any desire to know what the liberty of the people is, which J. M. pleads for, he resolves us, saying, that he that takes away from the people the right of choosing what form of government they please, takes away truly that in which all liberty doth almost consist. It is well said by J. M. that all liberty doth almost consist in choosing their form of government, for there is another liberty exercised by the people, which he mentions not, which is the liberty of the peoples choosing their religion; every man may be of any religion, or of no religion; Greece and Rome have been as famous for Polytheism, or multitudes of gods, as of governors; and imagining aristocracy and democracy in heaven, as on earth.

OBSERVATIONS UPON H. GROTIUS
DE JURE BELLI ET PACIS

IN most questions of weight and difficulty concerning the right of war, or peace, or supreme power, Grotius hath recourse to the law of nature, or of nations, or to the primitive will of those men who first joined in society. It is necessary therefore a little to lay open the variety or contrarity in the civil and canon law, and in Grotius himself, about the law of nature and nations, not with a purpose to raise any contention about words or phrases, but with a desire to reconcile or expound the sense of different terms.

Civilians, canonists, politicians and divines, are not a little perplexed in distinguishing between the law of nature and the law of nations: about *jus naturae*, and *jus gentium*, there is much dispute by such as handle the original of government, and of property and community.

The civil law in one text allows a threefold division of law, into *jus naturae, jus gentium* and *jus civile*. But in another text of the same law, we find only a twofold division, into *jus civile* and *jus gentium*. This latter division the law takes from Gaius, the former from Ulpian, who will have *jus naturale* to be that which nature hath taught all creatures, 'quod Natura omnia animalia docuit', but for this he is confuted by Grotius, Salmasius and others, who restrain the law of nature only to men using reason; which makes it all one with the law of nations; to which the canon law consents, and saith, that 'Jus Naturale est commune omnium Nationum: That which natural reason appoints all men to use, is the law of nations', saith Theophilus in the text of the civil law: and in the second book of the *Instit.* chap. 1, *jus naturae* is confounded with *jus gentium*.

As the civilians sometimes confound, and sometimes separate the law of nature and the law of nations, so other-whiles they make them also contrary one to the other. By the law of nature all men are born free, 'Jure naturali omnes liberi nascuntur'. But servitude is by the law of nations: 'Jure Gentium Servitus invasit', saith Ulpian.

And the civil law not only makes the law of nature and of nations contrary, but also will have the law of nations contrary to itself. War, saith the law, was brought in by the law of nations. 'Ex jure gentium introducta bella', and yet the law of nations saith, since nature hath made us all of one kindred, it follows it is not lawful for one man to lie in wait for another. 'Cum inter nos cognitionem quandam natura constituit, consequens est hominem homini insidiari nefas esse', saith Florentinus.

Again, the civil law teacheth, that from the law of nature proceeds the conjunction of man and woman, the procreation and education of children. But as for religion to God, and obedience to parents it makes it to be by the law of nations.

To touch now the canon law, we may find in one place that men are governed either by the law of nature, or by customs. 'Homines reguntur Naturali jure, aut moribus.' The law of nations, they call a divine law, the customs a humane law; 'Leges aut divinae sunt aut humanae; divinae naturâ, humanae moribus constant'. But in the next place the canon law makes *jus* to be either 'Naturale, aut Civile, aut Gentium'. Though this division agrees in terms with that of Ulpian in the civil law, yet in the explication of the terms there is diversity; for what one law makes to belong to the law of nature, the other refers to the law of nations, as may easily appear to him that will take the pains to compare the civil and canon law in these points.

A principal ground of these diversities and contrarieties of divisions, was an error which the heathens taught, that all things at first were common, and that all men were equal. This mistake was not so heinous in those ethnic authors of the civil laws, who wanting the guide of the history of Moses, were fain to follow poets and fables for their leaders. But for christians, who have read the scriptures, to dream either of a community of all things, or an equality of all persons, is a fault scarce pardonable.

To salve these apparent contrarieties of community and propriety, or equality and subjection, the law of *jus gentium* was first invented; when that could not satisfy, to mend the matter, this *jus gentium*, was divided into a natural law of nations, and a humane law of nations; and the law of nature into a primary and a secondary law of nature; distinctions which make a great sound, but edify not at all if they come under examination.

If there hath been a time when all things were common, and all men equal, and that it be otherwise now; we must needs conclude that the law by which things were common, and men equal, was contrary to the law by which now things are proper, and men subject.

If we will allow Adam to have been lord of the world and of his children, there will need no such distinctions of the law of nature and of nations: for the truth will be, that whatsoever the heathens comprehended under these two laws, is comprised in the moral law.

That the law of nature is one and the same with the moral, may appear by a definition given by Grotius. 'The law of nature (saith he) is the dictate of reason, showing that in every action by the agreeing or disagreeing of it with natural reason, there is a moral honesty or dishonesty, and consequently that such an action is commanded or forbidden by God the author of nature.' I cannot tell how Grotius would otherwise have defined the moral law. And the canon law grants as much; teaching that the law of nature is contained in the law and the gospel: 'Whatsoever ye will that men do, etc.,' Matthew vii.

The term of *jus naturae* is not originally to be found in scripture, for though T. Aquinas takes upon him to prove out of the second epistle to the Romans, that there is a *jus naturae*, yet Saint Paul doth not use those express terms; his words are, 'The Gentiles which have not the law, do by nature the things contained in the law, these having not the law are a law unto themselves': he doth not say, nature is a law unto them, but they are a law unto themselves. As for that which they call the law of nations, it is not a law distinct, much less opposite to the law of nature, but it is a small branch or parcel of that great law; for it is nothing but the law of nature, or the moral law between nations. The same commandment that forbids one private man to rob another, or one corporation to hurt another corporation, obliges also one King not to rob another King, and one commonwealth not to spoil another: the same law that enjoins charity to all men, even to enemies, binds princes and states to show charity to one another, as well as private persons.

And as the common, or civil laws of each kingdom which are made against treason, theft, murder, adultery, or the like, are all and every one of them grounded upon some particular commandment of the moral law; so all the laws of nations must be subordinate and reducible to the moral law.

The law of nature, or the moral law is like the main ocean, which though it be one entire body, yet several parts of it have distinct names, according to the diversity of the coasts on which they border. So it comes to pass that the law of nations, which is but a part of the law of nature, may be sub-divided almost *in infinitum*, according to the variety of the persons, or matters about which it is conversant.

The law of nature or the divine law is general, and doth only comprehend some principles of morality notoriously known of themselves, or at the most is extended to those things which by necessary and evident inference are consequent to those principles. Besides these, many other things are necessary to the well governing of a commonwealth: and therefore it was necessary that by humane reason something more in particular should be determined concerning those things which could not be defined by natural reason alone; hence it is that humane laws be necessary, as comments upon the text of the moral law: and of this judgment is Aquinas, who teacheth, that 'necessitas legis humanae manat ex eo, quod Lex naturalis, vel Divina, generalis est, et solum complectitur quaedam principia morum per se nota, et ad summum extenditur ad ea quae necessaria et evidenti elatione ex illis principiis consequuntur: praeter illa vero multa alia sunt necessaria in republica ad ejus rectam Gubernationem: et ideo necessarium fuit ut per humanam rationem aliqua magis in particulari determinarentur circa ea quae per solam rationem naturalem definiri non possunt. Ludo. Molin. de Just.' Thus much may suffice to show the distractions in and between the civil and common laws about the law of nature and nations. In the next place we are to consider how Grotius distinguisheth these laws.

To maintain the community of things to be natural, Grotius hath framed new divisions of the law of nature. First, in his preface to his books *De Jure Belli et Pacis*, he produceth a definition of the law of nature, in such doubtful, obscure and reserved terms, as if he were diffident of his undertaking: next in his first book and first chapter he gives us another distribution, which differs from his doctrine in his preface.

In his preface his first principle is, that the appetite of society, that is to say, of community, is an action proper to man. Here he presently corrects himself with an exception, that some other creatures are found to desire society, and withal he answers the objection thus, that this desire of society in brute beasts, comes from some external principle. What he means by 'Principium intelligens extrinsecum', I understand not, nor doth he explain, nor is it material, nor is the argument he useth to any purpose; for, admitting all he saith to be true, yet his principle fails; for the question is not, from what principle this desire of society proceeds in beasts, but whether there be such a desire or no. Besides, here he takes the appetite of society and community to be all one, whereas many live in society, which live not in community.

Next he teacheth, 'that the keeping of society (*custodia Societatis*) which in a rude manner (saith he) we have now expressed is the fountain of that law which is properly so called'. I conceive by the law properly so called he intends the law of nature, though he express not so much: and to this appetite of sociable community he refers *alieni abstinentia*, but herein it may be he forgets himself, for where there is community there is neither *meum* nor *tuum*, nor yet *alienum*; and if there

be no *alienum* there can be no *alieni abstinentia*. To the same purpose he
saith, that by the law of nature men must stand to bargains, ‘Juris naturae
sit stare pactis’./But if all things were common by nature, how could
there be any bargain?

Again, Grotius tells us, that from this signification of the law there
hath flowed another larger, which consists (saith he) in discerning what
delights us or hurts us, and in judging how things should be wisely
distributed to each one. This latter he calls the looser law of nature;
the former, *jus sociale*, the law of nature, strictly, or properly taken.
‘And these two laws of nature should have place (saith he) though men
should deny there were a God. But to them that believe there is a God,
there is another original of law, beside the natural coming from the
free will of God, to the which our own understanding tells us we must
be subject.’.

Thus have I gathered the substance of what is most material concerning the law of nature in his preface.

If we turn to the book itself, we have a division of the law, into

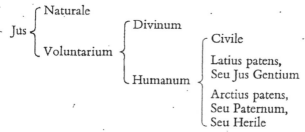

In the definition of *jus naturale* he omits those subtleties of *jus
naturae proprie dictum*, and *quod laxius ita dicitur*, which we find in his
preface, and gives such a plain definition, as may fitly agree to the moral
law. By this it seems the law of nature and the moral law are one and
the same.

Whereas he affirmeth, that the actions about which the law of nature
is conversant are lawful or unlawful of themselves, and therefore are
necessarily commanded or forbidden by God: by which mark this law
of nature doth not only differ from humane law, but from the divine
voluntary law, which doth not command or forbid those things, which
of themselves, and by their own nature are lawful or unlawful, but
makes them unlawful by forbidding them, and due by commanding
them. In this he seems to make the law of nature to differ from God’s

s

voluntary law, whereas in God necessary and voluntary are all one. Salmasius de Usuris in the twentieth chapter, condemns this opinion of Grotius: though he name him not, yet he means him, if I mistake not.

In the next place I observe his saying, that some things are by the law of nature, not *proprie* but *reductive*; and that 'the law of nature deals not only with those things which are beside the will of man, but also with many things which follow the act of man's will: so dominion, such as is now in use, man's will brought in: but now that it is brought in, it is against the law of nature, to take that from thee against thy will which is in thy dominion'.

Yet for all this Grotius maintains, that the law of nature is so immutable, that it cannot be changed by God himself. He means to make it good with a distinction, 'some things (saith he) are by the law of nature, but not simply, but according to the certain state of things; so the common use of things was natural as long as dominion was not brought in; and right for every man to take his own by force, before laws were made'. Here if Grotius would have spoken plain, instead of but not simply, but according to the certain state of things, he would have said, but not immutably, but for a certain time. And then this distinction would have run thus: Some things are by the law of nature, but not immutably, but for a certain time. This must needs be the naked sense of his distinction, as appears by his explication in the words following, where he saith, that the common use of things was natural so long as dominion was not brought in: dominion, he saith, was brought in by the will of man, whom by this doctrine Grotius makes to be able to change that law which God himself cannot change, as he saith. He gives a double ability to man; first to make that no law of nature, which God made to be the law of nature: and next, to make that a law of nature which God made not; for now that dominion is brought in, he maintains, it is against the law of nature to take that which is in another man's dominion.

Besides, I find no coherence in these words, by the law of nature it was right for every man to take his own by force, before laws made, since by the law of nature no man had anything of his own; and until laws were made, there was no propriety according to his doctrine.

'Jus Humanum voluntarium latius patens', he makes to be the law of nations, which (saith he) by the will of all, or many nations hath received a power to bind. He adds, of many, because there is, as he grants, scarce any law to be found common to all nations, besides the law of nature; which also is wont to be called the law of nations, being common to all nations. Nay, as he confesseth often, that is the law in one part of the world, which in another part of the world is not the law of nations.

By these sentences it seems Grotius can scarce tell what to make to be the law of nations, or where to find it.

Whereas he makes the law of nations to have a binding power from the will of men, it must be remembered, that it is not sufficient for men to have a will to bind, but it is necessary also to have a power to bind. Though several nations have one and the same law, for instance, let it be granted that theft is punished by death in many countries: yet this doth not make it to be a law of nations, because each nation hath it but as a national, or civil law of their own country, and though it have a binding power from the will of many nations, yet because each nation hath but a will and power to bind themselves, and may without prejudice, consent, or consulting of any neighbour-nation, alter this law if they find cause, it cannot properly be called the law of nations. That which is the foundation of the law of nations, is, to have it concern such things as belong to the mutual society of nations among themselves, as Grotius confesseth;* and not of such things as have no further relation than to the particular benefit of each kingdom: for, as private men must neglect their own profit for the good of their country; so particular nations must sometimes remit part of their benefit for the good of many nations.

True it is, that in particular kingdoms and commonwealths there be civil and national laws, and also customs that obtain the force of laws: but yet such laws are ordained by some supreme power, and the customs are examined, judged, and allowed by the same supreme power. Where there is no supreme power that extends over all or many nations but only God himself, there can be no laws made to bind nations, but such as are made by God himself: we cannot find that God made any laws to bind nations, but only the moral law; as for the judicial law, though it were ordained by God, yet it was not the law of nations, but of one nation only, and fitted to that commonwealth.

If any think that the customs wherein many nations do consent, may be called the law of nations, as well as the customs of any one nation may be esteemed for national laws; they are to consider, that it is not the being of a custom that makes it lawful, for then all customs, even evil customs, would be lawful; but it is the approbation of the supreme power that gives a legality to the custom: where there is no supreme power over many nations, their customs cannot be made legal.

* Lib. 2, c. 8.

[Here follow the ten pages which were taken from the *Patriarcha* MS., and which are printed as pp. 63-73 above.]

Concerning subjection of children to parents, Grotius distinguisheth three several times.

The first is the time of imperfect judgment.

The second is the time of perfect judgment; but whilst the son remains part of the Father's family.

The third is, the time after he hath departed out of his Father's family.

In the first time he saith, all the actions of children are under the dominion of the parents.

During the second time, 'when they are of the age of mature judgment, they are under their Father's command in those actions only, which are of moment for their parents' family. In other actions the children have a power or moral faculty of doing, but they are bound in those also to study always to please their parents. But since this duty is not by force of any moral faculty, as those former are, but only of piety, observance and duty of repaying thanks; it doth not make anything void which is done against it, as neither a gift of anything is void, being made by any owner whatsoever, against the rules of parsimony'.

'In both these times, the right of ruling and compelling is (as Grotius acknowledgeth) comprehended so far forth as children are to be compelled to their duty or amended, although the power of a parent doth so follow the person of a Father, that it cannot be pulled away, and transferred upon another, yet the Father may naturally pawn, or also sell his son if there be need.'

In the third time he saith, 'the son is in all things free and of his own authority: always that duty remaining of piety and observance, the cause of which is perpetual'. In this triple distinction, though Grotius allow children in some cases during the second, and in all cases during the third time to be free, and of their own power by a moral faculty: yet in that he confesseth, in all cases children are bound to study always to please their parents out of piety and duty, the cause of which, as he saith, is perpetual: I cannot conceive how in any case children can naturally have any power or moral faculty of doing what they please without their parents' leave, since they are always bound to study to please their parents. And though by the laws of some nations children when they attain to years of discretion have power and liberty in many actions; yet this liberty is granted them by positive and humane laws only, which are made by the supreme fatherly power of princes, who regulate, limit, or assume the authority of inferior Fathers for the public benefit of the commonwealth: so that naturally the power of parents over their children never ceaseth by any separation, but only by the permission of the transcendent fatherly power of the supreme prince, children may be dispensed with, or privileged in some cases, from obedience to subordinate parents.

Touching the point of dissolving the vows of children, Grotius in his last edition of his book hath corrected his first; for in the first he teacheth, that the power of the Father was greater over the daughter dwelling with him than over the son, for her vow he might make void, but not his: but instead of these words in his last edition, he saith, that the power over the son or daughter to dissolve vows, was not perpetual, but did endure as long as the children were a part of their Father's family. About the meaning of the text out of which he draws this conclusion, I have already spoken.

Three ways Grotius propoundeth, whereby supreme power may be had.

First, by full right of propriety.

Secondly, by a usufructuary right.

Thirdly, by a temporary right.

The Roman dictators, saith he, 'had supreme power by a temporary right; as well those Kings who are first elected, as those that in a lawful right succeed to Kings elected have supreme power by a usufructuary right: some Kings that have got supreme power by a just war, or into whose power some people, for avoiding a greater evil have so yielded themselves, as that they have excepted nothing, have a full right of propriety'.

Thus we find but two means acknowledged by Grotius whereby a King may obtain a full right of propriety in a kingdom. That is, either by a just war, or by donation of the people.

How a war can be just without a precedent title in the conqueror, Grotius doth not show and if the title only make the war just, then no other right can be obtained by war, than what the title bringeth; for a just war doth only put the conqueror in possession of his old right, but not create a new. The like which Grotius saith of succession may be said of war. 'Succession (saith he) is no title of a kingdom, which gives a form to the kingdom, but a continuation of the old, for the right which began by the election of the family, is continued by succession, wherefore so much as the first election gave, so much the succession brings.' So to a conqueror that hath a title war doth not give, but put him in possession of a right: and except the conqueror had a full right of propriety at first, his conquest cannot give it him: for if originally he and his ancestors had but a usufructuary right, and were outed of the possession of the kingdom by a usurper: here, though the re-conquest be a most just war, yet shall not the conqueror in this case gain any full right of propriety, but must be remitted to his usufructuary right only: for what justice can it be, that the injustice of a third person, a usurper, should prejudice the people, to the divesting of them of that right of propriety, which was reserved in their first donation to their elected King, to whom they gave but a usufructuary right, as Grotius conceiveth? Wherefore it seems impossible, that there can be a just war, whereby a full right of propriety may be gained, according to Grotius's principles. For if a King come in by conquest, he must either conquer them that have a governor, or those people that have none: if they have no governor, then they are a free people, and so the war will be unjust to conquer those that are free, especially if the freedom of the people be by the primary law of nature as Grotius teacheth: but if the people conquered have a governor, that governor hath either a title or not; if he hath a title, it is an unjust war that takes the kingdom from him: if he hath no title, but only the possession of a kingdom, yet it is unjust for any other man that wants a title also, to conquer him that is but in possession, for it is a just rule, that where the cases are alike, he that is in possession is in the better condition, 'In pari causa possidentis melior conditio', *lib.* 2, *c.* 23. And this by the law of nature, even in the judgment of Grotius. But if it be admitted, that he that attempts to conquer hath a title, and he that is in possession hath none: here the conquest is but in nature of a possessory action, to put the conqueror in possession of a primer right, and not to raise a new title, for war begins where the law fails: 'Ubi Judicia deficiunt incipit Bellum', *lib.* 2, *c.* 1. And thus upon the matter I cannot find in Grotius's book *De Jure Belli*, how that any case can be put wherein by a just war a man may become a King, 'pleno Jure Proprietatis'.

All government and supreme power is founded upon public subjection, which is thus defined by Grotius. 'Publica Subjectio est, qua se Populus homini alicui, aut pluribus hominibus, aut etiam populo alteri in ditionem dat', *lib.* 2, *c.* 5. If subjection be the gift of the people, how can supreme power, *pleno jure*, in full right, be got by a just war?

As to the other means whereby Kings may get supreme power in full right of propriety, Grotius will have it to be, when some people for avoiding a greater evil do so yield themselves into another's power, as that they do except nothing. It would be considered how, without war, any people can be brought into such danger of life, as that because they can find no other ways to defend themselves, or because they are so pressed with poverty, as they cannot otherwise have means to sustain themselves, they are forced to renounce all right of governing themselves, and deliver it to a King.

But if such a case cannot happen, but by a war only, which reduceth a people to such terms of extremity as compels them to an absolute abrenunciation of all sovereignty: then war, which causeth that necessity, is the prime means of extorting such sovereignty, and not the free gift of the people, who cannot otherwise choose but give away that power which they cannot keep.

Thus, upon the reckoning the two ways, propounded by Grotius, are but one way, and that one way, in conclusion, is no way whereby supreme power may be had in full right of propriety. His two ways are, a just war, or a donation of the people; a just war cannot be without a title, no title without the donation of the people, no donation without such a necessity as nothing can bring upon the donors but a war. So that howsoever Grotius in words acknowledges that Kings may have a full right of propriety, yet by consequence he denies it, by such circular suppositions as by coincidence destroy each other, and in effect he leaves all people a right to plead in bar against the right of propriety of any prince, either *per minas* or *per dures*.

Many times, saith Grotius, it happens, that war is grounded upon expletive justice, *justitiam expletricem*, which is, when a man cannot obtain that he ought, he takes that which is as much in value which in moral estimation is the same. For in war, when the same province cannot be recovered, to the which a man hath a title, he recovers another of the like value. This recovery cannot give a full right of propriety: because the justice of such a war reacheth no farther than to a compensation for a former right to another thing, and therefore can give no new right.

I am bound to take notice of a case put by Grotius, amongst those causes which he thinks should move the people to renounce all their right of governing and give it to another. It may also happen (saith he) that a Father of a family possessing large territories will not receive any man to dwell within his land upon any other condition. And in another place, he saith, that all Kings are not made by the people, which may be sufficiently understood by the example of a Father of a family receiving strangers under the law of obedience. In both these passages we have a close and curt acknowledgment, that a Father of a family may be an absolute King over strangers, without the choice of the people; now I would know whether such Fathers of families have not the same absolute power over their own children without the people's choice, which he allows them over strangers: if they have, I cannot but call them absolute proprietary Kings, though Grotius be not willing to give them that title in plain terms: for indeed to allow such Kings were to condemn his own principle, that dominion came in by the will of the people, and so consequently tó overthrow his usufructuary Kings, of whom I am next to speak.

Grotius saith, that the law of obeying or resisting Princes depends upon the will of them who first met in civil society, from whom power doth flow to Kings. And, that men of their own accord came together into civil society, from whence springs civil power, and the people may choose what form of government they please. Upon these suppositions he concludes that Kings elected by the people have but a usufructuary right, that is, a right to take the profit or fruit of the kingdom, but not a right of propriety or power to alienate it. But why doth he call it a usufructuary right? It seems to me a term too mean or base to express the right of any King and is derogatory to the dignity of supreme majesty. The word usufructuary is used by the lawyers to signify him that hath the use, profit, or fruit of some corporal thing that may be used without the property, for of fungible things (*res fungibiles*, the civilians call them) that are spent or consumed in the use, as corn, wine, oil, money, there cannot be a usufructuary right.

It is to make a kingdom all one with a farm, as if it had no other use but to be let out to him that can make most of it: whereas, in truth, it is the part and duty of a King to govern, and he hath a right so to do, and to that end supreme power is given unto him, the taking of the profit or making use of the patrimony of the crown is but as a means only to enable him to perform that great work of government.

Besides, Grotius will not only have an elected King, but also his lawful successors to have but a usufructuary right, so that though a King hath a crown to him and to his heirs, yet he will allow him no propriety, because he hath no power to alienate it, for he supposeth the primary will of the people to have been to bestow supreme power to go in succession, and not to be alienable; but for this he hath no better proof than a naked presumption, 'In Regnis quae Populi voluntate delata sunt concedo non esse praesumendum eam fuisse Populi voluntatem ut alienatio Imperii sui Regi permitteretur'.

But though he will not allow Kings a right of propriety in their kingdoms, yet a right of propriety there must be in somebody, and in whom but in the people? For he saith, the empire which is exercised by Kings doth not cease to be the empire of the people. His meaning is, the use is the King's, but the property is the people's.

But if the power to alienate the kingdom be in him that hath the property, this may prove a comfortable doctrine to the people: but yet to allow a right of succession in Kings, and still to reserve a right of property in the people, may make some contradiction: for the succession must either hinder the right of alienation which is in the people; or the alienation must destroy that right of succession, which, by Grotius's confession, may attend upon elected Kings.

Though Grotius confess that supreme power be *unum quiddam*, and in itself indivisible, yet he saith, sometimes it may be divided either by parts potential, or subjunctive. I take his meaning to be that the government, or the governed may be divided: an example he gives of the Roman Empire which was divided into the East and West: but whereas he saith, *fieri potest*, etc. 'It may be the people choosing a King may reserve some actions to themselves, and in others they may give full power to the King.' The example he brings out of Plato of the Heraclides doth not prove it, and it is to dream of such a form of government as never yet had name, nor was ever found in any settled kingdom, nor cannot possibly be without strange confusion.

If it were a thing so voluntary, and at the pleasure of men when they were free to put themselves under subjection, why may they not as voluntarily leave subjection when they please, and be free again? If they had a liberty to change their natural freedom, into a voluntary subjection, there is stronger reason that they may change their voluntary subjection into natural freedom, since it is as lawful for men to alter their wills as their judgments.

Certainly it was a rare felicity, that all the men in the world at one instant of time should agree together in one mind to change the natural community of all things into private dominion: for without such a unanimous consent it was not possible for community to be altered: for if but one man in the world had dissented, the alteration had been unjust, because that man by the law of nature had a right to the common use of all things in the world; so that to have given a propriety of any one thing to any other, had been to have robbed him of his right to the common use of all things. And of this judgment the Jesuit Lud. Molina seems to be in his book *De Justitia*, where he saith, 'Si aliquis de cohabitantibus, etc. If one of the neighbours will not give his consent to it, the commonwealth should have no authority over him, because then every other man hath no right or authority over him, and therefore can they not give authority to the commonwealth over him'.

If our first parents, or some other of our forefathers did voluntarily bring in propriety of goods, and subjection to governors, and it were in their power either to bring them in or not, or having brought them in, to alter their minds, and restore them to their first condition of community and liberty; what reason can there be alleged that men that now live should not have the same power? So that if any one man in the world, be he never so mean or base, will but alter his will, and say, he will resume his natural right to community, and be restored unto his natural liberty, and consequently take what he please and do what he list, who can say that such a man doth more than by right he may? And then it will be lawful for every man, when he please, to dissolve all government, and destroy all property.

Whereas Grotius saith, that by the law of nature all things were at first common, and yet teacheth, that after propriety was brought in, it was against the law of nature to use community. He doth thereby not only make the law of nature changeable, which he saith God cannot do, but he also makes the law of nature contrary to itself.

THE

ANARCHY

OF

A LIMITED

OR

MIXED MONARCHY

OR

A succinct Examination of the Fundamentals of *Monarchy*, both in this and other Kingdoms, as well about the Right of Power in Kings, as of the Originall or Naturall Liberty of the People.

*A Question never yet disputed, though most
necessary in these Times*

Printed in the Year, 1648.

(Thomason April 19th, 1648, i.e. the first of Filmer's publications on political obligation, four years earlier than the *Forms* or the *Original*. Published, though not acknowledged, by Royston, who bound up the unsold copies of this tract into the second issue of the *Original* in 1652. Reprinted in all the collected editions, 1679, 1680, 1684, 1695(?) and 1696, always in this position in the book, although it was written earlier than the tracts which precede it.

The *Anarchy* is very closely connected with *Patriarcha*, as is shown by the sub-titles of the two works. The texts run parallel in many places, and in at least one instance *Patriarcha* is quoted word for word. Locke quoted repeatedly from this tract in his attack on patriarchalism, particularly from the earlier part. In form it is a refutation of the arguments of Philip Hunton, perhaps the ablest exponent of the theory of the parliamentary cause, and an anticipator of Locke's own position. Both Filmer's tract and Hunton's were contributions to an extensive controversy being carried on by the publication of pamphlets.

The last nine pages of this work are irrelevant to its general thesis and are devoted to a criticism of the views of another of those engaged in this pamphlet battle — Henry Parker. Filmer calls Parker 'The Observator' because his contribution to the discussion was entitled *Observations on His Majesties late Answers and Expresses* (July 1642). The *Anarchy* is probably the most valuable of the works which Filmer printed, for it shows how much sharper and more critical his patriarchal ideas had become since the time of the composition of the *Patriarcha* MS.)

WE do but flatter ourselves, if we hope ever to be governed without an arbitrary power. No: we mistake; the question is not, whether there shall be an arbitrary power; but the only point is, who shall have that arbitrary power, whether one man or many? There never was, nor ever can be any people governed without a power of making laws, and every power of making laws must be arbitrary: for to make a law according to law, is *contradictio in adjecto*. It is generally confessed that in a democracy the supreme or arbitrary power of making laws is in a multitude; and so in an aristocracy the like legislative or arbitrary power is in a few, or in the nobility. And therefore by a necessary consequence in a monarchy the same legislative power must be in one; according to the rule of Aristotle, who saith, 'Government is in one, or in a few, or in many'.

This ancient doctrine of government, in these latter days, hath been strangely refined by the Romanists, and wonderfully improved since the reformation, especially in point of monarchy, by an opinion, 'That the people have originally a power to create several sorts of monarchy, to limit and compound them with other forms of government, at their pleasure.'

As for this natural power of the people; they find neither scripture, reason, nor practice to justify it: for though several kingdoms have several and distinct laws one from another; yet that doth not make several sorts of monarchy: nor doth the difference of obtaining the supreme power, whether by conquest, election, succession, or by any other way make different sorts of government. It is the difference only of the authors of the laws, and not of the laws themselves that alters the form of government, that is, whether one man, or more than one, make the laws.

Since the growth of this new doctrine, of the limitation and mixture of monarchy, it is most apparent, that monarchy hath been crucified (as it were) between two thieves, the Pope and the people; for what principles the papists make use of for the power of the Pope above Kings; the very same, by blotting out the word Pope, and putting in the word people, the plebists take up to use against their sovereigns.

If we would truly know what popery is, we shall find by the laws and statutes of the realm, that the main, and indeed, the only point of popery, 'is the alienating and withdrawing of subjects from their obedience to their prince, to raise sedition and rebellion'. If popery and popularity agree in this point, the Kings of Christendom that have shaken off the power of the Pope, have made no great bargain of it, if in place of one lord abroad, they get many lords at home within their own kingdoms.

I cannot but reverence that form of government which was allowed and made use of for God's own people, and for all other nations. It were impiety, to think, that God who was careful to appoint judicial laws for his chosen people, would not furnish them with the best form of government: or to imagine that the rules given in divers places in the gospel, by our blessed Saviour and his Apostles for obedience to Kings should now, like almanacs out of date, be of no use to us; because it is pretended, 'We have a form of government now, not once thought of in those days'. It is a shame and scandal for us Christians to seek the original of government from the inventions or fictions of poets, orators, philosophers and heathen historians, who all lived thousands of years after the creation, and were (in a manner) ignorant of it: and to neglect the scriptures, which have with more authority most particularly given us the true grounds and principles of government.

These considerations caused me to scruple this modern piece of politics, touching limited and mixed monarchy, and finding no other that presented us with the nature and means of limitation and mixture, but an anonymous author, I have drawn a few brief observations upon the most considerable part of his treatise, in which I desire to receive satisfaction from the author himself, if it may be, according to his promise in his preface; or if not from him, from any other for him.

THE ANARCHY OF A LIMITED OR MIXED MONARCHY

THERE is scarce the meanest man of the multitude, but can now in these days tell us, that the government of the kingdom of England is a limited and mixed monarchy: and it is no marvel, since all the disputes and arguments of these distracted times both from the pulpit and the press do tend and end in this conclusion.

The author of the *Treatise of Monarchy*[1] hath copiously handled the nature and manner of limited and mixed monarchy and is the first and only man (that I know) [who] hath undertaken the task of describing it; others only mention it, as taking it for granted.

Doctor Ferne gives the author of this *Treatise of Monarchy* this testimony, that 'the mixture of government is more accurately delivered and urged by this treatise than by the author of the Fuller Answer'.*[2] And in another place Doctor Ferne saith, 'He allows his distinction of monarchy into limited and mixed'.†

I have with some diligence looked over this treatise, but cannot approve of these distinctions which he propounds; I submit the reasons of my dislike to others judgments. I am somewhat confident that his doctrine of limited and mixed monarchy is an opinion but of yesterday, and of no antiquity, a mere innovation in policy, not so old as New England,[3] though calculated properly for that meridian. For in his first part of the treatise which concerns monarchy in general, there is not one proof, text, or example in scripture that he hath produced to justify his conceit of limited and mixed monarchy. Neither doth he

* p. 3.   † p. 13.

---

[1] Philip Hunton (*c.* 1604-82), puritan divine and later provost of Cromwell's Durham University. His *A Treatise of Monarchy*...was published in 1643, Thomason's date, May 24th. It was answered by Henry Ferne (1602-62), one of Charles I's favourite clergymen, in *A Reply unto Severall Treatises* . . . , 1643, Thomason, November 1st. Hunton replied to Ferne in *A Vindication of the Treatise of Monarchy* . . . , 1644, Thomason, March 26th. Filmer's work, therefore, came at the end of a controversy. It is interesting that Hunton's *Treatise* should also have been reprinted, with no indication of author, in 1689 (B.M. T. 1107 (6).)

[2] Ferne's first work had been *The Resolving of Conscience . . . whether subjects may . . . resist,* 1642. This had been answered by Charles Herle, 1598-1659, another puritan minister, in *A Fuller Answer to a Treatise written by Dr. Ferne entitled 'The Resolving of Conscience . . .',* 1642, Thomason, December 29th. Ferne in the work quoted here was replying both to Herle and to Hunton. Filmer's quotation is not word for word from pp. 3 or 13.

[3] This is Filmer's only direct reference in his published works to the American colonies, with which, as is known from his biography, he and his family were so closely connected.

afford so much as one passage or reason out of Aristotle, whose books of 'Politics', and whose natural reasons are of greatest authority and credit with all rational men, next to the sacred scripture. Nay, I hope I may affirm, and be able to prove, that Aristotle doth confute both limited and mixed monarchy,* howsoever Doctor Ferne think these new opinions to be raised upon Aristotle's principles.[1] As for other politicians or historians, either divine or humane, ancient or modern, our author brings not one to confirm his opinions; nor doth he, nor can he show that ever any nation or people were governed by a limited or mixed monarchy.

Machivell is the first in christendom that I can find that wrote of a mixed government, but not one syllable of a mixed monarchy: he, in his discourses or disputations upon the decades of Livy, falls so enamoured with the Roman commonwealth, that he thought he could never sufficiently grace that popular government, unless he said, there was something of monarchy in it: yet he was never so impudent as to say it was a mixed monarchy. And what Machivell hath said for Rome, the like hath Contarene for Venice. But Bodin hath laid open the errors of both these, as also of Polybius, and some few others that held the like opinions. As for the kingdom of England, if it hath found out a form of government (as the Treatise layeth it down) of such perfection as never any people could, it is both a glory to the nation, and also to this author, who hath first deciphered it.

I now make my approach to the book itself: the title is, *A Treatise of Monarchy*. The first part of it is 'Of Monarchy in general': where first, I charge the author, that he hath not given us any definition or description of monarchy in general: for by the rules of method he should have first defined, and then divided: for if there be several sorts of monarchy, then in something they must agree, which makes them to be monarchies; and in something they must disagree and differ, which makes them to be several sorts of monarchies. In the first place he should have showed us in what they all agreed, which must have been a definition of monarchy in general, which is the foundation of the treatise; and except that be agreed upon, we shall argue upon we know not what. I press not this main omission of our author out of any humour of wrangling; but because I am confident that had he pitched upon any definition of monarchy in general, his own definition would

* p. 6.

---

[1] Ferne, *Reply*, p. 6.

have confuted his whole treatise. Besides, I find him pleased to give us a handsome definition of absolute monarchy, from whence I may infer, that he knew no other definition that would have fitted all his other sorts of monarchy; it concerned him to have produced it, lest it might be thought there could be no monarchy but absolute.

What our author hath omitted, I shall attempt to supply, and leave to the scanning. And it shall be a real as well as nominal definition of monarchy. A monarchy is the government of one alone. For the better credit of this definition, though it be able to maintain itself, yet I shall deduce it from the principles of our author of the Treatise of Monarchy.

We all know that this word monarch is compounded of two Greek words, μόνος and ἀρχεῖν. ἀρχεῖν is *imperare*, to govern and rule; μόνος signifies one alone. The understanding of these two words may be picked out of our author. First, for government he teacheth us, it is *potestatis exercitium*, the exercise of a moral power;* next he grants us, that every monarch (even his limited monarch) must have the supreme power of the state in him, so that his power must no way be limited by any power above his; for then he were not a monarch, but a subordinate magistrate.† Here we have a fair confession of a supreme unlimited power in his limited monarch: if you will know what he means by these words supreme power, turn to his page 26, there you will find, 'Supreme power is either legislative, or gubernative, and that the legislative power is the chief of the two'; he makes both supreme, and yet one chief: the like distinction he hath before, where he saith, 'The power of magistracy, in respect of its degrees, is nomothetical or architectonical; and gubernative or executive':‡ by these words of legislative, nomothetical and architectonical power, in plain English, he understands a power of making laws; and by gubernative and executive, a power of putting those laws in execution, by judging and punishing offenders.

The result we have from hence is, that by the author's acknowledgment, every monarch must have the supreme power, and that supreme power is a power to make laws: and howsoever the author makes the gubernative and executive power a part of the supreme power; yet he confesseth the legislative to be chief, or the highest degree of power, for he doth acknowledge degrees of supreme power; nay, he afterwards teacheth us, that the legislative power is the height of power, to which the other parts are subsequent and subservient:§ if gubernative be subservient to legislative, how can gubernative power be supreme?

* p. 1.   † p. 12.   ‡ p. 5.   § p. 40.

T

Now let us examine the author's limited monarch by these his own rules; he tells us, that in a moderated, limited, stinted, conditionate, legal or allayed monarchy (for all these terms he hath for it) the supreme power must be restrained by some law according to which this power was given, and by direction of which this power must act;* when in a line before he said, that the monarch's power must not be limited by any power above his: yet here he will have his supreme power restrained; not limited, and yet restrained: is not a restraint a limitation? And if restrained, how is it supreme? And if restrained by some law, is not the power of that law, and of them that made that law, above his supreme power? And if by the direction of such law only he must govern, where is the legislative power, which is the chief of supreme power? When the law must rule and govern the monarch, and not the monarch the law, he hath at the most but a gubernative or executive power: If his authority transcends its bounds, if it command beyond the law, the subject is not bound legally to subjection in such cases,† and if the utmost extent of the law of the land be the measure of the limited monarch's power, and subject's duty,‡ where shall we find the supreme power, that *culmen* or *apex potestatis*, that prime ἀρχὺ, which our author saith, must be in every monarch? The word ἀρχὺ, which signifies principality and power, doth also signify *principium*, beginning; which doth teach us, that by the word prince, or principality, the *principium* or beginning of government is meant; this, if it be given to the law, it robs the monarch, and makes the law the *primum mobile*; and so that which is but the instrument, or servant to the monarch, becomes the master. Thus much of the word ἀρχεῖν.

The other word is μόνος, *solus*, one alone: the monarch must not only have the supreme power unlimited, but he must have it alone (without any companions). Our author teacheth us, 'He is no monarch, if the supreme power be not in one'.§ And again he saith, 'If you put the *apex potestatis*, or supreme power in the whole body, or a part of it, you destroy the being of monarchy'. ‖

Now let us see if his mixed monarchy be framed according to these his own principles. First, he saith, 'In a mixed monarchy the sovereign power must be originally in all three estates'. And again his words are, 'The three estates are all sharers in the supreme power ... the primity of share in the supreme power is in one'. Here we find, that he that told us the supreme power must be in one, will now allow his mixed monarch but one share only of the supreme power, and gives other shares to the estates: thus he destroys the being of monarchy, by putting

* p. 12.   † p. 14.   ‡ p. 16.   § p. 15.   ‖ p. 17.

the supreme power, or *culmen potestatis*, or a part of it, in the whole body, or a part thereof; and yet formerly he confesseth, that the power of magistracy cannot well be divided, for it is one simple thing, or indivisible beam of divine perfection:* but he can make this indivisible beam to be divisible into three shares. I have done with the word μόνος, *solus*, alone.

I have dwelt the longer upon this definition of monarchy, because the apprehending of it out of the author's own ground quite over-throws both his monarch limited by law, and his monarch mixed with the states. For to govern, is to give a law to others, and not to have a law given to govern and limit him that governs: and to govern alone, is not to have sharers or companions mixed with the governor. Thus the two words of which monarchy is compounded, contradict the two sorts of monarchy which he pleads for, and by consequence his whole treatise: for these two sorts of limited and mixed monarchy take up (in a manner) his whole book.

I will now touch some few particular passages in the treatise.

Our author first confesseth, 'It is God's express ordinance there should be government',† and he proves it by Genesis iii, 16, where God ordained Adam to rule over his wife, and her desires were to be subject to his; and as hers, so all theirs that should come of her. Here we have the original grant of government, and the fountain of all power placed in the Father of all mankind; accordingly we find the law for obedience to government given in the terms of honour thy Father: not only the constitution of power in general, but the limitation of it to one kind (that is, to monarchy, or the government of one alone) and the deter-mination of it to the individual person and line of Adam, are all three ordinances of God. Neither Eve nor her children could either limit Adam's power, or join others with him in the government; and what was given unto Adam, was given in his person to his posterity. This paternal power continued monarchical to the Flood, and after the Flood to the confusion of Babel: when kingdoms were first erected, planted, or scattered over the face of the world, we find, Genesis x, 11, it was done by colonies of whole families, over which the prime Fathers had supreme power, and were Kings, who were all the sons or grandchildren of Noah, from whom they derived a fatherly and regal power over their families. Now if this supreme power was settled and founded by God himself in the fatherhood, how is it possible for the people to have any right or title to alter and dispose of it otherwise? What commission can they show that gives them power either of

* p. 5.　　† p. 2.

limitation or mixture? It was God's ordinance, that supremacy should
be unlimited in Adam, and as large as all the acts of his will: and as in
him, so in all others that have supreme power, as appears by the judgment and speech of the people to·Joshuah when he was supreme
governor, these are their words to him, 'All that thou commandest us
we will do; whosoever he be that doth rebel against thy commandment and will not hearken unto thy words in all that thou commandest
him, he shall be put to death'. We may not say, that these were evil
councillors or flattering courtiers of Joshuah, or that he himself was a
tyrant for having such arbitrary power. Our author, and all those who
affirm that power is conveyed to persons by public consent, are forced
to confess that it is the fatherly power that first enables a people to make
such conveyance; so that admitting (as they hold) that our ancestors
did at first convey power, yet the reason why we now living do submit
to such power, is, for that our forefathers every one for himself, his
family, and posterity, had a power of resigning up themselves and us
to a supreme power. As the scripture teacheth us, that supreme power
was originally in the Fatherhood without any limitation, so likewise
reason doth evince it, that if God ordained that supremacy should be,
that then supremacy must of necessity be unlimited: for the power that
limits must be above that power which is limited; if it be limited, it
cannot be supreme: so that if our author will grant supreme power to
be the ordinance of God, the supreme power will prove itself to be
unlimited by the same ordinance, because a supreme limited power is a
contradiction.

The monarchical power of Adam the Father of all flesh, being by a
general binding ordinance settled by God in him and his posterity by
right of fatherhood, the form of monarchy must be preferred above
other forms, except the like ordinance for other forms can be shown:
neither may men according to their relations to the form they live
under, to their affections and judgments in divers respects, prefer or
compare any other form with monarchy. The point that most per-
plexeth our author and many others is, that if monarchy be allowed to
be the ordinance of God, an absurdity would follow, that we should
uncharitably condemn all the communities which have not that form,
for violation of God's ordinance, and pronounce those other powers
unlawful. If those who live under a monarchy can justify the form
they live under to be God's ordinance, they are not bound to forbear
their own justification, because others cannot do the like for the form
they live under; let others look to the defence of their own government:
if it cannot be proved or shown that any other form of government

had ever any lawful beginning, but was brought in or erected by rebellion, must therefore the lawful and just obedience to monarchy be denied to be the ordinance of God?

To proceed with our author, in the third page he saith, 'The higher power is God's ordinance: that it resideth in one or more, in such or such a way, is from human designment; God by no word binds any people to this or that form, till they by their own all bind themselves'. Because the power and consent of the people in government is the burden of the whole book, and our author expects it should be admitted as a magisterial postulation, without any other proof than a naked supposition; and since others also maintain that originally power was, or now is in the people, and that the first Kings were chosen by the people: they may not be offended, if they be asked in what sense they understand the word 'people' because this, as many other words, hath different acceptions, being sometimes taken in a larger, otherwhile in a stricter sense. Literally, and in the largest sense, the word people signifies the whole multitude of mankind; but figuratively and synecdochically, it notes many times the major part of a multitude, or sometimes the better, or the richer, or the wiser, or some other part; and oftentimes a very small part of the people, if there be no other apparent opposite party, hath the name of the people by presumption.

If they understand that the entire multitude or whole people have originally by nature power to choose a King, they must remember that by their own principles and rules, by nature all mankind in the world makes but one people, who they suppose to be born alike to an equal freedom from subjection; and where such freedom is, there all things must of necessity be common: and therefore without a joint consent of the whole people of the world, no one thing can be made proper to any one man, but it will be an injury, and a usurpation upon the common right of all others. From whence it follows that natural freedom being once granted, there cannot be any one man chosen a King without the universal consent of all the people of the world at one instant, *nemine contradicente*. Nay, if it be true that nature hath made all men free; though all mankind should concur in one vote, yet it cannot seem reasonable, that they should have power to alter the law of nature; for if no man have power to take away his own life without the guilt of being a murderer of himself, how can any people confer such a power as they have not themselves upon any one man, without being accessories to their own deaths, and every particular man become guilty of being *felo de se*?

If this general signification of the word People be disavowed, and men will suppose that the people of particular regions or countries have power and freedom to choose unto themselves Kings; then let them but observe the consequence. Since nature hath not distinguished the habitable world into kingdoms, nor determined what part of a people shall belong to one kingdom, and what to another, it follows that the original freedom of mankind being supposed, every man is at liberty to be of what kingdom he please, and so every petty company hath a right to make a kingdom by itself; and not only every city, but every village, and every family, nay, and every particular man, a liberty to choose himself to be his own King if he please; and he were a madman that being by nature free, would choose any man but himself to be his own governor. Thus to avoid the having but of one King of the whole world, we shall run into a liberty of having as many Kings as there be men in the world, which upon the matter, is to have no King at all, but to leave all men to their natural liberty, which is the mischief the pleaders for natural liberty do pretend they would most avoid.

But if neither the whole people of the world, nor the whole people of any part of the world be meant, but only the major part, or some other part of a part of the world; yet still the objection will be the stronger. For besides that nature hath made no partition of the world, or of the people into distinct kingdoms, and that without a universal consent at one and the same instant no partition can be made: yet if it were lawful for particular parts of the world by consent to choose their Kings, nevertheless their elections would bind none to subjection but only such as consented; for the major part never binds, but where men at first either agree to be so bound, or where a higher power so commands: now there being no higher power than nature, but God himself; where neither nature nor God appoints the major part to bind, their consent is not binding to any but only to themselves who consent.

Yet, for the present to gratify them so far as to admit that either by nature, or by a general consent of all mankind, the world at first was divided into particular kingdoms, and the major part of the people of each kingdom assembled, allowed to choose their King: yet it cannot truly be said that ever the whole people, or the major part, or indeed any considerable part of the whole people of any nation ever assembled to any such purpose. For except by some secret miraculous instinct they should all meet at one time, and place, what one man, or company of men less than the whole people hath power to appoint either time or place of elections, where all be alike free by nature? and without a lawful summons, it is most unjust to bind those that be absent. The whole people cannot summon itself; one man is sick, another is lame, a third is aged, and a fourth is under age of discretion: all these at some time or other, or at some place or other, might be able to meet, if they might choose their own time and place, as men naturally free should.

In assemblies that are by humane politique constitution, the superior power that ordains such assemblies, can regulate and confine them, both for time, place, persons, and other circumstances: but where there is an equality by nature, there can be no superior power; there every infant at the hour it is born in, hath a like interest with the greatest and wisest man in the world. Mankind is like the sea, ever ebbing or flowing, every minute one is born another dies; those that are the people this minute, are not the people the next minute, in every instant and point of time there is a variation: no one time can be indifferent for all mankind to assemble; it cannot but be mischievous always at the least to all infants and others under age of discretion; not to speak of women, especially virgins, who by birth have as much natural freedom as any other, and therefore ought not to lose their liberty without their own consent.

But in part to salve this, it will be said that infants and children may be concluded by the votes of their parents. This remedy may cure some part of the mischief, but it destroys the whole cause, and at last stumbles upon the true original of government. For if it be allowed, that the acts of parents bind the children, then farewell the doctrine of the natural freedom of mankind; where subjection of children to parents is natural, there can be no natural freedom. If any reply, that not all children shall be bound by their parents' consent, but only those that are under age: it must be considered, that in nature there is no *nonage*; if a man be not born free, she doth not assign him any other time when he shall attain his freedom: or if she did, then children attaining that age, should be discharged of their parents' contract. So that in conclusion, if it be imagined that the people were ever but once free from subjection by nature, it will prove a mere impossibility ever lawfully to introduce any kind of government whatsoever, without apparent wrong to a multitude of people.

It is further observable, that ordinarily children and servants are far a greater number than parents and masters; and for the major part of these to be able to vote and appoint what government or governors their fathers and masters shall be subject unto, is most unnatural, and in effect to give the children the government over their parents.

To all this it may be opposed, what need dispute how a people can choose a King, since there be multitude of examples that Kings have been, and are nowadays chosen by their people? The answer is: 1. The question is not of the fact, but of the right, whether it have been done by a natural, or by a usurped right. 2. Many Kings are, and have been chosen by some small part of a people; but by the whole, or major part of a kingdom not any at all. Most have been elected by the nobility, great men, and princes of the blood, as in Poland, Denmark and in Sweden; not by any collective or representative body of any nation: sometimes a factious or seditious city, or a mutinous army hath set up a King, but none of all those could ever prove they had right or just title either by nature, or any otherwise, for such elections. We may resolve upon these two propositions: 1. That the people have no power or right of themselves to choose Kings. 2. If they had any such right, it is not possible for them any way lawfully to exercise it.

You will say, 'There must necessarily be a right in somebody to elect, in case a King die without an heir'. I answer, 'No King can die without an heir, as long as there is any one man living in the world'. It may be the heir may be unknown to the people; but that is no fault in nature, but the negligence or ignorance of those whom it concerns. But if a King could die without an heir, yet the kingly power in that case shall not escheat to the whole people, but to the supreme heads and Fathers of families; not as they are the people, but *quatenus* they are Fathers of people, over whom they have a supreme power devolved unto them after the death of their sovereign ancestor: and if any can have a right to choose a King, it must be these Fathers, by conferring their distinct fatherly powers upon one man alone. Chief Fathers in scripture are accounted as all the people, as all the children of Israel, as all the congregation, as the text plainly expounds itself, 2 Chronicles i, 2, where Solomon speaks to all Israel, that is, to the captains, the judges, and to every governor, the chief of the Fathers: and so the elders of Israel are expounded to be the chief of the Fathers of the children of Israel, 1 Kings viii, 1, and the 2 Chronicles v, 2.

If it be objected, that Kings are not now (as they were at the first planting or peopling of the world) the Fathers of their people or kingdoms, and that the fatherhood hath lost the right of governing; an answer is, that all Kings that now are, or ever were, are, or were either Fathers of their people, or the heirs of such Fathers, or usurpers of the right of such Fathers. It is a truth undeniable, that there cannot be any multitude of men whatsoever, either great, or small, though gathered together from the several corners and remotest regions of the world, but that in the same multitude, considered by itself, there is one man amongst them that in nature hath a right to be the King of all the rest, as being the next heir to Adam, and all the others subject unto him: every man by nature is a King, or a subject: the obedience which all subjects yield to Kings, is but the paying of that duty which is due to the supreme fatherhood: many times by the act either of a usurper himself, or of those that set him up, the true heir of a crown is dispossessed, God using the ministry of the wickedest men for the removing and setting up of Kings: in such cases the subjects' obedience to the fatherly power must go along and wait upon God's providence, who only hath right to give and take away kingdoms, and thereby to adopt subjects into the obedience of another fatherly power: according to that of Aristotle, Πατρικὴ γὰρ ἀρχὴ βούλεται ἡ βασιλεία εἶναι. A monarchy or kingdom will be a fatherly government. *Ethic., lib.* 8, *c.* 12.

However the natural freedom of the people be cried up as the sole means to determine the kind of government and the governors: yet in the close, all the favourers of this opinion are constrained to grant that the obedience which is due to the fatherly power is the true and only cause of the subjection which we that are now living give to Kings, since none of us gave consent to government, but only our forefathers, act and consent hath concluded us.

Whereas many confess that government only in the abstract is the ordinance of God, they are not able to prove any such ordinance in the scripture, but only in the fatherly power, and therefore we find the commandment that enjoins obedience to superiors, given in the terms of honour thy Father: so that not only the power or right of government, but the form of the power of governing, and the person having that power, are all the ordinance of God: the first Father had not only simply power, but power monarchical, as he was a Father, immediately from God. For by the appointment of God, as soon as Adam was created he was monarch of the world, though he had no subjects; for though there could not be actual government until there were subjects, yet by the right of nature it was due to Adam to be governor of his posterity: though not in act, yet at least in habit. Adam was a King from his creation: and in the state of innocency he had been governor of his children; for the integrity or excellency of the subjects doth not take away the order or eminency of the governor. Eve was subject to Adam before he sinned; the angels, who are of a pure nature, are subject to God: which confutes their saying who in disgrace of civil government or power say it was brought in by sin: government as to coactive power was after sin, because coaction supposeth some disorder, which was not in the state of innocency: but as for directive power, the condition of humane nature requires it, since civil society cannot be imagined without power of government: for although as long as men continued in the state of innocency they might not need the direction of Adam in those things which were necessarily and morally to be done; yet things indifferent, that depended merely on their free will, might be directed by the power of Adam's command.

If we consider the first plantations of the world which were after the building of Babel when the confusion of tongues was, we may find the division of the earth into distinct kingdoms and countries, by several families, whereof the sons or grandchildren of Noah were the Kings or governors by a fatherly right; and for the preservation of this power and right in the Fathers, God was pleased upon several families to bestow a language on each by itself, the better to unite it into a nation or kingdom; as appears by the words of the text, Genesis x, 'These are the families of the sons of Noah, after their generations in their nations, and by these were the nations divided in the earth after the flood: every one after his tongue, after their families in their nations'.

The Kings of England have been graciously pleased to admit and accept the Commons in Parliament as the representees of the kingdom, yet really and truly they are not the representative body of the whole kingdom.

The Commons in Parliament are not the representative body of the whole kingdom: they do not represent the King, who is the head and principal member of the kingdom; nor do they represent the Lords, who are the nobler and higher part of the body of the realm, and are personally present in Parliament, and therefore need no representation. The Commons only represent a part of the lower or inferior part of the body of the people, which are the freeholders worth 40s. by the year, and the Commons or freemen of cities and boroughs, or the major part of them. All which are not one-quarter, nay, not a tenth part of the Commons of the kingdom; for in every parish, for one freeholder there may be found ten that are no freeholders: and anciently before rents were improved, there were nothing near so many freeholders of 40s. by the year as now are to be found.

The scope and conclusion of this discourse and argument is, that the people taken in what notion or sense soever, either diffusively, collectively, or representatively, have not, nor cannot exercise any right or power of their own by nature, either in choosing or in regulating Kings. But whatsoever power any people doth lawfully exercise, it must receive it from a supreme power on earth, and practise it with such limitations as that superior power shall appoint. To return to our author.

He divides monarchy into absolute and limited.

Absolute monarchy (saith he) is, when the sovereignty is so fully in one, that it hath no limits or bounds under God but his own will.* This definition of his I embrace. And as before I charged our author for not giving us a definition of monarchy in general, so I now note him for not affording us any definition of any other particular kind of monarchy but only of absolute: it may peradventure make some doubt that there is no other sort but only that which he calls absolute.

Concerning absolute monarchy, he grants, that such were the ancient eastern monarchies, and that of the Turk and Persian at this day. Herein he saith very true. And we must remember him, though he do not mention them, that the monarchs of Judah and Israel must be comprehended under the number of those he calls the eastern monarchies: and truly if he had said that all the ancient monarchies of the world had been absolute, I should not have quarrelled at him, nor do I know who could have disproved him.

Next it follows, that absolute monarchy is, when a people are absolutely resigned up, or resign up themselves to be governed by the will of one man. Where men put themselves into this utmost degree of subjection by oath and contract, or are born and brought unto it by God's providence. In both these places he acknowledgeth there may be other means of obtaining a monarchy, besides the contract of a nation or peoples resigning up themselves to be governed, which is contrary to what he after says, that the sole mean or root of all sovereignty, is the consent and fundamental contract of a nation of men.†

Moreover, the author determines, that absolute monarchy is a lawful government, and that men·may be born and brought unto it by God's providence, it binds them, and they must abide it, because an oath to a lawful thing is obligatory. This position of his I approve, but his reason doth not satisfy: for men are bound to obey a lawful governor, though neither they nor their ancestors ever took oath.

Then he proceeds, and confesseth that in Romans xiii, the power which then was, was absolute: yet the apostle not excluding it, calls it God's ordinance, and commands subjection to it. So Christ commands tribute to be paid, and pays it himself; yet it was an arbitrary tax the production of an absolute power.‡ These are the loyal expressions of our author touching absolute or arbitrary monarchy. I do the rather mention these passages of our author, because very many in these days do not stick to maintain, that an arbitrary or absolute monarch not limited by law, is all one with a tyrant; and to be governed by one

* p. 6.   † p. 12.   ‡ p. 7.

man's will, is to be made a slave. It is a question whether our author be not of that mind, when he saith, absolute subjection is servitude: and thereupon a late friend to limited monarchy affirms in a discourse upon the question in debate between the King and Parliament, 'That to make a King by the standard of God's word, is to make the subjects slaves for conscience sake.* A hard saying, and I doubt whether he that gives this censure can be excused from blasphemy. It is a bold speech, to condemn all the Kings of Judah for tyrants, or to say all their subjects were slaves. But certainly the man doth not know either what a tyrant is, or what a slave is: indeed the words are frequent enough in every man's mouth, and our old English translation of the Bible useth sometimes the word tyrant; but the authors of our new translation have been so careful, as not once to use the word, but only for the proper name of a man, Acts xix, 9, because they find no Hebrew word in the scripture to signify a tyrant or a slave. Neither Aristotle, Bodin, nor Sir Walter Raleigh (who were all men of deep judgment) can agree in a definition or description of tyranny, though they have all three laboured in the point. And I make some question whether any man can possibly describe what a tyrant is, and then tell me any one man that ever was in the world that was a tyrant according to that description.

I return again to our Treatise of Monarchy, where I find three degrees of absolute monarchy.

  1. Where the monarch, whose will is the law, doth set himself no law to rule by, but by commands of his own judgment as he thinks fit.

  2. When he sets a law by which he will ordinarily govern, reserving to himself a liberty to vary from it as oft as in his discretions he thinks fit; and in this the sovereign is as free as the former.

  3. Where he not only sets a rule, but promiseth in many cases not to alter it; but this promise or engagement is an after-condescent or act of grace, not dissolving the absolute oath of subjection which went before it.

For the first of these three, there is no question but it is a pure absolute monarchy; but as for the other two, though he say they be absolute, yet in regard they set themselves limits or laws to govern by, if it please our author to term them limited monarchs, I will not oppose him; yet I must tell him, that his third degree of absolute monarchy is such a kind, as I believe, never hath been, nor ever can be in the world. For a monarch to promise and engage in many cases not to alter a law, it is most necessary that those many cases should be particularly expressed

* p. 54.

at the bargain-making. Now he that understands the nature and condition of all humane laws, knows that particular cases are infinite, and not comprehensible within any rules or laws; and if many cases should be comprehended, and many omitted, yet even those that were comprehended would admit of variety of interpretations and disputations; therefore our author doth not, nor can tell us of any such reserved cases promised by any monarch.

Again, where he saith, 'An after-condescent or act of grace doth not dissolve the absolute oath of subjection which went before it'; though in this he speak true, yet still he seems to insinuate that an oath only binds to subjection, which oath, as he would have us believe, was at first arbitrary: whereas subjects are bound to obey monarchs though they never take oath of subjection, as well as children are bound to obey their parents, though they never swear to do it.

Next, his distinction between the rule of power, and the exercise of it,* is vain; for to rule, is to exercise power: for himself saith, that government is *potestatis exercitium*, the exercise of a moral power.†

Lastly, whereas our author saith, a monarch cannot break his promise without sin; let me add, that if the safety of the people, *salus populi*, require a breach of the monarch's promise, then the sin, if there be any, is rather in the making, than breaking of the promise; the safety of the people is an exception implied in every monarchical promise.

But it seems these three degrees of monarchy do not satisfy our author; he is not content to have a monarch have a law or rule to govern by, but he must have this limitation or law to be *ab externo* from somebody else, and not from the determination of the monarch's own will;‡ and therefore he saith, by original constitution the society public confers on one man a power by limited contract, resigning themselves to be governed by such a law. § Also before he told us, the sole means of sovereignty is the consent and fundamental contract; which consent puts them in their power, which can be no more nor other than is conveyed to them by such contract of subjection. If the sole means of a limited monarchy be the consent and fundamental contract of a nation, how is it that he saith, 'A monarch may be limited by after-condescent'? Is an after-condescent all one with a fundamental contract, with original and radical constitution? Why yea: he tells us it is a secondary original constitution; a secondary original, that is, a second first: and if that condescent be an act of grace, doth not this condescent to a limitation come from the free determination of the monarchs will? If he either formally, or virtually (as our author sup-

* p. 7.   † p. 1.   ‡ p. 12.   § p. 13.

poseth), desert his absolute or arbitrary power which he hath by conquest, or other right.

And if it be from the free will of the monarch, why doth he say the limitation must be *ab externo*? He told us before, that subjection cannot be dissolved or lessened by an act of grace coming afterwards:* but he hath better bethought himself, and now he will have acts of grace to be of two kinds, and the latter kind may amount (as he saith) to a resignation of absolute monarchy. But can any man believe that a monarch who by conquest or other right hath an absolute arbitrary power, will voluntarily resign that absoluteness, and accept so much power only as the people shall please to give him, and such laws to govern by as they shall make choice of? Can he show that ever any monarch was so gracious or kind-hearted as to lay down his lawful power freely at his subjects' feet? Is it not sufficient grace if such an absolute monarch be content to set down a law to himself by which he will ordinarily govern, but he must needs relinquish his old independent commission, and take a new one from his subjects, clogged with limitations?

Finally, I observe, that howsoever our author speak big of the radical, fundamental, and original power of the people as the root of all sovereignty: yet in a better mood he will take up, and be contented with a monarchy limited by an after-condescent and act of grace from the monarch himself.

Thus I have briefly touched his grounds of limited monarchy; if now we shall ask, what proof or examples he hath to justify his doctrine, he is as mute as a fish: only Pythagoras hath said it, and we must believe him; for though our author would have monarchy to be limited, yet he could be content his opinion should be absolute, and not limited to any rule or example.

The main charge I have against our author now remains to be discussed; and it is this, that instead of a treatise of monarchy, he hath brought forth a treatise of anarchy, and that by his own confessions shall be made good.

First, he holds: A limited monarch transcends his bounds, if he commands beyond the law; and the subject legally is not bound to subjection in such cases.

Now if you ask the author who shall be judge, whether the monarch transcend his bounds, and of the excesses of the sovereign power; his answer is, 'There is an impossibility of constituting a judge to determine this last controversy . . .† I conceive in a limited legal monarchy there

* p. 8.   † p. 16.

can be no stated internal judge of the monarch's actions, if there grow a fundamental variance between him and the community. There can be no judge legal and constituted within that form of government.'* In these answers it appears, there is no judge to determine the sovereign's or the monarch's transgressing his fundamental limits: yet our author is very cautious and supposeth only a fundamental variance betwixt the monarch and the community; he is ashamed to put the question home. I demand of him if there be a variance betwixt the monarch and any of the meanest persons of the community, who shall be the judge? For instance, the King commands me, or gives judgment against me: I reply, his commands are illegal, and his judgment not according to law; who must judge? If the monarch himself judge, then you destroy the frame of the state, and make it absolute, saith our author; and he gives his reason: for, to define a monarch to a law, and then to make him judge of his own deviations from that law, is to absolve him from all law. On the other side, if any, or all the people may judge, then you put the sovereignty in the whole body, or part of it, and destroy the being of monarchy. Thus our author hath caught himself in a plain dilemma: if the King be judge, then he is no limited monarch; if the people be judge, then he is no monarch at all. So farewell limited monarchy, nay farewell all government, if there be no judge.

Would you know what help our author hath found out for this mischief? First, he saith, that a subject is bound to yield to a magistrate, when he cannot, *de jure*, challenge obedience, if it be in a thing in which he can possibly without subversion, and in which his act may not be made a leading case, and so bring on a prescription against public liberty.† Again he saith, if the act in which the exorbitance or transgression of the monarch is supposed to be, be of lesser moment, and not striking at the very being of that government, it ought to be borne by public patience, rather than to endanger the being of the state.‡ The like words he uses in another place, saying, if the will of the monarch exceed the limits of the law, it ought to be submitted to, so it be not contrary to God's law, nor bring with it such an evil to ourselves, or the public, that we cannot be accessory to it by obeying.§ These are but fig leaves to cover the nakedness of our author's limited monarch, formed upon weak supposals in cases of lesser moment. For if the monarch be to govern only according to law, no transgression of his can be of so small moment, if he break the bounds of law, but it is a subversion of the government itself, and may be made a leading case, and so bring on a prescription against public liberty; it strikes at the

* p. 17.   † p. 14.   ‡ p. 17.   § p. 49.

very being of the government, and brings with it such an evil, as the party that suffers, or the public cannot be accessory to: let the case be never so small, yet if there be illegality in the act, it strikes at the very being of limited monarchy, which is to be legal: unless our author will say, as in effect he doth, that his limited·monarch must govern according to law in great and public matters only, and that in smaller matters which concern private men, or poor persons, he may rule according to his own will.

Secondly, our author tells us, if the monarch's act of exorbitancy or transgression be mortal, and such as suffered dissolves the frame of government and public liberty, then the illegality is to be set open, and redressment sought by petition; which if failing, prevention by resistance ought to be: and if it be apparent, and appeal be made to the consciences of mankind, then the fundamental laws of that monarchy must judge and pronounce the sentence in every man's conscience, and every man (so far as concerns him) must follow the evidence of truth in his own soul to oppose or not to oppose, according as he can in conscience acquit or condemn the act of the governor or monarch.*

Whereas my author requires, that the destructive nature of illegal commands should be set open: surely his mind is, that each private man in his particular case should make a public remonstrance to the world of the illegal act of the monarch; and then if upon his petition he cannot be relieved according to his desire, he ought, or it is his duty to make resistance. Here I would know, who can be the judge whether the illegality be made apparent? It is a main point, since every man is prone to flatter himself in his own cause, and to think it good, and that the wrong or injustice he suffers is apparent, when other moderate and indifferent men can discover no such thing: and in this case the judgment of the common people cannot be gathered or known by any possible means; or if it could, it were like to be various and erroneous.

Yet our author will have an appeal made to the conscience of all mankind, and that being made, he concludes, the fundamental laws must judge, and pronounce sentence in every man's conscience.† Whereas he saith, the fundamental laws must judge; I would very gladly learn of him, or of any other for him, what a fundamental law is, or else have but any one law named me that any man can say is a fundamental law of the monarchy. I confess he tells us, that the common laws are the foundation, and the statute laws are superstructive;‡ yet I think he dares not say that there is any one branch or part of the common law, but that it may be taken away by an Act of Parliament:

* p. 17.   † p. 18.   ‡ p. 38.

for many points of the common law (*de facto*) have, and (*de jure*) any point may be taken away. How can that be called fundamental, which hath and may be removed, and yet the statute laws stand firm and stable? It is contrary to the nature of fundamental, for the building to stand when the foundation is taken away.

Besides, the common law is generally acknowledged to be nothing else but common usage or custom, which by length of time only obtains authority: so that it follows in time after government, but cannot go before it, and be the rule to government, by any original or radical constitution.

Also the common law being unwritten, doubtful, and difficult, cannot but be an uncertain rule to govern by; which is against the nature of a rule, which is and ought to be certain.

Lastly, by making the common law only to be the foundation, Magna Charta is excluded from being a fundamental law, and also all other statutes from being limitations to monarchy, since the fundamental laws only are to be judge.

Truly the conscience of all mankind is a pretty large tribunal for the fundamental laws to pronounce sentence in. It is very much that laws which in their own nature are dumb, and always need a judge to pronounce sentence, should now be able to speak, and pronounce sentence themselves: such a sentence surely must be upon the hearing of one party only; for it is impossible for a monarch to make his defence and answer, and produce his witnesses, in every man's conscience, in each man's cause, who will but question the legality of the monarch's government. Certainly the sentence cannot but be unjust, where but one man's tale is heard. For all this, the conclusion is, every man must oppose or not oppose the monarch according to his own conscience. Thus at the last, every man is brought, by this doctrine of our authors, to be his own judge. And I also appeal to the consciences of all mankind, whether the end of this be not utter confusion, and anarchy.

Yet after all this, the author saith, this power of every man's judging the illegal acts of the monarch, argues not a superiority of those who judge over him who is judged;* and he gives a profound reason for it: his words are: 'It is not authoritative and civil, but moral, residing in reasonable creatures, and lawful for them to execute.' What our author means by these words (not authoritative and civil, but moral), perhaps I understand not, though I think I do; yet it serves my turn that he saith, that resistance ought to be made, and every man must oppose or not

* p. 18.

U

oppose, according as in conscience he can acquit or condemn the acts of his governor; for if it enable a man to resist and oppose his governor, without question, it is authoritative and civil. Whereas he adds, that moral judgment is residing in reasonable creatures, and lawful for them to execute; he seems to imply, that authoritative and civil judgment doth not reside in reasonable creatures, nor can be lawfully executed. Such a conclusion fits well with anarchy; for he that takes away all government, and leaves every man to his own conscience, and so makes him an independent in state, may well teach that authority resides not in reasonable creatures, nor can be lawfully executed.

I pass from his absolute and limited monarchy, to his division or partition (for he allows no division) of monarchy into simple and mixed, viz. of a monarch, the nobility and community.

Where first, observe a doubt of our author's, whether a firm union can be in a mixture of equality; he rather thinks there must be a priority of order in one of the three, or else there can be no unity.* He must know that priority of order doth not hinder, but that there may be an equality of mixture, if the shares be equal; for he that hath the first share may have no more than the others: so that if he will have an inequality of mixture, a primity of share will not serve the turn: the first share must be greater or better than the others, or else they will be equal, and then he cannot call it a mixed monarchy, where only a primity of share in the supreme power is in one: but by his own confession he may better call it a mixed aristocracy or mixed democracy, than a mixed monarchy, since he tells us, the Houses of Parliament sure have two parts of the greatest legislative authority;† and if the King have but a third part, sure their shares are equal.

The first step our author makes, is this, the sovereign power must be originally in all three; next he finds, that if there be an equality of shares in three estates, there can be no ground to denominate a monarch; and then his mixed monarch might be thought but an empty title: therefore in the third place he resolves us, that to salve all, a power must be sought out wherewith the monarch must be invested, which is not so great as to destroy the mixture, nor so titular as to destroy the monarchy;‡ and therefore he conceives it may be in these particulars.

First, a monarch in a mixed monarchy may be said to be a monarch (as he conceives) if he be the head and fountain of the power which governs and executes the established laws;§ that is, a man may be a monarch, though he do but give power to others to govern and execute the established laws: thus he brings his monarch one step or peg lower

* p. 25.   † p. 56.   ‡ p. 25.   § p. 26.

still than he was before: at first he made us believe his monarch should
have the supreme power, which is the legislative; then he falls from
that, and tells us, a limited monarch must govern according to law
only; thus he is brought from the legislative to the gubernative or
executive power only; nor doth he stay here, but is taken a hole lower,
for now he must not govern, but he must constitute officers to govern
by laws; if choosing officers to govern be governing, then our author
will allow his monarch to be a governor, not else: and therefore he
that divided supreme power into legislative and gubernative, doth
now divide it into legislative, and power of constituting officers for
governing by laws; and this, he saith, is left to the monarch. Indeed
you have left him a fair portion of power; but are we sure he may
enjoy this? It seems our author is not confident in this neither, and
some others do deny it him: our author speaking of the government
of this kingdom, 'saith the choice of the officers is entrusted to the
judgment of the monarch for ought I know':* he is not resolute in the
point; but for ought he knows, and for ought I know, his monarch is
but titular, an empty title, certain of no power at all.

The power of choosing officers only, is the basest of all powers.
Aristotle (as I remember) saith, the common people are fit for nothing
but to choose officers, and to take accounts: and indeed, in all popular
governments the multitude perform this work: and this work in a King
puts him below all his subjects, and makes him the only subject in a
kingdom, or the only man that cannot govern: there is not the poorest
man of the multitude but is capable of some office or other, and by
that means may some time or other perhaps govern according to the
laws; only the King can be no officer, but to choose officers; his subjects
may all govern, but he may not.

Next, I cannot see how in true sense our author can say, his monarch
is the head and fountain of power, since his doctrine is, that in a limited
monarchy, the public society by original constitution confer on one
man power: is not then the public society the head and fountain of
power, and not the King?

Again, when he tells us of his monarch, that both the other states,
as well *conjunctim* as *divisim*, be his sworn subjects, and owe obedience
to his commands: he doth but flout his poor monarch; for why are
they called his subjects and his commons? He (without any complement) is their subject; for they, as officers, may govern and command
according to law: but he may not, for he must judge by his judges in
courts of justice only: that is, he may not judge or govern at all.

* p. 38.

2. As for the second particular, the sole or chief power in capacitating persons for the supreme power. And

3. As to this third particular, the power of convocating such persons, they are both so far from making a monarch, that they are the only way to make him none, by choosing and calling others to share in the supreme power.

4. Lastly, concerning his authority being the last and greatest in the establishing of every act, it makes him no monarch, except he be sole that hath that authority; neither his primity of share in the supreme power, nor his authority being last, no, nor his having the greatest authority, doth make him a monarch, unless he have that authority alone.

Besides, how can he show that in his mixed monarchy the monarch's power is the greatest? The greatest share that our author allows him in the legislative power, is a negative voice, and the like is allowed to the nobility and Commons: and truly, a negative voice is but a base term to express a legislative power; a negative voice is but a privative power, or indeed, no power at all to do anything, only a power to hinder an act from being done.

Wherefore I conclude, not any of his four, nor all of them put into one person, make the state monarchical.*

This mixed monarchy, just like the limited, ends in confusion and destruction of all government: you shall hear the author's confession, †'That one inconvenience must necessarily be in all mixed governments, which I showed to be in limited governments; there can be no constituted legal authoritative judge of the fundamental controversies arising between the three estates: if such do rise, it is the fatal disease of those governments, for which no salve can be applied. It is a case beyond the possible provision of such a government; of this question there is no legal judge. The accusing side must make it evident to every man's conscience . . . The appeal must be to the community, as if there were no government; and as by evidence consciences are convinced, they are bound to give their assistance'. The wit of man cannot say more for anarchy.

Thus have I picked out the flowers out of his doctrine about limited monarchy, and presented them with some brief annotations; it were a tedious work to collect all the learned contradictions, and ambiguous expressions that occur in every page of his platonic monarchy; the book hath so much of fancy, that it is a better piece of poetry than policy.

* p. 26.   † p. 28.

·Because many may think, that the main doctrine of·limited and
mixed monarchy may in itself be most authentical, and grounded
upon strong and evident reason, although our author perhaps have
failed in some of his expressions, and be liable to exceptions: therefore
I will be bold to inquire whether Aristotle could find either reason or
example of a·limited or mixed monarchy; and the rather, because I
find our author altogether insists upon a rational way of justifying his
opinion. No man I think will deny, but that Aristotle was sufficiently
curious in searching out the several forms of commonwealths and
kingdoms; yet I do not find, that he ever so much as dreamed of either
a limited or mixed monarchy. Several other sorts of monarchies he
reckons up: in the third book of his *Politics*, he spends three whole
chapters together, upon the several kinds of monarchy.

First, in his fourteenth chapter he mentions four kinds of monarchy:

· The Laconic or Lacedemonian
  The Barbaric
  The Aesymnetical
  The Heroic. •

The Laconic or Lacedemonian King (saith he)·had only supreme·
power when he was out of the bounds of the Lacedemonian territories;·
then he had absolute power, his kingdom was like to a perpetual
Lord General of an army.

The Barbaric King (saith Aristotle) had a power very near 'to
tyranny; yet they were lawful and paternal, because the barbarians are
of a more servile nature than the Grecians, and the Asiatics than the
Europeans; they do willingly, without repining, live under a masterly
government; yet their government is stable and safe, because they are
paternal and lawful kingdoms, and their guards are royal and not
tyrannical: for Kings are guarded by their own subjects, and tyrants
are guarded by strangers.

The Aesymnetical King (saith Aristotle) in old time in Greece, was
an elective tyrant, and differed only from the barbarian Kings, in that
he was elective, and not paternal: these sorts of Kings, because they were
tyrannical, were masterly; but because they were over such as voluntarily elected them, they were regal.

The Heroic were those (saith Aristotle) which flourished in the
heroical times, to whom the people did willingly obey; and they were
paternal and lawful, because these Kings did deserve well of the multitude, either by teaching them arts, or by warring for them, or by
gathering them together when they were dispersed, or by dividing

lands amongst them: these Kings had supreme power in war, in sacrifices, in judicature.

These four sorts of monarchy hath Aristotle thus distinguished, and after sums them up together, and concludes his chapter as if he had forgot himself, and reckons up a fifth kind of monarchy; which is, saith he, when one alone hath supreme power of all the rest: for as there is a domestical kingdom of one house, so the kingdom of a city, or of one or many nations, is a family.

These are all the sorts of monarchy that Aristotle hath found out, and he hath strained hard to make them so many: first, for his Lacedemonian King, himself confesseth that he was but a kind of military commander in war, and so in effect no more a King than all generals of armies: and yet this no-king of his was not limited by any law, nor mixed with any companions of his government: when he was in the wars out of the confines of Lacedaemon, he was, as Aristotle styles him, Ἀυτοκράτωρ, of full and absolute command, no law, no companion to govern his army but his own will.

Next, for Aristotle's Aesymnetical King, it appears, he was out of date in Aristotle's time; for he saith, he was amongst the ancient Greeks ἐν τοῖς ἀρχαίοις Ἕλλησιν. Aristotle might well have spared the naming him (if he had not wanted other sorts) for the honour of his own nation: for he that but now told us the barbarians were of a more servile nature than the Grecians, comes here, and tells us, that these old Greek Kings were elective tyrants. The barbarians did but suffer tyrants in show, but the old Grecians chose tyrants indeed; which then must we think were the greater slaves, the Greeks or the barbarians? Now if these sorts of Kings were tyrants, we cannot suppose they were limited either by law, or joined with companions: indeed Aristotle saith, some of these tyrants were limited to certain times and actions, for they had not all their power for term of life, nor could meddle but in certain businesses; yet during the time they were tyrants, and in the actions whereto they were limited, they had absolute power to do what they list according to their own will, or else they could not have been said to be tyrants.

As for Aristotle's Heroic King, he gives the like note upon him, that he did upon the Aesymnet, that he was in old time κατὰ τοὺς ἡρωικοὺς χρόνους, in the Heroic times. The thing that made these Heroical kingdoms differ from other sorts of kingdoms, was only the means by which the first Kings obtained their kingdoms, and not the manner of government, for in that they were as absolute as other Kings were, without either limitation by law, or mixture of companions.

Lastly, as for Aristotle's barbaric sort of Kings, since he reckoned all the world barbarians, except the Grecians, his Barbaric King must extend to all other sorts of Kings in the world, besides those of Greece, and so may go under Aristotle's fifth sort of Kings, which in general comprehends all other sorts, and is no special form of monarchy.

Thus upon a true account it is evident, that the five several sorts of Kings mentioned by Aristotle, are at the most but different and accidental means of the first obtaining or holding of monarchies, and not real or essential differences of the manner of government, which was always absolute, without either limitation or mixture.

I may be thought perhaps to mistake, or wrong Aristotle, in questioning his diversities of Kings; but it seems Aristotle himself was partly of the same mind; for in the very next chapter, when he had better considered of the point, he confessed, that to speak the truth, there were almost but two sorts of monarchies worth the considering, that is, his first or Laconic sort, and his fifth or last sort, where one alone hath supreme power over all the rest: thus he hath brought his five sorts to two. Now for the first of these two, his Lacedemonian King, he hath confessed before, that he was no more than a generalissimo of an army, and so upon the matter no King at all: and then there remains only his last sort of Kings, where one alone hath the supreme power. And this in substance is the final resolution of Aristotle himself: for in his sixteenth chapter, where he delivers his last thoughts touching the kinds of monarchy, he first dischargeth his Laconic King from being any sort of monarchy and then gives us two exact rules about monarchy; and both these are point-blank against limited and mixed monarchy; therefore I shall propose them to be considered of, as concluding all monarchy to be absolute and arbitrary.

1. The one rule is, that he that is said to be a King according to law, is no sort of government or kingdom at all: Ὁ κατὰ νόμον βασιλεὺς οὐκ ἔστιν εἶδος πολιτείας.*

2. The second rule is, that a true King is he that ruleth all according to his own will, κατὰ τὴν αὐτοῦ βούλησιν.

This latter frees a monarch from the mixture of partners or sharers in government, as the former rule doth from limitation by laws.

Thus in brief I have traced Aristotle in his crabbed and broken passages, touching diversities of Kings; where he first finds but four sorts, and then he stumbles upon a fifth; and in the next chapter contents himself only with two sorts of Kings, but in the chapter following concludes with one, which is the true perfect monarch, who rules all by

* Aristotle, *Politics*, lib. 3, c. 16.

his own will: in all this we find nothing for a regulated or mixed monarchy, but against it.

Moreover, whereas the author of the Treatise of Monarchy affirms it as a prime principle, that all monarchies (except that of the Jews)- depend upon humane designment, when the consent of a society of men, and a fundamental contract of a nation, by original or radical constitution confers power: he must know, that Aristotle searching into the original of government, shows himself in this point a better divine than our author; and as if he had studied the book of Genesis, teacheth, that monarchies fetch their pedigree from the right of Fathers, and not from the gift or contract of people; his words may thus be Englished. At the first, cities were governed by kings, and so even to this day are nations also: for such as were under Kingly government did come together; for every house is governed by a King, who is the eldest; and so also colonies are governed for kindred sake. And immediately before, he tells us, that the first society made of many houses is a village, which naturally seems to be a colony of a house, which some call foster-brethren, or children, and children's children.

So in conclusion we have gained Aristotle's judgment in three main and essential points.

1. A King according to law makes no kind of government.

2. A King must rule according to his own will.

3. The original of Kings, is from the right of fatherhood.

What Aristotle's judgment was two thousand years since, is agreeable to the doctrine of the great modern politician Bodin: hear him touching limited monarchy: 'Unto majesty or sovereignty (saith he) belongeth an absolute power, not subject to any law . . . chief power given unto a prince with condition, is not properly sovereignty, or power absolute, except such conditions annexed to the sovereignty, be directly comprehended within the laws of God and nature . . . Albeit by the sufferance of the King of England, controversies between the King and his people are sometimes determined by the high court of Parliament, and sometimes by the Lord Chief Justice of England; yet all the estates remain in full subjection to the King, who is no ways bound to follow their advice, neither to consent to their requests . . . It is certain, that the laws, privileges, and grants of princes, have no force but during their life, if they be not ratified by the express consent, or by sufferance of the prince following, especially privileges . . . Much less should a prince be bound unto the laws he maketh himself; for a man may well receive a law from another man, but impossible it is in nature for to give a law unto himself, no more than it is to command a man's self in a matter depending of his own will. The law saith, "Nulla obligatio consistere potest, quae a voluntate promittentis statum capit". The sovereign prince may derogate unto the laws that he hath promised and sworn to keep, if the equity thereof be ceased; and that of himself, without the consent of his subjects . . . The majesty of a true sovereign prince is to be known, when the estates of all the people assembled, in all humility present their requests and supplications to their prince, without having power in anything, to command, determine, or give voice, but that that which it pleaseth the King to like or dislike, to command or bid, is holden for law: wherein they which have written of the duty of magistrates have deceived themselves, in maintaining that the power of the people is greater than the prince; a thing which causeth oft true subjects to revolt from their obedience to their prince, and ministereth matter of great troubles in commonwealths; of which their opinion there is neither reason nor ground: for if the King be subject unto the assemblies and decrees of the people, he should neither be King nor sovereign, and the commonwealth neither realm nor monarchy, but a mere aristocracy . . . So we see the principal point of sovereign majesty, and absolute power, to consist principally in giving laws unto the subjects in general without their consent.' Bodin de Rep., *lib. 1, c. 8.*

'To confound the state of monarchy with the popular or aristocratical estate, is a thing impossible, and in effect incompatible, and such as cannot be imagined: for sovereignty being of itself indivisible, how can it at one and the same time be divided betwixt one prince, the nobility and the people in common? The first mark of sovereign majesty, is to be of power to give laws, and to command over them unto the subjects; and who should those subjects be that should yield their obedience to the law, if they should have also power to make the laws? who should he be that could give the law? being himself constrained to receive it of them, unto whom himself gave it? so that of necessity we must conclude, that as no one in particular hath the power to make the law in such a state, that then the state must needs be a state popular . . . Never any commonwealth hath been made of an aristocracy and popular estate, much less of the three estates of a commonweal . . . Such states wherein the rights of sovereignty are divided, are not rightly to be called commonweals, but rather the corruption of commonweals, as Herodotus has most briefly but truly written . . . Commonweals which change their state, the sovereign right and power of them being divided, find no rest from civil wars and broils, till they again recover some one of the three forms, and the sovereignty be wholly in one of the states or other. Where the rights of the sovereignty are divided betwixt the prince and his subjects, in that confusion of state there is still endless stirs and quarrels for the superiority, until that some one, some few, or all together, have got the sovereignty.' Id., *lib.* 2, *c.* 1.

This judgment of Bodin's touching limited and mixed monarchy, is not according to the mind of our author, nor yet of the Observator, who useth the strength of his wit to overthrow absolute and arbitrary government in this kingdom; and yet in the main body of his discourse, lets fall such truths from his pen, as give a deadly wound to the cause he pleads for, if they be indifferently weighed and considered. I will not pick a line or two here and there to wrest against him, but will present a whole page of his book, or more together, that so we may have an entire prospect upon the Observator's mind: 'Without society (saith the Observator) men could not live; without laws men could not be sociable; and without authority somewhere to judge according to law, law was vain: it was soon therefore provided, that laws according to the dictate of reason, should be ratified by common consent; when it afterward appeared, that man was yet subject to unnatural destruction, by the tyranny of entrusted magistrates, a mischief almost as fatal as to be without all magistracy. How to provide a wholesome remedy therefore, was not so easy to be invented: it was not difficult to invent laws for the limiting of supreme governors; but to invent how those laws should be executed, or by whom interpreted, was almost impossible, 'Nam quis custodiet ipsos Custodes?' to place a superior above a supreme, was held unnatural; yet what a lifeless thing would law be without any judge to determine and force it? If it be agreed upon, that limits should be prefixed to princes and judges to decree according to those limits, yet another inconvenience will presently affront us: for we cannot restrain princes too far, but we shall disable them from some good: long it was ere the world could extricate itself out of all these extremities, or find out an orderly means whereby to avoid the danger of unbounded prerogative on this hand, and of excessive liberty on the other; and scarce has long experience yet fully satisfied the minds of all men in it. In the infancy of the world, when man was not so artificial and obdurate in cruelty and oppression as now, and policy most rude, most nations did choose rather to subject themselves to the mere discretion of their lords, than rely upon any limits; and so be ruled by arbitrary edicts, than written statutes. But since tyranny being more exquisite, and policy more perfect, especially where learning and

religion flourish, few nations will endure the thraldom which usually
accompanies unbounded and unconditionate royalty; yet long it was
ere the bounds and conditions of supreme lords was so wisely determined, or quietly conserved as now they are: for at first, when as
Ephori, Tribuni, Curatores, etc., were erected to poise against the
scale of sovereignty, much blood was shed about them, and states were
put into new broils by them, and in some places the remedy proved
worse than the disease. In all great distresses, the body of the people
were ever constrained to rise, and by force of the major party to put
an end to all intestine strifes, and make a redress of all public grievances:
but many times calamities grew to a strange height, before so cumber-
some a body could be raised; and when it was raised, the motions of it
were so distracted and irregular, that after much spoil and effusion of
blood, sometimes only one tyranny was exchanged for another, till
some was invented to regulate the motions of the people's moliminous
body. I think arbitrary rule was most safe for the world: but now,
since most countries have found an art and peaceable order for public
assemblies, whereby the people may assume its own power to do itself
right, without disturbance to itself or injury to princes; he is very unjust that will oppose this art or order. That princes may not be now
beyond all limits and laws, nor yet be tied upon those limits by any
private parties; the whole community, in its underived majesty, shall
convene to do justice; and that the convention may not be without
intelligence, certain times, and places, and forms, shall be appointed
for its reglement; and that the vastness of its own bulk may not breed
confusion, by virtue of election and representation, a few shall act for
many, the wise, shall consent for the simple, the virtue of all shall redound to some, and the prudence of some shall redound to all; and
surely as this admirably-composed court, which is now called a Parliament, is more regularly and orderly formed, than when it was called
mickle Synod of Wittenagemot, or when this real body of the people
did throng together at it: so it is not yet perhaps without some defects,
which by art and policy might receive further amendment: some
divisions have sprung up of late between both Houses, and some between the King and both Houses, by reason of uncertainty of jurisdiction; and some lawyers doubt how far the Parliament is able to
create new forms and precedents, and has a jurisdiction over itself; all
these doubts would be solemnly solved: but in the first place, the true
privileges of Parliament belonging not only to the being and efficacy
of it, but to the honour and complement of it, would be clearly declared: for the very naming of privileges of Parliament, as if they were

chimeras to the ignorant sort, and utterly unknown unto the learned, hath been entertained with scorn since the beginning of this Parliament.'

In this large passage taken out of the Observator which concerns the original of all government, two notable propositions may be principally observed.

First, our Observator confesseth arbitrary or absolute government to be the first, and the safest government for the world.

Secondly, he acknowledgeth that the jurisdiction is uncertain, and the privileges not clearly declared of limited monarchy.

These two evident truths delivered by him, he labours mainly to disguise. He seems to insinuate that arbitrary government was but in the infancy of the world, for so he terms it; but if we inquire of him, how long he will have this infancy of the world to last, he grants it continued above three thousand years, which is an unreasonable time for the world to continue under-age: for the first opposers he doth find of arbitrary power, were the Ephori, Tribuni, Curatores, etc. The Ephori were above three thousand years after the creation, and the Tribuni were later; as for his Curatores, I know not whom he means, except the Master of the Court of Wards, I cannot English the word Curator better. I do not believe that he can show that any Curatores or etceteras which he mentions were so ancient as the Ephori. As for the Tribuni, he mistakes much if he thinks they were erected to limit and bound monarchy; for the state of Rome was at the least aristocratical (as they call it) if not popular, when tribunes of the people were first hatched. And for the Ephori, their power did not limit or regulate monarchy, but quite take it away; for a Lacedemonian King in the judgment of Aristotle was no King indeed, but in name only, as generalissimo of an army; and the best politicians reckon the Spartan commonwealth to have been aristocratical, and not monarchical; and if a limited monarchy cannot be found in Lacedemon, I doubt our Observator will hardly find it anywhere else in the whole world; and in substance he confesseth as much, when he saith, now most countries have found out an art and peaceable order for public assemblies; as if it were a thing but new done, and not before; for so the word now doth import.

The Observator in confessing the jurisdiction to be uncertain, and the privileges undetermined of that court that should bound and limit monarchy, doth in effect acknowledge there is no such court at all: for every court consists of jurisdictions and privileges; it is these two that create a court, and are the essentials of it: If the admirably composed court of Parliament have some defects which may receive amendment,

as he saith, and if those defects be such as cause divisions both between
the Houses, and between the King and both Houses, and these divisions
be about so main a matter as jurisdictions and privileges, and power to
create new privileges, all which are the fundamentals of every court
(for until they be agreed upon, the act of every court may not only
be uncertain, but invalid, and cause of tumults and sedition), and if
all these doubts and divisions have need to be solemnly solved, as our
Observator confesseth: then he hath no reason at all to say, that now the
conditions of supreme lords are wisely determined and quietly conserved, or that now most countries have found out an art, and peaceable order for public affairs, whereby the people may resume its own
power to do itself right without injury unto princes: for how can the
underived majesty of the people by assuming its own power, tell how
to do herself right, or how to avoid doing injury to the prince, if her
jurisdiction be uncertain, and privileges undetermined?

He tells us now most countries have found an art, and peaceable
order for public assemblies: and to the intent that princes may not be
now beyond all limits and laws, the whole community in its underived
majesty shall convene to do justice. But he doth not name so much as
one country or kingdom that hath found out this art, where the whole
community in its underived majesty did ever convene to do justice. I
challenge him, or any other for him, to name but one kingdom that
hath either now or heretofore found out this art or peaceable order.
We do hear a great rumour in this age, of moderated and limited Kings;
Poland, Sweden and Denmark are talked of for such; and in these
kingdoms, or nowhere, is such a moderated government, as our
Observator means, to be found. A little inquiry would be made into
the manner of the government of these kingdoms: for these northern
people, as Bodin observeth, breathe after liberty.

First for Poland, Boterus saith, that the government of it is elective
altogether, and representeth rather an aristocracy than a kingdom: the
nobility, who have great authority in the diets, choosing the King, and
limiting his authority, making his sovereignty but a slavish royalty:
these diminutions of regality began first by default of King Lewis, and
Jagello, who to gain the succession in the kingdom contrary to the
laws, one for his daughter, and the other for his son, departed with
many of his royalties and prerogatives, to buy the voices of the nobility.
The French author of the book called *The Estates of the World*, doth
inform us that the princes' authority was more free, not being subject
to any laws, and having absolute power, not only of their estates, but
also of life and death. Since christian religion was received, it began

to be moderated, first by holy admonitions of the bishops and clergy, and then by services of the nobility in war: religious princes gave many honours, and many liberties to the clergy and nobility, and quit much of their rights, the which their successors have continued. The superior dignity is reduced to two degrees, that is, the Palatinate and the Chastelleine, for that Kings in former times did by little and little call these men to public consultations, notwithstanding that they had absolute power to do all things of themselves, to command, dispose, recompense and punish, of their own motions: since they have ordained that these dignities should make the body of a senate, the King doth not challenge much right and power over his nobility, nor over their estates, neither hath he any over the clergy. And though the King's authority depends on the nobility for his election, yet in many things it is absolute after he is chosen: he appoints the diets at what time and place he pleaseth; he chooseth lay-councillors, and nominates the bishops, and whom he will have to be his privy council: he is absolute disposer of the revenues of the crown: he is absolute establisher of the decrees of the diets: it is in his power to advance and reward whom he pleaseth. He is lord immediate of his subjects, but not of his nobility: he is sovereign judge of his nobility in criminal causes. The power of the nobility daily increaseth, for that in respect of the King's election, they neither have law, rule, nor form to do it, neither by writing nor tradition. As the King governs his subjects which are immediately his, with absolute authority; so the nobility dispose immediately of their vassals, over whom every one hath more than a regal power, so as they entreat them like slaves. There be certain men in Poland who are called earthly messengers or *nuntios*, they are as it were agents of jurisdictions or circles of the nobility: these have a certain authority, and, as Boterus saith, in the time of their diets these men assemble in a place near to the Senate House, where they choose two marshals, by whom (but with a tribune-like authority) they signify unto the council what their requests are. Not long since, their authority and reputation grew so mightily, that they now carry themselves as heads and governors, rather than officers and ministers of the public decrees of the state: one of the council refused his senator's place, to become one of these officers. Every palatine, the King requiring it, calls together all the nobility of his palatinate; where having propounded unto them the matters whereon they are to treat, and their will being known, they choose four or six out of the company of the earthly messengers; these deputies meet and make one body, which they call the order of knights.

This being of late years the manner and order of the government of Poland, it is not possible for the Observator to find among them that the whole community in its underived majesty doth ever convene to do justice: nor any election or representation of the community, or that the people assume its own power to do itself right. The earthly messengers, though they may be thought to represent the Commons, and of late take much upon them, yet they are elected and chosen by the nobility, as their agents and officers. The community are either vassals to the King, or to the nobility, and enjoy as little freedom or liberty as any nation. But it may be said perhaps, that though the community do not limit the King, yet the nobility do; and so he is a limited monarch. The answer is, that in truth, though the nobility at the choosing of their King do limit his power, and do give him an oath; yet afterwards they have always a desire to please him, and to second his will; and this they are forced to do, to avoid discord: for by reason of their great power, they are subject to great dissentions, not only among themselves, but between them and the order of knights, which are the earthly messengers: yea, the provinces are at discord one with another: and as for religion, the diversity of sects in Poland breeds perpetual jars and hatred among the people, there being as many sects as in Amsterdam itself, or any popular government can desire. The danger of sedition is the cause, that though the crown depends on the election of the nobility; yet they have never rejected the King's successor, or transferred the realm to any other family, but once, when deposing Ladislaus for his idleness (whom yet afterwards they restored) they elected Wenceslaus King of Bohemia. But if the nobility do agree to hold their King to his conditions, which is, not to conclude anything but by the advice of his council of nobles, nor to choose any wife without their leaves, then it must be said to be a commonweal, not a royalty; and the King but only the mouth of the kingdom, or as Queen Christina complained, that her husband was but the shadow of a sovereign.

Next, if it be considered how the nobility of Poland came to this great power; it was not by any original contract, or popular convention: for it is said they have neither law, rule, nor form written or unwritten, for the election of their King, they may thank the bishops and clergy: for by their holy admonitions and advice, good and religious princes, to show their piety, were first brought to give much of their rights and privileges to their subjects, devout Kings were merely cheated of some of their royalties. What power soever general assemblies of the estates claim or exercise over and above the bare naked act of counselling, they were first beholding to the popish clergy for it: it is they first brought Parliaments into request and power: I cannot find in any kingdom, but only where popery hath been, that Parliaments have been of reputation: and in the greatest times of superstition they are first mentioned.

As for the kingdom of Denmark, I read that the senators, who are all chosen out of the nobility, and seldom exceed the number of twenty-eight, with the chief of the realm, do choose their King. They have always in a manner set the King's eldest son upon the royal throne. The nobility of Denmark withstood the coronation of Frederick, 1559, till he swore not to put any nobleman to death until he were judged of the Senate; and that all noblemen should have power of life and death over their subjects without appeal; and the King to give no office without consent of the council. There is a chancellor of the realm, before whom they do appeal from all the provinces and islands, and from him to the King himself. I hear of nothing in this kingdom that tends to popularity; no assembly of the Commons, no elections, or representation of them.

Sweden is governed by a King heretofore elective, but now made hereditary in Gustavus's time: it is divided into provinces: an appeal lieth from the viscount of every territory to a sovereign judge called a Lamen; from the Lamens, to the King's Council; and from this council to the King himself.

Now let the Observator bethink himself, whether all, or any of these three countries have found out any art at all whereby the people or community may assume its own power: if neither of these kingdoms have, most countries have not, nay none have. The people or community in these three realms are as absolute vassals as any in the world; the regulating power, if any be, is in the nobility: nor is it such in the nobility as it makes show for. The election of Kings is rather a formality, than any real power: for they dare hardly choose any but the heir, or one of the blood royal: if they should choose one among the nobility, it would prove very factious; if a stranger, odious, neither safe. For the government, though the Kings be sworn to reign according to the laws, and are not to do anything without the consent of their council in public affairs: yet in regard they have power both to advance and reward whom they please, the nobility and senators do comply with their Kings. And Boterus concludes of the Kings of Poland, who seem to be most moderated, that such as is their valour, dexterity and wisdom, such is their power, authority and government. Also Bodin saith, that these three kingdoms are states changeable and uncertain, as the nobility is stronger than the prince, or the prince than the nobility; and the people are so far from liberty, that he saith, divers particular lords exact not only customs, but tributes also; which are confirmed and grow stronger, both by long prescription of time, and use of judgments.

THE
NECESSITY
OF
The Absolute Power of all KINGS:
And in particular
OF THE *KING*
OF
ENGLAND
BY
JOHN BODIN
A Protestant according to the Church of *Geneva*

At LONDON, Printed in the year, 1648.

(Thomason, August 21st, 1648. Typographical evidence shows that Royston certainly published it. The title page printed here is the rarer variant, but it is substantiated by the title of Sir Robert's original MS., of which the first part is in MS. Harl. 6867, 16. Omitted from the 1679 and 1680 collections, but issued on its own in 1680 under the title *The Power of Kings*, with an interesting introduction. This version was reprinted in the 1684 and 1696 collections, and shows greater variation from the original printed version than in the case of any of the other tracts. It is possible that the reprints were made from a manuscript source rather than from the 1648 impression.

The *Power* consists entirely of extracts from the *République*. It repeats some of the passages quoted in Filmer's other works, notably *Patriarcha*, and reveals the source of many of the arguments which he presents as his own, especially in the *Anarchy*. It is valuable as a measure of Filmer's dependence on Bodin, and of that thinker's influence on English Royalist thought. It also indicates the contemporary interest in the study of comparative institutions.)

To majesty or sovereignty belongeth an absolute power not subject to any law. It behoveth him that is a sovereign, not to be in any sort subject to the command of another; whose office is to give laws unto his subjects, to abrogate laws unprofitable, and in their stead to establish other; which he cannot do, that is himself subject to laws, or to others which have command over him: and this is that which the law saith, that the prince is acquitted from the power of the laws.

The laws, ordinances, letters-patents, privileges, and grants of princes, have no force but during their life; if they be not ratified by the express consent, or at least by sufference of the prince following, who had knowledge thereof.

If the sovereign prince be exempted from the laws of his predecessors, much less shall he be bound unto the laws he maketh himself; for a man may well receive a law from another man, but impossible it is in nature for to give a law unto himself, no more than it is to command a man's self in a matter depending of his own will: There can be no obligation which taketh state from the mere will of him that promiseth the same; which is a necessary reason to prove evidently, that a King cannot bind his own hands, albeit that he would: we see also in the end of all laws these words, 'Because it hath so pleased us'; to give us to understand, that the laws of a sovereign prince, although they be grounded upon reason, yet depend upon nothing but his mere and frank good will. But as for the laws of God, all princes and people are unto them subject; neither is it in their power to impugn them, if they will not be guilty of high treason against God; under the greatness of whom, all monarchs of the world ought to bow their heads, in all fear and reverence.

A question may be, whether a prince be subject to the laws of his country that he hath sworn to keep, or not? If a sovereign prince promise by oath to his subjects to keep the laws, he is bound to keep them; not for that a prince is bound to keep his laws by himself or by his predecessors, but by the just conventions and promises which he hath made himself, be it by oath, or without any oath at all, as should a private man be: and for the same causes that a private man may be relieved from his unjust and unreasonable promise, as for that it was so grievous, or for that he was by deceit or fraud circumvented, or induced thereunto by error, or force, or just fear, or by some great hurt;

even for the same causes the prince may be restored in that which toucheth the diminishing of his majesty: and so our Maxime resteth, that the prince is not subject to his laws, nor to the laws of his prede-cessors, but well to his own just and reasonable conventions.

The sovereign prince may derogate from the laws that he hath pro-mised and sworn to keep, if the equity thereof cease, and that of him-self, without consent of his subjects; which his subjects cannot do among themselves, if they be not by the prince relieved.

The foreign princes well advised, will never take oath to keep the laws of their predecessors; for otherwise they are not sovereigns.

Notwithstanding all oaths, the prince may derogate from the laws, or frustrate or disannul the same, the reason and equity of them ceasing.

There is not any bond for the sovereign prince to keep the laws, more than so far as right and justice requireth.

Neither is it to be found, that the ancient Kings of the Hebrews took any oaths, no not they which were anointed by Samuel, Elias and others.

As for general and particular, which concern the right of men in private, they have not used to be otherwise changed, but after general assemblies of the three estates in France; not for that it is necessary for the Kings to rest on their advice, or that he may not do the contrary to that they demand, if natural reason and justice do so require. And in that the greatness and majesty of a true sovereign prince is to be known, when the estates of all the people assembled together in all humility present their requests and supplications to their prince, with-out having any power in anything to command, or determine, or to give voice; but that that which it pleaseth the King to like or dislike, to command or forbid, is holden for law. Wherein they which have written of the duty of magistrates, have deceived themselves, in main-taining that the power of the people is greater than the prince; a thing which oft-times causeth the true subjects to revolt from the obedience which they owe unto their sovereign prince, and ministereth matter of great troubles in commonwealths; of which their opinion, there is neither reason nor ground.

If the King should be subject unto the assemblies and decrees of the people, he should neither be King nor sovereign, and the common-wealth neither realm nor monarchy; but a mere aristocracy of many lords in power equal, where the greater part commandeth the less; and whereon the laws are not to be published in the name of him that ruleth, but in the name and authority of the estates; as in an aristocrati-

cal seignory, where he that is chief hath no power, but oweth obeisance
to the seignory; unto whom yet they every one of them feign themselves to owe their faith and obedience: which are all things so absurd,
as hard it is to see which is furthest from reason.

When Charles VIII, the French King, then but fourteen years old,
held a Parliament at Tours, although the power of the Parliament was
never before nor after so great, as in those times; yet Relli, then the
Speaker for the people, turning himself to the King, thus beginneth:
'Most High, most Mighty, and most Christian King, our natural and
only lord; we poor, humble and obedient subjects, etc., which are
come hither by your command, in all humility, reverence, and subjection, present ourselves before you, etc., and have given me in charge
from all this noble assembly to declare unto you, the good will and
hearty desire they have, with a most fervent resolution to serve, obey
and aid you in all your affairs, commandments and pleasures.' All this
speech is nothing else but a declaration of their good will towards the
King, and of their humble obedience and loyalty.

The like speech was used in the Parliament at Orleans to Charles IX,
when he was scarce eleven years old.

Neither are the Parliaments in Spain otherwise holden, but that even
a greater obedience of all the people is given to the King; as is to be
seen in the Acts of the Parliament at Toledo by King Philip, 1552,
when he yet was scarce twenty-five years old. The answers also of the
King of Spain unto the requests and humble supplications of his people,
are given in these words: We will, or else, We decree or ordain; yea,
the subsidies that the subjects pay unto the King of Spain, they call
service.

In the Parliaments of England, which have commonly been holden
every third year, the estates seem to have a great liberty (as the northern
people almost all breathe thereafter), yet so it is, that in effect they proceed not, but by way of supplications and requests to the King. As in
the Parliament holden in October 1566, when the estates by common
consent had resolved (as they gave the Queen to understand) not to
treat of anything, until she had first appointed who should succeed her
in the crown; she gave them no other answer, but that they were not
to make her grave before she were dead. All whose resolutions were
to no purpose without her good liking, neither did she in that anything
that they requested.

Albeit by the sufferance of the King of England, controversies between the King and his people are sometimes determined by the high
court of Parliament; yet all the estates remain in full subjection to the

King, who is no way bound to follow their advice, neither to consent to their requests.

The estates of England are never otherwise assembled, no more than they are in France or Spain, than by Parliament-Writs and express commandments, proceeding from the King; which showeth very well, that the estates have no power of themselves to determine, command or decree anything; seeing they cannot so much as assemble themselves, neither being assembled, depart without express commandment from the King.

Yet this may seem one special thing, that the laws made by the King of England, at the request of the estates, cannot be again repealed, but by calling a Parliament which is much used and done as I have understood by Mr. Dale the English Ambassador, an honourable Gentleman, and a man of good understanding, who yet assured me the King received or rejected the Law as seemed best to himself, and stuck not to dispose thereof at-his pleasure as we see Henry VIII to have always used his sovereign power, and with his only word to have dis-annulled the decrees of Parliament.

We conclude the majesty of a prince to be nothing altered or diminished by the calling together, or presence of the estates: but to the contrary, his majesty thereby to be much the greater and the more honourable, seeing all his people to acknowledge him for their sovereign.

We see the principal point of sovereign majesty and absolute power to consist principally in giving laws unto the subjects without their consent. It behoveth, that the sovereign prince should have the laws in his power, to change and amend them according as occasion shall require.

In a monarchy everyone in particular must swear to the observation of the laws, and their allegiance to one sovereign monarch; who, next unto God (of whom he holds his sceptre and power), is bound to no man: for an oath carrieth always with it reverence unto whom, and in whose name it is made, as still given to a superior; and therefore the vassal gives such oath unto his lord, but receives none from him again, though they be mutually bound, the one of them to the other.

Trajan swore to keep the laws, although he under the name of a sovereign prince was exempted; but never any of the Emperors before him so swore: therefore Pliny the younger, in a panegyrical oration, speaking of the oath of Trajan, gives out, a great novelty, saith he, and never before heard of, he sweareth, by whom we swear.

Of these two things the one must come-to pass, to wit, the prince that swears to keep the laws of his country, must either not have the sovereignty, or else become a perjured man, if he should abrogate but one law contrary to his oath; whereas it is not only profitable that a prince should sometimes abrogate some such laws, but also necessary for him to alter or correct them, as the infinite variety of places, times and persons shall require: or if we shall say, the prince to be still a sovereign, and yet nevertheless with such condition, that he can make no law without the advice of his council or people; he must also be dispensed with by his subjects, for the oath which he hath made for the observation of the laws; and the subjects again which are obliged to the laws, have also need to be dispensed withal by their prince, for fear they should be perjured: so shall it come to pass, that the majesty of the commonweal inclining now to this side, now to that side; sometimes the prince, sometimes the people bearing sway, shall have no certainty to rest upon; which are notable absurdities, and altogether incompatible with the majesty of absolute sovereignty, and contrary both to law and reason. And yet we see many men, that think they see more in the matter than others, will maintain it to be most necessary, that princes should be bound by oath, to keep the laws and customs of their countries: in which doing, they weaken and overthrow all the rights of sovereign majesty, which ought to be most sacred and holy, and confound the sovereignty of one sovereign monarch, with an aristocracy or democracy.

Publication, or approbation of laws, in the assembly of the estates or Parliament, is with us of great importance for the keeping of the laws; not that the prince is bound to any such approbation, or cannot of himself make a law, without the consent of the estates or people (for even all his declarations of war, treaties of peace, valuations of the coin, charters to enable towns to send burgesses to Parliament, and his writ of summons to both Houses to assemble, are laws, though made without the consent of the estates or people); but it is a courteous part to do it by the good liking of the senate.

What if a Prince by law forbid to kill or steal, is he not bound to obey his own laws? I say, that this law is not his, but the law of God, whereunto all princes are more straitly bound than their subjects; God taketh a stricter account of princes than others, as Solomon a King hath said; whereto agreeth Marcus Aurelius, saying, 'the magistrates are judges over private men; princes judge the magistrates, and God the princes'.

It is not only a law of nature, but also oftentimes repeated among the laws of God, that we should be obedient unto the laws of such princes as it hath pleased God to set to rule and reign over us; if their laws be not directly repugnant unto the laws of God, whereunto all princes are as well bound as their subjects: for as the vassal oweth his oath of fidelity unto his Lord, towards and against all men, except his sovereign prince: so the subject oweth his obedience to his sovereign prince, towards and against all, the majesty of God excepted, who is the absolute sovereign of all the princes in the world.

To confound the state of monarchy, with the popular or aristocratical estate, is a thing impossible, and in effect incompatible, and such as cannot be imagined: for sovereignty being of itself indivisible, how can it at one and the same time be divided betwixt one prince, the nobility and the people in common? The first mark of sovereign majesty is to be of power to give laws, and to command over them unto the subjects: and who should those subjects be that should yield their obedience to the law, if they should have also power to make the laws? Who should he be that could give the law, being he himself constrained to receive it of them, unto whom he himself gave it? So that of necessity we must conclude, that as no one in particular hath the power to make the law in such a state, that there the state must needs be popular.

Never any commonwealth hath been made of an aristocracy and popular estate, much less of all the three estates of a commonwealth.

Such states, wherein the right of sovereignty is divided, are not rightly to be called commonweals, but rather the corruption of commonweals; as Herodotus hath most briefly but truly written.

Commonweals which change their state, the sovereign right and power of them being divided, find no rest from civil wars.

If the Prince be an absolute sovereign, as are the true monarchs of France, of Spain, of England, Scotland, Turkey, Muscovy, Tartary, Persia, Ethiopia, India, and almost of all the kingdoms of Africa and Asia; where the Kings themselves have the sovereignty, without all doubt or question, not divided with their subjects: in this case it is not lawful for any one of the subjects in particular, or all of them in general, to attempt anything, either by way of fact or of justice, against the honour, life, or dignity of the sovereign, albeit he had committed all the wickedness, impiety and cruelty that could be spoke. For as to proceed against him by way of justice, the subject hath not such jurisdiction over his sovereign prince, of whom dependeth all power to command, and who may not only revoke all the power of his magistrates, but even in whose presence the power of all magistrates, corporations, estates and communities cease.

Now if it be not lawful for the subject by the way of justice to proceed against a King, how should it then be lawful to proceed against
him by way of fact or force? For question is not here what men are
able to do by strength and force, but what they ought of right to do;
as not whether the subject have power and strength, but whether they
have lawful power to condemn their sovereign prince.

The subject is not only guilty of treason in the highest degree, who
hath slain his sovereign prince, but even he also which hath attempted
the same, who hath given counsel or consent thereto; yea, if he have
concealed the same, or but so much as thought it: which fact the laws
have in such detestation, as that when a man guilty of any offence or
crime, dies before he be condemned thereof, he is deemed to have died
in whole and perfect estate, except he have conspired against the life
and dignity of his sovereign prince. This only thing they have thought
to be such, as that for which he may worthily seem to have been now
already judged and condemned; yea, even before he was thereof
accused. And albeit the laws inflict no punishment upon the evil
thoughts of men, but on those only which by word or deed break out
into some enormity; yet if any man shall so much as conceit a thought
for the violating of the person of his sovereign prince, although he have
attempted nothing, they have yet judged this same thought worthy of
death, notwithstanding what repentance soever he have had thereof.

Lest any men should think [Kings or princes] themselves to have
been the authors of these laws, so the more straitly to provide for their
own safety and honour; let us see the laws and examples of holy
scripture.

Nabuchodonosor, King of Assyria, with fire and sword destroyed
all the country of Palestine, besieged Jerusalem, took it, robbed and
razed it down to the ground, burnt the Temple, and defiled the
sanctuary of God, slew the King, with the greatest part of the people,
carrying away the rest into captivity into Babylon, caused the image
of himself made in gold to be set up in public place, commanding all
men to adore and worship the same, upon pain of being burnt alive,
and caused them that refused so to do, to be cast into a burning furnace.
And yet for all that, the holy prophets [Baruch i; Jeremy xxix], direct-
ing their letters unto their brethren the Jews, then in captivity in Babylon, will them to pray unto God for the good and happy life of
Nabuchodonosor and his children, and that they might so long rule
and reign over them, as the heavens should endure: yea even God
himself doubted not to call Nabuchodonosor his servant, saying, that
he would make him the most mighty prince of the world; and yet was

there never a more detestable tyrant than he: who not contented to be himself worshipped, but caused his image also to be adored, and that upon pain of being burnt quick.

We have another rare example of Saul, who possessed with an evil spirit, caused the priests of the Lord to be without just cause slain, for that one of them had received David flying from him; and did what in his power was to kill, or cause to be killed, the same David, a most innocent prince, by whom he had got so many victories; at which time he fell twice himself into David's hands: who blamed of his soldiers for that he would not suffer his so mortal enemy, then in his power, to be slain, being in assured hope to have enjoyed the kingdom after his death; he detested their counsel, saying, 'God forbid that I should suffer the person of a King, the Lord's anointed, to be violated'. Yea, he himself defended the same King persecuting of him, when as he commanded the soldiers of his guard, overcome by wine and sleep, to be wakened.

And at such time as Saul was slain, and that a soldier, thinking to do David a pleasure, presented him with Saul's head; David caused the same soldier to be slain, which had brought him the head, saying, 'Go thou wicked, how durst thou lay thy impure hands upon the Lord's anointed? Thou shalt surely die therefore'.

And afterwards, without all dissimulation, mourned himself for the dead King. All which is worth good consideration: for David was by Saul prosecuted to death, and yet wanted not power to have revenged himself, being become stronger than the King; besides, he was the chosen of God, and anointed by Samuel to be King, and had married the King's daughter: and yet for all that, he abhorred to take upon him the title of a King, and much more to attempt anything against the life or honour of Saul, or to rebel against him; but chose rather to banish himself out of the realm, than in any sort to seek the King's destruction.

We doubt not but David, a King and a prophet, led by the spirit of God, had always before his eyes the law of God, Exodus xxii, 28. Thou shalt not speak evil of thy prince, nor detract the magistrate; neither is there anything more common in holy scripture, than the forbidding not only to kill or attempt the life or honour of a prince, but even for the very magistrates, although, saith the scripture, they be wicked and naught.

The Protestant princes of Germany, before they entered into arms against Charles the Emperor, demanded of Martin Luther, if it were lawful for them so to do, or not; who frankly told them, that it was not lawful, whatsoever tyranny or impiety were pretended: yet was he not therein by them believed; so thereof ensued a deadly and most lamentable war, the end whereof was most miserable; drawing with it, the ruin of many great and noble houses of Germany, with exceeding slaughter of the subjects.

The prince, whom you may justly call the Father of the country, ought to be to every man dearer and more reverend than any Father, as one ordained and sent unto us by God. The subject is never to be suffered to attempt anything against the prince, how naughty and cruel soever he be: lawful it is, not to obey him in things contrary to the laws of God, to flee and hide ourselves from him; but yet to suffer stripes, yea, and death also, rather than to attempt anything against his life and honour. Oh how many tyrants should there be, if it should be lawful for subjects to kill tyrants? How many good and innocent princes should as tyrants perish by the conspiracy of their subjects against them? He that should of his subjects but exact subsidies, should be then, as the vulgar people esteem him, a tyrant: he that should rule and command contrary to the good liking of the people, should be a tyrant: he that should keep strong guards and garrisons for the safety of his person, should be a tyrant: he that should put to death traitors and conspirators against his state, should be also counted a tyrant. How should good princes be assured of their lives, if under colour of tyranny they might be slain by their subjects, by whom they ought to be defended?

In a well-ordered state, the sovereign power must remain in one only, without communicating any part thereof unto the state (for in that case it should be a popular government and no monarchy). Wise politicians, philosophers, divines and historiographers, have highly commended a monarchy above all other commonweals. It is not to please the prince, that they hold this opinion; but for the safety and happiness of the subjects. And contrariwise, when as they shall limit and restrain the sovereign power of a monarch, to subject him to the general estates, or to the council; the sovereignty hath no firm foundation, but they frame a popular confusion, or a miserable anarchy, which is the plague of all estates and commonweals: the which must be duly considered, not giving credit to their goodly discourses, which persuade subjects, that it is necessary to subject monarchs, and to give their prince a law; for that is not only the ruin of the monarch, but also of the subjects. It is yet more strange, that many hold opinion, that the prince is subject to his laws, that is to say, subject to his will, whereon the laws which he hath made, depend; a thing impossible in nature. And under this colour, and ill-digested opinion, they make a mixture and confusion of civil laws, with the laws of nature and of God.

A pure absolute monarchy is the surest commonweal, and without comparison, the best of all. Wherein many are abused, who maintain that an optimacy is the best kind of government; for that many commanders have more judgment, wisdom and counsel than one alone. For there is a great difference betwixt counsel and commandment.

The counsel of many wise men may be better than of one; but to resolve, determine, and to command, one will always perform it better than many: he which hath advisedly digested all their opinions, will soon resolve without contention; the which many cannot easily perform: it is necessary to have a sovereign prince, which may have power to resolve and determine of the opinions of his council.

DATE DUE

AUG - 6 1992			
AUG - 2 1992			

Filmer, Robert, Sir, d 16
Patriarcha and other political   010101 000

0 1163 0229983 3
TRENT UNIVERSITY

JC153   .F513

Filmer, Sir Robert

Patriarcha and other political
works.

DATE	ISSUED TO
Filmer, Ser R.	8905

www.ingramcontent.com/pod-product-compliance
Lightning Source LLC
LaVergne TN
LVHW051651020125
800322LV00001B/73